UVEDALE PRICE (1747–1829)
Decoding the Picturesque

Garden and Landscape History

ISSN 1758–518X

General Editor
Tom Williamson

This exciting new series offers a forum for the study of all aspects of the subject. It takes a deliberately inclusive approach, aiming to cover both the 'designed' landscape and the working, 'vernacular' countryside; topics embrace, but are not limited to, the history of gardens and related subjects, biographies of major designers, in-depth studies of key sites, and regional surveys.

Proposals or enquiries may be sent directly to the editor or the publisher at the addresses given below; all submissions will receive prompt and informed consideration.

Professor Tom Williamson, School of History,
University of East Anglia, Norwich, Norfolk NR4 7TJ, UK

Boydell & Brewer, PO Box 9, Woodbridge, Suffolk IP12 3DF, UK

Previously published

UVEDALE PRICE
(1747–1829)

DECODING THE PICTURESQUE

CHARLES WATKINS and BEN COWELL

THE BOYDELL PRESS

First published 2012
The Boydell Press, Woodbridge
Paperback edition 2015

ISBN 978 1 84383 708 4 hardback
ISBN 978 1 78327 023 1 paperback

The Boydell Press is an imprint of Boydell & Brewer Ltd
PO Box 9, Woodbridge, Suffolk IP12 3DF, UK
and of Boydell & Brewer Inc.
668 Mt Hope Avenue, Rochester, NY 14620–2731, USA
website: www.boydellandbrewer.com

A CIP catalogue record for this book is available
from the British Library

The publisher has no responsibility for the continued existence or accuracy of URLs
for external or third-party internet websites referred to in this book, and does not
guarantee that any content on such websites is, or will remain, accurate or
appropriate

Designed and typeset by Tina Ranft

This publication is printed on acid-free paper

CONTENTS

LIST OF ILLUSTRATIONS

MAPS

PREFACE AND
ACKNOWLEDGMENTS

WE HAVE BOTH BEEN WORKING ON ASPECTS of the life of Uvedale Price for several years and many people have provided advice and assistance. One of us (CW) first encountered Price when working on a project on the lost country houses of Herefordshire in 1976. He subsequently researched the history of land management at Foxley with Stephen Daniels, and they both worked on the exhibition 'The Picturesque Landscape', which was held at Hereford and Nottingham in 1994 to celebrate the bicentenary of the publication of Price's *Essay of the Picturesque* and Richard Payne Knight's *The Landscape* in 1794. They also developed a research project with Dr Susanne Seymour, funded by the Leverhulme Trust, on picturesque landscaping and estate management in Herefordshire and the Wye Valley. Ben Cowell came across Price while working on his PhD at Nottingham and together we edited the volume *Letters of Uvedale Price*, which was published by the Walpole Society in 2006. On completion of that project we both felt that it was high time that a biography was written of this important figure in the history of aesthetics, landscape gardening and woodland and forest history. This biography draws on surviving letters, estate documents, drawings and paintings, and contemporary descriptions and accounts. We hope that the publication of this biography will bring to light other manuscript sources and letters which remain in private hands. The original spellings and punctuation are retained in all quotations.

We wish to thank and acknowledge the many individuals and organisations that have provided assistance, information and illustrations. We would particularly like to thank the following individuals: the Duke of Abercorn; Professor Brian Allen; Professor Marcia Allentuck; Dr Hugh Brigstocke; George Clive; Edward Clive; Dr Harry Cocks; Professor Stephen Daniels; Major David and Lindy Davenport; James Davenport; John Eisel; Dr Paul Elliott; Tony Jackson; Dr Joachim Jacoby; Dr Richard Hamblyn; Dr Cyril Hart; Rohais Haughton; Robin Hill; Dr Holger Hoock; Dr Stephen Legg; Christopher Lewis; Professor Judith Mossman; Professor Tim Mowl; Bernard Nurse; Professor Philip Olleson; Caroline Palmer; Dr John Phibbs; Dr Rogério Puga; Dr George Revill; Dr Susanne Seymour; Susan Sloman; Sir Roy Strong; Sir Keith Thomas; Dr Alex Vasudevan; Elaine Watts; Dr Sarah Webster; David Whitehead; and Professor Tom Williamson.

The principal primary sources used are as follows: Beinecke Rare Book and Manuscript Library, Yale University, Burney Family Collection. Bodleian Library, Oxford: Correspondence between Uvedale Price and E H Barker 1004–5. British Library: Letters from Uvedale Price to Lord Abercorn BM Add. MS 43228, ff. 98–167; Letters from Uvedale Price to Lord Aberdeen BM Add. MS 43228, ff. 1–97; Correspondence of Uvedale Price and Charles James Fox, BM Add. MS 47476. Herefordshire Record Office (HRO): Foxley Estate Papers, B47. Skippe Family of Ledbury, B38. Kentchurch AL40. Knight Papers T74. Biddulph Papers BC. Paul Mellon Centre, London, Brinsley Ford Archive. Pierpont Morgan Library New York: Letters from Uvedale Price to Sir George and Lady Beaumont, MA 1581. Public Record Office of Northern Ireland: Letter from Uvedale Price to Lord Abercorn D623/A/228/17. Royal Archives, Windsor Castle. Worcestershire Record Office (WRO) Berington Collection.

The following archives, libraries and galleries have been of great assistance: the British Library, London; the Pierpont Morgan Library, New York; the Bodleian Library, Oxford; Herefordshire Record Office; Herefordshire Libraries; the Public Record Office of Northern Ireland, Belfast; the Royal Archives, Windsor; the Soane Museum, London, the Achenbach Foundation for Graphic Arts, San Francisco; the Metropolitan Museum of Art, New York; Bayerische Staatsgemäldesammlungen, Neue Pinachotek, Munich; the Whitworth Art Gallery, Manchester; Corpus Christi College, University of Oxford; the Wernher Foundation, English Heritage; the Berger Collection, Denver Art Museum; Plymouth City Museum and Art Gallery; the Hallward Library, University of Nottingham; the National Monuments Record, Swindon; the London Library; the Society of Antiquaries of London; the Linnean Society of London; the Athenaeum Library; the National Gallery, London; the National Portrait Gallery, London; the Tate Gallery, London; the Boston Museum of Fine Arts, Jordan Collection; the British Museum; the National Library of Wales, Aberystwyth; Cadw, Cardiff; the Trustees of the Wallace Collection, London; the Museum of London; the Government Art Collection, London; the Courtauld Institute of Art Gallery, London; the National Art Library, Victoria and Albert Museum, London; the Beinecke Rare Book and Manuscript Library, Yale University; the Berg Collection, New York Public Library; Wordsworth Trust Archive; Christie's Archives, London.

Charles Watkins, School of Geography, University of Nottingham
Ben Cowell, National Trust

ABBREVIATIONS

BM	British Museum
HRO	Herefordshire Record Office
NAO	Nottinghamshire Archives Office
ODNB	Oxford Dictionary of National Biography
RIBA	Royal Institute of British Architects
TNA	The National Archives
WRO	Worcestershire Record Office

SIMPLIFIED PRICE FAMILY TREE

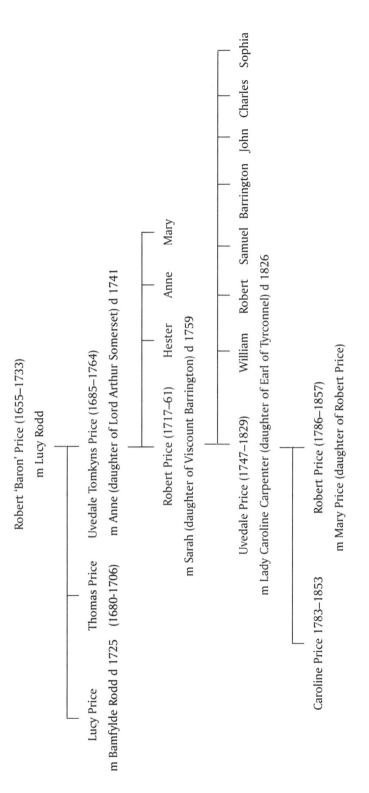

Robert 'Baron' Price (1655–1733)
m Lucy Rodd

Lucy Price   Thomas Price   Uvedale Tomkyns Price (1685–1764)
m Bamfylde Rodd d 1725   (1680-1706)   m Anne (daughter of Lord Arthur Somerset) d 1741

                    Robert Price (1717–61)   Hester   Anne   Mary
                    m Sarah (daughter of Viscount Barrington) d 1759

                    Uvedale Price (1747–1829)   William   Robert   Samuel   Barrington   John   Charles   Sophia
                    m Lady Caroline Carpenter (daughter of Earl of Tyrconnel) d 1826

Caroline Price 1783–1853   Robert Price (1786–1857)
                              m Mary Price (daughter of Robert Price)

INTRODUCTION

PICTURESQUE IDEAS CONTINUE TO FASCINATE long after they initially erupted onto the intellectual scene in the eighteenth century. David Watkin considers that 'the theory and practice of the Picturesque constitute the major English contribution to European aesthetics' and that between 1730 and 1830 the 'Picturesque became the universal mode of vision for the educated classes'.[1] John Macarthur has recently argued that 'at the moment of its emergence, and faithfully since, the picturesque has provided an ever-refreshing image of a precocious aesthetics' which infected the arts with an 'equivocation' and 'instability'.[2] Christopher Hussey's *The Picturesque: Studies in a Point of View* of 1927 reignited critical interest in the early twentieth century[3] and Nikolaus Pevsner extolled the value of picturesque principles for post-war planning. According to Pevsner, Uvedale Price (1747–1829) was 'the most brilliant of the theorists of the English Picturesque',[4] a view supported by Walter Hipple, who, in his review of British aesthetic theory, considered that 'Price may almost be said to have formed the taste of the early nineteenth century in gardening and architecture.'[5]

Price achieved greatest fame as the author of the influential *Essay on the Picturesque* of 1794, which had several subsequent editions. This sparked off a public controversy, drawing in Richard Payne Knight and Humphry Repton, which became a cause célèbre for several years.[6] The strength of the attack by Price on the work of Lancelot 'Capability' Brown resonated widely, as shown by conversations in Jane Austen's *Mansfield Park* (1814) and its satirical treatment in Thomas Love Peacock's *Headlong Hall* (1816). Price argued that the work of the greatest landscape artists should be used as models for the 'improvement of real landscape'. He considered that the category 'picturesque' should be added to Edmund Burke's aesthetic categories the sublime and the beautiful. He was strongly opposed to the extensive views of open parkland, with clumps of trees and surrounding plantations, deemed to be so characteristic of Brown. Instead, he urged landowners to respect the particularities of place, to cultivate the ancient trees and rutted tracks of their estates and to make only subtle, judicious alterations to the landscape in the interests of framing suitably picturesque compositions. Above all, he opposed the notion that alien styles of landscape could be imposed wholesale in the manner ascribed to Brown.

But Price himself remains an elusive figure and no full biography has ever been written. There are several reasons for this. His son became heavily involved in industrial investments in the mid nineteenth century which later failed, and he was eventually made bankrupt. This caused the sale of the Foxley estate and the collections of paintings and drawings. The family papers became dispersed and in many cases lost. The sale meant that there was little chance for friends or members of the family to write a biography in the middle years of the nineteenth century. While working on an edition of Price's surviving letters for the Walpole Society we decided that there was a need for a biography which set the development of his ideas and theories in the context of his social world in London, Herefordshire and Wales.[7]

Apart from his own published writings, the main sources for the biography of Price are his correspondence, estate papers and the surviving features of the landscapes on which he advised and worked. Price had a wide-ranging correspondence and friendships with key political figures such as Charles James Fox and Lord Aberdeen, poets such as William Wordsworth, Samuel Rogers and Elizabeth Barrett Browning, and connoisseurs and artists such as Sir George and Lady Beaumont and Richard Payne Knight. The letters provide much material on the publishing history of various editions of his essays, on his ideas of architecture and the relationship between literature and landscape, and on his responses to criticism.

Uvedale Price's ideas on aesthetics develop from a family background in western Herefordshire, close to the Welsh border. On his return from the Grand Tour in 1771 he was described by the young Fanny Burney as 'a young man of fashion … very intelligent, sensible and clever'. She later called him 'the macarony of the Age'.[8] Like his great-grandfather, grandfather and father, he made an extensive tour of France and Italy as a young man. The Prices had been at Foxley in Herefordshire since the 1680s and they became well-known patrons of art and landscaping. Gainsborough knew the family well and painted at Foxley. Uvedale Price's lifelong friendship with Charles James Fox placed him in the most fashionable Whig society; he married Lady Caroline Carpenter, the daughter of Lord Tyrconnel, in 1774.

Although recent research has helped to ground Uvedale Price's theories in his landscaping and agricultural improvements at Foxley, Price is still underestimated as a practical gardener and landscaper. Price was a keen improving landowner with interests in forestry and agriculture. Lady Caroline was an enthusiastic gardener and farmer. In about 1791 Price commissioned the then unknown John Nash to build an extraordinary gothic castellated villa at Aberystwyth. The house was triangular, with octagonal towers, and was built on the rocky shore, so that the sea could be seen directly from the drawing room. Price insisted that rooms should be built to take in particular views. His ideas on the integration of architecture and landscape had a significant influence on contemporary architects.

Price further developed his landscape ideas through practical experimentation in the construction of lakes and tree planting and management. He developed a 'picture gallery' composed of a sequence of real landscapes which were viewed from a sequence of 'stations' on a carriage ride which followed the rim of the bowl-shaped valley in which Foxley was situated. Views could be taken out across to the Wye valley and the Welsh hills or inwards over the estate. These views were carefully framed with trees 'cut to the nearest twig'.[9] Price gave personal advice on several gardens and parks including St Anne's Hill (1785–); Beech Grove (1790–); Holme Lacy (1790s); Bentley Priory (1797–); Dropmore (1823–); Cashiobury (1823–); Bowood (1793); Guy's Cliffe (1813); Packington (1796–); Coleorton (1803–); Sandwell Park (1806–) and Ingestre Hall (1828). Price's aesthetics were enthusiastically taken up by Sir Walter Scott at Abbotsford and by nineteenth-century landscape gardeners, including William Sawrey Gilpin and John Claudius Loudon. They became a normal way of seeing, understanding and appreciating landscape throughout the nineteenth and early twentieth centuries.

Recent research has explored the relationship between the design, representation and experience of landscape and the formation of personal, local and national identities in England from the eighteenth century to the present day. Studies have examined the work of key landscape artists, designers and theorists, and demonstrated the ways in which specific sites or components of landscape, such as gardens, trees and parks, refract and exemplify the politics and poetics of landscape.[10] Architectural historians have become interested in the reception of Price's ideas and the way they have affected modern culture, with one writer suggesting that 'Price's picturesque is the quotidian lived environment.'[11] Research has helped to ground Uvedale Price's theory in his landscaping and agricultural improvements at Foxley[12] and has identified the importance of the Price family as patrons of Gainsborough.[13] Two of Price's most important intellectual friends and correspondents have been the subject of biographies.[14] There is a compelling case, therefore, for the publication of the first biography of Price. We hope that this biography goes some way to providing an understanding of the context of the development of Price's practices and theories and the key interconnections between his roles as landowner, art collector, forester, landscaper, connoisseur and scholar.

CHAPTER 1

'THE GREATEST VARIETY OF PROSPECTS'[1]

UVEDALE PRICE WAS BORN INTO A FAMILY OF LANDOWNERS who over three generations displayed an intuitive feeling for the sensitivities of landscape and art. The intellectual context of the family was developed through friendships and contacts established on the Grand Tour, in London and in Bath. It was, moreover, strongly associated with the particular geography of the family estate at Foxley, Herefordshire, and linked to the Prices' Welsh ancestry and connections. Some knowledge of the Price family history, their long-term interests in collecting art, in drawing and architecture, and in estate management, forestry and gardening, is essential in developing an understanding of Uvedale Price's ideas and actions.

PATRIOT, JUDGE, POLITICIAN AND 'DETERMINED CAREERIST':[2] ROBERT PRICE (1655–1733)

The acquisition of the Foxley estate and the origins of the eighteenth-century Price family line were the legacies of Robert Price (1655–1733), a judge and leading lawyer in the court of Charles II who became Baron of the Court of the Exchequer in 1702.[3] To avoid confusion we refer to the successive generations as Robert Baron Price (1655–1733), Uvedale Tomkyns Price (1685–1764), Robert Price (1717–1761), Uvedale Price (1747–1829) and Sir Robert Price (1786–1857). Robert Baron Price was born in Giler in the parish of Cerrigydrudion in Denbighshire, and was said to have been 'a descendant from the ancient stock of one of the noble tribes of Wales' who could trace his lineage to Marchweithan, one of the Welsh princes.[4] Giler is just over a mile south of Rydlydan near Pentrefoelas, about five miles to the west of Cerrigydrudion, itself fifteen miles west of Llangollen on the Holyhead road. The small manor house with its tiny arched gateway survives today (Figure 1). The gatehouse is thought to have been built by Thomas the son of the poet Rhys Wynn and has a fireplace in the upper room over which is 'a large white-washed plaster panel framed and cut with strap decoration, it contains the date 1623 and the initials T p. W', standing for Thomas ap Prys Wynn, who became High Sheriff in 1624.[5] His son, also Robert, was Sheriff of Denbighshire in 1658 and his grandson, Thomas, who was Robert Baron Price's father, married Margaret Wynne, heir to the Bwllchybeudy estate, also in Denbighshire. There are monuments to Robert

Fig. 1 Gatehouse to
the Price's manor house
at Giler, near
Cerrigydrudion,
Denbighshire, 2007.
The small manor house
is about twenty miles
west of Llangollen. The
property at Giler was
sold by Uvedale Price in
the 1770s. (Photograph:
Václav Žaloudek)

Baron Price's parents Thomas Price (1668) and Margaret Price (1723) in Giler
Chapel, which is the south transept of St Mary Magdalene, Cerrigydrudion.

Robert Baron Price was educated at St John's College, Cambridge, and made
a Grand Tour in France and Italy from 1677 to 1679, a practice that would be
followed by his male descendants for at least the next three generations. He
stayed at Blois in 1677, where he learnt French, and then went to Rome. Here
some officials reportedly mistook one of the books he was carrying, *Coke upon
Littleton*, as a heretical English bible and he was taken before the pope.
According to Curll, 'Mr Price soon convinced his Accusers of their Error, and
made a Present of the Book to the Pope, who immediately assigned it a Place

in the Vatican Library, and, in the very same Press wherein are reposed Anne Boleyn's Letters to King Henry the VIIIth.'[6] On his return to England in 1679 Price was called to the Bar, and in the same year he married the wealthy Lucy Rodd, daughter of Robert and Anna Sophia Rodd of Foxley. Curll notes that 'Mr *Price* was then about Twenty Five Years of Age, and had, with this Gentlewoman, a Fortune of above thirteen thousand Pounds; besides, many considerable Advantages accruing from her Family.'[7] At Robert Rodd's death in 1691 Price acquired the nucleus of his estate at Yazor, including Foxley, and another at Monnington-on-Wye.

Robert Price had the political intelligence to be a successful Vicar of Bray. The *History of Parliament* considers that 'Price was a determined careerist, well able to adapt his principles to changing times. Starting out as a client of the Beauforts and an outspoken champion of high-flying constitutional legitimism, he made himself into a moderate, Harleyite Tory, and finally a willing servant of the Hanoverian regime.'[8] In pursuing his legal career Price cultivated his connections with prominent Tory and former Jacobite families and maintained close alliances with the Duke of Beaufort.[9] These connections served him well, and he was appointed first by Charles II as his Steward and then by James II as Steward to Charles II's widow, Queen Catherine of Braganza (1685–1702), and Queen's Counsel at Ludlow.[10] Price also served as MP for Weobley on the king's side in the parliament of 1685, and again in 1690, 1695, 1698 and 1701.[11] He was elected Town Clerk of Gloucester and Steward of Shrewsbury in 1685, and later Alderman of Hereford. However, his refusal to read the Declaration of Indulgence in 1686 caused him to be dismissed from his position in Gloucester, while his refusal to support the repeal of the Test Act meant that he lost the stewardship of Shrewsbury in 1688.[12]

Although a supporter of the revolution of 1688, Price, after his re-election in 1690, became a strong advocate of the Country party opposition to William III. In 1695 he was vocal in mounting a challenge in parliament to the granting of certain lands in Wales to the king's favourite, William Bentinck, earl of Portland. In a famous speech that earned him the title 'Patriot', Price criticised the appropriation of properties in his native Denbighshire, alleging that this was evidence of the pernicious influence of Dutch advisers at Court. The grant of the lands was subsequently annulled. He was appointed Exchequer Court judge in 1702, becoming known as Baron Price of Foxley. In 1702, after the king's death, his speech was published under the title *Gloria Cambriae, Or, The Speech of a Bold Briton in Parliament against a Dutch Prince of Wales*.[13] His strident and independent political views might have prevented him from rising any further, but he received promotion again in 1726 when he became a justice of the common pleas. In 1730 Alexander Pope wrote to the earl of Oxford concerning a nephew who had been born 'Born a Papist' and needed a favour from a judge to allow him to practise law without making a religious oath. Pope had been told 'that if possibly one of the Judges will be good naturd enough to do this, it would be Judge Price; with whom I think your Lordship has good interest …'.[14]

While his legal and political career blossomed, however, his marriage failed. He sued Thomas Neale in 1690 for enticing away his wife 'and keeping her, and getting her with child' and won £1,500 damages. They were legally separated and she received £400 a year. The three children (Thomas, Uvedale Tomkyns and Lucy) probably remained with their mother in Bristol.[15]

Robert's eldest son, Thomas, went to Westminster School and St John's College, Cambridge, becoming MP for Weobley in 1702 at the age of 22. He travelled extensively on the Continent, and his surviving letters demonstrate a keen interest in women, society, landscape and art. From Hanover, on 26 June 1705, he wrote to his sister that it was impossible to obtain meat in Westphalian post houses 'unless it be Westphalia-Ham which their Room or Barn is hung round with, instead of Pictures, it is that makes them keep the Smoak in, to smoak it; their Bread is as black as my Shoo, with Straws in it the length of my Finger'.[16] He made a politically expedient visit to the electress of Hanover at Herrenhausen, where he was introduced to her son and grandson, the future kings George I and George II, and shown around the famous gardens. Price was entertained to discover that the electress, aged 74, 'has all her Teeth, reads without Spectacles, works six Hours a Day, and, to my Sorrow, walked me two Hours about the Garden which is a very fine one'. He described the future George II, Prince George Augustus, as 'about my Size, has a face somewhat like young CORNWELL a very full Eye, he is a brisk good humoured Man 21 Years old'.[17] Writing from Berlin on 21 August 1705, he told his sister that he had been down a silver mine 'above five hundred Yards perpendicular under Ground' and that 'This is a very pleasant Place, encompassed with woods of Firs and Pines, of which we have more in these Countries than of any other Sort.' He thought 'The ladies are very Handsome, and early in conversation. Whether they wear Drawers, or not, I cannot tell; and if I knew, I should not.' He added that he was sorry he could not be with his family 'at Foxley to partake of the Pleasures the Country will afford. I am glad to hear that my Brother loves Rural-Sports for that will keep him in good Health.'[18] From Vienna, 19 October 1705, he told his mother that 'The Ladies here are very proud, as well as handsome … . The Emperor and Empress I see every Day; they are both affable. This Town is no larger than Bristol, tho' much finer built.'[19] But on the way from Vienna to Venice he had a 'quarrel' with a German count: 'His Wound is much more dangerous than mine, his being thro' the Thigh, and mine in the left-hand, of which I am cured; but the Mark, and a weakness in that Part, will always remain.'[20]

At Venice on New Year's Day in 1706, he found 'all the Pleasures that one can imagine, and much more Liberty than I thought. The Italians are jealous, but not so much as they are represented to be. Those I am acquainted with, have done me the Favour of their Wives Acquaintance.' He thought: 'The Women here, are more like Angels than Mortals … . Our Carnival begins a Week hence; here is a great Concourse of Strangers from all Parts; Gamesters, Pickpockets, Bauds and Whores; with some Honest Men I put Them last, because They are fewest in Number … .' He enjoyed the operas, which were 'every Night at Three Houses, and those all full. The Voices here are esteemed the best in Italy. All the Men are Eunuchs, except One, in every Opera, they sing Base or Tenor.' He intended to stay in Venice for two months and then go to Rome, 'which is about four hundred Miles further. I designed to have gone along with the Venetian Ambassador to Turkey from hence, and thence to Jerusalem, but I came too late.'[21] He told his mother on 12 March 1706: 'I pass my time very well here, being almost Master of the Tongue … I take so much Delight in Travelling, that was it not on the Account of my Friends, I would not see England this five Years.' But he decided to leave Venice and 'make a little Tour into Lombardy, to take off the Imputation of those scandalous Suspicions, which, very often, are not without Grounds'.[22]

By 12 June 1706 Thomas Price was in Florence and sent his father a full description of the Gallery of the Great Duke which 'joins, one End, to the Old Palace, and the other to the River'. He noted that 'The first Room, is furnished with 200 Pictures of the most famous Painters, done by their own Hands; they may be more esteemed for their Works than their beauty.'[23] He described the principal churches and palaces and observed that at Pratolino the 'Great Duke's House' had 'a large Grove walled in of about 25 acres, well stocked with pheasants'. But, 'as to the Government, it is altogether Despotick, their Taxes are much higher than Ours in England'.[24] He provided a detailed description of the 'Great Duke's Palace', which contained 'the largest Collection of Pictures in the World, being 7 Rooms full. Among which are, That of the VIRGIN by Raphael Urbin; BARTHOLOMEW by Giurchin de Ceuto … The Birth of our SAVIOUR by Corregio, covered with a Chrystal, near the Bed; VENUS by TITIAN, valued at 20,000 Pistoles'.[25]

Price died suddenly in Genoa in September 1706. The cause of his death is unknown, but Curll gives several versions, including one where 'he found himself greatly out of Order. Among other Symptoms, which caused the utmost Anxiety, his Hair came off by Handfuls, and, the many Fears he had grew too strong for him to bear; insomuch, that it cost him his Life', and another where 'he was pursued by Bravoes, and through the Lattices of his Chamber Window in the Inn where he lay, shot in his Bed the next Morning'. The 'Senate of Genoua seized all his Effects', and he was buried at sea, 'being a Protestant, alias Heretick'.[26] Edmund Curll reported that 'The Expression of Mr. Justice Price, to all his Relations and Friends, even to the Day of his own Death, was, that the Loss of his eldest Son Thomas was irreparable!'[27] Subsequently Uvedale Tomkyns Price became heir to the Foxley estate and eventually succeeded his elder brother as MP for Weobley in 1713 and 1727.

The Foxley estate comprised a richly wooded valley which had been granted to Roger de Lacy at the time of the Conquest, and which subsequently became part of the estate of Llanthony Priory. At the Dissolution the land reverted to the Crown and was sold to Thomas of Credenhill in 1549. Before the end of the sixteenth century it had been sold to James Price Rodd of Hereford, after which it descended through the Rodd line until the property was shared between Robert Baron Price and Lucy Rodd's two sisters in 1691. Foxley is in the central Herefordshire Plain, the soils being mainly heavy loams derived from the Old Red Sandstone. The mansion itself was situated in a small valley surrounded on all but its south-eastern side by a horseshoe-shaped belt of hills. The area was characterised by mixed arable and pasture with many large-scale livestock enterprises, especially cattle. Hop-growing and the production of apples for cider were also very important. The steeper hillsides in Herefordshire are characteristically wooded, and much of this woodland is ancient in origin, the establishment of new woodland by planting becoming popular in the late seventeenth and eighteenth centuries.[28]

By 1714 Robert Baron Price had bought out the other co-heirs and the estate was in his sole possession. Other properties surrounding the estate were purchased piecemeal during his lifetime: various cottages and orchards in the Yarsop valley were acquired in the period 1695–1709, nearby Bishopstone Court was purchased in 1705, and additional land was acquired at Byford on Wye (1716), Mansel Gamage (1730) and Burghill (1732). Other lands were also acquired through marriage: the manors of Turnastone and Poston came into the Price family when Robert Baron Price's second son, Uvedale Tomkyns Price, married Anne, daughter of Lord Arthur Somerset, who was second son of the duke of Beaufort, in 1714 at Chelsea.[29] In 1717 Robert Baron Price built a set of almshouses prominently sited on the main road from Holyhead to England at his birthplace Cerrigydrudion, with the Price arms and an inscription in Welsh with verses from Proverbs, Tobit and Luke (Figure 2).[30]

The extension of the bounds of the estate continued through the eighteenth century and, through judicious estate consolidation, the family was

Fig. 2 Plaque on Robert 'Baron' Price's Almshouses at Cerrigydrudion, 2007. These were built in 1717 and prominently sited on the main road from Holyhead to England at his birthplace Cerrigydrudion, with the Price arms and verses from Proverbs, Tobit and Luke. (Photograph: Václav Žaloudek)

able to enjoy the prosperity that made the creation of the landscape at Foxley possible. In a letter, probably of June 1715, to her aunt Lady Anne Coventry, Anne Price described Foxley 'to which Place my Mother was so kind to go with us and seem'd to think nothing wanting, to make the place perfitly agreeable but a good House the prospect quite Round being, by most allow'd Charming'. After dinner they walked 'to the Mount … and found it full as agreeable as could be discribed I must therefore beg Leave to tell your Ladyship the whole walk from the House in the best Manner I can'. From the house

> in the first place you go throw the garden, to a grove that's so
> shaded with trees that one may on the hottest day, walk
> without the least uneaseness, from thence the next is, on the
> side of a hill, which walk is very plain and from whence one
> sees all the country, above 16 miles one way, this Last's till,
> you go into the Mount, which has the advantage of being very
> Woody, and a vast many pretty walks in it.

She noted that 'Mr Price is Resolved to have a Summer House on the top'.[31]

The lack of a good house at Foxley was rectified by Robert Baron Price when the foundation stone of a neo-classical nine-bay brick house was laid on 9 April 1719 in the sheltered Yarsop valley.[32] Anne Price told Lady Anne Coventry that 'I intend to work mightily for the Furnishing of our New Grand House.'[33] The house was probably built by William Smith (1660–1724): Robert Baron Price's bank account at Gosling's Bank shows substantial payments to him in 1720–21.[34] Andor Gomme points out that additional payments were made to William Smith in 1727–30 after his death, which indicates that Francis Smith (1672–1738) was also associated with the house.[35] Francis Smith also built a stable block (1726) and a summer house to designs by James Gibbs (1728). Smith's style was later to be criticised by both Daines Barrington and Uvedale Price.[36] Daines Barrington told the Society of Antiquaries in 1785 that he had seen several houses by 'Smith of Warwick who, between 60 & 70 years ago, was employed by many gentlemen in his Neighbourhood in building their Mansion Houses' and all were 'convenient & handsome'; but that 'there is a great sameness in the Plans, which proves he had but little invention'.[37] Uvedale Price noted in 1828 that 'most of the houses throughout the county' were 'an unvaried lump of brick'.[38] Formal terraces and enclosed gardens were laid out to the north and east of the new house.

'PITTORESQUE BEYOND IMAGINATION':[39] UVEDALE TOMKYNS PRICE (1685–1764)

Uvedale Tomkyns Price, in a memorandum dated 1735, states that he 'invented' the plan of Foxley and also the 'disposition of offices and stables'.[40] Indeed, it is probable that Uvedale Tomkyns Price, rather than his father, who by now was in his mid sixties and mainly living in London, was largely responsible for the implementation of the new house and gardens at Foxley.[41] He also worked on wall paintings inside the house, noting that in 1729 he 'finished the historical part of the staircase painting'. The landscape and garden appear to have been very much a joint effort between father and son. Uvedale Tomkyns Price was responsible for sowing one coppice wood in 1718 and another in 1733, while Robert Baron Price planted the 'walk of lime trees in front of the house' in 1728 and several horse chestnuts in 1731, when he was 76.[42] Robert Baron Price 'spent most of the money, Uvedale only £700 or £800', but they shared several costs: the 1,600 yards of lead water pipe laid down in 1733, for example, was 'borne half and half'. The 'square pond in front of the house' was put in by Robert Baron Price in 1729, while the 'bason or round pond' was by Uvedale Tomkyns Price. The statues in the lower garden were 'sent down' from London by Robert Baron Price, while a gladiator was set in the upper garden in 1735.[43]

Strangely, there is no contemporary account of the construction of the principal landscape building, the Ragged Castle on the mount. It has usually been attributed to the early 1740s, but there is an argument for dating it to the 1720s or 1730s (Plate 1).[44] Susan Sloman has pointed out the interesting resemblance with the old gatehouse at Giler.[45] Certainly the Castle must have been built some time between June 1715, when Anne Price told her aunt 'Mr Price is Resolved to have a Summer House on the top' of the mount,[46] and 1744, when Robert Price made his pen and wash drawing *The Castle and Mount at Foxley in Herefordshire* (Figure 3).

It is thus certain that both father and son were involved in the landscaping and gardening at Foxley, and that Uvedale Tomkyns Price played a large role

Fig. 3 Robert Price, *The Castle and Mount at Foxley Herefordshire*, 1744 This drawing by Uvedale Price's father is the earliest representation of the strange folly at Foxley also known as the Ragged Castle. (See Plate 1) (Hereford City Library)

well before his father's death in 1733 in Kensington.[47] He continued to enlarge the estate at Foxley thereafter.[48] Many of his cultural tastes were informed by the Grand Tour he had made to France and Italy between 1709 and 1712,[49] which left him with a passionate interest in landscape and music. After his father's death he employed William or Francis Smith in additional building work at Foxley.[50] He noted 'The hall at Foxley when first built was no higher than the rest of the rooms upon that floor, but was raised to 2 storeys and finished after a design of Gibbs in 1735 at expense of Uvedale Price.'[51] He also built a library to his designs in the same year. In 1733 he published a parody, later mistakenly attributed to his grandson, *A New Catechism for the Fine Ladies*:

> The Maid is blest that will not hear
> Of masquerading Tricks,
> Nor lends to wanton Songs an Ear,
> Nor sighs for Coach and Six.
> To please her shall her Husband strive,
> With all his Main and Might,
> And in her Love shall exercise
> Himself both Day and Night.
> *She* shall bring forth most pleasant Fruit,
> He flourish still and stand,
> Even so all *Things* shall prosper well,
> That this Maid takes in *Hand*.
> No wicked Whores shall have such Luck,
> Who follow their own Wills,
> But purg'd shall be to Skin and Bone,
> With Mercury and Pills.
> For why, the pure and cleanly Maids
> Shall all good Husbands gain;
> But filthy and uncleanly Jades
> Shall rot in *Drury-Lane*.[52]

His wife, Anne, led a lively social life and was a friend of Martha Blount and Alexander Pope.[53] They had four children, but only Robert (1721–1761) survived childhood. Anne Price suffered from ill health and visited 'Aix la Chappelle, for the benefit of the Spaw' in 1731 and Spa in 1740; she died at Hampstead in 1741.[54] After her death Uvedale Tomkyns Price spent much of his time at Bath, where his friends included musicians and artists.

A key figure in the formation of the Price family's interest in art was Arthur Pond (1701–1758), who went on the Grand Tour from 1725 to 1727 (about ten years after Uvedale Tomkyns Price) with the painter George Knapton, the poet and artist John Dyer (1700–58) and the antiquarian Daniel Wray. They all became members of the Roman Club in London.[55] Pond emerged in the 1730s as a fashionable portrait painter, print seller and connoisseur. He partnered John and Paul Knapton in the production and sale of Italian Landscapes

(1741–46) after paintings by Gaspard Dughet, Claude Lorrain and others in English collections. Louise Lippincott argues that such prints 'broadened public interest in landscapes painted in the style of Claude Lorrain at a crucial moment in the development of English taste and garden design'.[56] Pond was also a member of the Common Room, a group of scholarly grand tourists with interests in classical studies, natural history and old master drawings. Other members included Benjamin Stillingfleet, William Windham, Richard Aldworth (later Neville) and Robert Price (1721–61).[57] According to Louise Lippincott, Arthur Pond's surviving accounts 1734–50 demonstrate the Price family to be 'stalwart' long-term patrons who purchased prints and drawings, commissioned portraits and lent paintings to be engraved.[58] Uvedale Tomkyns Price bought drawings in December 1737 and on many occasions thereafter through to Christmas Day 1749. He purchased two small 'Landskips Horizonti' in March 1740, several Paninis, two Rembrandt drawings in 1748 and a Polidoro pen and wash drawing in December 1749.[59] A drawing from Price's collection of a young man seated at a table, by Annibale Carracci, was engraved by Pond in 1747. Another of his drawings, 'Envy with her Toads', was formerly attributed to Veronese but is now thought to be by Pierino da Vinci and is in the British Museum.

Uvedale Tomkyns Price mainly lived in Bath from 1741 (when he was 55) until his death aged 79 in 1764. He was Lord of the Manor of Caldicot, which included the ruined medieval Caldicot Castle to the south-west of Chepstow, where the River Tregony joins the Severn.[60] He was a very keen collector of paintings and prints, and built up a considerable library.[61] He was also an enthusiastic scholar and author. His translation of Antonio Palomino de Castro y Velasco, *An Account of the Lives and Works of the Most Eminent Spanish Painters, Sculptors and Architects from the Musæum Pictorium*, was published in 1739.[62] His *An Account of the Most Remarkable Places and Curiosities in Spain and Portugal* appeared in 1749, with a second edition in 1760, under the name Udal ap Rhys, emphasising his Welsh ancestry and connection. In this travel guide he argues that 'Spain is not only the greatest Repository of fine Paintings; but the Face of the Country itself is rich, beautiful, and pittoresque beyond Imagination.' He included a catalogue of the cities, towns and villages with 'exact distances, after a new and accurate method. Many of which are not to be found in any Maps extant.'[63] There is no independent evidence that Uvedale Tomkyns Price visited Spain or Portugal, and the quarrelsome Philip Thicknesse argued that his book 'abounds with many flagrant falsehoods' and that 'it was written, indeed, as many modern travels are, over a pipe in his own chimney corner. DON UDAL, never was in Spain.'[64]

Susan Sloman has demonstrated conclusively the importance of Uvedale Tomkyns Price as a patron of Gainsborough at Bath.[65] Price and Gainsborough became friends from about 1758, when he was in his seventies and Gainsborough was 31. His portrait by Gainsborough (1761–63) shows him seated next to a collection of drawings, with a half-completed sketch of

Fig. 4 William Hoare, *Uvedale Tomkyns Price*, c.1760–61. Chalk on grey-green paper. Price's scholarly connoisseurship is indicated by the books, statuette of Minerva, classical relief and porte-crayon. (© Trustees of the British Museum)

shredded trees in his hand and a framed landscape on the wall over his shoulder. Another portrait by William Hoare (1707–92) is of a similar date but emphasises Price's scholarly interests, with several books, a statuette of Minerva and a classical relief (Figure 4).

'UNBOUND BY GLITTERING CHAINS':[66] ROBERT PRICE (1717–1761)

Uvedale Tomkyns Price's son Robert was a keen artist who also had strong links with Gainsborough. He had a great influence on the landscape of Foxley even though he never came into the family property himself, predeceasing his father by three years in 1761. Although relatively unknown now, he was an influential figure who was to leave a lasting impact in many areas of eighteenth-century cultural life, not least the 'naturalistic' mode of landscape drawing and gardening.[67] He knew Hogarth, his son Uvedale Price noting that: 'My father was very much acquainted with him, and I remember his telling me, that one day Hogarth, talking to him with great earnestness on his favourite subject, asserted, that no man thoroughly possessed with the true idea of the line of beauty, could do any thing in an ungraceful manner ... "He happened," said my father, "at that moment, to be sitting in the most ridiculously awkward posture I ever beheld".[68] Undoubtedly, Robert Price's passions for landscape and his patronage of artists such as Gainsborough and John Baptist Malchair had a significant influence on the theories developed by his son, Uvedale, who was to inherit Foxley.

Robert Price was 'of a robust and athletic make' and 'loved manly exercise and excelled in them all', including boxing. Indeed, according to William Coxe, Price 'would have been the first tennis player in England; but his father telling him one day, he feared exercise might make him into bad company, he never would take a racket afterwards'. Price could speak Italian and write French, although he did not prove himself to be a scholar at Winchester College, and was not 'of a precocious nature' with 'any brilliancy of parts'. He was of a 'serious aspect, and reserved behaviour', and yet he was 'a great lover of fun and merriment' and was keen to develop his knowledge and understanding by travel and conversation.[69] Robert Price's passion for landscape was informed greatly by his experience of the Grand Tour between 1738 and 1741, when he visited Turin, Florence, Rome, Naples, Venice and Geneva.[70] His travelling companions, who were to become lifelong friends and influences, included William Windham (1717–1761),[71] Windham's tutor Benjamin Stillingfleet (1702–1771) and Richard Pococke (1704–1765). In Rome the group took lessons from Giovanni Battista Busiri (1698–1757), 'one of the first masters in drawing landscapes with the pen'.[72] Busiri, a follower of Gaspard Poussin, was well known in the eighteenth century for his paintings and drawings of 'landscapes and classical ruins in Rome and the Campagna'.[73] Benjamin Stillingfleet noted that Price 'copied nature with unwearied diligence; he reflected much, reduced every part of drawing to clear and stable principles; and matured his knowledge by the conversation of virtuosi; and artists of the first order'.[74] Price also studied music at Rome with Andrew Basili, and some of Price's songs and trios, 'delicate and expressive' and 'composed in the Italian style', were 'much approved by the best judges'.[75]

The group studied history, natural philosophy and botany together while staying at the Academy in Geneva, and established the 'Common Room' (or The Bloods). The group also included Thomas, 7th earl of Haddington, and his brother George Hamilton, their tutor the Rev. John Williamson, Benjamin Tate of Mitcham in Surrey, and his tutor Thomas Dampier.[76] Coxe related that the group 'passed their leisure hours in amicable or literary discourse, admitting occasionally persons of different countries, distinguished either by any superior merit, or singular peculiarity'.[77] They achieved some reputation for theatrical performances, which they staged to great success, with Price arranging the orchestra, composing the music and helping Windham to paint the scenery. According to Coxe, Price was also a versatile actor: he played 'with great judgment and propriety' Banquo in *Macbeth*, Caled in the *Siege of Damascus* and Scaramouch in a pantomime which the group itself composed.[78]

A key moment of the tour was the group's expedition to the Alps in June 1741 to observe the glacier near Mont Blanc. This expedition, on which they were accompanied by the travel writer and naturalist Dr Richard Pococke, was later publicised in a report in *Mercure de Suisse* in 1743 and commemorated by the Swiss themselves with a large stone erected directly on the glacier.[79] The trip was significant in being one of the first ever made to the glacier purely in the pursuit of knowledge. Stillingfleet's biographer observed that it 'gave the first impulse to that curiosity which has since led travellers of every nation into the wildest recesses of the Alps and has produced discoveries highly valuable to the cultivation of Natural History in general and equally important towards ascertaining the structure and changes of the globe'.[80] Windham later published an account of the experience in London in 1744, describing the glacier as a 'Lake put in Agitation by a strong Wind, and frozen all at once', while Robert Price's drawing of the Mer de Glace broke new ground and was later engraved by Francis Vivares (1709–80).[81]

Robert Price's tour ended in Paris, where he met new artists and engravers and added to his collection of prints. He met Jacques-Philippe Le Bas (1707–83), who 'was just come in from walking … it is his custom when he walks out, to take his book with him, and in case he sees anything picturesque, to sketch it out'.[82] This gave Price the idea of carrying a sketchbook around at all times, an idea that was later in turn to be adopted by John Baptist Malchair.[83] Price, writing from Paris in November 1741, told William Windham: 'The other day I invited Laurent and Le Bas to breakfast with me, and to show them Busiris Landskapes; I was very agreeably surprised to see Soubeyran whom they brought along with them. They look'd over all Busiris things and were vastly pleas'd with them.' Price noted that

> Soubeyran, Laurent and Le Bas have been pressing me very
> much to engrave Busiri's things in aquafortis: I believe when I
> am settled in England I shall undertake it though I fear it is
> much beyond my force: I may hope at least that when I get to
> the last I shall know something of the matter.[84]

Back in London the following month, he wrote to Lord Haddington in Geneva: 'I would not give the worst of my Busiris watercolours, for the best picture I ever saw of him', referring to John Wooton (1681/2–1764), the fashionable landscape painter.[85] He also reported that 'I have shown my Father my Busiris things, my prints that I bought at Paris, and given him a noting of what he is to expect from my Collection of prints, and Musick, that is coming by Carrier.' He had smuggled several Busiri sketches back to England in a fiddle case. His father commended him 'for having lay'd out my money in so sensible a manner, and not having let slip an opportunity of buying what will be a continual source of pleasure to me'.[86]

A group family portrait of the Prices by Bartholomew Dandridge (1691–c.1754) recorded Robert Price in the year of his return to England in 1741, the year also of his mother's death (Figure 5).[87] When this painting was sold out of the Price family in 1893 it was described as showing 'Uvedale T Price of Foxley, Herefordshire, and Geeler, Denbighshire assisting his cousin Miss Rodd from a boat, his eldest son Robert leading another cousin Miss Greville, her sister Hester feeding Swans, their brother called Jockey Greville fondling a greyhound, other relations and attendants around'.[88] Susan Sloman considers that the lady is more likely to be Anne Price than Miss Rodd, but the identification of the individual members of the family still remains uncertain.[89] Price rented a house in Panton Square with William Windham, which they shared with Benjamin Stillingfleet.[90] In 1746 he married Sarah Barrington, daughter of Lord Barrington, and returned to live at Foxley, while his father lived mainly in Bath. Robert Price started to buy prints and drawing from Arthur Pond in June 1746; he also bought drawing equipment including 'plates, vernish and burnishers' in June 1746 and two quires of paper in June 1747. A portrait of 'Honble Miss price' of June 1746 is probably his wife Sarah, whom he married that month. In 1749 he paid Arthur Pond for another portrait of 'Mrs price and Master Price': his wife Sarah and the infant Uvedale Price, who was born in 1747. Over the next ten years the Prices had four other children who survived childhood, all boys: Robert, William, Samuel and Barrington.

Fig. 5 Bartholomew Dandridge, *Uvedale Tomkyns Price and members of his Family.* c. 1741. This group portrait shows Uvedale Tomkyns Price and other family members including his son Robert Price the year he returned from his Grand Tour. (Metropolitan Museum of Art New York, Rogers Fund 1920 20.40)

Robert Price continued the extensive landscaping at Foxley begun by his father and grandfather. The improvements were on a large scale and involved tree planting, woodland management, agricultural experimentation and the creation of rides and prospects.[91] He made shooting butts and planted trees about them in 1747; planted horse chestnut trees in the meadow by Yazor church in the same year; sowed a wood with acorns 'to the west of the firs on Ladylift' in 1759; and, the following year, planted a wood south of Burton Hill Common.[92] Two drawings of Foxley made by Robert Price in the 1740s document the Prices' activities. The first, signed and dated 1744, is 'The Castle and Mount at Foxley in Herefordshire', which shows the folly overlooking an apparently uncultivated valley, with the house hidden behind the mount. The second is 'A View of Foxley in Herefordshire' of 1753. The Ragged Castle is shown almost enveloped in trees above Foxley in this drawing, which also shows the house set in pasture fields with cattle, a plantation fenced against the cattle and wooded sheep pastures. Francis Smith's stables lie to the north-west of the house, and there are extensive barns and other farm buildings. This subtle move towards an appreciation of cultivation and husbandry reflects Robert Price's increasing interest in agricultural improvement.

A significant part in the changes made at Foxley at this time was played by Benjamin Stillingfleet, Price's companion on the Grand Tour. Stillingfleet moved to Foxley in 1746 and 'took up his residence in a neighbouring cottage, where he was perfectly master of his time and pursuits, and passed his leisure hours within the family'.[93] Price encouraged him in the development of his thinking, which was now heavily influenced by Linnaean principles.[94] Stillingfleet's *Miscellaneaous Tracts* (1759) gave Linnaeus's works greater notice in England at a time when they were still relatively obscure.[95] One advantage of his move to Foxley was that Stillingfleet was able to put into practice his theories on Linnaean investigation. He and Price took extensive tours together into the surrounding country to examine the local flora and to sketch from nature, including in 1759 a journey into Wales, where they rode to the top of Cader Idris and met Daines Barrington, Price's brother-in-law, at Ffestiniog.[96] F. I. McCarthy reconstructed the 1759 tour by studying the pencil drawings held at the National Library of Wales. The tour began and ended at Foxley and the principal towns visited were Knighton, Newton, Dolgellau, Barmouth, Harlech, Ffestiniog, Llanwrst, Denbigh, Ruthin, Bala and Montgomery. Many waterfalls were visited and McCarthy notes that 'the content of the drawings shows Price's love of mountain scenery, and a special felicity in depicting the gullies and roughnesses of ravines and waterfalls.' Although 'some of the scenes exhibit sublime subjects, most tend towards picturesque taste … a remarkably early manifestation of this kind of art in England', and the influence of Gaspard Poussin 'on Price's love of wild nature' is shown by his 'Water-break-its-neck in Radnorshire'. Several of Price's sketches from these tours survive, and a number were later engraved by Isaac Basire.[97] Stillingfleet wrote in March 1760 to his former Common Room associate, Mr Neville of Stanlake,[98] that he and

Price had come to London together (his children remaining in Foxley, having been inoculated), and that he had brought more than fifty drawings with him.[99] Price also made copies of drawings from other artists, including a landscape by Anthonie Waterloo.

Benjamin Stillingfleet described in detail the way – 'which I never saw practised anywhere else' – in which Robert Price made new walks at Foxley. 'He first walked over the whole ground, following, as well he could, the gentlest and most gradual ascent all the way, and pacing it to the top of the hill.' When the top was reached 'he took the whole height, and, by an easy operation in arithmetic, found out how much it rose in any number of feet or yards by the way he had marked.' Finally, with the

> help of a triangle and plummet, he made the path rise
> regularly, and, in some places, where the height did not bear a
> great proportion to the length of the walk, insensibly; so that
> you go to the top of a high and steep hill without any labour,
> and without knowing that you were not upon plain ground.

Stillingfleet argued that this method had two additional advantages. First, 'the walk was lengthened', which was a considerable benefit 'where space is wanted', and, second, 'that by the winding of the path you were constantly enjoying a new prospect'. Moreover, 'both these advantages were gained without affectation, which appears in all winding walks, upon a flat, however well managed, unless the plantation itself winds.'[100] Stillingfleet told Windham in 1757 that Price's 'walks or rather rides, for they will admit of wheel-carriages, will take in a compass of 6 or 7 miles diversify'd with different prospects'.[101] He also improved the local roads and 'condescended to fill the place of surveyor of the highways to two parishes each year: he fulfilled the duties of that inferior office with the strictest regularity and perseverance, acting with such disinterestedness, that he first finished those roads' furthest from Foxley.[102] Price also advised the map maker and land agent Isaac Taylor of Ross in the production of his maps of Herefordshire and the City of Hereford of 1757.[103]

Price's friend Richard Pococke visited the estate in September 1756 and wrote:

> The house is in a bottom on one side of the vale, which is
> form'd by a chain of hills in form of a circus, and covered with
> wood. He is practising a rideing all round the inside and
> outside of the hills, which within is at least six miles, and
> making sheep walks down from the wood, and corn fields are
> to be in the middle.

In addition to the rides, there were 'from the house … winding walks through woods of fine young oaks, up to the top of a little hill, which commands a view of the country'. The range of views over Herefordshire, Radnorshire and 'a great way farther into Wales' and towards Worcestershire formed 'altogether the greatest variety of prospects I ever saw without going two miles from the house'.[104] The principal route for the rides ran though Darkhill Wood and up to the Cold Bath, where the remains of a bath and spring with associated stone walling are still visible today. From there the ride took in the Ladylift clump, a prominent clump of old Scots pines whose origins remain obscure.[105] From Ladylift the ride progressed around the head of the valley through Walks Wood and Shukes Bank, and crossed open land before entering Bach Wood. It then passed the edge of Pole Wood and Merryhill Wood before reaching Mansel Lacy. Much of the route remains evident as a ride today, not least because in a number of places substantial walls and drains were required in order to lay out the rides. The development of the woodland rides was a particularly important feature of the changes made at Foxley by Robert Price. The winding routes through the woods created the illusion of scale while allowing extensive views across open countryside.

After Robert Price's death, Stillingfleet was offered and accepted the post of Master of the Barracks at Kensington by Lord Barrington, Price's brother-in-law; in response, Stillingfleet dedicated his *Calendar of Flora* to Barrington.[106] Stillingfleet wrote a series of sonnets to friends who were members of the Common Room. The first was addressed to Robert Price:[107]

TO PRICE

Grandson to that good man, who bravely dared
Withstand a Monarch's will, when crowds around
Of noble serving men stoop'd to the ground
Whene'er Corruption's guilty face appear'd;
Thou nobly firm, like him, hast ever rear'd
Thy front sublime; thou, with the giddy found
Steady and wise, hast kept thyself unbound
By glittering chains that others have ensnar'd;
So shall thy virtue due reward obtain,
While they, like Greeks and Trojans: heretofore,
Fright holy Virtue from her graceful seat;
Destroying each his rival, but to gain
A Phantom Helen; thou shalt her adore,
Her real, and enjoy in thy retreat.

In his memoir of Price, Stillingfleet describes how after marriage he 'retired to the country' and, 'besides his application to Music and Drawing, he paid particular attention to Agriculture'.[108] Robert Price encouraged Stillingfleet to conduct experiments into the planting of different sorts of grasses in order to determine which were the best species for the improvement of turf and the nourishment of cattle.[109] The findings of these experiments were later published as *Observations on Grasses*, the second edition of which in 1762 included seven engravings of different grass species drawn from nature by Robert Price (Figures

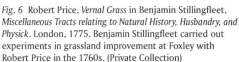

Fig. 6 Robert Price, *Vernal Grass* in Benjamin Stillingfleet, *Miscellaneous Tracts relating to Natural History, Husbandry, and Physick*. London, 1775. Benjamin Stillingfleet carried out experiments in grassland improvement at Foxley with Robert Price in the 1760s. (Private Collection)

Fig. 7 Robert Price, *Great Meadow Grass* in Benjamin Stillingfleet, *Miscellaneous Tracts relating to Natural History, Husbandry, and Physick*. London, 1775. (Private Collection)

6 and 7). Zoffany's portrait of Stillingfleet of c.1761 celebrates his botanising by showing him with a magnifying glass and with grasses on a table. The land agent Nathaniel Kent, who knew Stillingfleet, drew attention to these experiments and recommended them as examples of profitable estate improvements in his *Hints to a Gentleman of Landed Property* (1776).[110]

Price was 'constantly surrounded by his family and friends; for he pursued his studies in a room open to all, not finding the smallest interruption from the conversation of those who were present, or from the noise of children, who were allowed to divert themselves without undue restraint'.[111] His favourite musical instrument was the violin and 'he excelled in expression'. He wrote two musical treatises and 'set to music' Metastasio's oratorio *Guiseppe Riconosciuto* and 'Se mai turbo' from *Allessandro nell' Indie*, mentioned by Charles Burney as a pasticcio performed in 1756.[112] The composer John Christopher Smith (1712–1795) knew Robert Price and Benjamin Stillingfleet, and Price 'according to Burney, gave him "a taste for, and procured him admission into, good company; so that he formed his character on models of a higher class than that of a mere musician"'.[113] Another important relationship cultivated by Robert Price was with John Baptist Malchair (1730–1812). Born in Cologne and resident in England from 1754, Malchair was a professional violinist and drawing master. He worked for some time in Hereford before taking up the post of leader of the Oxford Music Room in 1760.[114] His talents for drawing and music drew him to the attention of Robert Price, and Malchair made several visits to Foxley over the period to draw from nature. Malchair's visit of June 1757 was to be particularly influential, since he learned from Price the practice of sketching directly into a sketch book rather than onto separate sheets of paper. A note in Malchair's own hand in his first sketchbook of 1757 states:

> The first lot of drawings after Nature. The few attempts I made before this were on single papers. The method of drawing in a book was adopted from Robert Price, Esqr. of Foxley Herefordshire. From him I received a deal of useful information respecting the art of drawing, for he was himself an excellent artist as well as patron.[115]

Fig. 8 Thomas Gainsborough, *Beech trees at Foxley*, 1760. Chalk, watercolour and body colour over pencil. The Price family were patrons of Gainsborough in Bath and this drawing was made on a visit to Foxley. The beech tree on the left side is recently pollarded. (Whitworth Art Gallery Manchester D. 1896, 1)

Malchair was to make several return visits to Foxley, including one in September 1772, not long after Uvedale Price had inherited the estate.

Robert Price was painted twice by Gainsborough in about 1758 and about 1761, the year of his death. The later of these paintings was engraved by Basire as after Zoffany 'from an original in the possession of his Son William Price Esq', but Susan Sloman has demonstrated that it was by Gainsborough.[116] The Prices' patronage of Gainsborough was to play a significant role in the development of Gainsborough's art and his success as a professional artist after his move to Bath in 1758/59. He visited Foxley in 1760 and his 'Beech trees at Foxley' is signed and dated in that year (Figure 8). This shows two beech trees growing on a pronounced knoll or tump, with a curving path leading to a distant tower, possibly the tower of old Yazor church. To the left is a recently pollarded tree, while to the right is a rustic fence. A later label on the back of the picture reads 'A study from nature, by Gainsborough when on a visit to Foxley'.

Gainsborough's acquaintance with the adult members of the Price family was to be cut short. Robert's wife, Sarah, died in 1759, and Robert Price died suddenly in 1761, at the age of just 44. According to Stillingfleet, his death was 'accelerated by undertaking a journey to attend his father, who was dangerously ill, at a time when he himself had scarcely recovered from a fit of gout'.[117] In the church at Yazor there are also memorials to Charles Price, aged 5, Sophia, aged 2 and John aged 9, who died in 1760 and 1761, all children of Robert and Sarah Price.[118] Robert's father Uvedale Tomkyns Price died three years later in March 1764, aged 79, leaving the estate to Robert Price's heir Uvedale, in minority. His memorial stone in Bath Abbey emphasises that the young Uvedale had 'succeeded to the antient family Estates of Geelar and Foxley'.[119] Two years before his death he gave a copy of Pine's *Horatii Flacci Opera* of 1733 to his grandson, then aged fifteen.[120] It was inscribed 'this curious copy of Pine's Horace belonged to Prince Eugene, and is presented by Uvedale Price to his Godson Uvedale Price, 1762': a portent of the extraordinary inheritance of landed property, prints, drawings, paintings, trees, ideas and landscapes that came to the young Uvedale Price.

CHAPTER 2

'MACARONY OF THE AGE'[1]

CHILDHOOD AND GRAND TOUR

Uvedale Price, who was born in 1747, was 12 when his mother died, 14 and still at Eton at the time of his father's death in 1761 and 17 when his grandfather died three years later in 1764. His school days at Eton were to exert a great deal of influence on him, and this must have been starkly emphasised by the early death of his parents and of two brothers and a sister. Writing to Lord Aberdeen in 1816, Price noted: 'I was bred at Eton, + have the strongest attachment to it.'[2] His headmaster at Eton was Edward Barnard (1717–1781), who taught Greek, including Greek plays, to both Price and his friend Charles James Fox. (Price later described him as 'an elegant, but by no means a deep scholar'.[3]) Another strong influence was that of his maternal Barrington uncles: William Wildman Barrington (1717–1793), second Viscount Barrington, politician; John Barrington (1719–1764), army officer; Daines Barrington (1727/8–1800), judge, antiquary and naturalist; Samuel Barrington (1729–1800), naval officer; and Shute Barrington (1734–1826), successively canon of Christ Church Oxford, bishop of Llandaff, bishop of Salisbury and bishop of Durham. The Barrington estate was at Beckett, near Shrivenham, Berkshire. Uvedale Price's youngest surviving brother was named Barrington Price, and there continued to be important financial and intellectual relations between the Prices and the Barringtons over the next century.

At Eton Uvedale Price's contemporaries included Charles James Fox, of whom Price recounted many years later that 'Our friendship and intimacy, which began at Eton, continued without interruption through life. While Etonians, we acted together in the plays given at Holland House' which 'had at the time great celebrity'.[4] Horace Walpole noted that he had been 'excessively amused' and that 'one Price, Lord Barrington's nephew, was Gloster, and acted better than three parts of the comedians'.[5] Uvedale left Eton for Oxford with Fox, attending Christ Church College, where his uncle Shute Barrington was Dean 1761–68. He matriculated without a degree from Christ Church in 1763. In addition to his uncle he knew John Baptist Malchair, who taught drawing at Oxford (Figure 9) and who led the Oxford Music Band from 1760 onwards. This friendship is likely to have done much to encourage his lifelong interest in music and art. He was a keen singer but did not, unlike his father, play a musical instrument or draw. The only report of his time at Oxford

is from an unreliable account written more than sixty years later by Lord Egremont who was 'about four years younger than him, and followed him at the university and the college was then fill of ridiculous stories of his selfishness'. He thought Price ought 'to be immortalised in a comedy. His extreme selfishness for his own sensual comforts, is not acquired … by indulgence, but is an innate instinct of the animal.'[6]

After leaving Oxford at the age of 17 Price continued to visit his grandfather Uvedale Tomkyns Price at Bath, whose portrait by Gainsborough was completed in 1764. In his *Essay* Uvedale Price recollects that when Gainsborough 'lived at Bath, I made frequent excursions with him into the country; he was a man of an eager irritable mind, though warmly attached to those he loved; of a lively and playful imagination, yet at times severe and sarcastic'. Price recalled that 'when we came to cottage or village scenes, to groups of children, or to any objects of that kind which struck his fancy, I have often remarked in his countenance an expression of particular gentleness and complacency'.[7] Price also remembered an occasion when he and Gainsborough visited a house to view a collection of pictures, which included a portrait of the owner said to be by Sir Joshua Reynolds. On closer enquiry, the housekeeper confirmed that every aspect of the picture apart from the face had been 'totally changed, and newly composed as well as painted, by another, and, I need not add, an inferior hand'.[8]

Fig. 9 J. B. Malchair, *The Garden of Shute Barrington, Canon of Christ Church*. Graphite with watercolour. Uvedale Price's uncle Shute Barrington was Dean at Christ Church College 1761–8. Price matriculated from the College in 1763 and this drawing is by his father's friend John Baptist Malchair who taught music and drawing at Oxford. (© Trustees of the British Museum)

After his grandfather's death in 1764 Price's guardian was Lord Barrington.[9] Thirty years later he felt unable to 'resist paying a tribute to the memory of a beloved uncle, and recording a benevolence towards all the inhabitants around him that struck me from my earliest remembrance; and it is an impression I wish always to cherish'. Price emphasised his uncle's compassion:

> It seemed as if he had made his extensive walks as much for
> them as for himself; they used them as freely, and *their*
> enjoyment was *his*. The village bore as strong marks of his and
> of his brother's attentions (for in that respect they appeared
> to have but one mind), to the comforts and pleasures of its
> inhabitants.[10]

This benevolent attitude at Beckett was one which Price saw himself as keen to emulate when he started to manage his own estate at Foxley.

Price toured Italy and France with Fox in 1767 and 1768, visiting Genoa (1767), Florence, Rome, Venice and Turin (1768).[11] Price noted that we 'were almost constantly together at Florence, where we studied Italian under the same master at the same time. From Rome we travelled together along the eastern coast to Venice, and thence to Turin, where we met by appointment our excellent friend and schoolfellow, Lord Fitzwilliam.'[12] Another member of the party was Richard Fitzpatrick, who had been at Westminster School and became a great friend of Fox after the marriage of his sister Mary to Fox's elder brother Stephen, later second Baron Holland, in 1766. In October 1767 Fox wrote a gossipy letter from Turin to Price in Florence. He mentioned delivering some music to Cortoni and that 'Kitty + Angelina are as charming as ever; I believe they will be my principal company while I am here: they are both sweet girls.' He planned, 'as the weather is so fine on taking the Grand Chartreuse in my way to Lyons, + I do not find that it will delay me at all'. He tells Price that he will have to 'continue to owe you the 25 Louis (I think that is the sum) till I see you in Italy next Spring'.[13] In December 1767 Price and Lord Fitzwilliam stayed at the English-style hotel in Florence run by Charles Hadfield, who was a dealer in art and father of the artist Maria Hadfield, later the wife of Richard Cosway.[14] They just missed meeting up with Price's friend John Skippe, who had travelled down to Rome 1766–67 and stayed in Florence in June 1767 on the way to Venice.[15] The wealthy Fitzwilliam returned home in 1769 with fourteen pictures by artists such as Canaletto, Guercino and Guido Reni.

Charles James Fox stayed in Nice for several months and wrote to Price in February 1768: 'I have scarce looked into an Italian book since I have been here …' and 'My Spanish I have in a manner left off, but I shall resume it'.[16] This is because of two women Fox had met: Mrs Holmes, an Irish woman he visits every morning 'exquisite entertainment for Charles', but, as she is chaste, 'not for Carlino'; and Madᵉ Castelnard, a silversmith's wife, whom he visited every evening. 'She is the woman who at present receives Carlino, who never desired, much less ever had, better lodging. I was a long time here before I could get a f… but in recompense for my sufferings I have now got a most excellent piece that must be allowed.' He promised to send Price a poem on the Pox and agreed to Price's suggestion to visit Voltaire at Ferney: 'I agree with you that it would be scandalous to go home without having seen Voltaire.' He then planned his journey to Rome, where he hoped to meet Price and Fitzpatrick. He was going to Genoa for three days: 'I will not forget to see the Pallavicini Palace. From Genoa I will go to Lerici, to Lucca, Pisa, Leghorn, + Sienna + so to Rome, where I probably shall be by April 15.' He hoped to find 'you + Fitz at Rome' and advised Price to travel 'to Naples now, that you may be back at Rome by that time'. He continued in laddish vein:

> I shall send Matcham to Florence to b…r Sir Horace[17] de ma
> part, + fetch my cloaths, + make him meet me at Sienna…
> G.d D…n the Cardinal Vicar, he is as bad as the Bishop here;
> but yet I f…k in spite of him, + so I hope you will in spite of
> his Eminence.

The letter ends in praise of friendship: 'I am beyond measure obliged to you all for wishing me with you, indeed friendship is the only real happiness in this world, + in that respect no one can be happier than myself.'[18]

The tour left a deep impression on Uvedale Price, and he reminisced about it in his seventies, writing to Sir George Beaumont, who was in Italy in 1822: 'How I long to be with you, + to see Rome again after an absence of above half a century, + to see it with you!'[19] Price recalled his purchase of six drawings by Salvator Rosa while travelling through Perugia in 1767/8:

> Gavin Hamilton, knowing I was going from Rome through
> Perugia said to me, if you can manage to find out a house
> where there is a very long drawing of Moses shaking the rock
> by Polydore over a door, + can tempt the owners to sell it,
> you will be a happy man. I did find the house, tempted the
> owner, + bought the drawing, which, however, was not a
> Polydore but a Beccafumi; + I dare say you remember it from
> its enormous length when open'd, + from its being folded
> several times on its paper hinges.[20]

The Beccafumi was purchased for the British Museum after the Price sale in 1854 and is now described as 'A frieze with Moses striking the rock, after Domenico Beccafumi (1501–1551) … on several sheets conjoined of buff prepared paper' (Figure 10).

Price purchased from the same man six drawings by Salvator Rosa which he considered to be 'admirable specimens of the unparalleled freedom + lightness of his pen':

> The man of the house then told me that he had some other
> drawings, which, having parted with this, he should be willing

Fig. 10 After Domenico Beccafumi, *A frieze with Moses striking the rock* (detail), Pen and brown ink, with brown wash on several sheets conjoined of buff prepared paper. Uvedale Price bought this drawing in Perugia in June 1768. (© Trustees of the British Museum)

to dispose of; + he carried me into a room hung round with them: besides 7 Salvators, there were several drawings of great merit, + some of very high relish: I fell in Paradise. We soon made a bargain; he wanted money, + I did not care for it; so I bought all but one drawing, which gold would not tempt him to part with.

These drawings were also purchased for the British Museum at the Price sale of 1854 and include 'Study of trees', 'Monks with Silenus and satyrs', 'Two figures in a rocky landscape', 'Study of stump of old tree', 'A magnificent study of a tree' and 'Four monks seated at the foot of a tree' (Figures 11 and 12). The depictions of trees in the 'Study of trees' show extraordinarily shattered and contorted stems characteristic of trees damaged by an ice storm or 'galaverna'. They epitomise aspects of the picturesque later to be theorised by Price.

In August 1768 he visited Voltaire at Ferney with Fox and Lord Fitzwilliam. They set out to Geneva from Turin 'but went out of our direct road to that most singular and striking place, the Grande Chartreuse, so finely described in Gray's Alcaic Ode. From Geneva Fox and I went to Voltaire at Ferny, having obtained a permission then seldom granted.' Price emphasised that it 'is an event in one's life to have seen and heard that extraordinary man: he was old and infirm, and, in answer to Fox's note and request, said that the name of Fox was sufficient, and that he could not refuse seeing us'. Voltaire, he remembered,

Fig. 11 Salvator Rosa, *Study of trees*. Pen and brown ink. This is one of six drawings by Salvator Rosa Uvedale Price bought in Perugia in June 1768. (© Trustees of the British Museum)

Fig. 12 Salvator Rosa, *Four monks seated at the foot of a tree*. Pen and brown ink, with grey-brown wash. Uvedale Price thought his Salvator Rosa drawings were 'admirable specimens of the unparalleled freedom + lightness of his pen.' (© Trustees of the British Museum)

conversed in a lively manner walking with us to and fro in a sort
of alley; and at parting gave us a list of some of his works, adding
'Ce sont des livres de quoi il faut se munir,' they were such as
would fortify our young minds against religious prejudices.

Fox returned from Geneva directly to England 'and commenced his political career', while Price went with Fitzwilliam 'through the finest parts of Switzerland, and then down the Rhine to Spa' and Paris.[21]

At Paris in November 1768 and April 1769 Price dealt with the artist and dealer Johann-George Wille, whose studio was a lively meeting place for artists and collectors. Price wanted to sell or exchange 'un dessein de Raphael' he had acquired in Italy and gained from Wille 'un des plus beaux desseins de P. Roos' and 'd'une très-beau paysage de Both, réprésentant une Ruine de Rome'.[22] Susan Sloman notes 'It seems inconceivable that Price could have exchanged a Raphael for a drawing by Phillipe Peter Roos (1657–1705) but it is perhaps a symptom of his overwhelming interest in landscape.'[23] The Roos drawing of 'a Shepherd Boy with sheep and goats in a landscape' was retained by Price in his collection and sold in 1854, and the Jan Both 'Tomb of Martius Curtius, Rome' in the same sale is probably the other drawing in the deal.

Price followed his father, grandfather and great-grandfather in undertaking a grand tour. For him, as for many wealthy young Englishmen, it was an essential part of his education. Although we have little evidence of what Price did for much of the time on his tour, he certainly enjoyed his time with Fox and other friends enormously and looked back on this time with much pleasure. He reinforced friendships developed during his schooldays and made new friends and acquaintances keen on art and collecting. In this he was very like his father, Robert Price. Fox mentions that it was Price's idea to visit Voltaire at Ferney, and although this was not an uncommon practice for English visitors it at least indicates Price's interest in enlightenment thought and literature. He also used his time profitably in learning languages, especially Italian and French, in which he remained skilled for the rest of his life. He was not wealthy enough, unlike his friend Lord Fitzwilliam, to buy the most expensive art, but he bought many old master drawings which became a central part of his collection and which provided a stimulus for the development of his ideas on art, landscape, gardening and estate management.

INHERITANCE AND MARRIAGE

Uvedale Price returned to England in 1769. We know he visited Oxford because he much later recorded that he first met Lord Aylesford there 'where he was a student + I just come from abroad: he happened to be in the tennis-court where I was playing'. Aylesford 'was a great admirer of that game though but a bad performer, + I a great admirer of drawing tho' no performer at all: we took to each other + from that time have always been on the most cordial terms'.[24] It was not long, however, before he took control of the estate at Foxley. He commissioned a full survey of the estate in 1770, which showed that although much of his land was concentrated around the mansion of Foxley, outlying portions of the estate were intermixed with the land of other owners, both large and small (Plates 2 and 3).[25] The estate had been under trustees since his grandfather's death in 1764 and once he gained full control its management remained central to Price's interest for the rest of his life.[26] Of his brothers, William and Barrington went into the army and Robert into the church; Samuel died in Jamaica in 1773.[27] His uncle and trustee Daines Barrington was an early visitor, calling at Foxley in September 1770 on his way back from a visit to 'Dolgelly', where he had been visiting the library of Edward Lhwyd.[28] Uvedale Price's enthusiasm for trees was demonstrated by his sowing of 'two fields on the left hand side of the road to Yazor' with acorns in 1771.[29] In the same year he employed James Cranston, of James Lee, the important Hammersmith nursery, as gardener.[30]

Price made considerable modifications to the house at Foxley using designs by Robert Adam in 1772–3. He noted his improvements in the same copy of James Gibbs's *Book of Architecture* as had done his father and grandfather: 'Hall altered after design of Mr Adam and a small room made over it by Uvedale Price, 1772; New eating room. The room above it, back staircase, housekeeper's apartment built 1773 with considerable alterations to offices by Uvedale Price.' In addition, the 'Great staircase' was 'converted' into an 'antechamber and billiard room, the former back staircase altered on a design of Mr Adam, 1773, by Uvedale Price'.[31] Mrs Davies of Henbury wrote to her daughter in May 1772 at Hereford congratulating her on her visit to Foxley and matchmaking:

> On Wednesday I had the satisfaction of reading my dear
> daughter's letter, and thank her for her good description of
> Foxly – it is to be hop'd, [that] the master of that elegant
> mansion will think of the best piece of furniture to compleat
> the whole, [that] he may enjoy his improvements with double
> relish.[32]

The costs of such improvements were offset by the sale of some of the Welsh properties at Giler, Denbighshire, in this year. This reduction in his Welsh patrimony and property was to be partially offset twenty years later by his building of Castle House in Aberystwyth.

It was in this period that Price's friendship with Richard Payne Knight (1751–1824) developed. And at exactly the time Price was modifying his existing mansion at Foxley, the much wealthier Knight was building his extraordinary new gothic castle at Downton (1772–78), near Ludlow, on the borders of Herefordshire and Shropshire. In the same period Mancel Lacy House was built for William Price, Uvedale Price's eldest brother, possibly being designed by Thomas Symonds, who also worked for Richard Payne Knight.[33] The network of architectural patrons which Price joined in Herefordshire included the trustees for the new Hereford Infirmary: Price was a trustee, as was his neighbour Sir George Cornewall of Moccas. The plan for the Infirmary, dated 26 December 1776, was by Thomas Symonds, who was surveyor for Richard Payne Knight at Downton.[34]

The connection between Richard Payne Knight, Uvedale Price and Foxley was made even closer by the fact that Knight's father Thomas Knight, although rector of Bewdley in Worcestershire, lived at Wormsley Grange, which directly adjoins Foxley to the north. The strong family connection with Wormsley is symbolised by the burial there, many years later, of both Richard Payne Knight and his brother Thomas Andrew Knight, rather than at Downton, where they had both lived for much of their lives. Knight was only three years younger than Price and had been educated at home, and although there is no direct evidence that they were childhood friends it seems unlikely that they would not have known of each other's existence and perhaps even been acquaintances. They both lost their fathers when they were in their early teens. When Robert Price died in 1761, Uvedale Price was 14 and Richard Payne Knight was 10. Knight's own father died only a few years later, when Knight was aged 13. But their education was very different: Knight was taught at home while Price was sent to Eton. Knight took his Grand Tour in 1772/3, when Price had returned to take over the Foxley estate, and went again in 1776 to Italy with John Robert Cozens and on an expedition to Sicily with the German landscape painter Jakob Philip Hackert and the wealthy amateur painter Charles Gore. The friendship between Price and Knight was to provide a stimulus for much discussion and writing about architecture and landscape aesthetics.[35]

Price did not restrict himself to developing his estate at Foxley and local connections, and he made a brilliant entry into London society. He was elected a member of the Society of Dilettanti in 1770, the same year as Lord Robert Spencer and Richard Fitzpatrick, who remained lifelong friends, and only a year after his other friends Charles James Fox and Stephen Fox.[36] Richard Fitzpatrick (1748–1813), who was later to become Secretary at War in 1783 and 1806, was a great friend of Charles James Fox: they were 'drawn together by a love of reckless gambling, fast living, and witty conversation'. Fitzpatrick acted for Fox at his duel with William Adam in Hyde Park on 29 November 1779. Fitzpatrick, a 'talented writer of satirical verse, bon viveur and a balloonist', also remained a close friend of Uvedale Price and they often stayed at each other's houses (Figure 13).[37]

Uvedale Price immediately made an impression on the young Fanny Burney. When he called on 8 May 1771 she wrote in her diary:

THE PARADE MACARONI.

Fig. 13 The Parade Macaroni. Richard Fitzpatrick (1748–1813). Satirical print published by M Darly 25 February 1772. Richard Fitzpatrick was a friend of Uvedale and Lady Caroline Price. The inscription on this caricature adds bitterly 'after losing all his patrimony – played most nights for the winning or losing of 8 to 10,000£ + at last realized a Fortune – but refused to pay many debts of Honour + Justice'. (© Trustees of the British Museum)

> After Dinner, Sir Thomas Clarges,[38] a modest young Baronet, & Mr Price, a young man of Fashion, called & sat about two Hours. The latter is lately returned from his

Travels, & was eager to compare Notes with my Father. He is a very intelligent, sensible & clever young man. He is a kinsman to Mr Grenville.[39]

Fig. 14 J. B. Malchair, *A view of Foxley in Herefordshire belongin to Uvedal Price Esqr Septr 16.1772/6.* Sheep graze on the Lawn in front of the mansion at Foxley with the stable block to the right. (Corpus Christi College, Oxford, MS CCC 443, Vol. III)

The next spring she again noted Price. They met at a music party at the Burneys' on Monday 4 May 1772, when Sir William Hamilton was present: 'Mr [Uvedale] Price, who I have mentioned formerly & who is the macarony of the Age, came with Sir William.'[40] Price, now aged 25, was clearly relishing opportunities for music and art. Towards the end of his life he reminisced about this period when he was 'a young man of wit and pleasure about town'.[41]

He also, like his father, encouraged visitors to his newly embellished Foxley. In September 1772 John Baptist Malchair made four drawings there (Figures 14, 15, 16 and 17). These were of the prominent hill called Lady Lift, and three drawings of the mansion itself and the views from the gardens.[42] Malchair also made several drawings of the banks of the Wye which adjoined the Foxley estate at Bishopstone. He had visited Foxley before, in 1757, when he had stayed with Price's father, Robert. His links with Herefordshire were reinforced by his role as leader of the second violins at the Three Choirs Festival.[43] He drew on walking tours and the visit to Foxley in 1772 was part of a tour which also included a visit to the artist and connoisseur John Skippe at Upper Hall, Ledbury. John Skippe (1741–1812) had been a pupil of Malchair and after leaving Merton College in 1760 he travelled widely in northern Italy and made

Fig. 15 J. B. Malchair, *A view from Foxley Garden. Mr Prices. Herefordshire Friday 18 of Sepr. 1772/7.* This view to the east from the gardens at Foxley showing many young trees planted by Uvedale Price's father and grandfather. (Corpus Christi College, Oxford MS CCC 443 Vol. III)

Fig. 16 J. B. Malchair, *at Mr Price's at Foxley. Herefordshire. wednesday Sep': 16 1772.* A view across the Lawn at Foxley with the village of Mancel Lacy surrounded by trees in the middle distance. (Corpus Christi College, Oxford MS CCC 443, Vol. III)

drawings from the old masters. His work includes studies made in 1773 from the frescoes by Andrea Mantegna in the church of the Eremitani at Padua.[44]

The Malchair circle also included Sir George Beaumont, later to become one of Price's greatest friends and correspondents, and William Crotch. The extent of Price's immersion in local musical culture is indicated by his important role in September 1774 with Archdeacon Clive as one of the two stewards at the Hereford Music Meeting. The works performed over three days included pieces by Boyce, Purcell and Handel. The instrumentalists included 'Giardini, the leader, Malchair, Fischer, Crosdill, Parke, &c.'.[45] The performers 'were desired' to dine at the Swan and Falcon in Hereford with the stewards.[46] The performances 'on the first and third evenings consisted of a *Miscellaneous Concert*; *Judas Maccabeus* was performed on the second evening, and *The Messiah* on Friday morning'. Mrs Sheridan was indisposed, but the stewards had 'engaged the celebrated Miss Cecilia Davies, whose extraordinary talents procured her an admission on the stage for the first theatres in Italy, where she went by the name of L'Inglesina, being the first English woman who had then been tolerated on the Italian stage'.[47] Price followed his father in maintaining a great enthusiasm for music throughout his life. He had been elected a member of the Noblemen and Gentlemen's Catch Club in 1770, and was regularly noted attending concerts and recitals in London.[48]

Price married one of the greatest society beauties, Lady Caroline Carpenter, on 28 April 1774. The marriage ceremony was performed by Price's uncle Shute

Fig. 17 J. B. Malchair, *A view of Lady Lift from a Meadow by Yazor. Herefordshire wednesday 16 of Sept: 1772/1.* A view through farmland trees at Yazor to the hill Lady Lift with its clump of Scots pine trees. (Corpus Christi College, Oxford MS CCC 443, Vol. III)

Barrington, then bishop of Llandaff.[49] Lady Caroline's portrait was painted by George Romney the same year.[50] Her family had strong Herefordshire connections: her great grandfather, George Carpenter (1657–1732), first Baron Carpenter of Killaghy, a strong supporter of the Protestant succession, was born at Ocle Pychard and the family had owned property in the county for 400 years.[51] Her father was George Carpenter (1723–62), who had been created first earl of Tyrconnel in 1761. He was formerly Baron Carpenter of Killagly and had been MP for Taunton from 1754 to 1762. He married in 1747/8 Frances, daughter of Sir Robert Clifton of Clifton Hall, Nottinghamshire. She died at the age of 56 on 8 November 1786 at the Homme, Dilwyn, Herefordshire.[52]

The Carpenters were a more raffish family than the Prices and strongly connected with court circles. Lady Caroline's brother was George Carpenter, 2nd earl of Tyrconnel (1750–1805) and MP for Scarborough (1772–96) and Berwick (1796–1802). He had married in 1772 Frances, first daughter of John Manners, heir to the duke of Rutland. However, they divorced in 1777 by act of parliament. He married again, in 1780, Sarah Hussey, sixth and youngest daughter of John Hussey (Lord Delaval), but she 'went off' with the earl of Strathmore in 1791 and lived openly with him.[53] It was noted that

> the Earl of Tyrconnel, might be said to contribute at this time,
> more than any nobleman about the court, to the recreation of
> the reigning family: for while his wife formed the object of the
> homage of one prince of the blood, his sister had long
> presided in the affection of another.[54]

Lady Caroline's elder sister, Almeria (1752–1809), was described by the *London Magazine* of 1774 as having 'like a celestial meteor … long streamed through the circles of the court – the admiration of the men, and envy of the women'.[55] The courtesan Perdita Robinson recollected in her memoirs that on one occasion 'As soon as I entered the Pantheon Rotunda, I never shall forget the impression which my mind received: the splendour of the scene, the dome illuminated with variegated lamps, the music, the beauty of the women, seemed to present a circle of enchantment.' She remembered 'that the most lovely of fair forms met my eyes in that of Lady Almeria Carpenter' and that the 'first Countess of Tyrconnel also appeared with considerable *éclat*'.[56]

Lady Almeria Carpenter was described by Nathaniel Wraxall as 'one of the most beautiful women of her time, but to whom nature had been sparing of intellectual attractions'. She 'reigned at Glocester House. The duchess remained indeed its nominal mistress; but Lady Almeria constituted its ornament and pride'[57] and was 'Famed for Disdain of Virtue … for Ridicule of Scruple, and Love of nothing but that Gaite de Coeur, which she learnt in her pupilage from the lessons of her Father'.[58] *The Female Jockey Club* satirised her as Prince William Henry, the duke of Gloucester's mistress, and as having acquired from him the habit of obscene and profane expressions.[59] Their sexual relationship began in the early 1780s and in January 1782 Lady Almeria 'gave birth to a daughter, Louisa Maria La Coast (d. 1835), who was brought up by Farley Edsir, Gloucester's steward who kept a dairy farm at Hampton Court'. The duke and duchess of Gloucester, with Lady Almeria, lived on the Continent at Geneva and Italy in the mid 1780s.[60]

But we have little hard evidence of Price's London life at this period. Much later he recollected one lively adventure from the mid-1770s which gives a colourful flavour. One evening at Vauxhall Gardens there was 'a party consisting of Lord Maynard, Sir John Stepney, L:[d] Derby[61] + myself en hommes, + of Lady Harcourt,[62] M[rs] North, L[y] Frances Fitzwilliam, L[y] Almeria + L[y] Caroline en femmes'. While 'we men were settling the bill' the ladies walked about 'according to the usual practice' but after a short time 'we heard a violent bustle + screaming below (for we were in an upper room) + soon after the Ladies scrambled up stairs with several young Bucks in pursuit of them.' The Ladies ran back to their party and 'M[rs] North got in first, + running up to me, who happened to be nearest to her, clasped me in her arms so closely, that, had I wished it, I could not have escaped.' Price recounts that as 'none of the other Ladies took the same sort of refuge as M[rs] North, the rest of the Gentlemen advanced towards these intruders, who immediately on finding their mistake slunk away', and that 'we were all very much diverted by a speech of M[rs] North's, I declare, said she, I never felt such happiness as when I found myself in M[r] Price's arms.'[63]

Although Price took on local and county duties such as magistrate and sheriff he was not, unlike his grandfather or many of his friends, in parliament. He was by no means uninterested in politics, however, and was a keen Whig. One of the few recorded instances of his speaking publicly at a political meeting was at Hereford Shirehall on 11 March 1780 at a meeting of 'Gentlemen, Clergy, Freeholders and Landholders of this County, concerned about the 'uncommon scarcity of money' consequent upon the wars with the colonies and with France and Spain 'the dangerous and inveterate enemies of Britain'. Price 'opened the business in a very pertinent speech' which was seconded by Richard Payne Knight. The petition addressed to the House of Commons was to stop the 'gross abuses in the expenditure of public money; to reduce all exorbitant emoluments; to rescind and abolish all useless places; sinecures, and unmerited pensions; and appropriate the produce thereof to the necessities of the State'. The meeting thanked 'Uvedale Price Esq. for opening the business of the Petition with a manly and spirited speech'.[64]

The Prices corresponded with artist friends such as John Skippe and John Baptist Malchair. John Skippe wrote to Price from Venice in 1776 that 'I wish I could tell you I had taken a resolution of returning to England ...'. When he eventually returned he made a series of woodcuts which were published in 1782, including one which was a copy of a Bandinelli drawing from Uvedale Price's collection. Price wrote to Skippe from Foxley saying he had showed the woodcuts to Sir Joshua Reynolds, 'who was very greatly struck with them, + interested to buy a set'.[65] In the following year John Baptist Malchair visited

Foxley and Skippe painted 'the portrait of Miss Price, painted the same year [1783], and sent to Foxley'; in 1784 he painted 'Joseph explaining Pharoah's Dream painted … for Lady Caroline Price' and sent it to Foxley.[66] It was during this period that Price became friends with Sir George and Lady Beaumont, who had returned from their Grand Tour in 1783.[67]

The Sheridans stayed at Foxley not long after their marriage. Richard Brinsley Sheridan (1751–1816) had married the famous singer and beauty Elizabeth (Eliza) Linley (1754–1792) on 13 April 1773. Price noted that 'no one who ever heard or saw her could ever forget' Miss Linley's 'beauty' of 'countenance and voice'. He was amused to note: 'They both of them passed some time with me here at Foxley: he has very little pleasure in music, none in scenery: for if this house had been placed in the midst of Hounslow Heath, he could not have taken less notice of all that surrounded it.'[68] He told Samuel Rogers: 'At one time I saw a good deal of Sheridan: he and his first wife passed some time here, and he is an instance that a taste for poetry and for scenery are not always united.' Neither was Sheridan much good at rural pursuits: 'His delight was in shooting all day, and every day, and my gamekeeper said that of all the gentlemen he had ever been out with he never knew so bad a shot.'[69]

On one occasion the Sheridans were joined by James Hare (1747–1804), the leading Whig social celebrity, who shared a house with Charles James Fox in St James' St.[70] Price describes 'excellent sparring between those doughty knights, and the more amusing from their play being – as you well know who knew them both – very different'. Price heard Miss Linley sing in private and in public and thought: 'Hers was truly 'a voice as of the cherub choir'', and 'she was always ready to sing without any pressing. She sang here a great deal, to my infinite delight.' He was particularly delighted that 'she used to take my daughter, then a child, on her lap and sing a number of childish songs, with such a playfulness of manner and such a sweetness of look and voice as was quite enchanting.'[71]

The Prices' first child, Caroline, was born in January 1783 (the painting of her by John Skippe is unfortunately lost), and their son Robert was born in August 1786. In 1787 Lady Caroline sat for her portrait by Sir Joshua Reynolds (Figure 18). There were three sittings in November, and the bill of £52 10s was paid in December 1787. Price and Lady Caroline frequently entertained at Foxley. They shared their friends. Indeed, the closeness of Lady Caroline's friendship with more than one of Price's friends, including Richard Fitzpatrick, was the cause of gossip. Lord Egremont told Lord Holland many years later, when Price was made a baronet in 1827, that

> I knew him soon after by his marriage with my first cousin,
> and this alliance advanced him very much in the world by her
> cuckolding him, with Hare and Fitzpatrick, and if all the
> connections arising from those two fortunate incidents had
> survived with him, I do not see why he should not have been a
> peer instead of a baronet.[72]

Fig. 18 Sir Joshua
Reynolds. *Lady Caroline
Price*. This mezzotint
was published by John
Jones 3 June 1788 the
year after Reynolds
painted her portrait in
1787, emphasising her
fame as a society beauty.
(© Trustees of the
British Museum)

Fitzpatrick certainly had a reputation and was cited in a scandalous divorce case of 1788 involving Mrs Foley of Stoke Edith in Herefordshire.

The Prices continued to attend parties and musical events in London through the 1780s. Price recalled one occasion when he turned down a dinner invitation from Sir Joshua Reynolds at which he could have met both Crabbe and Johnson: 'Crabbe, I once saw and that's all. I might have been acquainted with him, for Sir Joshua invited me to dinner, and told me I should meet Crabbe and Johnson.' He had another engagement 'probably' that he could not remember precisely 'at some fine house to meet fine gentlemen and ladies: whatever it was, I was blockhead enough not to break it, and I have never forgiven myself.' He had 'never thought from that time to this' of the dinner he went to but imagined that 'the dinner I did not go to I never should have forgotten, and if I had gone should now be recollecting every circumstance with pleasure and satisfaction, instead of crying, Oh, fool! fool! Fool!'[73] The Prices were also sighted at plays and operas. Lord Palmerston[74] wrote to his wife in 1787:

> I hear of nothing but the gaiety of London, suppers balls and
> concerts without end ... I called today on Lady Caroline Price
> and have been in her box this evening at *The School for
> Scandal*. They are determined to stay for an opera which is
> now deferred till Saturday. The burletta and the dancing I hear
> are likely to be pretty good ...[75]

The Prices had no permanent London house and later on some of his friends began to complain that he over-stayed his welcome. Many years later Samuel Rogers complained that

> Uvedale Price once chose to stay so long at my house, that I
> began to think he would never go away; so one day I
> ingeniously said to him, 'You must not leave me *before the end
> of next week*; if you insist on going before that, you may; but
> certainly not before.' And at the end of the week he *did* go.[76]

Visitors at Foxley in the 1780s included friends such as Richard Fitzpatrick, Fox and Hare and literary figures such as William Combe and Mr St John.[77] Price recollected in a letter to Samuel Rogers

> I am, as you know, a great admirer of Crabbe; so were Charles
> Fox and Fitzpatrick. The first poem of his I ever saw (I believe
> his first work) was 'The Library'. Charles brought it to Foxley
> soon after it came out and read a good deal of it to us, Hare
> being one of the audience.

Price remembered in particular 'his reading the part where Crabbe has described 'the ancient worthies of romance', and has given in about twenty lines the essence of knight errantry. When Fox came to 'And shadowy forms with staring eyes stalk round', Hare cried out (you remember his figure and eyes), 'That's meant for me." Philip Carter notes that while Hare was 'celebrated for his social ease and gentlemanly wit' he was 'rather less impressive on first meeting. He was, in Sir Alexander Clifford's view, 'the thinnest man I ever saw', with a face so pallid that it resembled a 'surprised cockatoo'.[78]

Samuel Rogers told of an occasion when Price asked William Combe to leave Foxley:

> Combe was staying at the house of Uvedale Price; and the
> Honourable Mr St John (author of *Mary Queen of Scots*) was
> there also. The latter, one morning, missed some bank-notes.
> Price, strongly suspecting who had taken them, mentioned

the circumstance to Combe, and added, 'Perhaps it would be as well if you cut short your visit here.' – 'Oh, certainly,' replied Combe with the greatest coolness; 'and allow me just to ask, whether henceforth we are to be friends or acquaintances?' – 'Acquaintances, if you please,' said Price.

This incident was apparently the cause of a complete fissure between Price and Combe, who was later to help write Humphry Repton's response to Price's *Essay*.[79] Rogers noted that: 'Long after this had happened, I was passing through Leicester Square with Price, when we met Combe: we both spoke to him; but from that hour he always avoided me.'[80]

The friendship between Price and Sir George Beaumont and Lady Beaumont also began in this period and the surviving letters from Price to the Beaumonts are of great value in documenting his life and opinions. Sir George Beaumont (1753–1827) was six years younger than Price. He also went to Eton and was taught drawing there by Alexander Cozens. He was a member of the Malchair circle at New College, Oxford, and played in Oldfield Bowles, amateur theatre at North Aston. He knew Joshua Reynolds and Richard Wilson through his Oxford connections. He married Margaret Willes (1756–1829) in 1778, having met her at a theatrical production at North Aston. She was described by Mary Hartley to William Gilpin as a 'young woman with some genius and a prodigious eagerness for knowledge and information' who was 'always learning something' but 'not negligent of her toilet'. According to Hartley 'her greatest object seems to be the preservation of her husband's affection.' Coleridge noted that 'one may wind her up with any music, but music it must be, of one sort or another.' The Beaumonts went on a joint grand tour in 1782–3, which enabled Sir George to develop his talents as a landscape artist as well as to purchase art for his collection. This collection was displayed in a purpose-built gallery at their London home, 34 Grosvenor Square. He served as Tory MP for Beer Alston (1790–96), but his interests were mainly artistic and his inspiration was fuelled by sketching tours of the Lake District and North Wales, where for several summers they stayed at Benarth, near Conway. Price and the Beaumonts had many literary, theatrical and artistic interests in common, and they often met up in London, with Price frequently staying at their house.[81]

GARDENING

During the 1770s Price's enthusiasm for horticulture and gardening flourished. It was in this period that he constructed a new walled kitchen garden. He also removed the old formal gardens around the house at Foxley, writing twenty years later, in his *Essay*, of 'having done myself, what I so condemn in others, – destroyed an old-fashioned garden'. In one of the few lengthy sections in his essays argued from direct personal experience he 'long regretted its destruction. I destroyed it, not from disliking it: on the contrary, it was a sacrifice I made against my own sensations, to the prevailing opinion.'[82] The garden was probably the one laid out for the house built in 1719 by Robert Baron Price and Uvedale Tomkyns Price. The old garden, according to Price, 'had an air of decoration and of Gaity, arising from that decoration; *un air paré*, a distinction from mere unembellished nature, which whatever the advocates for extreme simplicity may allege, is surely essential to an ornamented garden', although 'it was infinitely inferior to those of Italy.'[83] Indeed, the fact that he reiterates this comparison with Italy later in the *Essay* when he records the 'total destruction … even of a garden so inferior to those that I remember in Italy, though with many of the same decorations'[84] suggests that it was his ability to make a direct comparison between recently visited Italian gardens, and the garden he knew in his youth with imported statues which he now saw to be 'inferior', which prompted its destruction.

The old garden, he recollected, had a 'raised terrace' and

> a flight of steps with iron rails, and an arched recess below it,
> backed by a wood: those steps conducted you from the terrace
> into a lower compartment, where there was a mixture of fruit-
> trees, shrubs, and statues, which though disposed with some
> formality, yet formed a dressed foreground to the woods.

He regretted removing this walled compartment and the consequent loss of its 'seclusion and safety', as 'no man is more ready than myself to allow that the comfortable, is a principle which should never be neglected.' He was also concerned to recollect the effect of the removal of a wall:

> I cannot forget the sort of curiosity and surprize that was
> excited after a short absence, even in me, to whom it was
> familiar, by that simple and common circumstance of a door
> that led from the first compartment to the second, and the
> pleasure I always experienced on entering that inner, and
> more secluded garden.

When the door was opened 'the lofty trees of a fine grove appeared immediately over the opposite wall.' Although the 'trees are still there' the removal of the wall had taken away 'the striking impression'.[85] He also removed at this time an upper terrace and a 'wilderness of exotics' on which was a 'summer-house, with a luxuriant Virginia creeper growing over it: this summer-house and the creeper – to my great sorrow at the time, to my regret ever since, to my great surprize at this moment, and probably to that of my reader – I pulled down.' He had been told that the summer house, which was probably the one designed by James Gibbs, 'interfered too much with the levelling of the ground, with its flowing line and undulation, in short with the prevailing system, that it could not stand'.[86]

Pondering his reasons for destroying the old garden, Price argued that in addition to his need at the time to '[be] in the fashion', which will have been reinforced by his employment in 1771 of James Cranston, from the leading

London firm of James Lee of Hammersmith, he wanted to 'restore the ground to what might be supposed to have been its original state' – in other words, to remove the 'inferior' Italianate garden he found on his return from his continental tour. He concluded that 'after much difficulty, expence and dirt, I have made it look like any other parts of mine and all beautiful grounds; but with little to mark the difference ... between the habitation of man, and that of sheep.'[87]

He was certainly following the general fashion of the 1760s and 1770s when 'Capability' Brown's career was at its peak. Lancelot Brown (1716–83) developed his reputation working at Stowe for Lord Cobham in the 1740s. He then moved to Hammersmith in 1751 where the nurseries of Lee and Kennedy were one of his principal suppliers. He was appointed the king's Master Gardener in 1764 and lived at Wilderness House, Hampton Court. Over the course of his lengthy career he designed and advised at over 200 gardens and grounds and his ideas on the disposition of grassland, trees and water were enormously potent and dominant. Brown was well known for replacing old-fashioned walled gardens with ones where the house was set in lawns with unobstructed views of park and pasture. Price's detailed knowledge of Brown's work was brought home to him by local commissions, such as those at Berrington, near Leominster in north Herefordshire, where Brown was commissioned in 1775 by Thomas Harley – a relation of the earl of Oxford, whose estates at Brampton Bryan and Eywood were also in Herefordshire – to design and build with Henry Holland a house and park. Even closer to Foxley was Sir George Cornewall's Moccas estate, where Brown drew up a plan of 'intended alterations' in 1778.[88] As we shall see, this was at the time Price was implementing the remodelling of his own estate by Nathaniel Kent. Price's employment of an improving land agent and a gardener, James Cranston, with experience at one of the leading London nurseries shows indeed that he was at the height of agricultural and horticultural fashion. The four drawings of Foxley made by Malchair in 1772 show the house set in an expanse of pasture grazed by sheep, the views from the house depicting the well-established parkland trees planted by his father.

Charles James Fox remained a great friend of Price throughout this period, and made several visits. He wrote from Newmarket in July 1781 hoping that he would be 'able at last to make you the visit I have so long intended, but as I should not like to go a hundred and fifty miles and not see you (though I do not foretend to say that to see Foxley itself is not worth the journey)'. He was accompanied by Lord Robert Spencer[89] and they were both intending to go on to Bath.[90] Fox also visited Foxley in 1785, and Price enthused him with his horticultural knowledge and ideas about planting. Price sent Fox 'a cargo of plants' and Fox noted 'I know we settled all this at Foxley, but I have forgot it.' He went on: 'Your plants will be very welcome and I wish to God you were near enough to come and give me some advice too for there are great inconveniences in such ignorance as mine.' He wanted to 'ask you a thousand questions, but as I can not ask them all I give you my word I will only ask you to the end of this paper and no more'; and then asked many, including:

> What is that that grows on the library side of Foxley House
> and that was beginning to be in flower when I was there? In
> the thing that you call the Gem at Lord B's what are the
> principal things that give it the gaiety and brilliance you
> described? Does it consist chiefly of roses, honeysuckles +c,
> or is there much mixture of shrubs and what shrubs?[91]

He went on to ask many questions about specific species, such as American Oaks, Camellias, Azaleas and Canadian Poplars, and more general questions about the layout of screens, under-planting, nursery beds and so forth.

It is clear that by his late thirties Price was known, at least within his circle, both as an horticultural and a gardening expert, and one who could provide advice on garden design for someone like Fox, who was laying out his new garden at St Anne's Hill at this time. Price's advice was also liked because it could be set against that of professional gardeners, who could not necessarily be trusted. Fox told Price that 'I am afraid when I see the nursery man's bill it will be a good deal of money; for I hear of this plant costing 1^s. this 1^s.6^d. and so on and in one little walk which is all that I have finished there appear to me to be thousands of plants.' He was worried because 'There are two nursery men hereabouts both Scotchmen and my Gardiner is a Scotchman too, so that it is not impossible but I may be a little cheated into the Bargain.'[92]

Until recently it has been thought that Uvedale Price's first book was a translation of Pausanias published in 1780 by the leading bookseller T. Evans.[93] But we now know that this is another piece by Uvedale 'Tomkyns' Price which unaccountably appeared 16 years after his death. Uvedale Price told E. H Barker in 1825 the 'translation of Pausanias was made by my Grandfather + Godfather from whom I received the Christian name that has misled you: he was, like myself, passionately fond of the fine arts.' He wished he had shown it to Richard Payne Knight, but suspected that 'my grandfather was not a much better grecian than his grandson.' Price added in a later letter that his only copy was 'printed in 1758+ anonymous but the words by Uvedale Price are added in my grandfather's hand' so confusingly even he appears unaware of the 1780 edition.[94]

No surviving correspondence between Price and his Barrington uncles has been found. This is unfortunate, as the influence of these maternal uncles is likely to have been strong in this period, as it was in earlier years. Daines Barrington, with his wide-ranging and enthusiastic publications on architecture, gardening and music, will have encouraged Price to write by example if not by persuasion. He had been made a Fellow of both the Royal Society and Society of Antiquaries in 1767 and after his first paper on Welsh castles in 1770 in *Archaeologia* he published twenty four pieces on a variety of topics, including card-playing in England and the history of the Cornish language. He also published twelve pieces, mainly on natural history, in the Royal Society's *Philosophical Transactions*. In 1767 he established *The Naturalist's Journal*, a series of proformas to record natural phenomena such as weather and the dates plants flowered, and was influenced by Benjamin Stillingfleet's *Miscellaneous Tracts* (1762). The diversity of his writings and his inaccuracy provoked adverse criticism from Horace Walpole and, in *Peter Pindar's Peter's Prophecy, or, The President and Poet* (1788), Barrington was attacked in an imaginary exchange. Sir Joseph Banks asks Peter Pindar 'what think ye of our famous Daines?'; Peter replies: 'Think, of a man denied by Nature brains! … Who knows not jordens brown from Roman vases! About old pots his head for ever puzzling … Who likewise from old urns to crotchets leaps, Delights in music, and at concerts sleeps.' According to David Miller, 'Barrington symbolized a form of intellectual life, the virtuoso or dilettante, that came under attack from some quarters in the later eighteenth century.'[95]

Daines Barrington read a paper at the Society of Antiquaries in 1782 'On the progress of gardening', published in *Archaeologia* in 1785, which attacked Capability Brown and called for a greater understanding of the relations between literature, painting and gardens. He thought that

> the true test of perfection in a modern garden is that a
> landscape-painter would choose it for composition. Kent has
> been succeeded by Brown who hath undoubtedly great merit
> in laying out pleasure grounds, but I conceive that in some of
> his plans I see rather traces of the gardener of Old Stowe,
> than of Poussin or Claude Lorraine.

He wished 'that Gainsborough gave the design and that Brown executed'.[96] In his references to Tasso, Claude and Gainsborough he drew on the same sources as Price in his *Essay on the Picturesque* of 1794. We have noted that Daines Barrington visited Foxley in 1770 and the parish records of Mansel Lacy note the 'gift of a pump at the Blacksmith's shop by the Honble Daines Barrington' in 1788.[97] It is likely that he paid several visits to Foxley from his chambers in King's Bench Walk in the Inner Temple, and that Price visited him there. It is not clear whether Daines Barrington influenced Price or Price influenced Daines Barrington on ideas about garden design, but it is likely that the relationship between art and landscaping was a staple topic when Price and Barrington met, whether at Foxley or in London. Barrington's celebration of Gainsborough as the preferred model for a landscape designer was certainly central to the development of Price's ideas and practice. The next chapter examines how Price developed a practical understanding of the picturesque through agricultural and forestry practices at Foxley in the last thirty years of the eighteenth century.

CHAPTER 3

'THE IMPROVEMENT OF REAL LANDSCAPE'[1]

T HE MANAGEMENT OF THE FOXLEY ESTATE was central to Price's life. He inherited an estate in 1768 which was ripe for improvement, and we are lucky that two major estate surveys survive which show how he remodelled the estate in the early 1770s, just as he had transformed his garden and modernised his house. Perhaps more importantly, these surveys, together with later documents and writings, indicate how he used his estate as a practice ground for experimentation in local government, agricultural modernisation, the management of hedgerow trees and forestry. These experiments provided results which he later used later to expound ways of improving 'real landscape' based on the ideas and experience of drawings and paintings of the best artists, many of which he was familiar with from his own and other people's collections.

The first survey is 'A book of survey containing the Manors of Yazor, Mancellacy, Bishopstone ... with the contents and yearly estimates of Uvedale Price Esq. of Foxley ... in the year of our Lord 1770'.[2] It consists of a set of maps of the estate, together with a terrier giving the acreages of the different tenancies and the size of the fields. Denis Lambin suggested that this was by Nathaniel Kent, but the cartography employed in this survey is rather old-fashioned for that leading land agent.[3] The second survey, entitled 'A survey of Foxley and its appendages ... the estate of Uvedale Price Esq', was rediscovered in 1988 and is now known to be by Kent.[4] The last page of the survey is signed by Kent, who states that 'This estate was surveyed, modelled and sett out by me upon the agreements contained in this book in the year 1774.' The maps are much more accurately drawn than those in the 1770 survey. However, although the maps show the correct boundaries of the holdings, the field boundaries are in some cases those which Kent intended should be made during the tenancy, rather than those actually present in 1774. Unfortunately, one of the maps is missing and maps were not drawn for some of the farms, nor for the land kept in hand.

Why should two such expensive surveys have been drawn up for the same estate, for the same proprietor, within four years? The 1770 survey was made when Price was 23, a couple of years after he had come of age. It contains complete surveys of the remaining open fields, including land held by other proprietors, and would have formed a useful prelude for land exchanges with, or purchases from, these smaller owners. The 1774 survey, which was produced the year that Price married, was drawn up to assist the complete reorganisation of the estate by Nathaniel Kent. The survey includes copies of the leases, general hints to the landlord and specific hints relating to particular fields and farms. Although Kent's *Hints to Gentlemen of Landed Property* was not published until the following year, he was already well established as a land agent. While working on Foxley he was asked to value part of the earl of Hardwicke's Gloucestershire estate; in 1775 he was collecting rents on Sir Charles Cock's estates in Worcestershire and Gloucestershire. The precise reason for his employment at Foxley is probably his friendship with Benjamin Stillingfleet, who had carried out agricultural experiments at Foxley with Robert Price and whom he had got to know in Norfolk.[5]

Although Price was an important county figure – he was appointed sheriff of Herefordshire in 1774 and sat on several important committees – he was by no means the largest landed proprietor in the county.[6] The acreage of Foxley in 1774 was 3,537 and, following remodelling, this was set to produce an annual income of £2,461.[7] This places it firmly in the category of gentry estates, as later defined by F. M. L. Thompson, and in the nineteenth century over 40 per cent of the area of Herefordshire consisted of such estates of between 1,000 and 10,000 acres. Herefordshire, Shropshire and Oxfordshire were the only counties so dominated by gentry estates.[8] Price continued to exchange land and expand his estate throughout his life. Many of these exchanges were of open-field strips, so that Price could make new enclosures for his tenant farmers. An example includes an exchange between Thomas Berrington and Uvedale Price in November 1775 of lands in 'a field called Middle Lurcott' and another called 'Farther Lurcott' in the parish of Yazor.[9] In 1810 he acquired twelve acres of Mansell Common from the enclosure commissioners dealing with Mansell Lacy[10] and by the time his son sold the estate in 1855 it was virtually in a ring fence, indicating the success of Price's policy of consolidation.

THE INFLUENCE OF NATHANIEL KENT

At the time of the 1770 survey the estate consisted of at least 3,844 acres, while the area surveyed by Kent in 1774 was 3,537 acres; however, the areas are not comparable as the second survey did not included some of the outlying farms. As a result of his reorganisation, the rental on 'such parts of Mr Price's estate as have been modelled by N. Kent and are mentioned in this book' rose by a fifth (21 per cent), from £2,031 to £2,461. Kent achieved this by amalgamating farms and fields and consolidating holdings. Map 1 shows how, for example, the two holdings of Mr Allen and Mr Davis were simplified and consolidated by Kent. In addition, leases of fifteen years were introduced which included a series of covenants designed to encourage good farming practice.

Kent was an advocate of small farms and small farmers. He considered that as the small farmer 'has no great space to superintend, it lies under his eye at

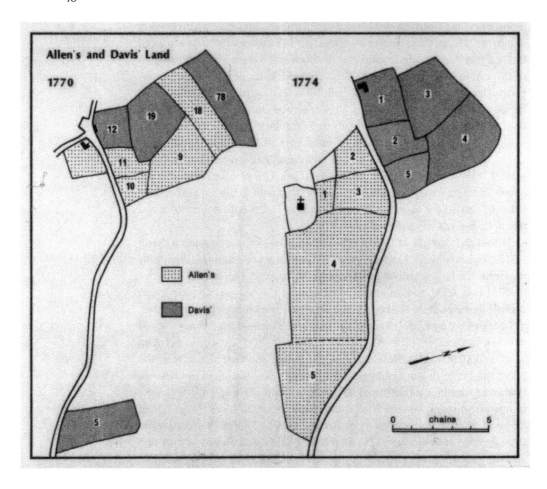

all times, and seasons; he seizes all minute advantages; cultivates every obscure corner'. In addition, small farmers encouraged independence and industriousness, which could be harnessed by the larger landlords, as the daughters of small farmers made 'the best dairy maids' while the sons made 'the best gentlemen's bailiffs'.[11] It is interesting to compare the distribution of farms at Foxley by value in 1770 and 1774 and compare these to those given by Kent in *Hints* for a model estate worth £2,000. At first glance, Foxley falls well short of Kent's (1775) model. Kent suggests that 12 per cent of farms should be over £100 in value, while the figure for Foxley is 41 per cent in both 1770 and 1774. As a corollary, Kent considers that 56 per cent of farms should be let at £30–60, while at Foxley the figure was 42 per cent in 1770, reducing to 25 per cent in 1774.

Kent's model suggests that an estate of £2,000 should support thirty-two farming families, while both before and after reorganisation by Kent there were only twelve families with farms valued at £30 or more at Foxley. However, Kent

Map 1 Map of the reorganisation of the holdings of Mr Allen and Mr Davis at Yazor by Nathaniel Kent between 1770 and 1774.

points out that 'estates of this value usually support less than a third' of the number he suggests, and so Foxley would seem to be just above par in this respect. The comparison changes remarkably, however, if smallholders, who do not figure at all in Kent's model, are also considered. Thus at Foxley in 1770 there were five tenants with holdings valued between £15 and £29, and this was increased to eight by the reorganisation of the estate. There were, moreover, twenty-nine tenants with holdings worth less than £15, but over five acres in area, although this number was reduced slightly by the reorganisation. If the Foxley smallholders are included in the calculations then the estate supported more tenants than Kent's model estate.[12]

As well as being a supporter of small farmers, Kent considered that 'cottagers are indisputably the most beneficial race of people we have' and argued in his *Hints* that cottagers should have from half to one acre so that they could keep a cow.[13] This is echoed in Kent's comment in his 1774 survey of Foxley about a smallholding of five acres in six enclosures at Stoke Lacy: 'This is a very comfortable little place for an industrious man being just enough to enable him to keep one cow.' It is difficult to be certain of the effect of the reorganisation on cottagers, as many holdings are not identifiable, but it does appear that the total number of cottagers with some land (but less than five acres) remained constant at about twenty-five, although there is some considerable turnover in tenants. Of the ten cottager holdings that can be identified at both dates, one increased slightly, three remained exactly the same size, but six became smaller.[14]

Most cottagers had to pay increased rents as a result of reorganisation, but in some instances Kent makes out specific cases as to why a cottager's rent should not be increased. In the case of a tenant who held a public house and ferry, for example, Kent notes that 'As the ferry is greatly fallen off since Bredwardine Bridge, it is dear enough at present rent which is to continue.' The independence of at least one cottager is indicated by the case of Richard Evans, who was paying £6 4s 6d for his holding of about ten acres, consisting of three enclosures and four open-field strips. Kent considered that it was worth £7 10s, but noted that '[Evans] would not give it and Ridgeway [the bailiff] intimated that he was a man which it would be imprudent for Mr Price to have any dispute with.'[15]

Kent's remodelling consisted of as far as possible putting farms and smallholdings within a ring fence. In addition, he suggested that the fields should be enlarged. With Good's Farm at Yazor, for example, Kent called for 'the hedges to be stubbed up so as to lay the fields as much like the map as may be found convenient.' The farm as remodelled consisted of 312 acres and was intended to have twenty-four enclosures; previously, excluding 22 acres in open fields, it consisted of 306 acres in forty-nine enclosures. Where fields were amalgamated the old boundary banks had to be removed and specific instructions were given for individual fields: 'No's 7, 9 and 10 have several banks in them should be levelled and mixed with lime for manure. As no 17 will now be a compleat inclosure all the banks which divided different persons land should likewise be levelled'.[16] Other recommendations in the 1774 survey include draining; the removal of hedgerows; the removal of alders and rushes which had spread onto fields; and the removal of pollards. Fields 27 and 28 at Wellson's Farm were 'miserably overspread with alders, bushes and lie wet. The former should be extirpated and likewise the pollards.'

The combined efforts of Nathaniel Kent and Uvedale Price completely to remodel the Foxley estate is an exemplar of what was happening on the most modern agricultural estates in the late eighteenth century. The precise, detailed and critical evaluation chimes with Price's exacting personality and he will have been keen to maximise the rental so that he could secure his income and the future of the estate. The detailed specification to retain cottagers and smallholders is a little more unusual but one which was congruent with his celebration of his remembrance of the relatively benevolent management of his uncle Lord Barrington's estate at Beckett.

WOODLAND MANAGEMENT

Throughout the eighteenth century successive generations of the Price family established new areas of woodland and planted ornamental trees (see Table 1). They had, moreover, by no means inherited a landscape devoid of trees. In addition to surviving ancient woodland, the Little Transcript indicates that a grove of trees next to the house had been sown c.1640 (probably by the Rodds) while the wood on the mount near the Grove 'was much older'. Further evidence of planting by the Rodds is shown by Gainsborough's *Beech trees at Foxley* of c.1760. Beech is not a native tree in this part of Herefordshire and, as the trees are around 120 years old, the painting suggests that tree planting was being carried out at Foxley in the mid seventeenth century. Robert Baron Price's contribution seems to have been mainly groups of ornamental trees, while Uvedale Tomkyns Price planted two coppice woods. His son, Robert, planted ornamental trees and two woods, one of which, on the brow of a hill, would have helped to complete the band of woodland forming a horseshoe around the house. Uvedale Price noted himself as planting up two fields in 1771, but the record provided by the annotations to Gibbs's *Book of Architecture* finishes in 1773.

The 1770 survey provides for the first time a complete list of the woodland on the estate, and maps of its disposition. There were about 500 acres of woodland and this was mainly found along the inside slopes of the Yarsop valley. Over half (57 per cent) of the land in hand at this time was woodland. The map evidence ties in quite well with the Little Transcript: an area of twenty-seven and a half acres called the 'New Coppiece' on the map is in the correct position to be the wood sown by Robert Price south of Burton Wood Common ten years previously. The evidence points to a number of conclusions. First, although no acreages are given, it is clear that the planting was not on a massive scale; a couple of fields were sown one year, while a few years later another planting would be made. Second, the successive members of the Price family all made important contributions to the development of the landscape. Third, the planting does not appear to have been made according to an explicit plan, although it is likely that the overall plan was determined to a large extent by the topography of the valley. Finally, the fact that some of the new areas were specifically named as coppices confirms that the planting was justified by commercial as well as ornamental considerations. By 1770 the woodland landscape of Foxley had already undergone over a hundred years of planting, most of which tended to emphasise the sense of enclosure of the horseshoe-shaped valley of Yarsop.

Table 1 *Summary of tree planting at Foxley as shown by the Little transcript*

c.1640	Grove next to the house sown [by the Rodds]
1718	Coppice wood sown by Uvedale Tomkyns Price
1728	Walk of lime trees planted in front of house by Baron Price
1729	Fir trees above house planted by Uvedale Tomkyns Price
1731	Horse chestnuts on rising ground on the left-hand side of road to Yazor Church planted by Baron Price
1733	Coppice wood between Grove and Bishopson's Hill sown by Uvedale Tomkyns Price
1746–47	Wood below tower towards Bishopson cut down
1747	Shooting butts made and trees round them planted by Robert Price
1747	Horsechestnuts in meadow by Yazor Church planted by Robert Price
1748	Other trees in pool meadow planted by Robert Price
1759	Wood on brow of hill to the west of the firs on Ladylift sown by Robert Price
1760	Wood south of Burton Hill Common sown by Robert Price
1771	Two fields on the left-hand side of road to Yazor, below butts sown with acorns by Uvedale Price

Kent's reorganisation allowed Price to increase the area of woodland under his direct control from around 500 acres in 1770 to about 700 acres in 1774. Most of this increase is due to the transfer of woodland growing on the hill slopes around the head of the Yarsop valley, which had been tenanted by Mr Prichard in 1770. Indeed, Prichard's farm was reduced in size by 221 acres by the reorganisation. Thus the remodelling was a vital instrument in enabling Price to take full control of both the woodland and the whole landscape at Foxley. More than half the woodland retained by Price was classed by Kent as 'open woods and groves'. This included such areas as the Upper and Middle Shoaks, managed as wood-pasture: the 400 acres of grove pasture was worth, at 1s 6d an acre, £30, and the 'necessary thinning' of the groves would result in a further £50 per year. Evidence that Price was producing timber for the naval market is given by an advertisement of March 1795 in the *Hereford Journal* giving oak timber 'fit for the navy' for sale at Yazor.[17] A further indication of commercial management is provided by a covenant in a farm lease of 1799 which allowed Price 'to make saw pits or to coal wood' on any part of the farm.[18]

Price extended his woodland acreage by the purchase of existing woodland, the planting of new areas and exchange. In 1773, for example, he purchased an area described as 'coppice wood ground' near to Lady Lift at Yazor from his neighbour Sir John Cotterill.[19] This purchase helped to thicken the existing border of woodland around Foxley. In addition, there is fragmentary evidence that he was planting new areas of woodland, or at least aspiring to do so. A covenant on a lease of 1781 on a farm at Mansell Lacy, for example, permitted the landlord 'to plant with wood and take into his own hands as coppice ground any parts of the before mentioned premises making a reasonable deduction in the rent for the same'.[20] This particular covenant had not been put in any of the leases devised by Kent seven years earlier in 1774.

The grove woodland was supplemented by about 300 acres of coppice. There was a very strong market for coppice products in late eighteenth-century Herefordshire. Kent noted in the 1774 Foxley survey that 'Wood under regular course of felling is the most profitable estate in the county of Hereford, being always a ready money article, and the management of it is so well known that it is needless for me to give any particular direction about it.' This high price was partly due to a local demand for hop poles, but Clark noted in his *General View* that, in addition, a 'vast quantity of wood is sent down the Severn to Bristol and other markets for making hoops and hop poles.'[21] This high demand was reflected in the value of the coppice at Foxley. Kent suggested that about twelve acres should be felled each year and that the coppice should be worth 12s per acre, which was three times the value of the groves and considerably more than the average value Kent gave to 'profitable land good and bad'. The market for coppice products held up and, if anything, increased through the last two decades of the eighteenth century: Clark gave its value at between 12s and 15s an acre per year in 1794 and Duncumb in 1805 gave a range of 11s to 22s per acre, though there is some evidence that there was a decline around 1810.[22]

HEDGEROW TREES AND POLLARDS

In addition to the groves and coppices, the estate at Foxley had many trees in orchards, hedgerows and scattered over fields. Many of these, apart from the fruit trees, would be pollarded: cut off at above head height on a regular cycle to produce crops of poles for fuel, hop poles and fencing material. A pollarded tree was depicted by Gainsborough to the left of his *Beech trees at Foxley*. Other trees, especially elms, although not pollarded, would be stripped of almost all branches, often to a great height. The practices of pollarding and stripping were increasingly seen throughout the eighteenth century as ones which destroyed potentially valuable timber trees and moreover ones which transferred the control of 'timber' trees, legally owned by the landlord, to the tenant. Duncumb, in his *General View* of 1805, noted that 'the natural strong constitution of the elm, which enables it to recover from the wounds it receives in lopping', had encouraged the spread of the practice to other trees, including even firs, which were less able to bear it: 'yet all are often obliged to submit to this fashionable dressing'. He felt, however, that 'The lopping of hedge-row timber, while it hurts the beauty of the county by doing violence to nature, proves beneficial to all vegetables that are placed immediately under the trees: and since the boughs are requisite to mend the hedges, to abolish the practice would be impossible.'[23]

Kent's survey of 1774 showed how widespread pollards and other trees were on the farms at Foxley. He considered, for example, that the alders found growing in seven of the low-lying fields on Wellson's Farm should be extirpated, and similar comments are found for most of the farms. His view was that pollards growing within fields should be removed. On one holding, for example, he noted that 'Pins meadow should be cleared of pollards, ferns and bushes' and that 'there is an oak in the little Clanley and one oak and five elm which are utterly spoiled by being stripped of their limbs and therefore had better be taken down and sold. A great many withey pollards of a considerable size should likewise be taken down.'[24] Where the land was very wet, Kent suggested that the alders should be cut down and the blank parts set with withy stakes. In some cases tenants had already done this. On Deroy's farm, for example, where the 'land is generally kind for hops', the tenant 'has lately planted in his meadows near the brook a considerable number of withey stands of the best sort which thrive prodigiously, yield very profitable tops, and show that it is more advantageous for hop poles than any other wood'.

A clear distinction was made by Kent: he was pleased to see plantations of such coppice, but was much less happy when the alders and willows were scattered about the farm seemingly at random. 'Brook Meadow and Hale Leasows are all overrun with alder pollards and bushes. A great part of this land would make good pasture if cleared and kept free from wood which I suppose the tenant will never agree to as his hops induce him to encourage the growth of wood though in the most slovenly manner and at every other expense.' In this instance he thought it would be 'for the advantage of the estate to plant the blank parts of such pieces which are now thickest and fence them off for wood entirely; and to clean and clear such parts as are now thinned of wood and keep it pasture only'.[25] Kent was happy when a conscious effort has been made by a farmer to establish *plantations* of alder and willow coppice; he was unhappy when areas of pasture had been allowed to become overgrown with such coppice. Most of the leases introduced by Kent, as was increasingly common in the eighteenth century, included covenants controlling the cutting of pollards and timber by tenants.[26] A lease of 1774 allowed the tenant the tops of all pollards standing in the hedgerows, provided they were not cut before ten years' growth, and alders provided they are not cut under seven years' growth.[27] Pollards and alders growing away from hedges and in the middle of fields were treated differently, Price being allowed to cut these down for his own use. In one lease of 1781 the pollarding arrangements were brought under stricter control, with the tenant being allowed to cut only 'eight pollard trees every year during the whole of the term the said trees to be marked by the said Uvedale Price on any part of the estate which he may think advisable'.[28]

It was Price's direct experience of owning and managing such trees that encouraged him to publish his first essay on the management of trees and landscape. His 1786 essay 'On the bad effects of stripping and cropping trees' was published in the *Annals of Agriculture*, a major periodical venture launched by Arthur Young in 1784 to publicise the views of the leading agriculturalists, including the duke of Grafton and Arthur Young himself.[29] The essay is interesting as Price combines practical knowledge with aesthetics, a concern for the protection of property, sound management for profit and the control of tenants and their workmen. It also demonstrates his use of a mixture of careful personal observation, judicious use of anecdote and example, and humour and exaggeration which he later used so effectively in his *Essay on the Picturesque*. It is interesting that Thomas Ruggles (1745–1813), of Spains Hall, Essex, who later wrote the influential *The History of the Poor, their Rights, Duties and the Laws Respecting Them* (1793–94), wrote two short pieces in the *Annals of Agriculture* on picturesque agriculture in the 1780s; this may well have been one of the factors that spurred Price on to write the much fuller treatise on the picturesque he published in 1794.

Price opened his essay by expressing surprise at how 'little attention should be paid to timber trees that grow on farms, both in the hedgerows, and upon open pieces'. Such trees were 'generally left to the discretion of the tenant, who is too apt to consider them merely as furnishing him with fuel, and hedge-wood, and to send his workmen to cut off their boughs in what manner they please.'[30] He made a clear distinction between pollarding and stripping. With the former, 'cutting off the head of the tree causes it to shoot vigorously both at the top, and at the sides' and, if such trees were allowed to grow again, they could 'swell to a great bulk' and 'make a noble appearance' and even 'produce very valuable timber for purposes that do not require length'. Pollarding, then, could be 'less disfiguring to the country' although 'in one respect' it was 'still more pernicious' than stripping, as it generally affected oaks, which were 'the most valuable of timber'.[31] Thomas Hearne, when at Downton, drew just such an overgrown oak pollard in 1784–6 for Richard Payne Knight (Plate 7). On the other hand, Price thought that 'Stripping a tree to the top (as chiefly practised with elms)' was 'the most pernicious, as well as the most disfiguring' practice. Once stripped, 'the lower part of it shoots out very strongly' but 'the top hardly pushes at all' and if the tree is repeatedly stripped it 'at last decays.' He backed up this argument by reporting a 'very observing timber merchant' who told him that stripped elms being 'full of holes' were particularly unfit 'for what they are most used in the neighbourhood of London, that is for pipes, as the water is frequently bursting out at the knots unless they are secured by lead.'[32]

He went on to argue that although it was 'a very general notion among the common people, that the stripping an elm makes it grow faster' this was a misconception derived from the 'shoots being longer and fresher the first year after it is stripped'; overall, the growth of a tree was in fact checked by the removal of boughs, as trees need leaves to grow. To give greater strength to this argument he reported an experiment 'that was made to convince a gentleman of large property, at Ledbury, in Herefordshire, that the custom of stripping elms was extremely hurtful to the timber'. This was most probably either Price's friend and artist John Skippe's father, who owned the extensive Upper Hall estate at Ledbury, or his neighbour John Biddulph of Ledbury Park.[33] To demonstrate the effect of stripping, this person

> desired that an elm might be felled that was known to have
> been stripped to the top twice within a certain number of
> years, and the particular years when it was stripped exactly
> remembered. It is well known that trees when sawed across
> show the increase of each year by circles, and that when a tree
> grows much in any one year the circle is enlarged, and the
> contrary when it grows but little; when this elm was felled,
> the person showed that the year after it was stripped the
> circle was very contracted, the next year it was wider, and the
> circles continued to increase with the quantity of boughs till
> the next stripping, when the circle was again contracted in the
> same manner.

Price recounted that the 'gentleman was so struck with the truth of this experiment, that from that time he never allowed a tenant to touch any of his trees' and that 'the size and beauty of the elms about Ledbury' were a 'standing proof' of the 'effect this experiment produced in that neighbourhood'.[34]

Price was particularly concerned that landlords were losing their property rights over timber trees. He noted that 'it is a common opinion among tenants, that they have a right (unless restrained by their leases) to crop or strip any tree that has once been stripped or cropped. This makes it in their material interest to convert every timber tree into a tree of that description.' This was made easier by landlords who were either 'careless about their trees' or lived at a distance from their estate and were unable to keep a close watch over it. This gave tenants 'constant opportunities' to strip or pollard and if they were 'not observed all the time, it is extremely difficult to detect them afterwards'. By this lack of interest or observation by landlords 'the profit of trees on each farm is, in a manner, transferred from the landlord to the tenant.' Furthermore, Price considered that the capital value of the estate was reduced as 'a number of healthy growing timber trees must be a great inducement to any purchaser, whether considered in the light of beauty, or profit; and the mean, and wretched look of a number of mangled trees that can never become timber, must be a great discouragement.'[35]

The key point of the essay was to develop a way in which the landlords could maintain their control of timber trees and at the same their tenant farmers could make use of boughs which caused damage to their crops. Price recognised that tenants would 'object, that if they are not allowed to crop or strip their trees, they can neither get fuel nor hedge-wood, and that their hedges will be hurt by the trees growing over them'. He makes use of an anecdote to show that sometimes it was the farm workers rather than the tenants that were to blame. 'I was told by several farmers … that they did not wish them to be stripped so high, but that their workmen made it a point of honour to get as high as possible, and that they despised a workman who left many boughs at top.'[36]

Price argued that a compromise could be made that would allow 'the tenant both hedge-wood and fuel, and not materially hurt the landlord's timber, that is to allow the tenant to take off the lower boughs to a certain height, as one quarter, one third, or at most one half of the height of the whole tree'. He noted that this was the 'the practice in some parts of England, where the heads of the trees make a noble figure, and the bodies are enabled to swell to a large size'. The benefit of this practice was that the farmer would be able 'to cut off constantly those boughs that would hang too close over his hedge and a large part of the loppings that formerly went to repair the damage the tree itself had done to the hedge, would go for fuel'.[37] Price felt that this could be achieved by modifications to tenancy agreements. In addition, however, he argued that landlords themselves had to be much more active in their management of timber on farmland to the extent that every tree, whether in a hedge or a field, should be documented.

His principal recommendation was 'to number all the trees on each farm, and in every piece of ground, and to enter them in a book, distinguishing the sorts, as oak, elm, ash &c. those that have been cropped, and those that are in hedge-rows from those in the open parts'. He thought it would be 'very useful to have each tree measured in the girth, and roughly valued', which would allow 'the encrease of each tree, both in size and value' to be 'seen from the time the account was taken, and it would be extremely convenient when timber was wanting for any purpose, to be able to turn to a book that shewed the size and situation for each tree on the estate'. These suggestions were put into practice a few years later by Price's friend John Biddulph of Ledbury Park. In his 'Timber Book' of July 1817 there is a 'Survey and Valuation of all the Timber Trees and young trees growing on the several Estates in the parishes of Ledbury and Donnington'.[38] Every tree on the farms was 'blazed and numbered with white paint'; the totals listed were 'Maiden Oak Trees': 493; 'Pollard Oaks': 320; 'Elm Trees': 619; 'Ash Trees': 181; 'Poplar Trees': 31; and one 'Wich Elm'. The profusion of pollard oaks and elms is remarkable. Sales of trees were noted in this book through the 1820s until 1829, and an additional benefit of this level of management was that 'all tenants would be very cautious how they cropped, stripped, or felled any tree without leave, when there was so certain a method

of detecting them.' He identified one weakness in this approach, namely that
'tenants have it in their power either to preserve young trees in their hedgerows, or to prevent their becoming timber.' In other words, they could cut out
young oak or elm saplings rather than allow them to grow on to become timber
trees, and hence the supply of new young timber trees 'over and above those
that were marked when he first entered upon the farm' would dry up. Price
recommended that landlords should 'agree to give each tenant a certain sum
for every tree he had preserved in his grounds'; this would reward those tenants
who 'from a good principle, are very careful of young timber'. while 'others who
are not naturally careful, might become so by means of such encouragement'.[39]

Price's essay on the bad effects of stripping was an important contribution
to a national debate on the preservation of timber and the rights of tenants to
crop, lop and pollard trees. This type of tree management was increasingly
vilified by agricultural improvers in the eighteenth century, and Price was very
active in trying to stop this traditional form of management both on his own
estate and through his writings and publications.[40] Price encouraged landlords
to take a minute control of timber trees through documentation and
surveillance. He certainly practised what he preached: an advertisement in the
Hereford Journal in December 1783 records that one of his tenants, Judith
Davies, made an apology for felling a pollarded ash and an oak which Price had
marked to stand. Price advertised that he had 'generously' terminated a
prosecution.[41] Price's article was commended as 'judicious' by John Lodge, a
local cleric, who noted that Uvedale Price was 'a gentleman whose extensive
plantations, conducted by the truest taste, contribute highly to adorn and
beautify the neighbouring country'.[42]

One effect of the cessation of pollarding was the development of the type
of large overgrown pollards which Price so valued and praised a few years later
in his 1794 *Essay on the Picturesque...* for their characteristic variety of form,
shade and colour. Price recognised that the animation and picturesqueness of
such old pollards was the consequence of the 'indiscriminate hacking of the
peasant' and the 'careless method of cutting, just as the farmer happened to
want a few stakes or poles'. Compared to the:

> Tameness of the poor pinioned trees (whatever their age) of a
> gentleman's plantation drawn up strait and even together, there
> is often a sort of spirit of animation, in the manner in which old
> neglected pollards stretch out their limbs across these hollow
> roads, in every wild and irregular direction: on some, the large
> knots and protuberances, add to the ruggedness of their
> twisted trunks; in others, the deep hollow of the inside, the
> mosses on the bark, the rich yellow of the touch-wood, with
> the blackness of the more decayed substance, afford such
> variety of tints, of brilliant and mellow lights, with deep and
> peculiar shades, as the finest timber tree, however beautiful in
> other respects, with all its health and vigour cannot exhibit.[43]

Price added covenants to some of his leases to restrict the number of pollards which could be regularly cut, and the consequence of this was that the remaining trees, as marked by Price, would develop into large overgrown pollards. In one lease of 1799, for example, the tenant was not allowed to crop any of the pollards which 'stand in the middle of any of the fields, or clear of the hedge rows'.[44] This policy would reduce the power of the tenants and increase the shading effect of the trees on their land, but it would, according to Price's ideas, benefit the landscape.

COURT CONNECTIONS

We know little of Uvedale Price's relationship with his brothers. The Reverend Robert Price was prebendary and residentiary canon at Salisbury (1785–1823). He was a keen musician and Thomas Twining told Charles Burney that he was 'the best Dilettante player on the Violincello … that I ever heard'. Twining met him in Northamptonshire in 1783 and thought him 'as little like a Doctor of any kind as can be imagined: a young, lively clergyman, in his own hair + buckskin breeches'.[45] For some years he appears to have lived at The Lodge, Haslemere, and his daughter was to marry Uvedale Price's son Robert Price.[46] Colonel Barrington Price lived at Beckett, Berkshire, and married Mary, daughter of the 7th earl of Strathmore and Mary Bowes, on 11 May 1789.[47] Major William Price lived at Mansel House and had land which he farmed on the estate at Foxley. He served as an equerry to George III, reluctantly resigning in 1787 on grounds of ill health, and from 1792 became vice-chamberlain to Queen Charlotte. His close relations to the royal family contrast with Uvedale Price's support of the Foxite Whigs. Samuel Rogers recounts that Major William Price was 'a great favourite with George the Third, and ventured to say any thing to him'. One story is that when walking in the grounds of Windsor Castle the following dialogue took place. 'I shall certainly,' said the King 'order this tree to be cut down.' 'If it is cut down, your majesty will have destroyed the finest tree about the Castle.' – 'Really, it is surprising that people constantly oppose my wishes.' 'Permit me to observe, that if your majesty will not allow people to speak, you will never hear the truth.' – 'Well, Price, I believe you are right.' On another occasion, when the duke of Clarence (later William the Fourth) was a young man, 'he happened to be dining at the Equerries' table. Among the company was Major Price. The Duke told one of his facetious stories. "Excellent!" said Price; "I wish I could believe it." – "If you say that again, Price" cried the Duke, "I'll send this claret at your head." Price *did* say it again. Accordingly the claret *came*, – and it was *returned*.'[48]

Major Price's role as an equerry is described in the diaries of his friend Robert Fulke Greville: 'Major Price was nephew to the Bishop of Durham an excellent & Most Worthy Man – He was one of My Fast Bosom Friends through Life.'[49] In March 1789, for example, Price walked with the king to Richmond Workhouse, while in 1794, during 'a stag chace, & when attended by Major Price at that time one of His Equerrys & at this time in Waiting' when the king was 'crossing the

Mill Dam in Blackwater His Majesty's Horse frightened at the rush of water, gave a sudden and violent start, & threw H.M. into the Pool. Tho' not out of his depth, H M: in the first Instance disappeared under the water'. Luckily 'His Faithful Equerry instantly dashed in, & laying hold of the King, supported Him, not however before He had Swallowed some Water and was become a little confused. No serious consequence however ensued … .'[50] While at Weymouth in September 1794, Greville and Price visited 'the Pebbly Beach', Chesil Beach. 'As soon as We got on the Beach & turn'd our Eyes to the Wide ocean, We both enjoy'd the scenery & felt our thoughts free, which they had not been for some time – All géne, all hurry, all interruption were now at rest, & We felt ourselves, Ourselves again.'[51] They collected pebbles. A few days later, on 18 September 1794, they went to Chesil Beach again, but were too late for the ferry. 'On our return a violent Shower of rain overtook us. We were ill prepared for it, however, We contrived for about half an hour to shelter ourselves tolerably well. My friend by getting under the Lee of a Hay Stack + I by thrusting Myself in a thick Hedge.'[52]

William Price was closely concerned with King George's interest in agricultural improvement and was himself keen to experiment on his farm at Foxley. In October 1786 he was so keen to grow the racine de disette, also known as the French beetroot or the mangel wurzel, which had very recently been introduced, that he asked Sir Joseph Banks for some to be sent to him at Hereford. Banks was keen to know what quantity the major required and Dr James Lind at Windsor was able to reassure him that 'the quantity of seed of the French Beetroot he wishes you to provide for him, is only a single handful.'[53] Princess Elizabeth, commenting on William Price's management of the Mansel Lacy property, said in 1790 that he had 'become quite a farmer. They say his house in Herefordshire is the neatest thing that ever was. I forget how much cyder he made last year, but it was, I do remember, a very large quantity, and that he was very much pleased with it.'[54]

It is difficult to be certain of the extent to which William Price, after he became vice-chamberlain, was responsible for introducing alterations to Queen Charlotte's house at Frogmore, Windsor, and whether he drew upon his brother Uvedale Price's advice and guidance in carrying out these changes. Jane Roberts has analysed the account book that William Price maintained for Queen Charlotte in respect of the gardens at Frogmore, and has concluded that he was the 'guiding spirit' behind the enlargement of grounds between 1792 and 1819, even if Christopher Alderson and possibly Humphry Repton may have been the most significant aesthetic influences on the landscaping of the site.[55] There are records of William Price directly supervising work, requesting two of the royal horses for use 'in digging the grounds for the intended River at Frogmore' in May 1795[56] and ordering nursery plants for the Queen's garden.[57] It is unlikely, therefore, that Uvedale Price was unaware of the improvements and he may well have influenced them through his brother's connection.

In the early 1790s Price started his lengthy connection with John James

Hamilton (1756–1818), the first marquis of Abercorn. Lord Abercorn was a leading Tory influence and friend of William Pitt who had a great interest in theatre and literature. He was one of the earliest patrons of Thomas Lawrence, who acted in plays at Bentley Priory. Walter Scott described his 'evenings of modern fashion' at Bentley Priory with guests such as Richard Payne Knight and Lord Aberdeen as resembling 'a Greek symposium for learning and literature'. The house was partially rebuilt in 1788 by John Soane and Price provided some personal advice on the plantings in the grounds. Abercorn's three marriages were the cause of considerable gossip, especially as his second wife eloped with her cousin. Abercorn was to provide much editorial and stylistic advice on drafts of Price's writings over the next ten years. Their surviving correspondence starts with a letter of 1792 which is the first documented reference to Price's meeting Humphry Repton, who had been advising on several estates in Herefordshire, including Garnons (1791) and Stoke Edith (1792).[58] Price relished telling Humphry Repton of the continuing prevalence of the stripping of elm trees in the view from William Pitt the Younger's estate at Holwood, Kent. Price told Abercorn that he had asked Repton

> to shew a proper horror for stript Elms, + told him he would deserve a statue if he could inspire Mr Pitt with such an aversion to them as to make him exert his great authority + eloquence to put an end to such a horrid practice. If I remember right there are some striking instances of their deformity in the view from Holwood. I don't know how far Mr Pitt is interested by natural beauties, or likely to listen to such a man as Mr Repton, but if you my Lord were to take up this cause in earnest, I should not despair of singing the nunc dimittis for an act that would do more towards beautifying the face of England than all the sums that ever have, or will be laid out in improvements.[59]

The next year, 1793, Price was busy writing his *Essay on the Picturesque* and planning his new house at Aberystwyth. He recollected later that just before the *Essay* was published he had been with Richard Payne Knight on a visit to Lord Lansdowne at Bowood. It was in this period that 'Fox and Lansdowne edged closer. Their rapprochement was assisted by Fox's friendly treatment in the House of Commons of Lansdowne's son Lord Wycombe, which contrasted with Pitt's scorn.'[60] 'Price remembered that Lord Lansdowne 'used to look at us with some surprise when we were making very bold remarks on all that we saw. 'He does not know,' said Knight to me, 'that we are great doctors.'' Price noted as an aside that 'this visit of ours was at the early part of the French Revolution; we found at Bowood the Duchesse de Levis,[61] and her mother; the next day Talleyrand arrived while we were at dinner.'[62] The turbulent political situation was to underlie Price's writings and ideas for at least the next twenty years.

CHAPTER 4

'THE GREAT GUNS OF TASTE'

THE PICTURESQUE

By the early 1790s, as he approached his 50s, Price could have contented himself with life at Foxley and the endless round of social engagements with neighbours. He was a well-respected figure in the county, and his architectural experiment and patronage of Nash at Aberystwyth (see Chapter 5), as well as his art collection, demonstrated his commitment to continuing the legacy of his father and grandfather in promoting architecture and the arts. The estate at Foxley was in good order, and was being further consolidated as Price bought up additional pockets of land in order to enhance his curatorial authority over the landscape. Yet this was the point at which Price chose to court national attention by publishing the work that was to define his reputation. The *Essay on the Picturesque* of 1794 was also the start of a new round in contemporary debates on the interpretation of art and landscape that was to lead, ultimately, to a very public falling out with Price's close ally Richard Payne Knight.

Price's *Essay* was the product of a lifetime's interest in the practice and philosophy of art, on the one hand, and the management of land and landscapes, on the other. His motive in publishing the *Essay* was a sincerely held conviction that the face of the country was being steadily diminished by the mania for the 'improvement' of landscape on the part of landowners and the garden designers they employed, chief among them 'Capability' Brown and his disciples. A key moment, equivalent to his meeting with John Nash at Aberystwyth at about the same time, was his meeting with Humphry Repton, who had set himself up as the heir to Brown, in Herefordshire. Price's first impressions of the man were vividly captured in his letter to Lord Abercorn of July 1792: 'I have lately had an opportunity of seeing a good deal of Mr Repton a layer out of grounds, or as he styles himself a Landscape Gardener.' Price felt that Lord Abercorn would 'guess at his manners by his title which I believe is of his own creation, but tho a coxcomb he is very ingenious in his profession, + seems to me to have infinitely more resources, + better principles, than his predecessors.' He reported that Repton 'has been making plans of improvement for some Gentlemen in my neighbourhood at whose houses I saw him, + afterwards went down the Wye with him', and was delighted to discover 'that he really admired the banks in their natural state, + did not desire to turf them, or remove the large stones'. Price confirmed that Knight had also met him and 'thinks about him as I do, + we both rejoice that he has some respect for picturesque beauty which has hitherto been treated with great indignity'.[1] It was these meetings with Repton and discussions with Knight that impelled Price to write on the subject of the picturesque.

Price had already written on the subject of stripped trees in his 1786 essay for the *Annals of Agriculture*, but his encounters with Repton and his discussions with Richard Payne Knight had stirred in him new ideas on landscape and its significance. Price and Knight had, however, been discussing aesthetics for several years. Indeed, they both visited Franz Hemsterhuis (1721–1790), the Dutch philosopher of aesthetics, at the Hague sometime in the late 1780s. Price recorded that the meeting was 'on a very hot evening in June; we were ushered into a long room with one immense window that filled up the whole of the narrow end, while the setting sun in the very centre of it filled the whole room with one blaze of light.' Moreover, the window, 'as is always the case in Holland, was shut close, + probably had been so the whole day, or perhaps the whole year'. Price's relatively low threshold for high theory is indicated by his decision to leave the two Greek scholars together as 'I had not the advantage of being either a dutch man, or a Savant, or a cucumber.'[2] It is possible, too, that Price's desire to commit his thoughts to the published page once more was driven by a competitive urge to prove himself as the worthy heir of his father and grandfather, as the equal of his talented uncles and, above all, as the intellectual match of his neighbour, Knight. As we have seen, there was a strong family tradition of publishing, particularly on art and landscape. The account by Uvedale Tomkyns Price, Price's grandfather, of Spain and Portugal (published in 1749) includes descriptions of the 'pittoresque' face of the country. Among Price's uncles, Daines Barrington's diverse literary output must have been a particular influence. His paper 'On the progress of Gardening', read in 1782 and published in *Archaeologia* in 1785, is especially relevant in the context of explaining the origins of Price's *Essay*. As both Denis Lambin and Susan Sloman have noted, Daines Barrington's paper pre-empts several themes of Price's *Essay* in its extolling of Gainsborough as heir to Claude and Poussin and, even more significantly, in its critique of 'Capability' Brown as a desecrator of landscape.[3] Brown had died in 1783, but the arrival of an able, proficient and increasingly popular successor, in the form of Humphry Repton, spurred Price to write on the subject himself.

Price's ideas on the picturesque were developed in response to not only the influence of his family and neighbours but also a series of published interventions on the nature of art, beauty and landscape which appeared in various forms from the 1740s onwards. His *Essay* was in many ways an extended response to Edmund Burke's *Philosophical Enquiry into the Origin of Our Ideas of the Sublime and Beautiful* (1757; revised and expanded in 1759). Price, indeed, declaimed that the very intention of the *Essay* was 'to shew … that the picturesque has a character not less separate and distinct than either the sublime or the beautiful, nor less independent of the art of painting'.[4] William

Shenstone, in his *Unconnected Thoughts on Gardening*, published in 1764 – although they were written in 1759 – made use of his experience in gardening on his farm at The Leasowes in south Shropshire near Halesowen. He divided up gardening into 'three species', namely 'kitchen-gardening', 'parterre-gardening' and 'landscape, or picturesque gardening', which formed the basis of his essay. He argued that landscape or picturesque gardening 'consists in pleasing the imagination by scenes of grandeur, beauty, or variety' and further, drawing on Burke, thought that 'Garden-scenes may perhaps be divided into the sublime, the beautiful, and the melancholy or pensive … .'[5] These works were informed by William Hogarth's *Analysis of Beauty* of 1753, which argued that the eye preferred variety and intricacy to symmetry and that 'those lines which have the most variety themselves, contribute towards the production of beauty.' His 'line of beauty' was not simply a curved line but a 'precise serpentine line' which was neither 'too bulging nor too tapering'.[6]

In addition, Price was reacting to important contemporary works on gardening and landscape, many of which were published in the 1770s at the time he was transforming his own gardens at Foxley. William Chambers' *Dissertation on Oriental Gardening* of 1772 criticised the 'new manner' of gardening which had been 'universally adopted' in England and where 'our gardens differ very little from common fields, so closely is common nature copied in most of them.' He identified 'such a poverty of imagination in the contrivance, and of art in the arrangement, that these compositions rather appear the offspring of chance than design'. Visitors found themselves 'cursing the line of beauty', the repetition, the lack of shade and all that was 'insipid and vulgar' associated with the modern garden style of gardeners such as William Kent and Lancelot Brown.[7] Other key works were Thomas Whately's *Observations on Modern Gardening* (1770) and Whately's friend William Mason's poems *An Heroic Epistle to Sir William Chambers* (1773) and *The English Garden* (1772–81). William Mason had 'absorbed some of his garden tastes from an early love of poetry', but was also very familiar with the gardens and parks designed by William Kent and Capability Brown. When Brown died it was Mason who wrote his epitaph for Fenstanton church. Jules Smith argues that 'Mason's gardens were themselves very literary, with classical and modern busts, memorials, and verse inscriptions taken from Milton, Marvell, Gray, and Rousseau, to give a melancholy, sentimental atmosphere; his gardens were to be places of spiritual refreshment and aesthetic contemplation.' The most famous of the gardens he designed was for Lord Nuneham, later Earl Harcourt, at Nuneham Courtney in Oxfordshire:

> Mason created a series of points of interest in the picturesque
> manner (later more associated with his friend William Gilpin),
> and irregularly shaped flower beds containing wild, native,
> and imported flowers. The gently sloping ground was covered
> with patches of flowers including roses, lupins, tulips,
> hollyhocks, and sweet-scented mignonette; and trailing

garlands of clematis, bryony, and creepers draped the
surrounding trees, in imitation of Julie's garden in Rousseau's
Julie ou La nouvelle Héloïse (1760).

This garden is described in the fourth book of Mason's *The English Garden*.[8]

Horace Walpole published his *The History of the Modern Taste in Gardening* in 1780 as the fourth and last volume of his *Anecdotes of Painting in England*. It has a complicated publication history: it is dated as completed on 2 August 1770 and was actually printed at Strawberry Hill in 1771, but publication was delayed. A second edition was published in 1782 and this included a new note on French gardening. A third edition, the first separate edition of the work, was published in 1785 and a fourth appeared in 1786 as part of a new edition of *The Anecdotes of Painting in England*. The link between painting and landscaping is made as explicit in the text as in the mode of publication. In the third volume of *Anecdotes* (printed in 1763), Walpole noted that 'I have not been able to please myself with a single term that will express ground laid out on principles of natural picturesque beauty, in contradistinction to symmetrical gardens' and suggested '*Landscape-gardens*' for 'want of a happier appellation'.[9] He stressed the importance of understanding and seeing gardens with the eye of an artist or poet. Taking the garden of Alcinous in the *Odyssey* as an example, he asks 'Is there an admirer of Homer who can read his description without rapture; or who does not form to his imagination a scene of delights more picturesque than the landscapes of Tinian or Juan Fernandez?'[10] The works of Whately and Chambers had both been translated into French and Walpole felt that the French had underestimated the importance of English gardening. He argued that 'The French have of late years adopted our style in gardens, but chusing to be fundamentally obliged to more remote rivals, they deny us half the merit, or rather the originality of the invention, by ascribing the discovery to the Chinese, and by calling our taste in gardening Le Gout Anglo-Chinois.'[11] He stressed that it was the English who had brought about this revolution in gardening. 'We have discovered the point of perfection. We have given the true model of gardening to the world; let other countries mimic or corrupt our taste; but let it reign here on its verdant throne, original by its elegant simplicity … .' Moreover, he emphasised that this was unlikely to spread on to the Continent, as the expense 'is only suited to the opulence of a free country, where emulation reigns among many independent particulars'. Tying the new style of gardening directly to his project of encouraging English painting, he asked that if 'we have the seeds of a Claud or a Gaspar amongst us, he must come forth. If wood, water, groves, vallies, glades, can inspire poet or painter, this is the country, this is the age to produce them.'[12]

Walpole traced the line in the development of modern gardening from Charles Bridgeman, who 'first thought' of the 'capital stroke' of the 'sunk fence', to William Kent, who was 'painter enough to taste the charms of landscape, bold and opinionative enough to dare and to dictate, and born with a genius to strike out a great system from the twilight of imperfect essays. He leaped the fence, and saw all nature was a garden.' Walpole emphasised the importance of Kent's painterly knowledge and skill:

> the pencil of his imagination bestowed all the arts of landscape on the scenes he handled. The great principles on which he worked were perspective, and light and shade. Groupes of trees broke too uniform or too extensive a lawn; evergreens and woods were opposed to the glare of the champain …

By 'selecting favourite objects, and veiling deformities by screens of plantation; sometimes allowing the rudest waste to add its foil to the richest theatre, he realised the compositions of the greatest masters in painting'. Walpole noted that some of the newly created gardens and parks were directly comparable to the greatest art. At the earl of Halifax's Stanstead, for example, he relished that 'great avenue' which traversed 'an ancient wood for two miles' and the 'very extensive lawns at that seat, richly inclosed by venerable beech woods, and chequered by single beeches of vast size', but he was particularly taken by the view from 'the portico of the temple' where 'the landscape that wastes itself in rivers of broken sea, recall such exact pictures of Claud Lorrain, that it is difficult to conceive that he did not paint them from this very spot.' Walpole approved of much of Lancelot Brown's landscaping, noting that Kent had been 'succeeded by a very able master', although he could not name him as 'living artists' were not included in his history. Although he was concerned that 'the pursuit of variety' threatened the modern style of gardening, he stressed that 'In the mean time how rich, how gay, how picturesque the face of the country!' There had been so much improvement brought about by the modern style of gardening, he thought, that 'every journey is made through a succession of pictures …'.[13]

It was William Gilpin, however, who was to prove a more important and influential writer in the spread of the idea of the picturesque in the second half of the eighteenth century, through the publication of his *Essay on Prints* (first edition 1768) and his subsequent tour books which offered observations on 'picturesque beauty'. Gilpin, who combined careers as school master, vicar, philanthropist, scholar and artist, first developed his views on the picturesque in an early essay *A Dialogue upon the Gardens of the Right Honourable the Lord Viscount Cobham at Stowe* (1748), which characterised it as 'a term expressive of that peculiar kind of beauty, which is agreeable in a picture'.[14] Gilpin attempted to develop his theory of the picturesque in the *Essay on Picturesque Beauty*, written in 1776, though criticism from Reynolds, to whom he sent the work in manuscript, compelled him to delay publication until 1792.[15] The general idea was that certain qualities present in nature – roughness and ruggedness, variety and irregularity, chiaroscuro – could combine to form 'picturesque beauty' – a phrase that Gilpin admitted was 'but little understood', but by which he meant 'that kind of beauty which *would look well in a picture*'.[16] The fullest exposition of Gilpin's concept of the picturesque came from his various tours: along the River Wye (1770; published 1782), in the Lake District

(1772; published 1786), in North Wales (1773; published 1809) and in Scotland (1776; published 1789). Gilpin's ambition for these tours was to 'examine the face of a country *by the rules of picturesque beauty*: opening the sources of those pleasures which are derived from the comparison'.[17]

William Gilpin ran his school successfully at Cheam for several years until 1777, when it was taken over by his son William. The small garden there was designed by his friend Thomas Whately, the author of *Observations on Modern Gardening*.[18] Gilpin took advantage of the school holidays to take a series of short tours in the early summer between 1768 and 1776. In 1777 he moved to Vicar's Hill in the New Forest and became vicar of Boldre. Gilpin was fascinated by the ancient trees of the New Forest, and on his first visit there exclaimed in a letter to his friend, the poet William Mason: 'Such Dryads! Extending their taper arms to each other, sometimes in elegant mazes along the plain; sometimes in single figures; & sometimes combined! What would I have given to be able to trace all their beauteous forms on paper!!' But, he continued, 'Alass! My art failed me. I could only sketch: and a sketch amounts to no more, than, N.B. Here stands a tree.'[19] The manuscript versions of Gilpin's tours received wide circulation among an influential group of friends and acquaintances. Thomas Gray, who saw the manuscript of the Wye tour just before his death in July 1772, praised Gilpin's work, and this seal of approval from the leading poet of the sublime was publicised in a note that William Mason made in an influential edition of Gray's poems of 1775. The circle of friends and acquaintances who read and approved of Gilpin's picturesque tours, and encouraged their publication, included William Mason, William Mitford, William Lock, the duchess of Portland, Mrs Delany and Queen Charlotte, to whom the tour of the Lakes was dedicated when it was published in 1786.

Uvedale Price would have been familiar with the work of Gilpin published from 1782 onwards, but may well have known the manuscript versions of the tours, as he also had connections with Gilpin through his family and friends. His brother William, equerry to King George and later vice-chamberlain to Queen Charlotte, would have known of Gilpin's popularity with the queen. Gilpin also knew Price's old friend Thomas Johnes of Hafod, near Aberystwyth. Gilpin told William Mason that on the publication of the Wye tour Johnes

> paid me a visit; & brought me a large port-folio, full of
> paintings (on paper) of a variety of views around his house.
> They were done by [Thomas] Jones, a pupil of Wilson. On the
> whole they were not amiss, considering he is one of your
> religious copyists. But tho I could have criticized the
> paintings, I very much admired the views; which were both
> great and beautiful … . He told me … The walks & lawns were
> laid out by Mr. Mason; whose English garden he took in his
> hand; & wanted no other direction. So if you want to see an
> exact translation of your book into good Welsh, you must go
> to Mr. Johnes's seat in Cardiganshire.[20]

An even more important connection between Gilpin and Price in the 1780s was through the diocese of Salisbury. Price's brother, Robert, was a prebendary of the cathedral, as was Gilpin, while Price's uncle, Dr Shute Barrington, was the bishop of Salisbury from 1782 until he became bishop of Durham in 1791.

Gilpin was a regular correspondent with Barrington from 1783 until 1803. Barrington asked Gilpin's opinion on James Wyatt's plans for improving Salisbury Cathedral, and Gilpin wrote that

> The Bishop gave me Wyatt's plan in my hand, and desired I
> would go into the Cathedral alone, and examine them at my
> leisure; which I did. To one capital part of the intended
> improvement, I ventured to object; and gave the Bishop my
> reasons in writing; which he sent to Wyatt: and I have reason
> to believe, Wyatt had the candour to be convinced ...[21]

Wyatt had proposed to fill 'three grand Gothic arches ... with tracery-work in the manner of the great window at Carlisle'. Gilpin thought this would introduce 'a nugatory' and an 'inharmonious ornament' and that it would destroy 'a great beauty; for the view of the pillars &c, of St Mary's Chappel through the great arch, was both a very beautiful piece of perspective; and gave space to the Choir'. He added with confidence that although 'there is great appearance of vanity in setting my opinion against the architect of the Pantheon. – But Mr Wyatt was probably never engaged in any Gothic work before; whereas I have in a degree studied it.' Barrington supported Gilpin's charitable work in Boldre. Gilpin 'started to advertise his charitable projects in 1791–92, by arranging for sets of his drawings to be displayed at the London residences of the Speaker and of the Bishop of Durham', asking Mrs Jane Barrington for this assistance in a letter of 20 July 1792. Eventually he set up a sale sponsored by his friends, including the earl of Dartmouth, the bishop of Durham, Col. William Mitford and Sir George Beaumont.

> The last was by far the most willing and active of his 'puffers',
> as he called them. Sir George increasingly took charge of the
> final arrangements. He favoured Christie as the most suitable
> auctioneer ... He saw to the advertising, read through the
> catalogue, and was consulted on the order of the presentation
> of the various lots.[22]

Thus, although there is no direct evidence of Price and Gilpin ever actually meeting, it is clear that they knew of each other and their ideas and publications through a web of friends and relatives.

By the early 1790s the picturesque was a topic of considerable public debate. While Reynolds had dismissed its importance within the artistic canon in his correspondence with Gilpin, others were attracted by the idea that the picturesque offered a new approach to the appreciation of art and landscape. John Baptist Malchair's unpublished 'Observations on Landskipp Drawing' of

1791 characterised the picturesque as that which was 'Accidental or mixed', consisting 'of a greater variety of objects, with a Capricious mixture of Arte and Nature, producing such fortuitous beauties as the reachest immagination and fancey cannot come up to'. Malchair emphasised the cultural relativism at the heart of this understanding of the picturesque, stating that 'even a Pig-Staiy with a single Elder bush is a Landskipp.'[23] The word 'picturesque' did not appear in the sixth edition of Johnson's dictionary of 1785, but the 1801 edition gave multiple definitions: 'what is pleasing to the eye; what strikes viewer as singular; what appeals with force of a painting; what is expressible in a painting or wd afford a good subject for a painting'.[24]

PUBLISHING *THE LANDSCAPE* AND THE *ESSAY*

Price and Knight were both swimming with the tide when they decided in the early 1790s to write on landscape and the picturesque. They had extensive personal experience of gardening, forestry and estate management on their own estates, they were connoisseurs and collectors of art and they were not reticent in criticising the estates they visited. Lord Lansdowne had been surprised by the boldness of their remarks to him on a visit to his estate at Bowood. The park had been redesigned in the 1760s by Lancelot Brown with a characteristic belt of trees, a lake and clumps of trees: all traits which both critics deplored. The even-aged plantations would have been about thirty years old at the time of Price and Knight's visit, an age when few trees would have shown the individual characteristics which Price valued. Price noted that it was not long after this visit that 'we laid our respective claims before the public.'[25]

But what did Price, writing many years later to the poet Samuel Rogers, mean by 'our respective claims'? It is clear that they had discussed their ideas with each other over several years and that they knew they were writing on related topics, but the mode of publication, and the way in which they appeared so close together, appears to have caused an immediate rift between the two authors. This antagonism was soon stilled, but was to reappear in following years when further publications publicly demonstrated the philosophical differences between them. The precise chronology of publication is important. *The Landscape* was published in February 1794 and the *Essay* was published early in June.[26] Knight's didactic poem was 'Addressed to Uvedale Price, Esq.' on the title page and the opening stanza refers directly to Price:

> How best to bid the verdant Landscape rise,
> To please the fancy, and delight the eyes;
> Its various parts in harmony to join
> With art clandestine, and conceal'd design;
> To adorn, arrange; — to separate, and select
> With secret skill and counterfeit neglect;
> I sing. ———— Do thou, O Price, the song attend;

Instruct the poet, and assist the friend:
Teach him plain truth in numbers to express,
And shew its charms through fiction's flowery dress.

Price's intervention on the subject, and the work that made his name, was
*An Essay on the Picturesque, as Compared with the Sublime and the Beautiful; and,
on the Use of Studying Pictures, for the Purpose of Improving Real Landscape,*
published in June 1794. The Preface is extraordinary because it tells the reader
that the work they are about to start is incomplete:

> This unfinished work (and such I fear it is in every respect) I
> did not intend publishing till it was more complete, and till I
> had endeavoured, at least, to render it more worthy the public
> inspection. I have, however, been induced to send it into the
> world earlier than I wished, from the general curiosity which
> my friend Mr. Knight's poem has awakened on the subject.

Price explained that 'I had mentioned to Mr. Knight that I had written some
papers on the present style of improvement, but that I despaired of ever getting
them ready for the press, though I was very anxious that the absurdities of that
style should be exposed.' This accords with Price's method of writing, which
entailed circulating drafts of sections of his works around friends and carefully
modifying them over several years. Price was never one, as his later works show,
to rush into print. Following this discussion, 'Knight conceived the idea of a
poem on the same subject; and having all the materials arranged in his mind,
from the activity and perseverance which so strongly mark his character, he
never delayed or abandoned the execution, till the whole was completed.'[27]
Knight was an author of a very different cast and a much less practical bent.
His early fascination with Greek architecture, such as the temples at
Agrigentum and Selinus, is displayed in his unfinished *Expedition into Sicily* of
1777, which also shows a prescient interest in the picturesque: at Lipari 'The
Houses are plaster'd white, with Roofs quite flat, which rising one over another,
form some very pictoresque Groupes; but when one enters the town the
prospect changes, and all is filth and misery.'[28] His first published work, for the
Society of Dilettanti, was *An Account of the Remains of the Worship of Priapus* in
1786. This could not have been more dissimilar to Price's work on tree
management of the same year. It included Price's old friend Sir William
Hamilton's 1781 account of the wax phallic votive offerings seen at Iserno in
Abruzzo, included a startling representation as a frontispiece and argued that
sexual symbolism was at the heart of religion. Although published for private
subscribers this first work scandalised many readers, including Horace Walpole,
and gave Knight a notorious reputation. Knight's scholarly credentials were
sharpened by the publication of his analytical essay on the Greek alphabet in
1791 in which he scrupulously examined ancient Greek letters to discover 'how
to pronounce the sounds they denoted'.[29] Price recounted that, when Knight's
The Landscape

was nearly finished, he wrote to me to propose, what I
consider as the highest possible compliment, and the
strongest mark of confidence in my taste, – that my papers
(when properly modelled) should be published with his poem,
in the same manner as Sir Joshua Reynold's notes were
published with Mr. Mason's Du Fresnoy.

Price is referring to William Mason's verse translation of Charles Alphonse Du
Fresnoy's *History of Painting*, which had been published with extensive notes
by Reynolds in 1783.[30] But Price argued that

This proposal, could it have been made at an earlier period, I
should have accepted with pride; but my work had then taken
on too much of a form and character of its own to be
incorporated with anything else; for indeed the whole of what
I have now published had been written some time before.[31]

Price was clearly emphasising here the long gestation of his ideas on the
picturesque, and contrasting his approach with that of Knight.

Price was also keen to emphasise that, although 'the plan' of his work was
'totally different' to Knight's and they disagreed 'in some particulars', 'the
general tendency is so much the same, and our notions of improvement are
upon the whole so similar, that my work may, in many points, serve as a
commentary on his.' He then judiciously and carefully argued that he thought
it better 'that what I had arranged should appear in its present state, now that
curiosity is alive, than in a less imperfect one when the subject might have
become stale'. He correctly realised that the furore caused by the publication
of *The Landscape* would improve the impact of his *Essay*. He then, as if walking
on a knife edge and expecting an adverse response from Knight, added that

in the light of a commentary it may possibly have more effect,
when each person publishes his own ideas (tinctured as they
must always be with the peculiarities of different minds, yet
tending to the same general end) than when two works are
modelled to agree and coincide with each other.

Price may have thought his carefully wrought preface explaining why his
Essay had had to be published prematurely would assuage Knight's possible ire
at the implicit public exposure of their differences of opinion both in the mode
of publication and philosophical position. Instead, however, according to the
artist and diarist Joseph Farington, it provoked an instant and angry response
from Knight, who was unhappy at the implication that his poem had been
adapted from ideas originally expressed by Price. Knight wrote Price 'a strong
letter, which caused Mr. P to call on him when the difficulties were explained
away'. Farington argued that Knight had tried to steal Price's thunder: 'The
fact is Mr Knight very likely forseeing the subject when mentioned to him by
Mr. Price was likely to be popular, pushed for the reputation of it.' He thought

that 'Mr. Prices preface shews that He had only adopted the Ideas of Mr. P.'[32]
Although the publication procedure was cack-handed it could not have been
better stage-managed to create an immediate public interest in the subject
and probably boosted the sales and impact of both books. A second edition of
Knight's poem was published in 1795 and an enlarged and modified version of
Price's *Essay* in 1796.

Knight's notorious reputation, derived from his publication of *Priapus*, no
doubt added to the intensity of interest, as did a spat between Knight and
Humphry Repton. Repton was in the process of completing his own work on
landscape gardening by subscription and was horrified to see that Knight
satirised his plan for Tatton Park, Cheshire. Knight claimed that Repton
'suggests many expedients for shewing the extent of property, and among
others, that of placing the family arms upon the neighbouring mile-stones'.
Repton placed an advertisement in the *Morning Chronicle* of 17 February 1794
immediately after *The Landscape* was published. This stated that,
'notwithstanding the flattering manner which Mr. Knight has been pleased to
mention my name, in his elegant Poem', it included a section 'said to be taken
from one of my manuscripts' which contained gross errors and
misrepresentations. He asked subscribers to 'suspend their judgment' until
publication. This public dispute further added to the surprisingly frenetic
reception of Price's *Essay* when it appeared in June. It was also a precursor to
the much longer printed exchange of views between Price and Repton over
the next few years.

The intellectual achievement of Price's *Essay* was to add a further dimension
to aesthetic theorising on the nature of the picturesque by placing it in the
context of the everyday business of cultivating and tending land. Price's *Essay*
and Knight's poem offered two quite distinct interpretations of the
picturesque. As well as being an assault on the prevailing conventions of
landscape design, in particular those exemplified by the work of Brown and
Repton, Knight's poem was a paean in praise of all that was dynamic, turbulent
and elemental in nature, a sensibility informed by the landscape of Knight's
own estate at Downton. The virulence of Knight's attack drew sharp rebuke
from contemporaries such as Horace Walpole, who called Knight a 'trumpery
prosaic poetaster' who 'Jacobinically would level the purity of gardens, as
malignantly as Tom Paine or Priestley guillotine Mr Brown'.[33] The allusion to
contemporary events in France was intentional, given the political analogies
made by Knight in his poem between the repression of the Brownian mode of
gardening and the revolutionary liberties of picturesque beauty. Price's more
moderate contribution to the debate was an attempt to ground ideas of the
picturesque in the tangible experience of landscape. His vision of the
picturesque represented a more domesticated and conservative version of that
presented in *The Landscape*. 'Where Knight's rhetoric was rousing, calling for
the liberation of repressed nature', writes Andrew Ballantyne, 'Price's is
affecting and sentimental and conservative in its tenor.'[34]

The *Essay* is not a slight work, the first edition consisting of 288 pages, but it has a simple structure, with Part I laying out the theoretical basis of Price's ideas and Part II discussing how these might be applied to parks, gardens and woods. It opens with a chapter examining why one should study pictures as well as nature when deciding how to make improvements and arguing that 'the general principles of both arts' are the same. It then attempts to show how the 'current system' as exemplified by Brown was opposed to these principles. Two chapters define the word picturesque and provide concrete examples of the difference between the picturesque and beautiful in buildings, water, trees, animals, birds, men, women 'the higher order of beings' and paintings. The *Essay* then considers the sublime and demonstrates that this was beyond 'our contracted powers' and that 'the art of improving therefore depends on the beautiful and the picturesque'. The last chapters of Part I consider themes of smoothness, light and shadow, colour and ugliness and deformity. Part II of the *Essay* is more practical, discussing the clumps, belts and avenues of the Brown system, trees and plantations, lawns and parks and, finally, water.

Price stated that the aim of his *Essay* was to adduce whether 'the present system of improving (to use a short though often an inaccurate term) is founded on any just principles of taste'.[35] For Price, the study of nature and the works of great artists – such as the landscapes of Claude, Salvator Rosa and Poussin, but also those of Dutch and Flemish artists such as Wouwerman and Ruysdael – was essential to understanding how to lay out grounds. Price saw the Brownian mode of gardening as thoroughly unnatural, and as a repudiation of the 'connection' between landscape and place: 'A painter, or whoever views objects with a painter's eye, looks with indifference, if not with disgust, at the clumps, the belts, the made water, and the eternal smoothness and sameness of a finished place.'[36] His emphasis on connection and local knowledge implicitly validated the authority of informed landowners (such as Price himself) as those best placed to effect changes to the landscape. 'He therefore, in my mind,' wrote Price, 'will shew most art in improving, who leaves (a very material point) or who creates the greatest variety of landscapes' and 'not he who begins his work by general clearing and smoothing, or in other words, by destroying all those accidents of which such advantages might have been made; but which afterwards, the most enlightened and experienced artist can never hope to restore'.[37]

Rather than considering the picturesque as a purely subjective interpretation of landscape, as Knight did, Price believed it to be an innate quality in the very atomic structure of certain objects and items.[38] Price introduced a third category of 'picturesqueness' to the Burkean ideas of the beautiful and the sublime. This stood for ruggedness, variety and character: 'intricacy in the disposition, and variety in the forms, the tints and the lights and shadows of objects … the two opposite qualities of roughness, and of sudden variation, joined to that of irregularity, are the most efficient causes of

the picturesque'.[39] According to Price's definition, 'the picturesque fills up a vacancy between the sublime and the beautiful, and accounts for the pleasure we receive from many objects, on principles distinct from them both'.[40] While the main purpose of the *Essay* was to show how landowners needed to draw inspiration from both art and nature in drawing out the picturesque qualities of their estates, this did not imply any particular mode of gardening or landscape design. Rather, it allowed Price to speak up for those aspects of the landscape that he saw were being cleared away by the mania for improvement: 'old neglected bye roads and hollow ways', 'old, mossy, rough-hewn park pales', rugged old oaks and rustic hovels, mills and cottages.[41] This picturesque aesthetic was one which Malchair delighted in on his visits to Foxley, and several of the drawings in Price's collection provide evidence of his fascination with this aspect of the picturesque, perhaps best exemplified by Hobbema's *Watermill* (Figure 19).

Although Price was less strident in his views than Knight, he hardly held

Fig. 19 Meindert Hobbema, *A Watermill*. This drawing from Uvedale Price's collection demonstrates roughness, irregularity and variety of forms, tints and light which Price saw as 'efficient causes' of the picturesque. (© Trustees of the British Museum)

back in his attacks on Brown for his uniformity, narrowness and vanity. Brown and those who followed him had a 'narrow pedantic manner of considering all objects'.[42] Price was scathing in his opinion of the trademark signs of a Brownian landscape – the clump, the belt and the open expanse of grassland. Price envisaged clumps as 'compact bodies of soldiers' and suggested that taking the first letter away from the name of the clump 'would most accurately describe its form and effect'.[43] The belt of trees around the perimeter of Brownian parks, meanwhile, was likened to a snake swallowing its own tail. While Price admitted that he had never met Brown, and therefore could 'have no personal dislike to him', he could not resist repeating in a footnote the opinion of a fellow gentleman (perhaps Knight): 'Former improvers ... at least kept near the house; but this fellow crawls like a snail all over the grounds, and leaves his cursed slime behind him wherever he goes.'[44]

RECEPTION OF *ESSAY ON THE PICTURESQUE*

Price's *Essay* attracted immediate attention. On receiving a copy from Price, Burke sent an encouraging reply, thanking him for a 'most pleasing, ingenious and instructive Book' and stating that 'It gave me a few hour's very seasonable relief from Books of a very different kind, which teach but too clearly, the art, not of improving, but of laying waste a Country, and of defacing the Beauties both of nature and of contrivance.'[45] It was somewhat astonishing that Burke found time to read Price's book and respond to him on 1 June 1794, as he was in the middle of his speech of reply to the defence in the Warren Hastings trial, which was spread over nine days between 28 May and 16 June 1794 and which 'ranged widely over the matter that had now occupied nine years of parliamentary time and culminated in a direct comparison between Hastings and the Jacobins in France'.[46] Burke largely concurred with Price about Brown, going as far as saying that 'I have the happiness to agree with you in almost everything you have said about Brownism', arguing that 'The Master of that School understood in my opinion, the art of producing a considerable Effect on the first entrance into a Park – but, as I conceive, you gained nothing upon a further aquaintance with the place.'[47] Later Burke told Mrs Crewe that he 'admired many parts of Mr. Price's Book, and thought both he + Mr Knight often discovered much genius in their observations'. However, he also thought that like 'most System-mongers they had pursued their Theories to a dangerous length'.[48] Benjamin West was very positive about Price's *Essay* and told Farington that he 'intended Major Price and Col. Greville to hear his discourse at the Royal Academy' in which he 'was pursuing the ideas of Mr Uvedale Price in his Essay on picturesque beauty'.[49]

A fascinating account exists of the reading of the *Essay* and *The Landscape* by Anna and John Larpent, who studied the books together over a three-week period in July and August. John Larpent was the inspector of plays for the Lord Chamberlain and so had a professional interest in reading literature, although these pieces were not within his official remit. His wife Anna scrupulously recorded what they read, providing an insight into the way the poem and the prose were both read and how they were discussed. On 21 July 1794 Anna Larpent recorded that at their country home in Ashtead, Surrey, 'Mr Larpent red loud the Landscape.' The following day they 'read the Newspapers and the Landscape near an hour'. On 23 July 'Mr Larpent read loud Price – on Picturesque Beauty prayer to bed at 11', and two days later 'Mr L read loud Price.' On 1 August 'I heard Mr L[arpent] read The Landscape. Supper and bed at 11', and on 6 August the reading of Price's essay aroused much discussion among the whole family: 'Then read <u>Price on Picturesque Beauty &c</u> + conversation arose in consequence in our family Circle. Supt. To bed at 11.' On the evening of Thursday 7 August Anna Larpent 'read the European Magazine 'till tea. Then worked at the tambour handkerchief whilst Mr. Larpent read loud <u>Price</u>. Supper prayers to bed at 11.' The next day, she 'walked to the Farm before Tea – returned home, worked at the handkerchief, And Mr L read loud Price which we now finished.' Finally, we reach her critical assessment of the work:

> This book gave us great pleasure, there is much Elegant knowledge in it, taste, + brilliancy, is often in the Images, extremely poetic. It is very spirited – perhaps the Condemnation on Modern improvers is too much strained, if they have carried art too far Mr Price would leave nature too wild – I think throughout his book be does not enough distinguish between the domestic comforts of a garden or <u>improved</u> Grounds, + the delightful romantic enjoyment of mere country. – Which fills the mind with a different sort of enjoyment.

This percipient distinction is one that forms the basis of much criticism of both Price and Knight's work. However, Anna Larpent felt that 'perhaps my own feelings accord with his. – He is Gentlemanlike in his Condemnation, happy in his Quotations, Animated in his observations on the Arts, in that this is a most pleasing work.' She went on to summarise her views of Knight's *The Landscape*, which they had finished 'sometime ago'. Knight would have been horrified to know that Mrs Larpent felt that it

> should be considered almost as a part of <u>Prices</u> book – There are some good lines, + poetry flows, rather than expressing strong Ideas. – it is splenetic – yet a chastened Elegant composition, I do not think there is much poetic Fire. His severity on Repton is not amiable in the stile, + I have since heard Repton had been unfairly dealt with, by His betraying private conversations.

It is clear that the way the two books had been published, and their titles, whatever the intentions of the authors, led readers to compare and contrast their approaches, styles and arguments. There is no doubt in this case that Anna Larpent preferred Price's volume, even though he might 'leave nature too wild'.[50]

Both *The Landscape* and Price's *Essay* provoked a series of counter-publications from others keen to impress their opinions on landscape. William Marshall's scathing review of both works appeared as a single volume in February 1795: 'Who but a man totally ignorant of all scenery, except that of a picture gallery, or the wild coppices of the Welch mountains, could have imagined that woods were, in nature, raised with the same facility that they were on canvas.' Marshall's tract was a dismissal of claims to finding beauty in the quotidian and picturesque: 'By mere *dint of neglect* places, heretofore beautiful, have been rendered picturesk, and highly irritating.'[51] Writing to Sir George Beaumont, Price claimed to find Marshall's attack 'as clumsy as it is coarse', and noted that it was he, rather than Knight, who bore the brunt of Marshall's assault.

> I find from Knight that controversy goes on merrily …
> [Marshall] has taken it into his head, or some wag has put it
> into his head, that Knight is a sort of needy Poet, + I his patron
> + that having some odd quirks of my own about improvement
> which I thought of printing I order'd my Bard to write some
> verses in order to try the taste of the public + finding his poem
> was well received, followed it up with my prose.[52]

Others drew more favourable comparisons between Price's work and Knight's poem. John Matthews, another Herefordshire landowner, published the satirical *A Sketch from Landscape* in late 1794 to lampoon Knight's ideas. According to Farington, whereas Matthews thought only 'very moderately' of Knight's poem, 'which is a Didactic poem only in title', he considered Price's book to be written with information and spirit.[53]

Price and Knight were also attacked by George Mason (1735–1806), who in 1768 had published anonymously an *Essay on Design in Gardening*, which tried to 'draw a line between desirable contrast and undesirable incongruity'. He 'lived comfortably at Porter's, Shenley, near St Albans, Hertfordshire, as a country gentleman, landscape gardener, and bibliophile'. His 'greatly augmented' edition of 1795 included 'a Revisal of several later publications on the same subject'. This included a very extensive review of Price's *Essay on the Picturesque*. Mason was concerned about the 'opinion' that 'seems to run through it' that 'none should presume to garden, who have no previous knowledge of painting'.[54] He argued that the 'poor rural proprietor, under an implied interdiction for not being initiated into the mysteries of the pencil, feels himself disheartened from the prosecution of a beneficial and civilizing amusement'.[55] In an appendix published after reading Price's modified *Essay* of 1796, Mason criticised Price's understanding of the link between terror and the sublime.[56]

A more powerful critic was William Mason, who was so incensed by Price's and Knight's publications that he published several sonnets on the subject.[57] The dispute was so intense that it eclipsed a prolonged dispute between William Mason and Horace Walpole that had started in 1788.[58] One sonnet accused Price and Knight of being pedants who prated of 'picturesqueness'; the other celebrated the pleasures of gravel walks over 'cart ruts and quarry holes'.

'SONNET IX.

Occasioned by a late Attack on the present Taste of
ENGLISH GARDENS.

When two Arcadian* Squires in Rhyme and Prose
Prick'd forth to spout that dilettanti lore.
Their Cicerronis long had threadbare wore,
TASTE from his polish'd lawn indignant rose,
And cry'd, "as Pedants are true Learning's foes,
"So, when true Genius ventures to restore
"To Nature, scenes that Fashion marr'd before,
"These travelled Cognoscenti interpose
"And prate of PICTURESQUENESS,† – Let them prate,
"While to my genuine Votaries I assign
"The pleasing task from her too rustic state
"To lead the willing Goddess; to refine,
"But not transform, her charms, and at her shrine
"Bid Use with Elegance obsequious wait."
*This epithet is rather hazarded, but if they be not Pastori
D'Arcadi, they ought to be so, for they are most certainly
Arcades Ambo.
† Had Dr. Johnson heard this word used, he would certainly
have said, "Sir, the term is cacophonous."

SONNET X.

To a GRAVEL WALK,

Relative to the preceding Subject.

Smooth, simple Path! Whose undulating line,
With sidelong tufts of flow'ry fragrance crown'd,
"Plain in its neatness,"* SPANS MY GARDEN ROUND;
What, tho' two acres thy brief course confine,
Yet sun and shade, and hill and dale are thine,
And use with beauty here more surely found,
Than where, to spread the Picturesque around,
Cart ruts and quarry holes their charms combine!†
Here, as thou lead'st my step thro' lawn or grove,
Liberal tho' limited, restrain'd tho' free,

Fearless of dew, or dirt, or dust I rove,
And own those comforts, all deriv'd from thee!
Take then, smooth Path, this tribute of my love,
Thou emblem pure of legal Liberty!

*A phrase that MILTON uses to express simplex munditiis. See
his Translation of Hor. Ode 5. L. 1. Mr. T. WARTON, in his
edition of MILTON'S Poems, criticises the expression. It is
however MILTON'S, and, if it does not fully express HORACE'S
meaning, seems to serve my purpose perfectly.
† See MR. PRICE's Description of a Picturesque Lane.'

Another critic was Thomas Mathias, who wrote in his satire *Pursuits of Literature*:

With Price and Knight grounds *by neglect* improve,
And banish use, for naked Nature's love,
Lakes, forests, rivers, in one landscape drawn,
My park, a county, and a heath, my lawn;

He noted that for 'Price and Knight – See the various treatises, all curious and
in some degree pleasant, on the subject of landscape, and the art of laying out
grounds. Knight and Price, versus Mason and Brown, Repton, Moderator'.[59]
Price later acknowledged that, compared with Knight's poem, his was the less
theoretical exposition of the picturesque, and that his outlook reflected 'a little
more of a materialist, perhaps for want of a proper education'.[60] Many, however,
saw the practical application of the *Essay* as the work's great strength, and
identified it as an influence on their own gardening. John Westcomb
Emmerton, a Nottinghamshire squire, wrote to his brother in Essex in 1796:

I wish you would get Mr. Price's Essay on the Picturesque, you
will find it of use to you in your improvements. He is a friend
to old Pollards and detests Belts and Clumps – you should see
it before you advance too far in the improvement of your lane
– if you are not going to Town soon, you might get it from
Chelmsford – It is printed for Robson in Bond Street.[61]

PRICE AND REPTON

Perhaps the most striking response to Price's publication came from Humphry
Repton, whose *A Letter to Uvedale Price Esq.* appeared just a month after the
Essay in July 1794. Repton attempted to reclaim Brown's reputation and to
point to the implications of Price's professed love of wild and untrammelled
nature. Although he acknowledged that Brown's designs were sometimes badly
imitated, and that the country near Foxley was indeed picturesque and
romantic in character, Repton insisted that '*Beauty*, and not '*picturesqueness*', is
the chief object of modern improvement.' For Repton, Price's advocacy of the
picturesque had more than the whiff about it of revolutionary sentiment: 'I

cannot help seeing great affinity betwixt deducing gardening from the painter's studies of wild nature, and deducing government from the uncontrouled opinions of man in a savage state ... let experiments of untried, theoretical improvement be made in some other country.'[62]

Repton claimed that he had prepared his *Letter* while travelling to Derbyshire, and that it was a 'hasty production – written on the spur of the moment'. However, it later emerged that the *Letter* was co-authored by William Combe, Price's former friend. Price dismissed Repton's *Letter* as 'a sort of mongrell' that neither Repton nor Combe 'had a perfect claim to, or are very proud of claiming': 'He would have been somewhat surprised had I sent him word that I had just learned that this <u>hasty</u> production of his, written on the <u>spur</u> of the occasion, was the calm, + deliberate performance of a professed writer.'[63] Combe himself was said to have begun an ironical poem on Price and Knight, 'making pictures their model for gardening, but had not time to proceed with it'. The shenanigans between Price, Combe and Repton interested Joseph Farington, who noted that 'Coombes regulated and corrected Reptons letter to Price, but the *matter* was entirely Reptons. – Coombes has also assisted him in the work preparing for publication', and thought that 'Repton has strong fears of the consequences of Knights enmity & Prices report, which checks him in answering them.'[64] The connection with Repton's letter apparently did not cause irreparable damage to Price's opinion of Combe. In June 1795 he told the Beaumonts that he would be very happy to see Combe again, 'for he is a very amusing person', though he acknowledged that 'he has not spared me in writing.' 'There is a sort of malicious ingenuity in the manner of asserting the most direct falsehoods, that can only belong to a steady veteran in the art of lying, + which nobody has had more ... <u>seen-service</u> ... than my old friend Combe.'[65]

The exchange continued in 1795 with Price's *A Letter to H. Repton, Esq. On the Application of the Practice as well as the Principles of Landscape-Painting to Landscape-Gardening: intended as A Supplement to the Essay on the Picturesque*, which was prefixed with *Mr. Repton's Letter to Mr. Price*.[66] As with his other published works, Price circulated the text in advance to trusted friends who acted as informal copy editors, suggesting changes and alterations in advance of printing. Price wrote to Beaumont from Foxley on 28 November 1794 to inform him that he would be sending the last but one part of the manuscript of his reply to Repton's letter: 'it includes all I have said on prospects + on views down steep hills in both of which I am happy to find how well we agree.' He asked Beaumont to 'attend to them both', adding the acknowledgement that if he had just one good quality as a writer it was 'that of receiving criticisms not only with docility but with thankfulness, + in having great readiness + perseverance in changing what I am convinced may be alterd for the better'.[67] Price sent another two sheets to Beaumont at the start of December 1794 – 'positively the last' – asking for them to be returned to him at Sunning Hill since they were his only copies and his 'female secretary' had not been available to make another copy. He wrote:

I hope you will think that tho I may have clawed Repton a
little in the body of my letter … I have at least taken a good
humourd leave of him, + made my apologies very prettily for
having scratched him. I don't believe a man feels much
obliged to you for offering him a plaster after you have broke
his head, but it is right to make the offer + if he wont accept
of it it is his fault.[68]

Price thanked Lady Beaumont for her comments and told her he had needed
to correct a gross error made by the printer, Mr Robson, on the title page. He
had transposed 'Landscape-painting' and 'Landscape-gardening', 'so that by the
title it appears as if I recommended the application of the principles of
gardening to painting, + you will witness for me that no book ever gave a
more direct lie to its title'.[69]

Price argued that Repton had misrepresented him: though he was a lover
of freedom, Price was at pains to point out that he was no lover of anarchy
and confusion in the manner in which he had been cast. Rather, freedom's
'steady and settled influence, like that of the atmosphere on a fine evening,
gives at once a glowing warmth, and a union to all within its sphere'. Price
emphasised the importance of connection:

The mutual connection and dependance of all the different
ranks and orders of men in this country; the innumerable, but
voluntary ties by which they are bound and united to each
other (so different from what are experienced by subjects of
any other monarchy,) are perhaps the firmest securities of its
glory, its strength and happiness.[70]

Price, indeed, explicitly addressed this issue in a note to the original *Essay*, in
which he declared that a 'good landscape' comprised of 'free and
unconstrained' but varied parts was a metaphor for good government in which
the variety of the constituent elements was necessary to the 'beauty, energy,
effect, and harmony of the whole'. Conversely, Price added, 'he who clears and
levels every thing round his own lofty mansion, seems to me to have very
Turkish principles of improvement.'[71]

Repton claimed that the appendix to his *Sketches and Hints*, which appeared
in February 1795, represented a softening of his response to Price. Yet he
argued that Price had stolen his ideas. For Repton, the picturesque was just
one of sixteen possible sources of pleasure in landscape. The book ends with
a letter from William Windham supporting Repton in the face of 'these wild
improvers'.[72] Price was amused by this paper debate, writing to Lady Beaumont
in February 1795 that

If we don't understand landscape gardening it will not be for
want of books. Knight writes me word that he means to attack
many parts of Repton's letter to me in the notes of his new

edition of his poem of the landscape so our game at controversy will now be as regular as a game at whist' with 'Knight + Price partners against Repton, with Brown as a <u>Dummy</u>, whose cards of course Repton must manage: if Sir George will now + then look over my hand, + advise me, I think we shall win a bumper.[73]

1796 AND 1798 EDITIONS: 'WHAT GOOD FUN IT IS TO BE AN AUTHOR'[74]

Price had hoped that the explanation in his letter to Repton where he distinguished 'between the general and more confined sense of beauty' might 'obviate many objections that have been made to Mr Burke as well as to myself + particularly by our friend Knight, + I shall feel very happy if I should be able to reconcile our opinions on almost the only point of difference between us'. He told Sir George Beaumont that he thought Knight wished to show in the new edition of *The Landscape* that 'the distinction I have made between the beautiful + the picturesque is unfounded' and that 'he means to do it (but without quoting me,) by proofs from the theory of vision'. Price imagined '(for I have not yet seen this note to his second edition)' that Knight's argument would be 'too refined + metaphysical for common understandings', but felt that 'If I get any deeper into the unfathomable gulph of metaphysicks I shall bother your head + my own.'[75] The 'advertisement' to Knight's second edition of *The Landscape* in 1795 did draw attention to important differences in Price's and Knight's aesthetic theories, and Knight's views were laid out in a lengthy note to the poem.[76] At the heart of their differences was the fundamental issue of whether the picturesque was an innate quality or a subjective experience. Price told Sir George Beaumont that he hoped that even those who had

> metaphysical heads will think that however true it may be that
> a man born without the sense of feeling could not distinguish
> rough from smooth, yet that in those who can feel, the sight
> takes so many lessons from the touch, that it soon grows
> quicker in distinguishing them that it's master, + from
> sympathy receives the same kind of sensations from them.[77]

Knight considered that one person, such as Price, might find 'his principles in a division of the sublime, the picturesque, and the beautiful', while another, such as Knight, might find them 'in a certain unison of sympathy and harmony of causes and effects'. Both, however, could 'agree in what is, or is not good taste, and approve or disapprove the same objects'. Indeed, Knight emphasised in his new edition that Price had fully explained 'the true principles of picturesque improvement of grounds … in a very masterly manner'. He referred all 'dissatisfied readers' of *The Landscape* to read his friend's *Essay*, 'expressing at the same time his entire approbation of the general system of picturesque improvement which is there so happily enforced and illustrated'. He concluded that the differences between them belonged 'rather to philosophical theory, than to practical taste'.[78]

Andrew Ballantyne argues that Price, in trying to establish underlying principles of the picturesque, was 'utterly misguided at a theoretical level' and contrasts this with Knight's view, following Hume, 'that beauty lay in the mind of the beholder'. Ballantyne considers that a 'genealogical network can be traced to show the relations between the picturesque and wider culture' and suggests that Burke and Price were more 'scholastic' than 'scientific': 'Burke's idea of the sublime came from Longinus, Price's picturesque from Gilpin; they both drew directly on Lucretius, another part of whose influence they felt indirectly through Newton.'[79] He points out that 'Ironically Price's lasting influence was effective precisely in so far as he escaped giving abstract answers about the 'essential' picturesque: his iteration of concrete examples, embodied in the particular and contingent, actually communicated his vision and taste, and did so very effectively.' Knight and others were able 'to endorse Price's taste and his practical recipes for the production of picturesqueness whilst repudiating completely the theory which he thought underpinned his enterprise'.[80]

Price enjoyed writing and discussing improvements, additions and modifications to drafts of his texts. He told Sir George Beaumont that 'You can't conceive what good fun it is to be an author; I really think I have doubled my mass of happiness by it, as well as of ideas.'[81] His surviving letters provide compelling evidence of his desire to share his ideas with friends and critics. In November 1794, for example, he reported how he had discussed a section of his *Essay* on the relationship between the picturesque and music with Charles James Fox. He had asserted

> that objects of <u>hearing</u>, that music according to the general
> principles I have laid down may be as truly picturesque as any
> visible object. You know that Charles Fox wrote down some
> criticisms on my essay while it was in MS. when he came to
> that part Mrs Armstead told he burst into a loud laugh.

Fox 'wrote down, "questo e un poco troppo, I am afraid my Uncle Toby would whistle Lilleburlero."' Price continued:

> I believe however on reading on he was convinced it was
> more a paradox in appearance then in reality + was only such
> when considered as having a mere reference to painting +
> visible objects. In reality if it is a separate character why
> should it not be applied as sublime + beautiful are, + who
> scruples to call a chorus of Handel sublime or an air of Hasse
> or Paesiello beautiful if such be their character? Even in the
> extended sense I have given to the term picturesque it is still
> more limited than that of beautiful.[82]

The development of Price's thinking on the picturesque led him to prepare a 'new edition, with considerable editions' of the *Essay*, printed for J. Robson of New Bond Street in 1796. He was close to finishing the new edition when he took it to the radical politician John Horne Tooke at his Wimbledon home, Chester House, in early May 1796, to ask for Tooke's views. According to Farington's account, Tooke 'had not observed any defects in the grammar &c that He recollected or if He had they wd. be found in the margin it being his custom thus to point out inaccuracies'. Farington noted that Hoppner thought Tooke to be 'destitute of taste, having no feeling for poetry or painting; and that his conversation is generally of a mixed quality exhibiting a radical want of taste'.[83] Price also shared his work in progress with Lord Abercorn on 31 May, at which point his new Preface was 'going on prosperously'.[84] But in response to comments from both Abercorn and Knight, Price prevaricated over whether or not to include the Preface.[85] Similarly, Price consulted Abercorn over changes he proposed to make to his letter to Repton.

In 1798 Price published a second volume of essays, noting that 'These three Essays which I here offer to the public, though detached from each other, and from the Essay on the Picturesque, are, in respect to the matter they contain, and the suite of ideas they present, perfectly connected.' The essays were on 'Artificial Water', including methods for devising picturesque banks, on 'Decorations near the House', and on 'Architecture and Buildings, as Connected with Scenery'. Again Price discussed his ideas widely. Farington noted in March 1797, for example, that Price had sent Sir George a

> printed Copy of a new work to inspect. The subject of it is to propose a method of laying out ground, and of forming banks for water in a more picturesque manner. – To make his works correct, Price consults many friends on different points of his publication. – Lord Abercorn corrects his expression and Sir George says is remarkably well qualified to do it.[86]

Price had finished the *Essay on Artificial Water* by 13 January 1797[87] and showed it to Beaumont as well as to Abercorn, who at the time Price was writing was creating Summerhouse Lake at Bentley Priory. He also showed the essays to Charles James Fox, Paul Sandby and Sir Harry Englefield, 'the omniscient Baronet' as Price termed him.[88] According to Price, Fox

> read it without making any objection: as to praise or approbation, he rarely bestows any at the time, but perhaps three or four months hence when you would suppose he had forgot every thing about it, he may say, if he happen to think so, – you were quite right about that ideal motion in bridges; + then will canvas the whole subject.[89]

Several small sections appear to have been drafted from Beaumont's ideas. In November 1797 he sent him a proof 'that with alterations + additions is half a manuscript; why the devil did not I think of them in the Ms itself?' Price regretted the death of Burke and told Beaumont that he hoped to add something 'on what I truly feel – my regret for the loss of Burke'. Price had just read the third letter from Burke's *Letters on a Regicide Peace*, published in 1797, in which Burke attacks Jacobinism. He felt that it included the 'most wonderful strains of eloquence, + of keen ridicule, as well as of strong + just reasoning', and tells Beaumont, a Tory, that his friends 'have still more reason to smart under his lash than mine'. He then told Beaumont that 'Your account of the town of Tivoli is admirable; I have a place ready for it', and that if 'you go on writing as you have done, my Essay will increase pretty considerably in size and very much indeed in goodness'.[90] In the *Essay on Architecture and Buildings* Price noted: 'Amidst all the interesting circumstances at Tivoli, nothing is more striking … than the manner in which the general outline of the town appears to yield and vary according to the shape of its foundation … . Not a projecting rock or knoll, no "coigne of vantage" but is occupied … .'[91] Price hoped 'to egg you on to write a book', but realised that Sir George was more likely to enjoy painting his 'real Ruysdal' – he had been copying one from Benjamin West's collection – than writing.[92] A few weeks later he told Sir George that 'I have sharped a little bit from your letter about the pillars on Black Friar's bridge: this is the third piece of larceny in one essay.'[93]

Price by no means always deferred to the views of his correspondents. This was particularly true for topics such as the choice of trees, where he could fall back on his extensive practical knowledge. When Sir George commented on Price's encouragement of the planting of exotic trees near cottages, Price retorted that his

> criticism with respect to acacia + foreign trees would be perfectly just, if I had proposed to have them planted by cottages; but if you had not had a Billion of account books haunting you, you would have perceived that I was talking of villages …, my worthy Mr Cocker, + of dressed villages.

He clarified his case:

> I had in my mind an acacia in the garden of a smart parsonage in a village not far from a Gentleman's seat, in this county where there are many exotics: The tree itself gave the parsonage a remarkably chearful dressed appearance, + the neighbourhood of other plants of the same kind justified its being there. Indeed in many of the villages twenty miles round London (which of course are included in my idea of villages), exotics are perfectly naturalised. I dare say you have often examined the cedar at Hillington, a mere village, + never objected to its exotic appearance: even in this distant county lilacs, laurels, laburnums laurustinus, bays +ca +ca are seen in the gardens of very ordinary houses + cottages.

In fact, the famous cedar tree at Hillingdon had blown down in 1790. It had been planted by Samuel Reynardson, a botanist who lived there from 1678 to 1721. William Gilpin thought 'The best specimen of this tree, I ever saw in England, was at Hillington, near Uxbridge. The perpendicular height of it was fifty three feet; it's horizontal expanse ninety six; and it's girth fifteen and a half.' When he saw it in 1776 'it was about one hundred and eighteen years of age; and being then completely clump-headed, it was a very noble, and picturesque tree. – In the high winds about the beginning of the year 1790, this noble cedar was blown down. It's stem, when cut, was five feet in diameter.' John Claudius Loudon noted that Sir Joseph Banks then had a table made from its timber.[94]

Price also enrolled Sir George as a researcher for his project. In January 1798 he informed Sir George that 'I shall have occasion to mention your picture of Sebastian Bourdon, as an instance of the great judgment with which he has introduced picturesque circumstances where the subject, + the general style of the picture is grand + solemn.' This is Sébastian Bourdon's (1616–1671) *The Return of the Ark*, which Sir Joshua Reynolds had left to Sir George Beaumont on his death in 1792 (Plate 4). Price recalled that Reynolds 'thought that the grandeur of its style … was of so peculiar a cast, and so far removed from obvious common nature, as to be incapable of being truly relished, except by minds of strong original feeling, and long accustomed to contemplate the higher excellencies of art'. Price told Sir George that he had described the picture in some detail in his text, but as 'I have described the particulars from memory, I beg you will examine my description' and compare it either to Lady Beaumont's 'excellent copy' or the original if 'you should happen to go to town'. Sir George approved of the description and a few weeks later Price wrote: 'The proof you will receive after the one that accompanies this letter, will I trust be the last; + high time it should. I shall then have nothing to do but the contents, + perhaps a little bit of a preface, + then shall get published.'[95]

The new edition was printed in Hereford in February 1798 and then sent to Robson in London for publication. Price told Sir George with relief that the

> The job is at last done, + I am (as a body may say,) now in the
> Hereford waggon on my road to London, partly in boards, +
> partly in sheets. I shall be published I trust early next week, +
> if I can get sold just enough to <u>cover</u> the impression as it is
> called, I shall think myself a lucky man.

He asked Sir George 'how do you like yourself in print? don't you think that part about sculpture + painting in Mr Price's preface uncommonly ingenious? somebody will ask you: a develish good account that of Wovermans picture; is it not Sir George? how well he has described it!'[96] This referred to a section of the preface where Price asserts that subjects which are relished as picturesque in paintings would be considered 'detestable' if portrayed 'in marble ever so skilfully executed'. He reported that 'A writer of eminence lays great stress on the advantage which painting possesses over sculpture, in being able to give value to insignificant objects, and even to those that are offensive.' The example he cited had clearly been provided by Beaumont: 'I remember a picture of Wovermans, in which the principal objects were a dung-cart just loaded; some carrion lying on the dung; a dirty fellow with a dirty shovel; the dunghill itself, and a dog, that from his attitude seemed likely to add to it.' Price argued that these 'unsavoury materials' had been 'worked up with so much skill, that the picture was viewed by every one with delight'.[97]

Price's preface to the 1798 edition re-emphasised his attack on Lancelot Brown and Humphry Repton. His previous 'censure of modern Gardening and Mr. Brown' had drawn upon him 'an attack from the most eminent professor of the present time, together with a defence of his predecessor' and he turned the table on Repton by arguing that 'Nothing could be more fortunate than such an opportunity, for discussing the practicability of what I had proposed.' He knew that some people would think he 'had already bestowed more time upon' the subject of 'modern Gardening' than it merited, but argued that his attack on it remained necessary and important. This was because 'the present style of laying out places is not a mere capricious invention, but a consistent and regular system, founded on the most seducing qualities.' He was greatly concerned about the 'almost universal admiration with which the exclusive display of smoothness, serpentine lines, &c. in our gardens and grounds has been viewed for almost half a century', and felt that there were 'scarcely any bounds to the sort of idolatry which prevailed, and still prevails on that subject'. He noted that 'English gardening has been considered as an object of high and peculiar national pride', that Brown had been celebrated in prose and verse and that 'marbles with inscriptions, have been erected to the memory of Mr. Brown and his works.'

Price ended his preface by lampooning Brown's success. He reported an old anecdote of the poet and wit Owen Cambridge, a school friend of Horace Walpole who also had a villa at Twickenham.[98] Cambridge 'very pleasantly laughed at Brown's vanity' and told Price that when Brown was 'vapouring … about the change he had made to the face of the country' he replied that he hoped Brown outlived him, as he (Cambridge) 'would like to see heaven before you had improved it'. Price argued that such was the enthusiasm of some admirers for Brown's work that they 'would wish, that "the great globe itself" could be new modelled upon that system'. If the popularity of such gardening continued, then 'there would really be a very curious similarity between Mr. Brown's finished state of the world, and the world in a state of chaos, as described by the poet – Unus erat toto naturae vultus in orbe.' The line from Ovid's *Metamorphoses* can be translated as 'the face of nature showed alike in her round.' The quotation continues 'quem dixere chaos': 'which state have men called chaos'.[99] Price was very pleased with this ending: he told Lord Abercorn, who checked the final version for him, not to 'take from me my finishing line from Ovid, + my two Chaosses'. He added: 'I hope to be actually published in a fortnight, + I find Buonaparte does not mean to come till just before the first leaf; so that if the spring is not very forward I shall be before him.'[100]

CHAPTER 5

PICTURESQUE DESIGNS

W HILE PRICE WAS WRITING HIS *ESSAY ON THE PICTURESQUE* in the early
1790s he was also building an extraordinary gothic villa called Castle
House at Aberystwyth. He and his wife started to take summer holidays in the
late 1780s at Aberystwyth, which was at that time beginning to become a
fashionable bathing resort. In mundane terms, this made every sort of sense:
Foxley adjoined the main road from Hereford to Kington, which formed the
principal route west to Aberystwyth.[1] The town and its surrounding
countryside was fast becoming a key focus of picturesque tours popular with
the gentry and aristocracy of Wales and the Midlands. But the Prices took more
than a passing interest in Aberystwyth: they decided to build a substantial villa
there in the early 1790s and here Price experimented practically, and very
publicly, with his ideas and understandings of picturesque architecture. This
chapter examines how Price commissioned the then relatively unknown John
Nash to design his marine villa, which was an eye-catching model example of
the integration of architecture and landscape. It also explores how these ideas
were used when advising the Beaumonts on their new house at Coleorton,
Leicestershire.

ABERYSTWYTH

Aberystwyth had developed by the mid eighteenth century into one of the
principal fishing ports of west Wales. In the 1770s John Campbell noted that
the 'Herring Fishery here is in most Years so exceedingly abundant, that a
thousand Barrels have been taken in one Night' and that in the autumn there
was 'such a Glut of Cod, Pollack Whiting' and other fish that 'they set but little
Value upon them'.[2] The custom house was moved to Aberystwyth from Aberdyfi
in 1763 and in 1762 the *Banc y Llong* (the Ship Bank) was established: a 'natural
concomitant of the considerable wealth which shipping and mercantile
interests had generated in the town during the mid-eighteenth century'.[3] Lead
ore, timber and bark also went through the port, but Campbell thought that
the harbour was crying out for improvement and that trade could be much
improved.[4]

Tourists began to visit the town in some numbers in the second half of the
eighteenth century. Richard Bolt, in his poem *Cambria*, had praised the natural

setting of the town, with its views over Cardigan Bay and of cliff scenery, as early as 1749, and by 1797 the town was fashionable enough to be called the Brighton of Wales by Henry Wigstead, who reported that in 'September players attend here; and the town hall is then the theatre. In winter months there are frequent assemblies. This town is a fashionable watering place, to which most families in the vicinity resort in the season.'[5] Advertisements and editorial comments in the *Hereford Journal* demonstrate the increasing popularity of the resort in the late eighteenth century. On 7 August 1781 there was mention of the discovery of mineral waters equal to those of Spa or Pynnont. The first reference to 'seabathing' at Aberystwyth is in an advertisement for the Talbot's Head Inn (9 June 1785). On 17 June 1789 the *Hereford Journal* stated that Aberystwyth 'has been much resorted to … in late years' because of the discovery of a chalybeate spring thought to contain more steel than 'any yet found in the island'. By 1791 (8 August) there was an editorial praising Aberystwyth: 'This season' it became 'a fashionable resort' and 'several gentlemen have built bathing houses at their own expense.' The *Journal* went on to extol the erection of 'numerous bathing machines' which were 'judiciously placed in situations where they are alike able to ensure personal safety and afford convenience'.[6]

The popularity of Aberystwyth as a resort continued into the nineteenth century, contemporary guides praising the 'grand coast' and the fineness of the 'marine prospect' at Aberystwyth. Benjamin Malkin considered that 'The town, though generally represented in the tours and directories as irregular and dirty, appeared to me rather above than below the level of Welsh towns in general' and notes that 'it is much frequented as a bathing place, especially by Shropshire and Herefordshire families.'[7] The seventh edition of *The Cambrian Tourist, or post-chaise companion, through Wales*, which included a Wye tour, stated that

> *Aberystwith* has of late years been in all respects greatly
> improved; for being the principal place of summer resort for
> bathing and pleasure from North Wales and the adjacent
> English counties, every inducement has been held forth that
> could attract company from its new competitors: the roads are
> now good, and the inns and accommodations excellent.

The town had a population of around 2,500 people by 1830. 'During the season assemblies are held here as at Brighton, Ramsgate, and other English sea-bathing places.' A substantial assembly room, designed by G. S. Repton, was built in 1820.[8]

The coast and sea bathing were not the only reasons for the increasing popularity of Aberystwyth. Only sixteen miles inland the agricultural improver and bibliophile Thomas Johnes (1748–1816) was establishing his Hafod estate as one of the most famous picturesque ensembles in Britain. Thomas Johnes' mother was Elizabeth, daughter of the wealthy industrialist Richard Knight of

Croft Castle, near Ludlow. This connection formed a strong link between the Johnes family, Aberystwyth and the Herefordshire and Shropshire gentry. Lord Viscount Bateman, of Shobdon Court, Herefordshire, and a friend of Thomas Johnes senior, was made a burgess of Aberystwyth as early as 1760.[9] Thomas Johnes himself was brought up at Croft Castle in Herefordshire and was influenced and encouraged by his cousin Richard Payne Knight and probably Uvedale Price to 'embellish his barren patrimony according to "picturesque" principles'.[10] Thomas Johnes was MP for Cardigan in 1774 and later for Radnorshire and also Cardiganshire, and had influential friends such as Lord Chancellor Thurlow and William Windham.[11] He radically transformed the farms and tenancies on his estate and made many new plantations.

His new mansion, designed by Thomas Baldwin of Bath, was completed in 1788 and, although Uvedale Price told Lord Aberdeen that 'there are some picturesque scenes, + a very pretty cascade, but I think the place has been over-rated', many visitors examined the picturesque elements of the estate, as well as the modern farming and forestry practices, often staying at the nearby Devil's Bridge Inn.[12] Johnes was keen to encourage the tourist trade at Aberystwyth. Mark Willett describes the town in 1810 as having 'cheap accommodation' and that Johnes 'aimed at bringing a more distinguished clientele who, once having tasted its delights, would return again year after year'.[13] Johnes' correspondence confirms that he had an interest in the tourist trade. In September 1798, writing to James Edward Smith, the Norwich botanist, he noted that he had had visits from his cousin Richard Payne Knight and the duke of Norfolk (both Herefordshire residents) and pointed out that 'Aberystwith has been fuller this Summer than ever known.' In September 1805 he wrote to George Cumberland in Somerset that

> Aberystwith has literally overflowed; people have been forced
> to sleep in carriages. They are going to erect a Theatre and a
> self-appointed master of the Ceremonies of the tribe of Levy
> means to commence his operations of Coupee and Bouree
> next summer ... I never remember so many *curious* travellers
> as this year.[14]

In 1788, the year that the mansion at Hafod was completed, twenty-four new burgesses of Aberystwyth were appointed, including Lord Berwick, of Attingham Park near Shrewsbury; Sir Richard Hill, of Hawkstone Park, Shropshire; Sir Watkin Williams Wynne, of Wynstay, Denbigh; the Rt Hon Lord Kensington; and 'Uvedale Pryse of Foley, Hereford'.[15] Several of these landowners had significant aesthetic and landscaping interests. Sir Richard Hill owned the picturesque landscape at Hawkstone; Lord Berwick died, aged 44, in the following year, but his son travelled widely in Italy and employed Nash and Repton at Attingham.[16] A list of gentry visiting Aberystwyth in the *Hereford Journal* of 8 August 1791 includes Lord and Lady Clive, Lord Somers and the Hon Richard Cocks (Eastnor Castle, Herefordshire), and Mr Price.

Travel to Aberystwyth was frequently difficult. The first turnpike Act for Cardiganshire was in 1770 and 'until 1807 the only post-chaises in the whole county were in Aberystwyth and the Hafod Arms.' In that year there was a 'plea for the road from Brecon via Builth, Rhayader and Cwmystwyth to be opened to carriages so that visitors might see the glories of Hafod and Devil's Bridge on their way to Aberystwyth'. In 1816 it still took the Kington coach from 5 a.m. to 7 p.m. to travel to Aberystwyth, but this allowed visitors from the western parts of counties such as Herefordshire and Shropshire to reach Aberystwyth in one day.[17] Thomas Johnes was keen to tell his correspondents of improvements in road and postal communications at Hafod and Aberystwyth. In June 1796 he wrote to George Cumberland at Egham, Surrey, that 'You will be surprised when I tell you there are two diligences as I hear coming to the Devil's Bridge & Aberystwyth from Leominster and Ludlow by different roads.' In 1805 he announced that 'A Mail Coach runs once a week from Ludlow, and you will see on the cover of this we have a post office at the Devil's bridge.'[18]

The rise of Aberystwyth as a resort, the improvement of agriculture and the enclosure of common lands did not preclude undercurrents of resistance and outside threats. Aberystwyth was, after all, not that far from the site of the landing on the Pembrokeshire coast of French troops in 1797. There were, moreover, several domestic disturbances in Aberystwyth itself in 1795. Lead miners entered the town at night, breaking into stores and carrying away the corn supplies destined for export. In 1816 soldiers intervened in a riot in Aberystwyth when a mob attacked an attorney and ignored the reading of the Riot Act. Soldiers were ordered to fire upon the crowd but it would appear that only the hat of one of the ringleaders was grazed. After this the main protagonists were quickly rounded up. Further disturbances followed the passing of Acts in 1812 and 1815 for the enclosure of 10,000 acres of land near Aberystwyth. Riots broke out when surveyors attempted to measure Mynydd Bach, the hilly land lying between Aberystwyth and Lampeter. The surveyor, John Hughes, was 'repeatedly assaulted' and the enclosure commissioners threatened. Soldiers were called in to Lampeter and Aberystwyth, but they were only partially effective in containing disorder, and protests against the enclosures (including the levelling of fences) continued until 1821.[19]

The increased importance of tourism in Aberystwyth led to pressure to develop and build on the common land around the town. The Court Leet had been opposed to this but the demand became so great that permission to build began to be given. Intriguingly, Uvedale Price was the first person to be given such permission; this was in 1788, when he was also made a burgess of Aberystwyth.[20] Price, then aged 42, purchased for £100 the lease of a piece of land 132 yards in length, bounded on its northern side by the rocky sea shore. The plot was situated between the ancient and picturesque ruins of Aberystwyth Castle, owned by Thomas Johnes, and Weeg Street in the town. A new road was laid out on the south side of the plot. He purchased the lease from the mayor of Aberystwyth, Mr John Jones, who had leased the land from the Corporation of Aberystwyth at a Court Leet in 1780.[21] The lease had ninety years left to run and was made with the condition that a house was to be built within two years. There were delays, however, and in 1791 Price was given leave by the Court Leet to complete the house by May 1794.[22]

Price later told Sir George Beaumont of his search for a suitable site for his house:

> I have thought a great deal of a situation for a sea-bathing place, + have looked over a great deal of the coast both of North + South Wales with that idea, + I have never yet seen any spot, take it all in all, that I have liked so well. In the first place every beautiful + romantic spot near the sea, will not do for a house, for of all solitariness that of a single house close to the sea is the most compleat, but by no means the most agreeable; + yet it [is not] pleasant to be in the midst of a town, even if one does enjoy a fine [view] of the sea. Now I really think my house is perfect in that respect; it is close to the town, so as to have all the advantage of a market + habitation near me; + is at the same time completely detached from it, + commands all the sea view without a possibility of interruption, all the land being mine on which any object could be built that might interrupt it, + I have no despicable walk by the sea side on my own domain ...[23]

The site he chose thus had the benefits of a town setting without suffering from the problems of being overlooked by people from the town, or 'fashionables'.

A PICTURESQUE EXPERIMENT: JOHN NASH AND CASTLE HOUSE

The architect that Price chose for his new house was John Nash, who was at this stage re-establishing his career from a base in Carmarthen following his earlier bankruptcy in London. Richard Suggett has argued that the years 1785–1796 were the 'lost decade' of Nash's professional career, but a period in which he established the basis for his later enormous success by taking commissions from the gentry of south-west Wales and from a variety of public bodies. He was commissioned to build three gaols – Carmarthen (1789–92), Cardigan (1791–7) and Hereford (1792–96) – to repair the west front of St David's Cathedral in 1790–93 and to build bridges at Aberystwyth (1793 and 1797) and the iron Stanford Bridge, Worcestershire (1795 and 1798). Suggett demonstrates that Nash designed a small group of Gothic buildings in the early 1790s, including the gateway to Clytha House at St David's in 1790, a school at St David's built to resemble a Gothic chapter house (1790–91), Castle House Aberystwyth (1791–94), Emlyn Cottage (1792) and the library at Hafod (1793).

His domestic buildings included Priory House at Cardigan, which, crucially, was built for Elizabeth Johnes of Croft Castle, Thomas Johnes's mother. This commission may well have led to the work that Nash was soon to do for Uvedale Price at Castle House, Aberystwyth, and at Hafod. However, the web of connections between Nash and the Herefordshire gentry is so complex it is difficult to disentangle who introduced who to whom. The locality and wide variety of Nash's commissions meant that he was likely to be considered by Price as a designer for his new house; it is most probable that they were introduced through members of the Johnes and Knight families. Following the design of Castle House there were several Herefordshire and Worcestershire commissions which have a direct link to Price. For example, Price sat on the committee for the Hereford Lunatic Asylum (1793–98), which was built by public subscription and for which Nash claimed fees of £143 in December 1793; the foundation stone was laid on 25 July 1794. The single-arch iron Stanford Bridge, Worcestershire, was on the estate of Sir Edward Winnington, who was a friend of both Richard Payne Knight and Price.[24] Moreover, David Whitehead has conclusively demonstrated that it was the commission for the new parlour at Stoke Edith, Herefordshire (1792–96), which led the owner Edward Foley to introduce Nash to Humphry Repton, which was a key moment in the development of both men's careers.[25]

Perhaps even more important than this fertile group of commissions, however, was the impact of Uvedale Price's ideas on Nash. Richard Suggett has argued that the 'remarkable coincidence' of Nash confronting the picturesque aesthetic at 'a crucial point' in its development was one which 'profoundly changed Nash's life'. He describes Castle House as the first of 'three key buildings' which show John Nash's work to have 'special and experimental significance' in the problem of relating buildings to scenery. The other two buildings were The Cottage, Newcastle Emlyn, with its 'remarkable floor-level sash windows' which allowed the owners 'to wander from the house through the vaulted portico into the garden to enjoy a composed view', and the library at Hafod.[26] John Summerson considered Nash's 'initiation' into the picturesque to be an important stage in the development of his career. He points out that Price's commission made 'it ... beyond dispute that Nash was in the midst of this circle of romantic, scholarly, innovating land-owners. It is equally beyond dispute that he adopted their views; the whole of his later career proves it.'[27]

Three of Uvedale Price's letters describing the design of Castle House and the reason for its situation survive. Two of these, from Price to Sir George Beaumont, one written in 1798 and the other twenty-one years later in 1819, provide detailed reasons for its commission. Another, written to Lord Aberdeen in 1810, gives an additional description of the views from the house.[28] In the autumn of 1797 and early 1798 Price was working on his *Essay on Architecture and Buildings* and sending extracts on the beauty of buildings, the grouping of buildings at Tivoli and their relationship with the underlying topography and also a new section on bridges to friends, including Charles James Fox, Mrs

Armitstead, Lord Abercorn, Sir Harry Englefield and Sir George Beaumont. He was staying at Sunning Hill from November until early January 1798. On 15 January, writing from Sunning Hill, he asked Sir George to compare a passage he had written on the introduction of 'picturesque circumstances where the subject + general style of the picture is grand + solemn' with Sir George's painting *The Return of the Ark*, by Sébastian Bourdon.[29] He wanted Beaumont to notice the way Bourdon had 'with great truth marked the intricacy of the wheels, + the effect of water in motion'. A few days later, on 28 January, writing from Foxley, Price told Sir George Beaumont that 'I am particularly glad that you are struck with what I have said about the idea of motion in a bridge', which Charles Fox had also read 'without making any objection'. Moreover,

> I have just seen Nash the architect, + he was struck as you
> were, + told me he had mentioned it to Repton, not as an
> idea of mine but as something he had lately read in a book; +
> he told me Repton was also very much delighted with it; so
> altogether my ideal motion a fait fortune.[30]

This is particularly interesting, as it shows that Nash visited Foxley in early 1798 and was commenting on Price's new *Essay on Building and Architecture* several years after the completion of Castle House. This is towards the end of the period when Nash was working on Hereford Lunatic Asylum (1793–98). He was also working on the modification of the north front of Corsham Court for Paul Cobb Methuen, and on the new gaol at Hereford. Indeed, Nash had to apologise to Methuen for breaking off an engagement at Corsham on 17 February because he had to visit the magistrates at Hereford concerning the new prison.[31] It is possible that Price was discussing with Nash the 'improvements' at Aberystwyth mentioned by Sarah Jones later in 1798: Lady Caroline had asked her whether she would like to spend a month or six weeks there in June 1799, 'Mr Price having some improvements in view'.[32] It also indicates that at this stage Nash was close enough to Price and aware of the difficulty between Price and Repton to the extent that he is happy not to mention Price's ideas directly to Repton. It is at this period that Repton's son George, who worked with Nash, probably drew the 'cottage for U. Price featuring a five columned loggia' which survives in a notebook watermarked 1798.[33]

In 1798 Sir George Beaumont asked Price to visit him at his Haverhill estate on the borders of Suffolk and Essex to discuss his 'house + cottages'. Price could not go but suggested that 'Should you think of doing enough there to employ an architect, let me recommend my little friend Nash to you; + I do it as much for his sake + that of the public as for yours.' Price stressed that Nash was 'very far from being bigotted to the independence of his art but wishes to unite it with scenery. I believe I have done him good but you would do him much more, particularly if you intend to make any alterations in the form of Haverhill.' Price remained on good terms with Nash after the completion of Castle House at Aberystwyth, and characteristically was keen to recommend him somewhat proprietarily to Beaumont, feeling that both would benefit from the introduction. Price considered that Beaumont 'would manage the form yourself much better than any other person but you would probably not make such drawings as a workman might proceed by. You would find Nash uncommonly quick + full of resources taking your ideas rapidly + very docile.' He concluded that Nash was 'reasonable in his charges' but hinted that his estimates should not be trusted and that it would be wise to 'get some other person to execute his designs'.[34] This was to be a familiar comment on Nash: the next year Methuen was complaining to Nash that he was exceeding his estimates at Corsham.[35]

Ten days later, Price wrote to Sir George with a very full description of his new house and the commissioning of Nash. He complained that 'Here am I somewhat pinched + squeezed because forsooth I must take a fancy for building at Aberystwith!' He:

> did resist as long as I could, I believe at least two years after I
> had got the ground; but Lady Caroline and I found ourselves
> always at the spot, always looking at the waves breaking
> against the near rocks, and at the long chain of distant
> mountains with their monarch Snowden at their head, and we
> thought how charming it would be [to] look at it comfortably
> from ones own window in all weathers, instead of being
> driven away "when the stormy winds do blow" just when the
> waves are the most magnificent; + I must say we have
> enjoyed it even more than I expected.[36]

Writing four years after the probable completion date of Castle House, Price stated that he at first thought 'merely of running up two or three nutshells of rooms, + got a plan from a common welch carpenter' but that then John Nash was mentioned to him. Nash 'had a mind to build me a larger house indeed, but a square bit of architecture', perhaps like the villa at Dolaucothi he refronted and replanned for John Johnes (1792–96).[37] Price continued:

> I told him however, that I must have not only some of the
> windows, but some of the rooms turned to particular points,
> + that he must arrange it in his best manner. I explained to
> him the reasons why I built it so close to the rock, shewed
> him the effect of the broken foreground + its varied line, and
> how by that means the foreground was connected with the
> rocks in the second ground; all which would be lost by placing
> the house further back. He was exceptionally struck with
> these reasons, which he said he had never thought of before
> in the most distant degree, + he has I think contrived the
> house most admirably for the situation, + the form of it is
> certainly extremely varied from my having obliged him to turn
> the rooms to different aspects. At first, as I told you, I meant

only to have some nutshells, but I now thought I would have one good room; + so I magnificently ordered one of 30 by 20; a charming room it is.[38]

In his *Essay on Architecture and Buildings as connected with Scenery* of 1798, Price argued that owners should do exactly what he had just done at Aberystwyth: 'if the owner … were to insist upon having many of the windows turned towards those points where the objects were most happily arranged, the architect would be forced into the invention of a number of picturesque forms and combinations, which otherwise might never have occurred to him.' This would mean the architect would have to 'do what so seldom has been done – accommodate his building to the scenery, not make that give way to his building'. Price went on to suggest that many advantages 'both in respect to the outside and the inside' might result from this approach. 'It is scarcely possible that a building formed on such a plan … should not be an ornament to the landscape, from whatever point it might be viewed.' The blank spaces where there is no view could be 'transformed into beauties' by climbing plants, trees and shrubs. He thought that the 'arrangement of the rooms, would oftentimes be at least as convenient as in a more uniform plan', while 'With respect to the improvement of the view, there can be no doubt.'[39]

Castle House was a triangular building with an octagonal tower at each corner, rising from square bases. The style of the house was a 'restrained Gothic': the windows were not gothic, and the parapets of three towers 'lacked machicolations and crenellations', though they were supported by corbels. Plans of the house have been reconstructed by Richard Suggett from mid nineteenth-century drawings made when the house was altered. The house was not large; there was a dining room, morning room, drawing room, six bedrooms, two dressing rooms and servants' quarters. The house was designed to provide well-composed views of the sea, the coast and the castle ruins. The drawing room was on the first floor and faced directly out to sea; doors led on to a balcony which had a large 'audacious hemispherical canopy without apparent means of support', where views could be taken of the ruins of the ancient castle to the south-west and of the cliffs and distant mountains to the north-east.[40] The extraordinary canopy allowed direct contemplation of the action of the sea on the rocks in almost all weathers. Similar views were obtained from the dining room on the ground floor, with its large bay window. Immediately below the balcony was the rocky shoreline, with its rock platforms, seaweed and pools, and to the north was the large sandy bay which later became the principal tourist beach of Aberystwyth. The extreme closeness of the house to the sea was emphasised by Price in 1810 in a letter to Lord Aberdeen. He explained how he had made 'a projection' in front of the house on the seaward side and that this was 'very necessary' as 'without such a buttress, the rock, and consequently the house, would have been in great danger. I did mean, + still mean, to put some sort of balustrade round it, both for ornament + and security.'[41]

Samuel Ireland noted that the house was 'recently erected on the shore and commands an extensive prospect of the sea, the only one in fact it does command'.[42] The house very conspicuously turned its back on the town of Aberystwyth and none of the main rooms had windows facing the town. The entrances to the house were from the newly built roadway. There was a private walk along the shoreline towards the ruins of the castle, the site of which was owned by Thomas Johnes of Hafod. Two small walled garden enclosures, decorated with castellated turret follies, ensured further privacy for the Prices. Price himself pointed out that there was a 'good kitchen garden, and a little field'.[43] The enclosures may have provided some protection for garden plants, although the exposed site must have made any gardening difficult. After fifteen years or so of direct experience Price noted that 'no plant will stand against the winds on that coast' and a commentator, writing of the adjoining castle ruins in 1802, regretted that 'every attempt to plant this interesting spot, has hitherto been unsuccessful' because of wind and saline air.[44] (Figure 20).

Walks were made about the castle ruins, although it is difficult to determine the extent to which Price was able to integrate the ruins into his garden.[45] George Lipscomb, in his tour of 1802, states that Uvedale Price, 'the proprietor of a whimsical castellated mansion' near the castle, made a gravel walk among the ruins and that the tower of the castle was repaired 'and converted into a prospect room which commands a view of the sea, and its fine bold shore, as far as the northern horn of the bay of *Cardigan*'.[46] However, guide books of 1810 and 1824 stated that the castle ruins were laid out with walks by Mr Probert, steward to the Earl Powys, who had obtained it on a long lease from Thomas Johnes. Probert, it was said, 'converted it to a delightful purpose, having made walks in it, in the most judicious places, and it is now the promenade of the fashionables, who retire to Aberystwyth during the summer season'.[47] He completed these works in 1810 and a guide was able to describe the castle as a 'picturesque heap of ruins' with splendid views of the coast and mountains in 1824.[48] As Price nowhere mentions the making of paths through the castle ruins, it is most likely that he was happy enough to appropriate the view of the ruins from his new house rather than the castle itself.

Price equated castles with 'suspicious defiance; the security of strength and precaution' in his *Essay on Architecture and Buildings, as connected with Scenery* and celebrated the 'ruins of these once magnificent edifices' as the 'pride and boast of this island: we may well be proud of them; not merely in a picturesque point of view: we may glory that the abodes of tyranny and superstition are in ruin.' He considered that the 'most picturesque *habitable* buildings, are old castles which were originally formed for defence as well as habitation: they in general consist of towers of different heights, and of various outworks and projections'.[49] The southern view from Castle House certainly allowed Price to take in views of Aberystwyth Castle at his leisure, but he remains remarkably silent about the outward appearance of his strange new residence, which John Andrews conjectures became the 'most striking architectural feature of the

town'.[50] In a view of the town ascribed to 1793, the house certainly appears strikingly dominant, dwarfing most of the other buildings in the town. It is quite distinct from the other domestic buildings and protected by substantial walls and two curious isolated watch towers or gazebos. According to Sir Richard Colt Hoare, who visited in 1796, the house was 'in the form of a castle projecting immediately over the rocks near the old castle'.[51] Samuel Ireland described Castle House in 1797 as the 'castellated dwelling of Uvedale Price, Esq; a man not less distinguished for the elegance with which he cultivates the fine arts, than for his powers of discrimination, and the accuracy with which he defines them'.[52] It appears in the background of his 'Market at Aberystwith', one of the images in *Picturesque views on the River Wye*. In this image the house appears rather forbidding with blank walls on the ground floor facing the town contrasting starkly with a lively market scene in the foreground with tented booths, pigs, a harpist and performers on a stage.

The dominant position of Castle House is clearly shown in W. M. Turner's 1798 sketch of Aberystwyth Castle and the town. This sketch also emphasises the house's cliff-edge position and its strangely separate yet symbiotic relationship with the ruins of the castle and the nearby church. A more detailed view is J. P. Neale's engraving of c.1818–29, which is a view from the ancient castle. This shows the line of cliffs and hills to the north, as well as the small walled gardens, one of the Gothic watch towers with lancet windows and the

Fig. 20 Castle House, Aberystwyth. Mid nineteenth century photograph of Aberystwyth showing Castle House directly facing the sea. Castle House predates the promenade and all other buildings in the photograph. (RCAHMW transparency)

Fig. 21 China model of Castle House, Aberystwyth. This model shows the canopied viewing platform which overlooked the sea immediately to the front of the house and representations of the three octagonal towers. (RCAHMW transparency)

extraordinary canopied viewing platform on the first floor of the seaward-facing side of the house. This canopy is again emphasised in the strange ceramic model of the house which survives at Aberystwyth Museum: an early example of kitsch seaside pottery which demonstrates that Castle House was itself a tourist attraction up to the mid nineteenth century (Figure 21). An anonymous drawing of c.1800 shows the two town-facing sides of the house with two large porches and recently planted creepers beginning to cover the walls of the towers and the internal faces of the garden walls.[53]

It is possible that Castle House was seen as the first in a series of marine villas that would hasten Aberystwyth's development into an important resort. Elizabeth Inglis-Jones thought that 'Uvedale Price's villa at Aberystwyth must have encouraged' Thomas Johnes to believe that others would build houses.[54] Thomas Johnes himself built a 'good comfortable small house' three miles to the north of Aberystwyth as 'a bathing house' in the early 1790s, but found it 'more convenient at Aberystwyth'.[55] But in fact few new large villas were built, and it was later in the nineteenth century, with the arrival of the railway, that the town began to grow rapidly. Castle House remained notable in the 1830s. In the *Cambrian Tourist* (1830) the house is described as a 'fantastic house in the castellated form, intended merely as a summer residence' erected 'close to the site of the old castle' by Price.[56] Not all contemporaries viewed Castle House with pleasure, however. Lewis states that the house 'excited interest' but that 'comments were often uncomplimentary to the house and to its owner-designer, Sir Uvedale Pryse (sic), who was said to be very critical of the tastes of others.'[57] Irrespective of whether people liked the house, its design, size and location announced to residents and visitors the wealth and aesthetic beliefs of the author of the *Essay on the Picturesque*.

LIVING THE PICTURESQUE

The little documentary evidence we have on the use of Castle House by the Prices suggests that it was always intended to be used as a summer villa. In 1795, for example, the Prices stayed there in August and September, and took as a guest Miss Glasse, who was a keen singer and musician. Her father wrote 'Mrs. Glasse accompanied her [Catherine] to Foxley about six weeks ago, + after a short stay there, Mrs. Glasse returned home, + Lady Caroline Price took my daughter to Aberystwith, where they continued a Month, + returned to Foxley a few days before the Hereford music-meeting.'[58] The next year they visited Aberystwyth for the whole of August. Price told Lord Abercorn that, after a strenuous election campaign in Herefordshire, his canvassing for Mr Scudamore

> will require a whole month of seabathing to wash off the
> scent of all the greasy butchers, + fusty tailors + and
> cobblers, fat alewives +ca whose particular paws I have been
> squeezing for the good of my country. As I shall not see you
> till my return from Aberystwith, I believe you may safely give
> me your hand without fear of any remains of canvassing.[59]

They went again for the summer in 1797, but Price began to regard the house as something of a luxury in 1798. He told Sir George Beaumont in March of that year that he had 'just contrived by degrees to squeeze enough money out of my income to pay for this house' but had suddenly become concerned about the costs of running the new establishment. This worry was caused by the introduction of the triple tax assessment by William Pitt in his budget of November 1797 to help pay for the French war. Price told Beaumont that the increase in taxation meant that he could not 'afford such a luxury' and would 'be obliged to let it, and hopefully, if the times don't mend, to sell it.' He wondered whether the Beaumonts were interested in it because of their 'love of mountains' and 'cascades' and offered it to them 'at a reasonable rent upon trial for a year, + if at the end of it you should be disposed to buy, and I to sell, we can talk further about it'.[60] Although Price was persuasive, the Beaumonts did not take him up on this offer, and instead for several years rented Benarth Hall at Conwy in north Wales.

An advertisement in the *Hereford Journal* on 9 May 1798 states that 'a house lately built by Uvedale Price at Aberystwyth' is 'to be let for the season or by the year ready furnished'. There is further evidence that Price was regularly letting Castle House for three months of the year, at six guineas a week.[61] On 6 August 1806 the *Hereford Journal* noted that

> The beautiful lodging house called the Castle, on the edge of
> the sea at Aberystwyth, built by U. Price Esq. of this county, is
> now fully occupied and as the charges of that place are no
> longer exorbitant, it is expected that it will very shortly be
> completely filled with visitors.[62]

But the Prices continued to stay at Castle House; in 1799, for example, they were staying there in the late autumn.[63] It became known locally as Lady Caroline's House and Oliver argues that the house was built for Price's 'delicate but sea-loving wife Lady Caroline'. The house was used by the Prices at least until 1823, when a diary entry of Mr Jones for September 1823 states that he 'Called on Mr Uvedale and Lady Price at Castle House'.[64]

The main attractions of the place for the Prices were the sea bathing and the scenery. Price felt that although the town was improving in the 1790s, with among other things the construction of a new five-arched stone bridge designed by John Nash in 1797,[65] some problems remained:

> The town of Aberystwith is a shabby little town, some of the
> streets however have lately been new paved which has much
> improved its appearance + its cleanliness, + a new stone
> bridge is now building. The general face of the country, like
> most others near the sea, is bare, + ugly ...

He greatly valued the scenery around the town, however, stressing to Sir George Beaumont that there are 'many charming wooded scenes on both the rivers that meet at the town' and celebrating the Devil's Bridge and its cascades 'within 12 miles on a good turnpike road' as 'one of the most surprisingly romantic scenes in all the principality', commenting that 'Knight raves about it.' Indeed, Price suggests that he has even thought of selling Foxley ('this beautiful, but expensive place'), maintaining a house at Aberystwyth and one in London, and purchasing a 'small farm' close to Devil's Bridge so that he could 'build a cottage to come for a few days at a time + make communications to the depths + chasms'.[66]

A letter from Uvedale Price to Sir George Beaumont written from Aberystwyth on 5 August 1819, when Price was 72, confirms that the Prices continued to visit Castle House well into the nineteenth century. He was replying to a letter from Sir George in Switzerland which contained descriptions of Mont Blanc, and he provided a lengthy description of the advantages of Aberystwyth and his considered views on the choice of the site for his house, twenty-five years after its completion. He started by emphasising the benefits of his visits to Castle House to his own health: the air of Aberystwyth was

> the most salubrious of any in the whole island; it has twice
> restored me from a miserably weak + emaciated state, as you

may believe when I tell you that I weighed only 8 stone 9
pound: my bones did keep within my skin, but they had a
great mind to come through it.

He built Castle House 'in gratitude to the air, + the sea, which is not less pure,
+ also from falling in love with one particular spot':

The spot I took such a fancy to was part of a small common
that went down to the sea, but quite close to the town: about
a hundred yards from it, a rocky promontory, on which stand
the ruins of Aberystwith Castle; projects into the sea almost at
right angles; + directly opposite to us, it's base has been worn
into several deep coves; at full tide the sea comes roaring into
the most distant, of which we only see the opening; then out it
comes, + dashes round the partition rock (the foam often
rising over the top of it) into the second cove, which is wider
+ deeper, + of which we see the whole: after rolling all round,
it dances about the foot of the next partition rock, climbs up it,
enters into cavities, pours down from them upon a number of
projecting ledges, + makes a thousand little cascades of all
sorts of shapes: then enters a third cove, + dashes away to the
same tune: + as it was never tired of playing these antics, so
we were never tired of looking at them.[67]

The Prices' fascination with the action of the sea over the rocky promontory
encouraged them 'to come in spite of wind + weather + stand by the hour'
and they used 'to think how pleasant + comfortable it would be to see the
same sight from a good comfortable room'. Eventually they 'got a long lease
from the corporation of all we wanted, + built the house so close to the sea
that I can almost spit into it from my window at high water'. He described in
full the views from his 'drawing-room 30 feet long with a bow window, go to!':

The part of it that looks to the south, has the view just
described, of the promontory: the centre part being full west,
looks towards the setting sun; + we often watched him as he
descends into Thetis' lap

Arraying with reflected purple + gold
The clouds, that on his western throne attend.

To the north we have first a level beach where the bathing
machines stand, then the land rises suddenly into a high hill
with a rocky base; above which the surface is turf mixed with
fern + furze + a tall broken cliff appearing beyond it. From
the base of this hill, the eye is led on to some more distant
projections into the sea, to the general line of the
Merionethshire coast bending strongly to the west, + forming
the northern part of the bay of Aberystwith: The outline of the

coast is not ill varied: about the middle of it is a depressed part that takes rather a long sweep; + what do you think appears behind it? Why Snowden, placed exactly where you would have placed him; + then the whole range of his Carnarvonshire subjects descending gradually to the level of the sea, the low island of Bardsey ending the sweep of the bay. The outline of these montagnette – they know themselves to be nothing more – is really very beautiful …[68]

This letter, with its classical allusion, reference to *Paradise Lost* and precise descriptions of compositions of mountain scenery with individual peaks 'placed exactly where you would have placed' them, provides an excellent insight into Price's picturesque sensibility. The great importance placed on the view of Snowdon emphasises the role of this mountain as an exemplar of picturesque north Wales. The letter confirms the importance of Castle House, to Price, as a place to recuperate and to enjoy the marine picturesque. It also provides further evidence for the extent to which the design and precise position of the house distanced it from the increasingly popular resort of Aberystwyth, whose existence is merely hinted at by the reference to the 'level beach where the bathing machines stand'.

But the growth of the town started to impinge on the grounds of Castle House towards the end of Price's life. The Rebuilding Committee of St Michael's Church wrote to Price in October 1825 to open negotiations for an extension to the church's burial ground at the same time as they wrote to Charles Cockerell asking him to be the architect of the new church. In 1828, the year before he died, Price was one of only two contributors from outside Wales on the list of subscribers to the new church.[69] A guide to the town of 1824 described Castle House as 'pre-eminent among the structures of the present day' and a 'unique and beautiful pile' which was a 'singularly handsome edifice, in the Gothic style' commanding 'a gratifying view of the Ocean and Castle Ruins on one side, and of the Church, Assembly Rooms, and part of the town on the other'. Before some modifications made at this time it was 'enveloped in ivy' and the 'general opinion' was that the house 'lost much of its original beauty by being modernised, as the ivy has been torn away, and the outside walls (which intermixed with brick, are of rough mountain stone, peculiar to this country) stuccoed'. The ivy would certainly have reduced its austerity and increased its picturesqueness. Some tourists did not appreciate the house. The Rev. Mr Evans 'could not suppress a smile' when he compared Castle House to the 'dilapidated fragments of the time worn building by its side' – Aberystwyth Castle. He thought that the 'heroes of antiquity' would survey with 'contempt' this 'mimickry of the antique'.[70] Soon after Price's death the house became a lodging house; it was then incorporated within a hotel and later became part of the University College of Wales, being for many years the principal's house, before it was finally demolished in 1897.[71]

THE MARINE PICTURESQUE

Castle House was constructed in the early 1790s at a key point in the development of Aberystwyth as a coastal resort for the gentry of Wales and the Welsh border counties. The Wye tour had already become a popular picturesque itinerary and Aberystwyth, with its surrounding mountains, rivers and waterfalls, became a convenient centre for the picturesque traveller, as well as for sea bathing. Price's interest in the Welsh picturesque would also have been strongly influenced by his Welsh ancestry and knowledge of his father's botanical and drawing tours of Wales with Benjamin Stillingfleet in the 1750s and 1760s. At Aberystwyth he was able put into practice his picturesque architectural theories in terms of both the extraordinary external appearance of the house as well as, and more fundamentally, the positioning of rooms and windows to capture particular compositions. Although he appears to have valued the views obtained from the windows of his drawing room over and above the external appearance of the house, the latter was certainly novel if not bizarre. Aberystwyth gave Price the ability to experiment boldly, something he was not rich enough to do at Foxley, where the house remained, during his lifetime, a rather severe classical building, devoid of gothic or picturesque treatment.

It is difficult to know whether Price or Nash was responsible for the extravagant and exuberant gothic treatment of the villa. Perhaps the demands by Price for a sequence of marine and coastal views, together with the restricted site, encouraged Nash to make use of the triangular plan. One of Price's key tenets was that an architect should 'accommodate his building to the scenery'.[72] J. Mordaunt Crook suggests that 'The habit of regarding buildings as scenery ... encouraged not only irregular skylines and asymmetrical plans, but triangular, hexagonal and octagonal features, eyecatchers, and all manner of follies', and places Castle House within a tradition of triangular follies and prospect towers.[73] The triangular plan at Castle House may also have been influenced by the plan of the adjoining, ancient, ruined Aberystwyth Castle and by the form of the Ragged Castle at Foxley, drawn by Robert Price in 1744. The house was built on former common land and its design allowed the Prices to turn their backs on the 'shabby little' town. Its prominent position, however, could not fail to advertise Price's picturesque ideas and social position. Whatever the reasons for its extraordinary design, Castle House was valued by Price until his old age and provided a highly visible demonstration to visitors and tourists of the exclusivity of his picturesque.

The Aberystwyth venture also provides an insight into Price's enthusiasm and experience of the sea shore. By building Castle House, Price was able to enjoy what Foxley conspicuously lacked: rocks and water. Wordsworth, writing in 1811 to Sir George Beaumont, noted that 'wanting rocks and water [Foxley] necessarily wants variety'.[74] In his *Essay on the Picturesque*, Price argued that 'the sea alone' formed an exception to his rule that 'the great art of improvement' lay in 'the arrangement and management of trees'. The sea's

sublimity absorbing all idea of lesser ornaments; for no one
can view the foam, the gulphs, the impetuous motion of that
world of waters, without a deep impression of its destructive
and irresistible power. But sublimity is not its only character;
for after that first awful sensation is weakened by use, the
infinite variety in the forms of the waves, in their light and
shadow, in the dashing of their spray, and above all, the
perpetual change of motion, continue to amuse the eye in
detail, as much as the grandeur of the whole possessed the
mind … the intricacies and varieties of waves breaking against
rocks, are as endless as their motion.[75]

This passage bears a strong resemblance to several of his descriptions of
the view of the sea from Castle House. For example, in a letter to Lord
Aberdeen he hopes that 'when you are at Aberystwith you will contrive to get
into my house + into the room with a bow window at high water: the sea
dashes very finely against the promontory on which the ruin of the old castle
stands.' He was critical of the 'rocks themselves', which were of a 'bad form'
and a 'shivery stone', but there were

deep coves, into which the waves rush most magnificently,
raising the spray above the top of the rocks, then roll round
into the nearer coves, mount up the sides, + tumble back in
such an endless variety of forms, that I used to sit in that side
of the bow by the hour.[76]

Castle House gave the Prices the ability to enjoy views of the sea, and
particularly the action of the sea against rocks, in comfort and security. In his
Essay on the Picturesque, Price illustrates his agreement with Burke's view, that
terror is strongly associated with the sublime, by arguing that the 'grandeur'
of the sea is increased during a thunder storm; and that 'rocks and precipices
[are] more sublime, when the tide dashes at the foot of them, forbidding all
access, or cutting off all retreat, than when we can with ease approach, or retire
from them.'[77] In one way, by building Castle House, Price was able to reduce
the sublime qualities of the sea to the picturesque. It allowed Price to enjoy a
picturesque which was more in tune with Salvator Rosa than the Georgical
picturesque he created and managed at Foxley, but one in which danger was
not an essential ingredient. Price was even able to argue, to Beaumont, that
the rocky coastline provided security from the French: 'There is another
circumstance that is not unpleasant to reflect on in these times of threatened
invasion; the country has not any riches to tempt invaders + the coast is such
as must prevent them from making any attempt, for it is uncommonly rocky +
dangerous'.[78]

Alain Corbain has argued that by the mid eighteenth century 'the shore no
longer appeared solely as something utilitarian.' People visited the coasts 'to
wonder about the earth's past and the origins of life. There, more than

anywhere else, it was possible to discover the multitude of temporal rhythms, to sense the duration of geological time, and to observe the indecisiveness of biological borderlines ... .'[79] Coastal features became recognised as 'the products of age-old wear' rather than 'relics of a cataclysm'. For some coastal scenery provided a sublime pleasure; storms and squalls brought waves crashing down on rocks and provided a frisson of danger. Corbain argues that the vogue for the paintings of Salvator Rosa 'helped to extend a taste for rocky shores bathed in chiaroscuro and bordered with stormy mountains and wild chasms'. Later in the century, a 'marine picturesque' developed in parallel with picturesque enjoyment of mountain scenery, woodland and parkland. The picturesque way of viewing landscape, Corbain suggests, 'is part of a strategy of distinctions; it implies a vocabulary of exclusion and demands a culture without which ... it is impossible to appreciate a landscape. Distinguishing the picturesque element within a natural scene is based on notions of composition and effect.'[80] The design, structure and use of Castle House epitomise several aspects of the development of this marine picturesque. It was, moreover, an astonishing experiment which had far-reaching implications for ideas of architecture and landscape. It helped Price consolidate his ideas on architecture and scenery, and ideas which sprang from his experiences at Aberystwyth rapidly informed his writings. They also influenced his later advice to friends such as Sir George Beaumont at Coleorton, which will be discussed in the next section. Perhaps more importantly, the exposure of John Nash to Price's forceful and precise ideas helped transform Nash into the exceptionally fertile architect he so soon became.

ASPECTS OF COLEORTON

Sir George and Lady Beaumont decided to build a house on their Coleorton estate in north-west Leicestershire in 1801, towards the end of a long legal dispute with their former agent and coal tenant Joseph Boultbee.[81] They commissioned George Dance to design a house for around £8,000 and expected that he would incorporate part of the old house into the new one. Dance provided a series of designs, one of which retained an octagonal tower from the old house. Price was sent some plans in December 1801 and in February 1802 he was agreeing with Sir George about the 'danger of attempting picturesque groups of buildings' and the need to caution 'all excentric architects, + to teach them a proper love and respect for chaste buildings'. He then uses the example of Moccas Court, designed by Anthony Keck, which Sir George Cornewall had built 1775–78, set in a park modified by Capability Brown in 1778. He told Beaumont

> that the most unchaste imitation of a picturesque group could
> hardly be more disgusting, even when new, than my
> neighbour Sir George's chaste erection at Moccas; but it
> would be much less so to our grandchildren; some of whom

might be tempted to make sketches from the first when it got
a little patina + accompaniments.[82]

The importance of ageing in the establishment of picturesque effects in ruins
had been emphasised in his 1794 essay: 'time ... converts a beautiful object
into a picturesque one. First, by means of weather stains, partial incrustations,
mosses, &c. it at the same time takes off from the uniformity of the surface,
and of its colour; that is, gives it a degree of roughness, and variety of tint.'[83]
In the same letter he expressed concern over the proposed new house
designed by John Nash at Conway for Mr Griffith, a neighbour of the Beaumonts
at Benarth, stating that 'I was quite sure he could not build either of Nash's for
anything like the sum he had thought of laying out' and wondering whether
other plans had been proposed.[84]

George Dance was not happy with the rather dreary situation of the house
at Coleorton. He told Farington in November 1802 that he had 'designed a
House for Sir George Beaumont, but had advised him not to build at Cole-
Orton, which He says He intended to do on a rising ground, before which Coal
pits and circumstances belonging to such works are principal objects'.[85] Sir
George Beaumont characteristically delayed taking a decision and the
resumption of the war with France in May 1803 caused further uncertainty.
Price recommended his former gardener James Cranston to help with the laying
out of the new grounds in the summer. In July 1803 Dance made a drawing of
Sir George and he told Farington in October 1803 that 'the spot was fixed upon
where the new House is to be built', but in November thought 'the
neighberoud bad, & the situation chosen for the House (the best they can fix
upon) places one front that of the principal rooms to the North, North-east,
on which there will be little sun'.[86] The debate over the building of the new
house erupted again in the spring of 1804, with Price emphasising the need
to place the house so that particular rooms had particular views. In January
1804 Lady Beaumont sent Price a model of the proposed new house. He
complained in jest that 'the texture was so flimsy, + the surface so glutinous,
that the top of one of the towers got loose, + stuck so close to the basement,
that it required as much care + patience to separate them, as to unfold the
leaves of one of the Herculean manuscripts.' However, he was impressed by
the overall design and thought that 'the effect of the whole will be very striking
from whatever part of the place, or of the country it is seen, the general outline
being so well varied; particularly that of the summit, on which you know I lay
a great stress.'[87]

The key dispute at this stage concerned the western aspect of the main
rooms of the new house. Price characteristically marshalled his arguments using
a variety of anecdotes, allusions and jokes. He started by asserting that 'As to a
western aspect, I persist in my opinion, that as a principal aspect, + at the time
it most deserves it name from the sun being full upon it, it is (con rispetto
parlando) the devil of an aspect.' He argued 'as my welch blood is up' against
Lady Beaumont's defence of 'the beauties of a setting sun on a fine evening' by

pointing out that when the sun shone directly into the windows it made them intolerable to the extent that when the sun 'places himself directly opposite my eyes, + looks at me through a glass window, I am inclined to say to him, what Lord Pembroke used to say when the sun plagued him in a Tennis-court, "Why ar'n't you ripening cucumbers at Chelsea".' As a further example of the appalling horrors of a west-facing room he recalled the visit to Franz Hemsterhuis, the Dutch philosopher of aesthetics, with Richard Payne Knight at the Hague: 'It was on a very hot evening in June; we were ushered into a long room with one immense window that filled up the whole of the narrow end, while the setting sun in the very centre of it filled the whole room with one blaze of light.' (Chapter 4) He argued, quoting from Lucretius *De Rerum Natura*, that

> you must also allow that there is a great difference between
> looking at a setting sun when the light is diffused all round
> you, + looking at it when you are pent up, + placed in a
> focus, + all the rays, the lucida tela diei, are all darting to that
> one point.

As an example he noted that 'My Library is to the west, + a very pleasant room till the sun gets too low, when to me it is no longer habitable' and that 'the glare of a western sun goes on encreasing till it is absolutely set'. However, he also gives Lady Beaumont space for manoeuvre by admitting that 'my eyes, + my nerves are very irritable, + strongly averse to all glare.' By March Dance wished that 'Sir George would desist from building'.[88]

The discussions over the new house continued during Price's visit to London in the spring. Farington's diary of April and May 1804 shows that Price met up with the Beaumonts in London and that, in addition to several dinner parties, including one hosted by Farington, he made excursions to see several pictures and engaged in politics of the Royal Academy. On 12 May Farington

> went with Sir George & Mr. Price & His Son to Mr. Crew's in
> Lower Grosvenor St & saw the Portrait of His Son when a Boy
> in the Character of Henry 8th. by Sir Joshua Reynolds – very
> fine – also several other portraits. From thence we went to
> Madame Le Brun's & saw Her pictures.

A few days later, on 15 May, Farington 'called on Sir George & found Mr Price & Lady Susan Bathurst there. – I conversed with Sir George & Mr Price abt. Thomas Hope's business and sufficiently informed them the situation in which the Academy stood and the Cause of the Council's complying with Wyatts wish.' Earlier on 16 April Farington had reported that at a large party at Lord Lowther's 'Sir George was 'not in spirits'' but Lady Beaumont was there and 'She brings every body to see the Plans of Sir George's House – among the rest T. Hope.' The Beaumonts, and especially Lady Beaumont, were avidly gathering advice and comment from a wide variety of friends. Price visited Coleorton again to discuss the position of the house and various planting schemes. By

Fig. 22 Uvedale Price by unknown artist c. 1805. Pencil and chalk. This unattributed drawing was made at about the same year as one by George Dance that is lost. (National Portrait Gallery 6810)

10 June 1804 Dance told Farington that Sir George 'at last determined to add two excellent rooms and Offices to the Old House at Coleorton. Mr. Price recommended this Plan & Dance approved it. As it is it will cost Sir George £10,000 to make the place complete.'[89] Price wrote to Lady Beaumont that 'Lady Caroline highly approves the scheme of adding to the old house + so does Knight + both are much pleased with Mr Dance's arrangement.' Indeed, Price and Dance appeared to get on very well and Dance made a portrait of Price which, however, Dance decided to keep (Figure 22). Price told Lady Beaumont to tell Dance that

> I am too much flattered by his motive for keeping my portrait, to wish for it myself, but that as he seemed to think that there was a more favourable view of the face, though he had then proceeded too far to begin again, perhaps at some future opportunity he may have the complaisance to make a second drawing for Lady Caroline.[90]

However, a significant dispute arose between Price, the Beaumonts and Dance about the positioning of the windows and the views from the main rooms.

> I am very happy to find that you continue to be so well
> satisfied with the plan of adding to the old house, but I am
> rather alarmed at what you tell me about the bows: if Mr
> Dance spoils my favourite composition from the eastern
> window of the bow in the drawing room, I mean that where
> the principal hill is seen between the Elms + the W. Elm, I
> shall do, what would be very difficult on any other occasion,
> quarrel with him; + likewise with you + Sir George + what is
> more never come into the said drawing room.[91]

He was less concerned about the 'library bow', which 'you may manage as you please', but was very worried that 'by compressing the house you will have less variety + play of outline but of that you are the best judges.' A few weeks later, in June, Price, writing from Foxley, was agitated and concerned: he had hoped 'that I should see Coleorton before you began to build, that we might discuss all the circumstances of placing the house' and argued that, 'although the general scenery round the house is the first object of attention', 'the choice of the particular compositions from the principal windows, mark the difference between a person who has formed his taste on the principles of painting, + a mere lover of prospects.' He went on to emphasise that 'the composition from the intended place of the eastern window of the Bow in the drawing room, was particularly happy, as the best feature you had among all the distant hills, came in between the finest trees you had in your foreground.' Moreover, 'a foot or two in the placing such a window, makes the whole difference, + that such a distant object either comes in between the trees as a Painter would wish it, or, on the other hand, is disagreably cut + divided by their stems.'[92]

Price was deeply affected by the proposed changes and stated that if

> you destroy this favourable composition of mine + I trust of
> yours also, you will do, what I am sure you will be sorry for;
> you will very much diminish the great pleasure I had in
> looking forward to all you were going to do, + the great
> interest I should otherwise take in it.

He would have 'the mortifying reflexion, that I had been of so little use with regard to the principal point on which I had been consulted'. More importantly, he argued, Lady Beaumont would 'always repent it if you should give way to what you must allow me to call, an ill judged peice of economy'. By way of analogy he compared the current choices being made by the Beaumonts with those Price and Lady Caroline had made at Aberystwyth.

> When I built my small house at Aberystwyth, Lady Caroline +
> I consulted day after day about the exact position of the
> principal windows so that the composition might be precisely

what we liked; by considering it so much we have succeeded in our own opinions, + have often congratulated ourselves upon it, as a perpetual source of satisfaction, + have often said how mortified we should constantly have been, if we had placed them, as we now + then had thought of doing.[93]

Writing to Sir George early in July, Price noted that

Lady Beaumont has of course received my Philippic on the proposed compression of the house: Demosthenes + Cicero had subjects of more importance, + may have been more eloquent, but they could not be more in earnest: it ill require ten times their eloquence to convince me that my favourite composition ought to be sacrificed to compress.[94]

But Price's eloquence was soon redundant: when the old buildings were examined by Sir George's surveyor it was found that 'the execrable old mansion, as Sir George calls it, be fit for nothing but offices' and the new house had to be moved 'near the old apple tree' which Price thought would allow the Beaumonts to 'gain in point of situation'. Indeed, this, according to Price, 'was the spot I was fondest of' and he was keen to know whether Mr Dance had 'quitted his churches, prisons, Lords, Baronets' and visited Coleorton to confirm the situation of the new mansion.[95] Dance began to lose heart entirely and told Farington on 19 July that 'Sir George has again altered His mind & proposes to build on a spot not before considered. – Dance said He should rejoice to give £200 to have nothing more to do with it'. Indeed, he said he would 'never take another Commission of the building kind'.[96]

It must have seemed as if the house would never be built, and Price expressed relief when he heard from Lady Beaumont that the work had started 'And so the foundations are actually begun! I sincerely hope you will never wish to alter one tittle of the present plan: I shrewdly suspect however that you have been obliged to sacrifice what I was so anxious about.' He could not work out from her description 'if any window of any room had been directed to my favourite composition'. He guessed that 'a good squinter, a Guerci no, a strabo, may see it pretty well, but not a man with strait-colour'd eyes.' Indeed, he was still so keen to understand the final design that he asked for Dance to send him a plan and sketch:

The slightest view of the slightest plan would give me a clearer idea than if Vitruvius + Palladio, + Mr Dance were to put their heads together to give me a description, + therefore, as I am still very anxious about the house, I will wish that the last mentioned gentleman would take the trouble of making just such a rough plan as he made at Cole Orton; + it would be still more amiable in him if he would add the slightest possible scetch of the elevation, + send them me …[97]

A plaque at Coleorton states that the first stone was laid on 21 August 1804 and that it was 'erected on the Site of the Old House' and 'inhabited for the first time on Friday the 12th Day of August 1808'. As if to placate Dance for the lengthy discussions, disputes and changes of plan, the plaque adds that the architect 'has manifested as much friendship by his attention to the Execution of the work, as he has shewn good sense, taste and genius in the Design'.[98] Coleorton Hall has been called Dance's 'most memorable Gothic house' and similarities with William Wilkins' Donington Hall, Leicestershire, have been pointed out.[99] None of the principal rooms, other than Sir George's study, face towards the glaring setting sun in the west; most of the principal windows of the house face south and east towards Bardon Hill in Charnwood Forest, the aspect which Price so prized.

The discussions and debate relating to Coleorton show both how tenacious Price was in trying to persuade the Beaumonts to place the new house to allow views to be taken of the surrounding scenery. He brought to bear all his experience of building at Aberystwyth, as well as marshalling arguments from his *Essay on Architecture and Buildings*. Bardon Hill, although described by John Throsby as 'the Olympus of Leicestershire, or the Jupiter of the county', hardly compared with the mountains of north Wales or indeed the Herefordshire hills, but it was the only significant hill in direct view of Coleorton.[100] Moreover, its importance was magnified by the contrast with the immediate setting of the house, where the farmland was bespattered with coal pits. Aspects of the principal rooms were a key factor, and Price convinced Beaumont of the need to place the house in relation to the landscape (Figure 23).

Fig. 23 Coleorton Hall 2005. The Hall has been converted into apartments and although several new houses have been built much of the garden remains. (Photograph, Charles Watkins)

Price popularised and imposed on architects and friends his ideas on the positioning of houses in a landscape. At Aberystwyth his views had a strong influence on John Nash just as his career was beginning to flourish. The effect of his ideas on the well-established George Dance is less clear, and is confused by the complicated interplay between the many people whose advice Sir George and Lady Beaumont sought and received, the lengthy gestation of the building programme and Sir George's vacillation. The conflicts between Price and Dance are a prelude to later debates about the role of Price as critic and connoisseur as compared with professional architects and artists, which became more intense in the first decades of the nineteenth century.

CHAPTER 6

PROPERTY AND LANDSCAPE

INVASION AND DEFENCE

The literary war over picturesque landscapes took place at the same time as military conflict was spreading across Europe. Poor harvests and poverty at home exacerbated the sense of domestic insecurity felt by many in Price's position. The fear of a French invasion gained potency with the unsuccessful landing at Fishguard, Pembrokeshire, of 1,000 or more French soldiers in February 1797. This was rather too close for comfort for Price, whose new house at Aberystwyth was only forty miles up the coast to the north. He also got to know at first hand of the effect of revolution from French émigrés whom he met in London, some of whom visited him at Foxley. Price started to correspond with his friends about the possibility of an invasion in June 1796 when he told Lord Abercorn that Knight had mentioned 'a strong report of an invasion, + of vast preparations for that purpose in Holland + Flanders'; Price joked that 'I should at any time be very sorry to see the French here en masse … . I hope they will at least put off their visit till your's is over.' In August he reminded Lord Abercorn that 'Knight had very serious apprehensions of a french invasion' and then told him of some London intelligence:

> I have just heard that a military man of great celebrity (not George Hanger)[1] has given a very singular proof of the firmness of his belief. He has written down in the club-book at Brooks s; 'General Tarleton[2] gives any member of this Club leave to spit in his face, or kick him, if the French do not invade England before Christmas next'.

Price hoped that 'our Coasts, and consequently the general's front and rear, are in no such immediate danger, but should an invasion take place, I would not be answerable that among so many members, some one might not avail himself of the general's permission'.[3]

Concern over a French invasion from 1794 led to the formation of many voluntary military associations. These were 'organizations of armed civilians' who 'committed themselves to full-time military service in local defence in the event of an invasion or internal insurrection but … remained citizens exercising only occasionally'. The government provided these officially sanctioned corps with 'arms and allowances for uniforms, and exempted them from militia service and some taxation'. There was a resurgence of interest in volunteering after the French landing in Pembrokeshire in 1797 and the naval mutinies of April and May in the same year 1797. Austin Gee argues that fears of invasion were strengthened and 'a run on the country banks led the Bank of England to restrict payments in cash'.[4] In response to this threat Price started to write what became, following considerable agonising over its form and content, *Thoughts on the Defence of Property*.

On 11 March, only three weeks after the French landing, he told Lord Abercorn that 'you will receive by tonight's post another proof of my defence of property, with many corrections + one considerable addition.'[5] This suggests that Price had been writing on this topic for a while and that the landing encouraged him to go to press. He waited four days for comments from Abercorn, but then wrote on the 15 March that 'your silence puzzles me … . If you disapprove of my thoughts on defence in toto, I think you would tell me so, with your reasons + not let me guess at your disapprobation from your silence.'[6] He received a reply a few days later and told Lord Abercorn that although he 'was strongly bent on publishing' his 'defence of property' he had been very concerned that 'you disapproved of it but hardly liked to tell me so' and that this worry 'had thrown a damp on all my proceedings'. He welcomed the detailed critique from Abercorn and as a result had changed the title, addressing it 'only to the County of Hereford. I think it more modest to address my own county only, + also more likely to make the thing itself attended to, than if I fired my little squib at the whole kingdom.' In addition, regarding

> the stoppage of the bank, I fear that the public opinion is so
> strong, that my words would add very little to it; but as there
> are arguments enough for pursuing my plan without any
> drawn from that … stoppage, + as you wish it not to be
> mentioned, I shall very readily yield to your objection, + shall
> totally expunge it.

He noted more generally that 'the uncertain state of public affairs, the difficulty of getting money, which already begins to be felt, + the use I may be of in my neighbourhood' prevented him from thinking of going to London that year, although in fact he did make a lengthy visit.[7]

By April he told Lord Abercorn that 'I am now engaged in writing both on politics, + improvement' and sent him a draft asking his 'opinion of it before it is offered to the County at large'.[8] At this stage he felt that the 'paper' would 'not appear in my name', but when published it did. The title page is dated 1797 and it was published at Hereford by and sold by 'J Allen in the High-Town; and all other booksellers.' The pamphlet received sufficient attention for a second printing, identical with the first other than for the title page, to be issued by a prominent London bookseller. An advertisement of 2 June 1798 states that 'This day is published price 1s. Thoughts on the Defence of Property by Uvedale Price Esq. printed for J. Debrett, opposite Burlington House

114

Piccadilly'. It was recommended as a 'safe, easy and constitutional Plan of Defence' for 'Men of Property of every description, particularly as some Associations, formed on the principles that are explained in it, have received the sanction of Government'.[9]

Price opened his essay arrestingly: 'The sudden and total revolution of property in France, has created very just apprehensions in other countries, where they never existed before: for the successful invasion of other men's property, and its confirmed possession, are examples and temptations of a very dangerous kind.' He argued that 'Property, then, marks its possessor as a victim; every degree of it is exposed, for lawless men seize what is at hand – in the cottage and the palace. Rapine soon unites the plunderers into bands' and 'Flight is difficult, is full of danger, and leads only to exile and poverty.' He thought that 'the danger is sufficient to make immediate precautions highly necessary, yet not so pressing as to afford no time for preparation.' He argued that the 'most agonising thought that can arise in the mind of man, is, that of being left, with all who are dear to him, exposed to the outrages of a savage rabble, who had just begun to taste the horrid pleasure of being able to pillage and insult the peaceful and unprepared inhabitants … .' By the time 'a distant military force' might eventually arrive they would do so 'only to pity and revenge'.[10]

Price, who was a local magistrate, wrote that when he had heard

> the French had landed in Wales, I went to most of the Yeomen and Farmers in my neighbourhood, and stated to them the danger that might arise from profligate and desperate men, who, having no property, and fancying themselves screened by the protection of a foreign enemy, and by the confusion which their coming would occasion, might attack those who had property.

He reported that they 'were all perfectly sensible of the danger and of the remedy' and that they all offered to be 'prepared with arms and horses' to 'assist the Civil Magistrate in suppressing Riots and Disturbances'. Price argued that this was, 'without any figure of rhetoric', a 'cheap defence' of the nation. Moreover, if it could be established effectively and quickly 'in a district of six parishes', why should not 'the circle extend itself through the whole of this county' or indeed 'through the whole kingdom?'[11] He celebrated the success of the Yeomanry Cavalry, but noted that the 'spirit of that corps' in offering their services to 'Government, to be employed out of the county' during an 'actual invasion' strengthened the need for a 'fixed, internal voluntary defence'. There was, he argued, 'no law which prevents twenty, thirty or more neighbours, from meeting together on horseback, without arms or accoutrements … . Both men and horses would be accustomed to each other, and well prepared for acting against an undisciplined mob.'[12]

The key to his argument was that all those who held property, especially agricultural property, and who by the nature of their occupations were tied to the land, had a special interest in protecting it, and protecting each other. Leslie Mitchell has argued that 'property and its defence was the central pre-occupation of eighteenth-century politics. It gave men status and a claim to a voice in politics.'[13] Price considered that the

> striking difference between this and every other Monarchy, is,
> that there are more gradations of property; that they are all
> equally secured, and equally favoured by the laws; and that
> intercourse between the highest and lowest is less separated
> by the pride of rank or fortune, than in any other kingdom.

To promote that union and intercourse 'men of the greatest, and of the smallest property, should, in the defence of it, serve together on equal terms.' He argued that those with the largest properties were not necessarily more pre-disposed to have an attachment to their locality: 'Vast possessions may give ambitious views, and ambition destroys local attachments', whereas

> the cottager, with a few acres which he has tilled and manured
> – who sees part of their produce in his small barn and
> flourishing on the ground – has at least as much attachment
> to his little spot, as the greatest lord to his immense domain;
> and that attachment is much less liable to weakened by
> outward circumstances.[14]

What of the landless farm labourers? Price recognised that some people might be concerned that 'many indigent and disaffected men' would 'seize the same pretext and opportunity for arming themselves' as those with property. But he argued that 'the labouring poor' were 'in general a patient, and much-enduring race'. Moreover, those 'who can scarcely buy bread, will hardly buy arms, unless driven to despair by long ill-treatment', which he did not consider to be the case, at least in Herefordshire. In addition, he argued that 'the whole property of the parish is interested to watch over them.' He returned to this point at the end of his address, which he admitted was 'confined to those persons, who, from their property, have visibly a stake, and an interest in their country'. He noted that 'there is a class of men which have little or none, whose welfare is intimately connected with our own: I mean the industrious labouring poor.' His view was that in Herefordshire, as 'in every other throughout the kingdom', there had been, even 'in very trying times', many 'proofs of attention and benevolence' towards the industrious poor. He concluded that his 'own sentiments' were that one of the effects of 'our union' would be 'a general and encreased attention to the welfare of that most useful and necessary body of men – the labourers; for without their genuine attachment, however firmly we may be united to each other, our union would be far from complete.'[15]

Price was so certain of the benefits of his scheme that he argued that, 'were the worst to happen' and there was a French invasion, and 'that powerful and irritated nation' refused all terms and 'were our resources to sink at last in the struggle', if 'property was armed and united, all would not be lost' and agriculture, which he termed 'the surest resource of every country', would continue 'under the guard of those who exercised that art'. He thought that even if Britain lost 'our great boast and triumph, our brave and victorious navy, and with it our extensive commerce, and all foreign possessions' it would still be possible 'in the midst of poverty' to 'possess freedom, security and happiness'. And there would be hope for the future: 'while the proprietors and occupiers of land are sure of enjoying its produce in security, the seeds of national prosperity, like those of the various grains by which we are nourished, may lie unproductive for years, yet not lose their productive power.'[16]

Thomas Beddoes, in his *Alternatives Compared: or What shall the Rich do to be Safe?* of 1797, strongly supported Price's proposals as 'an easy and cheap plan for securing internal tranquillity in case of sudden alarms' and thought they should be applied to cities as well as the country.[17] Before the second printing of the *Defence* Price wrote to Lord Abercorn to ascertain how he and his 'little troop', which 'except myself, + one other person' consisted of farmers who could not 'go beyond a certain distance without great injury to their affairs', could be of 'service to government'. He felt that such associations might be improved if they could 'meet + exercise <u>with</u> arms, provided they sent their names to the Lord Lieut[nt]: + offered to reject any person or persons whom he might disapprove of.' This might allow his 'local troop' to be deployed to greater effect in securing the 'internal tranquillity of the nation', so that the regular army could 'be used against the enemy'. The troop would 'be ready at the call of the civil magistrate to act under his orders in quelling any riots + disturbances within 8 miles around us'. A great benefit of his plan was that there was no 'expence to government. Those who compose my small troop have paid for their arms + accoutrements.' Price asked Abercorn to 'sound some of your friends in the administration' to see whether he should approach the government through the Lord Lieutenant with his ideas and was 'encouraged to make this request, as you so entirely approved of my pamphlet'.[18] Lord Abercorn's response does not survive, but a letter from a local resident in October the following year suggests that Price's troop, as with most such associations, was relatively short-lived. Sarah Jones told her husband that the 'Foxley troop were considered useless put under military discipline, useless + as they thought themselves highly accomplished as well as accoutered it was expedient that they should not trouble themselves to plough up the Lawn any longer.'[19]

TOURISTS AT FOXLEY

People had visited the gardens, grounds and walks at Foxley throughout the eighteenth century, and it was mentioned in several guides. In 1789, for example, the hill called Lady Lift topped with a clump of pines had been described by the Rev. Stebbing Shaw:

O nature how supreme! O Queen of hills
Enchanting Lady-Lift! Thy beauteous form,
Art ne'er with her insipid vest hath veil'd.[20]

With the popularity of Price's *Essays*, picturesque enthusiasts began to visit and describe the estate. John Britton (1771–1857), the antiquary who was to produce with Edward Brayley the monumental county-by-county topographical survey *The Beauties of England and Wales* from 1801 onwards, visited the estate in the summer of 1798 and, intrigued by the 'picturesque controversy', described how he spent 'a few hours in the house and about the grounds, with much gratification'. Although he described the house as 'a large, brick building, without any pretension to architectural ornament' he was pleased 'by the fine works of art and library it contains'. He noted that 'Most of the apartments are elegantly fitted up, and decorated with a good collection of paintings, by the first masters.' These included 'an Old Man's Head, by Titian; a fine head of OLD PARR, supposed by Rubens; a large battle piece by Berghem, exceedingly well colored; a Storm at Sea by Vandervelde; and an upright picture of Ruins and Statues'.[21]

He thought that there was 'so much to engage the eye and attention' in the 'features of the park scenery and country around' that 'a hasty traveller will not have time to examine or appreciate the artificial works of the landscape-gardener, in what he has done to the ground and plantations immediately around the house' where 'all seemed formed, disposed, clustered, and laid out with due regard to the picturesque.' Britton also recorded a 'timber lodge with a rustic gate at the entrance to the park', and 'several wild thickets and clumps of stones' by the roadside.[22] Foxley was also described in the Herefordshire volume of the *Beauties of England and Wales*, published in 1805:

> a ride of about two miles on the side of the eminence,
> conducts through the grounds and plantations to the summit
> of the Lady-Lift, the views from which form a most delightful
> close to the picturesque and interesting scenery of the
> desirable abode. The beautiful woods of Foxley were chiefly
> planted by the late Mr Price; but the improvements made both
> in the woods and grounds by the present possessor, most
> eminently display his superior knowledge in the difficult
> science of landscape gardening.[23]

In 1799 another description of Foxley was written by James Plumptre in his *Pedestrian Journey*.[24] Plumptre was a clergyman who wrote several plays and whose best-known work, *The Lakers: a Comic Opera*, was published in 1798. He took a copy of Price's *Essay on the Picturesque* with him on his first visit to the Lakes. His comic opera was dedicated 'to tourists' and was a satire on enthusiast botanists and 'picturesque travellers': Miss Beccabunga Veronica gushes over 'the peeping points of the many-coloured crags of the head-long mountains, looking out most interestingly from the picturesque luxuriance of the bowery foliage, margining their ruggedness, and feathering the fells; the delightful differences of the heterogeneous masses; the horrific mountains, such scenes of ruin and privation!'[25] Plumptre stayed overnight at the Red Lion at Yazor and asked the landlady about Price. She said that 'he never suffered his house and grounds to be seen while he was at home, that he was a very odd man, and never suffered any person to come near him.' However, Plumptre later discovered that she was a tenant in dispute with Price and he thought that 'every lover of good order must rejoice when a public house is so much under the control of an excellent landlord, that the keeper of it may be turned out at any time for misbehaviour.'

Plumptre delivered a note and was immediately sent Price's compliments 'and I was welcome to see anything I wished; he was going out with company, or he would have attended me himself round the grounds … the undergroom, an intelligent lad, was sent with me.' The house was 'of red brick and is covered with creeping plants'. They looked at the flower garden behind the house 'filled with fine plants, and creeping & trailing plants trained up the small pillars and the framework. A small alcove at the back had seats round made of straw work in the same manner as beehives. Before the house is a grass plot of flowers in irregular and picturesque situations.' Plumptre walked around the grounds, taking in Lady Lift and the views out across the countryside. He thought 'the trees are the largest and of the greatest variety growing in groups with underwood of holly, thorns, brambles and under these ferns, gorse and luxuriant growing plants.' He noted that 'broken roads and mouldering banks, dells and mounds' varied the spot, but that 'as a landholder I think I should at least clear my premises of weeds.' Coming down from the hillside he entered the farmland of the Yarsop valley. 'This valley is finely cultivated and here Lady Caroline Price has her farm: here are meadows, cornfields and hop-grounds.' He then passed a 'pond surrounded by trees and crowned with an island planted with Arbutus, alder, honeysuckle &c &c according to the principles laid down in the *Essay on the Picturesque*; the whole place indeed is a practical illustration of that work.' Finally, he was taken to the 'Managerie where there was a collection of choice birds'. This was 'planted with different kinds of trees whose branches overhang the grass plot, on which was seen the golden pheasant, the ringnecked and the common pheasant running across or peeping from beneath the shrubs'. There was a pair of Damasels 'so tender' they were kept in a house 'lined with carpeting'. Other poultry included 'silver pheasants', 'common, pied and Japan Peafowls', 'Guinea fowls' and 'Bantams'. He was offered refreshments after a tour of the house, which was 'fitted up in a style of simple elegance'.

A briefer account of Foxley was given by the collector Sir Richard Colt Hoare, who was shown around the grounds by Price when he visited in 1802. Although Hoare described the house as 'of brick, old, and indifferent in every respect', he declared the grounds to be 'highly gratifying to the lover of picturesque scenery'. Hoare noted the horseshoe shape of the estate and described how 'The declivities on each side are cloathed with very fine wood through which the distant prospect often introduces itself with a very happy effect.' Hoare also observed that the approach to the house was 'through an extensive and irregular lawn'. Summarising his impressions from the visit, Hoare recorded: 'The chief beauty of Foxley consists in the irregularity of its hills and woods, the variety in which the different sorts of trees are grouped and the extensive views it commands from the high grounds', and he memorialised the view from Foxley with a sketch in his notebook.[26]

Foxley also attracted French visitors, including several literary émigrés. Alexandre de Laborde, the authority on French gardens, visited Foxley in 1796: he was brought over from Downton by Richard Payne Knight, and Price reported that 'we really liked him very much: he is very natural + cheerful + unassuming.' His arrival was delayed by a week as 'we were afraid of bringing him here', as Lord Abercorn, who was staying at Foxley, 'is such an antigallican'.[27] Several years later, in 1808, Laborde quoted Price in his section on garden theory in his *Nouveaux jardins de la France*.[28] Jaques Delille (1738–1813), who had become famous with his translation of the *Georgics* of Virgil (1769), published his popular didactic poem *Les jardins ou l'art d'embellir les paysages* in Paris in 1782. Following the revolution he emigrated to Switzerland and Germany and then stayed eighteen months in London, where he translated *Paradise lost*. A new edition of *Les jardins*, 'revue, corrigée, et considérablement augmentée', was published by Le Boussonnier, Soho Sq, London in 1801 and was the first to recommend Foxley as a model for the improvement of rural estates.[29] He returned to Paris in 1802. The subscribers to this new edition, headed by 'Le Roi de France', included Uvedale Price and many of his friends and acquaintances, such as the marchioness of Abercorn; Mgr. De Boisgelin, archbishop of Aix; Lady Almeria Carpenter; Lord and Lady Holland; Thomas Hope, Esq.; R Payne Knight, Esq.; S. E. le Comte Ludolf; earl of Moira; George Moore, Esq.; earl of Upper Ossory; Samuel Rogers, Esq.; and Josiah Wedgwood, Esq. The poem emphasises both the contrast between Downton and Foxley and the friendship between their owners:

> Combien j'aime Parkplace, où content d'un bocage,
> L'ambassadeur des rois se plaît à vivre en sage;
> Leasowe de Shenstone autrefois le séjour,
> Où tout parle de vers, d'innocence et d'amour;
> Hagley, nous déployant son élégance agreste;
> Et Pain'shill si charmant dans sa beauté modeste;
> Et Bowton et Foxly que le bon goût planta,
> Fier d'obéir lui-même aux loix qu'il nous dicta;
> Tous le voisins, tous deux aimés des dieux champêtres,
> Et malgré leur contratse, amis comme leurs maîtres.

The first English version to mention Foxley is that 'translated from the French of the Abbé de Lille', by Mrs. Montolieu. Second Edition, London, 1805:

> Oh! How I love those scenes where Malmsbury woos,
> Escaped from cares of state, the sylvan Muse.

The Leasowes, erst whose gentle echoes rung
With love and innocence when Shenstone sung.
The polished lawns and temples of Pain's Hill;
Hagley's wild elegance more striking still.
Foxley and Downton both for beauty famed,
Where proudly Taste obeys the laws she framed;
Near, and in spite of contrast both approved.
Both by the rural deities beloved. (p. 17)

One of the subscribers to *Les Jardins* was Jean de Dieu-Raymond de Cucé de Boisgelin (1732–1804), who was archbishop of Aix from 1771 to 1801. A leading churchman during the Revolution, he was expelled to England and returned to France in January 1802. That year he became archbishop of Tours, and then cardinal.[30] Price told Lady Beaumont in 1800 that the

> Arch-Bishop of Aix has done me the honour of translating my
> first volume into French, + lent me the MS. to correct any
> misconceptions: it is extremely well translated, but there are
> some qui pro quos that are rather comical particularly the one
> that I have just met with. In a note in the 4th chapter I have
> observed that 'when a bald head is well plaisterd + flour'd, +
> the boundary of the forehead distinctly marked in pomatum
> + powder, it has as little pretention to picturesqueness as to
> Beauty.[31] The worthy Arch Bishop has mistaken the meaning of
> flour'd, + has translated it, 'quand une tête chauvre est bien
> enduite de pommade, + couronnèe de fleurs' fancy my head,
> first well pomatum'd, + then stuck round with flowers![32]

Artists continued to visit Foxley. Benjamin West, President of the Royal Academy, told Joseph Farington in August 1799 that he would be with Price on an extended visit to the west of England which also took in William Beckford at the newly constructed Fonthill and the duke of Norfolk at Holme Lacy. West, 'with his Grace, Mr Knight & Price is to go down the Wye'.[33] Price almost had to pull out of a visit to the duke of Norfolk's through a 'very ludicrous but disagreeable + painful accident' brought about by landscaping:

> You must know that I am thinking of making a way for carts
> +ca over the gravel walk, by making a bridge across from
> bank to bank: by way of seeing whereabouts the line of the
> bridge would come, I had placed some uprights with strings
> across: the night before this engagement at the Duke's I was
> riding home in the dark, when suddenly I found myself almost
> pulled off my horse: I had quite forgot this string across the
> road + it happened that it was exactly on a level with my
> mouth into which it forced its way; + never was poor animal
> more roughly bridled.

But he did manage to attend a dinner for the Corporation of Hereford given by the duke: 'A fine lively turtle however made amends for their dulness, + I found there a guest, still less used to Corporations than myself, the President of the Royal Academy.' The duke 'was in his perfect element' and

> was quite pathetic, + had almost tears in his eyes, when he
> talked of his attachment to the county, + the antient town of
> Hereford, + what a proud day it was for him when he saw the
> Corporation at his table + Mr Mayor (graciously clapping him
> on the shoulder) on his right hand.

When Charles James Fox's health was drunk 'you may imagine what an eulogium he made upon him, + afterwards, without drinking his health, he pour'd forth as bitter a philippic against Pitt'. Price 'sat between him + the Worshipful the Mayor, + divided my favours between them; talked of old cyder to my right, + old masters to my left'. Benjamin West told Price that 'he would have gone any distance to have seen, + heard' the duke.[34]

West then stayed two days with Price at Foxley, 'but the weather was most unlucky; not one ray of sun the whole time, nothing but cold fogs + rain: + the instant he was gone, the finest lights I ever saw.' The party at Foxley included 'Mr. Knight, Genl. Fitzpatrick and Mr Biddulph. The weather was very bad.' West told Farington that he was 'charmed with the scenery on the River & at Chepstow'.[35] John Hoppner also visited Foxley, but Price met him only briefly on the road in heavy rain. He told Sir George Beaumont: 'Since the President's departure I have had a visit from a royal Academician, who would not have been much pleased to have met him: you guess I mean Hoppner; he does indeed hate him with a black hatred + does not disguise it.' John Hoppner was known to have a horrible temper. Price complained

> I wish these artists would give one some notice of their
> coming; Hoppner arrived in the afternoon with his wife + son
> in the middle of a most settled rain; I was at Lord Oxford's:
> with much pressing he came in + staid all night. The next day
> (observe all these crosses + misfortunes) I met him on the
> road to Ld Oxford's as I was returning to Foxley; I should have
> turned back with him, but was obliged to go on through hard
> rain on horseback because Foley was to dine with me, + the
> first thing I saw on coming home was his excuse.[36]

SOCIAL LIFE IN TOWN

While the picturesque debate resounded, and Price drew up plans against a French invasion, he continued to enjoy life, mainly at Foxley but often in London. Evidence is thin but his attendance at musical events was not missed by the assiduous Burney family. Susan Burney noted him at a party where 'Mrs Raper was so good as to stick to one like a burr the *whole eve*^g – She is not my passion' but 'Mr Graham, one of Giardini's most celebrated Scholars was there, & played 2^d violin very well – his daughter, a pretty looking young Lady, Mr Uvedale Price – the two Mr Eckardts, Mr Christian La Trobe, & a few more whom I did not know made up the party'.[37] In May 1799 Price met Charles Burney, who noted 'I was at the opera on Saturday, & in the Pitt, under a Chandelier, was almost drowned by a shower of molten wax.' Burney told his daughter Fanny that

> in my distress I heard a well-known voice (that of L^y Clarges)
> call kindly out of a box to me – 'Dr Burney, w^d not you be
> better here?' thinking it likely, I with difficulty got out of the
> crowd, & heard the rest of the op. in comfort, with the dear L^y
> C. her daughter – L^d & L^y St Asaph & Mr Uvedale Price.[38]

Joseph Farington's copious diary provides frequent glimpses of Price's London life. The friends he stayed with included Sir George and Lady Beaumont in Grosvenor Square, but he also often stayed out of town at Sunning Hill near Windsor with Richard Fitzpatrick. He was regularly invited to the annual Royal Academy Dinner held in April, joining a group of well-known connoisseurs such as Charles Long, Samuel Lysons and Richard Payne Knight. Price's well-known role as a leading Whig and friend of Charles James Fox is indicated by a kerfuffle over the seating plan at the dinner in April 1796. Farington records that after the dinner George Dance

> came to me to mention his concern that Mr. Fox was so
> improperly situated, on which I went to Downman &
> requested He wd. come & sit by me which wd. leave an
> opening for Mr. Fox between Mr. Price & Mr. Knight, witht.
> Downman being obliged to leave his place …

After an opening sufficient had been made for the kindly and pliable Mr Downman,

> I then spoke to Mr. Price & Mr. Knight who were very happy at
> the proposal. I then went to Mr. Fox & requested He wd.
> remove to a seat prepared for him, He very good humouredly
> said He was very well situated but on my repeating my wish
> went with me & took his seat between Mr. Price & Mr. Knight.

Farrington was pleased with his diplomacy and 'observed this attention to Mr. Fox was much approved of. Malone told me it was a good maneouvre.'[39]

Price actively added to his collections throughout this period. He bought several drawings from the sale of Sir Joshua Reynolds, including a reclining nude male after Michelangelo in red chalk (Plate 5), and in 1790 he purchased a study in chalk for a portrait of Endymion Porter drawn by Anthony van Dyck in c.1635. On the back of the drawing is a note that he purchased it 'at Myers the miniature Painters Sale, March 1790'. The subject, who was 'one of the most cultivated

Fig. 24 Anthony van
Dyck, *Portrait of
Endymion Porter,* MP and
Royalist, c. 1633. Chalk
drawing from Uvedale
Price's collection
Endymion Porter was a
friend of van Dyck and
Rubens. His son Philip
was committed for high
treason during the
Interregnum.

and widely travelled members of the Caroline court, with a particular interest
in the fine arts', will have been particularly attractive to Price (Figure 24). He
also had a pen and brown ink drawing of a shepherd and flock with a horseman.
This had an inscription on the back of an old mount: 'Vandyck, thought so by
Mr West. It was a very favourite drawing of Gainsboroughs'.

His role in modern terms as a public intellectual became more marked in
the late 1790s and the early years of the new century, and this became
increasingly contentious.[40] Price not only regularly attended sales but became
involved in the politics of art. His connoisseurship was tested in 1797 by the
Venetian process affair. Benjamin West PRA exhibited 'Cicero discovering the

tomb of Archimedes', which he painted using the methods of the Venetian renaissance masters as described in an old manuscript shown to him by the artists Ann and Thomas Provis. Other artists, such as John Hoppner, Richard Westall and Joseph Farington, were also taken in by this scam, although Hoppner was a member of an 'ad hoc group which investigated the validity of the notorious "Provis's process" or the "Venetian secret", a recipe for mixing paints in the manner of Titian'.[41] In May, Knight and Price had a discussion about the Venetian process with the painter Robert Smirke, who 'defended the new process', and Farington reported, rather ambiguously, that 'Price was glad of it.'[42] A few days later, however, Hoppner told Farington that 'Price knows more than any other Connoisseur. – The Connoisseurs oppose the Venetian Process … . Hoppner, spoke to Price of Wests Landscape as being very bad. Price agreed, Hoppner wondered Knight should recommend it.'[43] In November Farington met Hoppner again at the Academy Club and reported that 'Hoppner thinks Price much superior to Knight in judgment on subjects of taste – the latter is writing against some of the opinions of Price.'[44] Although Price's opinion on the validity of the Venetian process is obscure from Farington's account, it is clear that he did not approve of West's painting. But Price did enjoy his drawings and engaged West while this controversy was brewing to draw a sketch of a Cyclops. Price was always concerned about his eyesight and became fascinated by the position of the Cyclopian eye. He told Lord Abercorn that 'West has made a scetch of a head after it which Knight + Sir George Beaumont think one of the best things he ever did, + I entirely agree with them.' West gave the drawing to Price; 'it is now in the Library at Foxley. It is really, un gran' bel' mostro; his eye, instead of being blind, is full of speculation, + the whole character is very poetically conceived + expressed.'[45]

In September 1797 Price told Sir George of his plans to visit Downton and then to take a tour with Knight of the picturesque sights of midland England, stopping at Coalbrookdale and Ironbridge, then on to Kenilworth and Warwick Castles, before arriving at Lord Abercorn's house, the Priory, at Stanmore.[46] By November Price had moved on to Beaumont's home in Dunmow, Essex (the Clock House), en route to Sunning Hill, from where he wrote to Beaumont in December 1797 to describe a visit to view Hogarth's 'Strolling Players Dressing in a Barn' of 1738, owned by Col. Thomas Wood of Littleton, Staines. Price's description is consciously ludicrous, bathetic and pungent and is a good example of his most humorous style.[47] Wood had purchased the painting at the auction of Hogarth's work in 1745. The original probably does not survive, although the engraving was well known (Figure 25). Horace Walpole thought that 'For wit and imagination without any other end … [it was] the best of all his works.'[48] Price rode to Littleton with his friend Richard Wyatt (1731–1813), who was an active collector of pictures and patron of contemporary artists including John Opie and Paul Sandby, and was 'the man I mentioned to you sometime ago, as having some very good drawings, + a fine picture of Borgognone, + as having formerly quarrelled with, knocked down, + pissed

Fig. 25 William Hogarth,
*The strolling players
dressing in a barn,* 1738.
Engraving. The original
painting viewed by
Uvedale Price has been
lost. (© Trustees of the
British Museum)

upon Joseph Mawbey', the vinegar distiller and supporter of John Wilkes.[49]
Price expertly drew out Sir George's patience:

> We got to Littleton about two O Clock: the servant said his
> master was dressing, but would be with us presently; I
> immediately proposed to him to carry us to the Hogarth, but
> he told me it was in a room that was locked up, + master had
> the key. We waited near an hour, + I began to be very
> impatient at the length of M.ʳ Wood's toilet, when at last the
> door opened, + in came a little old man in a brown scratch
> wig, one lock of which (it was not a curl) had got loose from
> the rest, + hung down to his neck: the poor old creature was
> a quarter of an hour in getting from the door to the chimney. I
> am glad to see you so stout says M.ʳ: Wyat, leaning towards
> him: the old gentleman looked up in his face with a sort of
> dismal smile; stout says he! why that's the greatest speed I can
> make: you have seen my best pace; just one foot before the
> other, that's all. After some little talk we proposed to look at
> the picture, with excuses for the trouble it would give him;
> but instead of moving, he entered into a history of the room
> in which it was locked up, of the writings + parchments that
> were there, of his attorney, his house in town, + a room that

was locked up there, + how his son took the wrong keys, + yet they were labelled –, + as his speed in walking + talking were much upon a par – just one word before the other, – that was all – + as it was 3 O Clock, + I had ten miles to go back to dinner, I cut short his narrative, + made him take the same journey reversed, from chimney to door: that being opened, he had a passage to cross to an opposite door; what a time it did take! one might have found out the north-east passage in less! at length he produced the key, put it in the key hole, + unlocked the door, through which I brushed, + got to the picture.

Even after he had got into the room the picture was difficult to examine because it was hung so high and the light poor: 'It is unfortunately placed in a dark room to the north, + the day, which had been bright, was becoming cloudy; another misfortune was, that being fixed in the pannel over the chimney, there was no taking it down.' Although difficult to view, he was able to provide a connoisseur's assessment of the painting:

> It is not painted with the force or the effect of those of Marriage a la Mode, but as far as I could distinguish in so bad a light, the expressions are fine + some of the faces are very beautiful in his whorish style of beauty, + very prettily coloured.

Price was particularly concerned about the conditions in which the painting was kept and the treatment it received:

> The old gentleman finding it so dark, in spite of remonstrances, would have candles: two hand candlesticks were brought accordingly, one of which Mr Wyat raised to the top of the barn where Cupid is getting his bootikins: Mr Wood, with much ado reached with the other (had it been Wyat, it would given him a diabetes) to the place where the monkey is pissing in the helmet; + I in the middle was so bothered with these two false lights that I could hardly see monkey or Cupid. I am somewhat alarmed for the fate of this poor picture, for on Wyat's saying it was dirty, Wood replyed, aye, but I'll never trust it out of my own hands; + so far so good: but then he added, I learned to clean pictures of my old Lord Portsmouth;[50] he cleaned all his own pictures: I put a little salt, + then a little water, + then a little oil, + then, I expected, a little mustard, + a little vinegar, but he stopped at the oil, saying he did not recollect what oil it was. I ventured to give him some caution, but found I was no match for my old Lord Portsmouth. I trust however that the picture will

remain in it's original pannel unnanointed, unanealed; for
indolence, which sometimes prevents so much good (of which
I could give an instance) in revenge does prevent a power of
mischief.[51]

Price was perhaps wise to be concerned, because the painting is no longer
known to exist; indolence appears not to have protected it.

In 1798 Farington reported on 2 June, the date that the new printing of
the *Defence of Property* and the new edition of the *Essay* were advertised in *The
Times*, that Price had breakfast with his Tory friend Sir George Beaumont and
then went on to Lord Robert Spencer's to meet his old Whig colleagues and
friends Fox, Sheridan, Fitzpatrick and Hare.[52] The following year he was
involved in two Royal Academy issues. Price's views of the industrious and
deserving poor are shown by his attention to the description of Sir George
Beaumont's *Elizabeth Woods, of Creeting Hills, Suffolk*, which was exhibited at
the Royal Academy in April. Sir George told Farington at the Society of
Antiquaries that he was advised by both Price and Richard Cosway, the artist
and collector, 'to have the *long acct.* of the Old Woman, put into the Exhibition
Catalogue'.[53] The painting shows the 89-year-old Mrs Creeting in her hovel,
which is clean and well swept, with a cat to accompany her by the fire. The
long account was

> Portrait of Elizabeth Woods of Creeting Hills, Suffolk, born of
> respectable parents in the year 1710, and now living. This
> singular character, having been by degrees deprived of the
> greatest part of her house, rather than quit possession,
> persevered in residence with her two daughters in the
> remaining ruins, an open chimney, and an oven, that served as
> their storeroom and wardrobe, having nothing to defend
> themselves from the weather, in a high and bleak situation,
> but a screen of bushes, which they shifted according to the
> direction of the wind. Here they lived sixteen years. At the
> time this sketch was made, the humanity of the neighbours
> had added a slight shed, and they are, at present, protected
> from the inclemency of the weather.[54]

This description positively celebrates the way in which the three women
overcame their impoverished condition, stressing the benefits of benevolent
neighbours and the gritty determination of the family to stay put in their
derelict cottage under terrible conditions.

The London art world was fascinated by William Beckford's purchase for
6,500 guineas of two Claudes from Rome in 1799. The two landscapes, *The
Landing of Aeneas* and *The Sacrifice of Apollo*, were known as the Altieri Claudes.
Farington took Lord Walpole to 'Mr Beckfords at Eleven oClock to see the
Altieri Claudes. – I staid there till near 5 oClock. Much Company there',
including 'Mr. Uvedale Price, Lady Caroline Price, Coll. Fitzpatrick, S. Rogers,

Lord and Lady Bathurst, Mr Annesley, Sir H Englefield, Coll Greville etc'.[55] A couple of days later he called on Sir George Beaumont, where he met Price and Anne and Lucy Bowles. They all discussed the paintings and 'Sir Geo thinks they are Claudes in the cold manner, which He fell into as he grew old, His *golden warmer Manner* is preferable.'[56] But such aesthetic judgments and discussions by connoisseurs were not welcomed by some of Farington's other friends. Nathaniel Dance thought too many people were invited to Academy dinners and that 'persons such as Pybus, Annesley, Sir H. Englefield, Price &c were not of sufficient distinction to be selected.'[57] This point was discussed a month later at the architect George Dance's house. Nathaniel Dance strengthened his argument. He thought 'Sir Geo: Beaumont falls off in his painting, – is all for producing pictures as a writing Master would flourish, all by dexterity & slight. – Thinks Sir George confines himself to trifling subjects instead of exerting himself on some considerable composition.' William Dance added that 'Artists judge ill in allowing some Connoisseurs such as K[night] & P[rice] to dictate to the town opinions.'[58] But Beaumont was to continue to have a strong influence in the new century, especially in his support of English artists. He told Farington in May 1800 'of a proposal to make an Exhibition of deceased English Artists' and, tantalisingly, Farington adds that 'Mr. Price wrote the proposal.'[59]

COUNTRY LIFE AND POLITICS

The Prices also had a very active social life in Herefordshire, welcoming local friends such as Miss Glasse, the daughter of Mr and Mrs John Glasse of Pencombe, and visiting neighbours such as Knight at Downton and the Oxfords at Eywood, where they met Lord Abercorn and his daughters.[60] On one occasion, Price, who was always excellent at turning his illnesses and injuries into anecdote, recounted how an energetic game of Blind Man's Buff caused him to dash his head against the chimneypiece:

> When it came to my turn to be blinded, I felt so impatient, +
> so tired of being in the dark, that I flew about the room like a
> madman, + in one of my most rapid movements encounterd
> three chairs which were placed to guard the chimney,
> dispersed them to right + left, fell over, or between them, +
> bent a brass fender in my fall, + pitched head foremost
> against the edge of the marble, which cut a deep gash just
> above my eye: You may imagine how near the eye it was,
> when I tell you that a peice of my eyebrow was found in the
> handkerchief which I had applied to my face just after the
> accident. I am now getting well, my wound is healed, + the
> swelling of my eye gone down, but I have very odd nervous
> sensations about my head, one side of which was quite
> numbed for the first ten days, so that I had no sensation in it;

+ I almost wish I had none now, for I feel as if a number of
insects were crawling over my head + often take out my glass
to see whether there are any.[61]

He tried 'to lure' Miss Copley, a sister of Lord Abercorn's first wife, to Foxley
in the summer of 1796 by advertising that 'there is a Clergyman at Hereford
who often comes to Foxley, + who is son + brother to the two famous
Philosophers of the name of Walker; one of whom, Corpetto! exhibits the
Eidouranion.' Price described Adam John Walker as 'a very pretty dilettante in
philosophy, + (what is more to my taste) in music. He expects his Father and
brother in the Autumn, + Miss Copley shall have them all three to herself; for
I will not ask Lady Beaumont, lest she should puzzle them in algebra.'[62] The
Walker family were famous for their entertaining astronomical lectures and
were painted by Romney. The Eidouranion was a mechanical form of
transparent orrery representing the motions of the heavenly bodies. Adam John
Walker was appointed vicar of Yazor, under Price's patronage, in 1809 and also
rector of Bishopstone, adjoining the Foxley estate, where he built a substantial
new rectory with a small park in 1812.[63] He remained vicar of Yazor until 1839.
Wordsworth, a friend of Walker's, wrote a sonnet *Roman antiquities discovered
at Bishopstone, Herefordshire* in 1835 and added a note: 'My attention to these
antiquities was directed by Mr. Walker, son to the itinerant Eidouranian
Philosopher. The beautified pavement was discovered within a few yards of the
front door of his parsonage.' Wordsworth thought that it 'appeared from the
site' as if 'it might have been the villa of the commander of the forces' as it
was 'in full view of several hills upon which there had formerly been Roman
encampments', at least 'such was Mr. Walker's conjecture'.

One of the more unexpected effects of the war with France was William
Pitt's imposition of a tax on the wearing of hair powder. John Barrell shows
that this was introduced to limit the conversion of flour to powder in the
famine year of 1795 and was presented as a tax on luxury. A side effect was
that those opposed to Pitt could demonstrate this publicly, as well as save
money, by having their hair cut. The tax was proposed in Pitt's budget speech
of 1795; Charles James Fox criticised it, arguing that leaders of taste could
choose to stop wearing powder and it was uncertain to produce income: 'he
who relied upon the fashion of the day built upon a slippery foundation.'[64] The
cropping of hair did, indeed, soon become a fashion, both to those who
enjoyed Greek architecture and to those who opposed the continuing war
against France. In August 1795 the duke of Bedford, Fox's principal supporter
in the upper house and leading Whig, cropped his hair and said that he and
his servants would stop wearing powder until after the next harvest.[65] In
September at a shooting party he formed a crop club and many gentlemen in
Bedfordshire followed the example. The fashion for cropping spread widely in
Whig circles. Those who were balding, like Price, had their pig-tails removed.
Price, never one since his days as a macarony not to follow Whig fashion, had
his cut off in November 1796 and his portrait by Sir Thomas Lawrence, painted

Fig. 26 Sir Thomas
Lawrence, *Uvedale Price*,
1798 (Boston Museum
of Fine Arts, Jordan
Collection, 24.212)

in late 1798 and exhibited at the Royal Academy in 1799, displayed his politics
and reaffirmed him as a leader of taste (Figure 26).

He told the Tory Lord Abercorn of the loss of his pig-tail in an extraordinary
flight of fancy, relating its demise to the loss of tails by humans:

> I am not sure whether you will know, or acknowledge me
> when you see me next. I have just parted with that, which
> Lord Monboddo[66] probably considers as the type + emblem
> of the most distinguishing feature of man in his original state;
> in a word, I have cut off my pig-tail, + am become a crop. I
> must say that if our primitive tails were no longer + thicker
> than my late cue, we have been very lucky to have got rid of
> them, at the same time I can easily conceive that they may
> have had their uses + comforts, if they were in proportion to

those of our quondam relations the monkeys. How pleasant
for instance to twist it round a bough + hang from it in the
air; + what a pretty sight to see a party of Ladies +
Gentlemen in a large tree, all suspended by their tails, +
gracefully swinging about. When flies were troublesome,
instead of giving oneself a great slap in the face, we should
lightly brush them off with our natural fly trap. On horseback
we should have no need of a whip, nature having furnished us
with so excellent a lash. How very amusing it would be to see
all the different passions expressed by that most pliant part of
our person; how we should lash ourselves with it in rage; tuck
it between our legs from fear; writhe it in jealousy; flirt it
about with pleasure. It would never be necessary to see the
face of a lover to know whether he was kindly received; if he
was low + desponding, that serpent-like part would extend
itself, and droop to the ground; but if his Mistress was kind,
we should say of it, as Milton does of Eve's serpent, 'hope
elevates, + joy, Brightens his crest'.[67]

He goes on to imagine what it would be like for both males and females to
have tails:

We all talk of the pleasure of being entwined, or as Milton
rapturously expresses it, 'imparadised in one another's arms'[68]
but how differently our caudated ancestors must have felt!
how little we can know of the joys of entwining compared
with them, who in addition to their arms (if indeed they ever
deigned to use them for such a purpose) the fibres of two
such elastic flexible parts were mingled together in a
thousand amorous twines, + expressed mutual delight by a
thousand rapturous vibrations. Here I will drop the subject, ·
for I begin to grow quite melancholy at thinking of our
degenerate state; + if I were not afraid of being thought
profane, I might give an interpretation of our bodies being
raised in a more glorified state, that would not be perfectly
orthodox.

He composed a 'panegyric upon crops' and sent it to Lord Abercorn, as he knew
'neither you, nor Lady Abercorn have any objection to nonsense':

How charming 'tis to be a Crop!
Dressed in a crack! while silly Fop
Frizzled + curl'd like doll in shop
Is all day fiddling at his top.
When the dank air is all of a slop
His flagging curls for want of prop

At every step go flippety-flop;
So drenched with moisture, such a sop
That you might wring them like a mop.
Not so the weather – braving Crop.
Adieu pig-tail! no more thou'lt hop
About my shoulders, change + chop
From side to side; then slily drop
Beneath my cape; there wouldst thou stop,
Till with much shaking of my cop
At length I forced thee out to pop.
I therefore wisely did thee lop,
And now I swear I would not swop
For twenty cues my honest crop.

The following year Price told Sir George with relish of Richard Payne Knight
having his pig-tail cut off while staying with Lord and Lady Oxford: 'Knight has
at last cut off that mark of loyalty + aristocracy ycleped a pigtail. The operation
was performed in great ceremony at the house of that Arch-rebel the Earl of
Oxford + Mortimer – revolted Mortimer.'[69] This was such a good story that he
embellished it the next day when writing to Lord Abercorn: 'you probably have
not heard of a change that has lately taken place in our friend's appearance;
he is become a crop: I wish I could reverse the last sentence + say that a crop
becomes him, but he has unfortunately what the Irishman calls, a strait
coloured head of hair + it does look somewhat bristly.' Knight was 'delighted
however at the change' and Price wondered how 'a man who has always been
poring over antique head-dresses, should so long have endured so gothic an
appendage as a cue.' The hair was cut by Lady Caroline Price and Lady Oxford:

> No common barber, I assure you, had the honour of this deed;
> it was performed in great ceremony at Lord Oxford's. After he
> had given his consent, Lady Caroline brought in a napkin +
> put it over his shoulders, + he looked like Don Quixote at the
> Duke's, when they were preparing to shave him. Lady Oxford
> then produced her scissors, + a most complete crop she
> made of him, for he is now as closely shorn behind as he was
> before. He is ordered to let his hair grow behind his ears till
> next Sunday, when he is to meet his two Dalilas at Foxley, +
> they are to decide about his accomodage.[70]

Two examples from Price's letters to Sir George Beaumont indicate that his
enthusiasm for Whiggish politics remained unabated in this period. In January
1798 he sent a copy of 'the only two latin verses I have made these thirty years.
They are meant as an inscription on the sword given by the Whig Club to
Kosciusco.'

> Kosciuscum hoc gladis Libertas Anglica donat.
> O, numquam ipsa sui muneris indigeat. UP.[71]

Thaddeus Kosciusko (1746–1817) was a Polish general who fought for the colonists during the American Revolution and then, on returning to Poland, fought for Polish independence. Kosciusko was much fêted by the Whigs, who presented him with a commemorative sword when he visited England in 1797. An indication of the heightened political atmosphere in 1798 is in a note Price sent to Sir George on 17 February 1798. Price includes 'a somewhat splenetic epigram' criticising the role of Capability Brown in influencing the king's taste at Windsor:

> On his M^{ys} Improvements in private + public.
> Windsor! thy injur'd towers, parks, forests groan.
> England! thy wealth, power, freedom, all are flown.
> What various ruin from his petty tricks,
> Whose taste was form'd by Brown; by Bute his politics.

Lord Bute (1713–1792) was a confidant of the king, prime minister 1761–63 and notorious for his anti-parliamentary and anti-Whig views; and George III employed Brown at Windsor. Price joked that if Sir George 'has a mind to get me sent to Botany Bay. Why do – a good safe place I believe.' The note concludes 'I wont sign my name.'[72]

DOMESTIC LIFE AT FOXLEY

An intimate view of the domestic life of the Prices is provided by letters from Sarah Jones to Harford Jones (1764–1847), who worked for the East India Company as its president in Baghdad 1798–1806.[73] They had married in 1796, and when Harford Jones went to Baghdad his wife rented Mancel House from Major William Price and wrote regularly to her husband from July 1798 to June 1805, providing a vivid picture of life at Foxley.[74] Sarah Jones was soon welcomed by the Prices: 'Mr Price, Lady Caroline, + Miss Price came in the chair here last night to ask me + all the children to dine there today.' Lady Caroline

> insisted on my going an airing with her yesterday round her
> fields + kitchen garden. Their melons are most prodigious I
> never saw any thing in this country to equal them. The
> smooth green persian sort ... on one bed I think these are
> now fine of the finest vigour I ever saw.[75]

Price presented the Jones with a copy of the new edition of his *Essays* and by December 1798 Sarah Jones told her husband that Lady Caroline 'begins I think to love me, she is so good + tender + very thoughtful on every occasion she can give me the smallest satisfaction'. The Prices took

> great pains to give the young folks as much pleasure as
> possible, during their holidays they spent three different
> evenings there twice dancing. – I assure you they were quite

in style + I sent the carriage each time with them, lamps light, the three girls + Henry to hand them out + very prettily they conducted themselves.[76]

The Jones's children enjoyed visiting Foxley, but Laura's 'horror at the Turkey Cocks, + Pea-fowls, is not to be described, if they come near her'.[77] In April 1799 Sarah Jones copied a poem of Price's written to celebrate Lady Caroline's birthday:

> So charming thy face, + thy shape + thine air
> That I fear to my shame I'd been caught in the snare
> Though thy mind had been foul, as thy person is fair
> But lodged in that form such rare Virtue I find,
> A judgment so true, with such tenderness join'd
> That stript of thy beauty I'd marry thy mind,
> Still more + more dear each return of this day
> Since Time who thy charms must at length bear away,
> Makes the Soul full amends for its mansions decay.[78]

Sarah Jones and Lady Caroline 'often laugh together she is charming. I cannot think of quitting this place but with a tender regret', but she was beginning to find the house and gardens too small: 'this dry summer my cows, + horses, are famishing – for want of a change of pasture. – it is so very confined.'[79] When the Prices went to Aberystwyth, however, 'Lady Caroline gave orders to the game keeper to supply me with whatever I wanted in their absence + also Spraggs she desired would take fruit to Mancel every day.'[80] She increasingly found her landlord Major William Price difficult,[81] but enjoyed the company of the Prices and sent on requests for seeds and other products from Baghdad: 'they leave Foxley next Monday sennight for Town where they have taken lodgings, for two months. M[r]. Price requests if it is in your power, to send them some coffee as they think prized as it is in Turky it cannot be so dear as in this country thay say 8d for the best.'[82] There were frequent parties. One celebrated 'Miss Prices birth day last week + had, a very pleasant evening', the guests including neighbours such as Mr and Mrs Parry from the Weir, Mr Biddulph from Ledbury, Miss Glasse and five children: 'they all danced away except Lady C. + myself M[rs] Parry as gay as a lark.'[83] Sarah Jones considered Lady Caroline to be 'the cleverest woman I ever knew'.[84]

This picture of domestic happiness was soon to be darkened by the illness of Caroline Price. Price's daughter had some sort of illness before 1797, when she was 14, and in late December 1797 Price wrote to Lord Abercorn from Sunning Hill that his daughter had had a relapse which had kept him in a state of 'great anxiety + uncertainty', though she was beginning to recover.[85] This kept the Prices at Sunning Hill over the New Year, until in early January 1798 she was well enough to manage the journey back to Foxley.[86] In the summer of 1800 Price himself was not well: Sarah Jones said 'Mr Price has been unwell, + I think thinner, + broke, which I am sorry to see … .'[87] But in November

Our friends at Foxley are under great affliction on account of
Miss Price, whose health has been but indifferent you know, at
any time, but ... she is however within these few, days in, a
deranged state, + betrays such symptoms of the disorder
increasing, that I fear the worst, consequences must be, had
recourse to + she will be confined.

Mrs Jones

can think of little else, an only daughter, fast becoming a
companion, Lady Caroline bears it with Heroism, – I do
conjecture that they must have had doubts ... before, or I am
sure from The shock I felt at first seeing her raving, a Mothers
feelings had they not been led on by, imperceptible degrees,
could not have stood it, with the resolution Lady C. has.

Lady Caroline told her that 'Mr Price ... is her sole comfort in her afflictions
his tenderness, +, firmness, is excessive, what a Prospect, for them, if she
should not recover her reason.'[88]

Caroline Price continued to be 'much deranged' throughout November.
There was 'little hope of her, ever recovering to, be secure from, the dread of
her, relapsing, I fancy there was always some thing wrong, but Lady C. had
conducted her so far so well, as to, rule her on all occasions, when she would
have been disobedient.' There was talk of 'keeping her confined, with a person
constantly to attend her'. Sarah Jones reported that Lady Caroline would then
'be relieved from the slavery of constant attendance on her' but that 'living at
Foxley ... will now be much less pleasant for M^r. Price who enjoyed poor
Carolines company + accomplishments, to pass the time (all that I fear is over),
+ will leave a sad blank.'[89] In January 1801 there were signs of improvement,
although 'she has a regular female keeper from a, Mad House in Town'.[90] Sarah
Jones felt there was 'no hope of her ever recovering, her reason. They keep
trying Experiments, but I fear to little Success.'[91] By April, however, she stated:
'Miss Price is quite recovered, + in better health + plumper than I ever saw
her, Lady Caroline, received me as if she had been my sister, + I am convinced
was happy to see me at home. Mr. Price is in Town.'[92] In September, Sarah Jones
was happy to report: 'Miss Price continues hearty. don't forget her Pearls she
asks every week about them +, expects to have them next week ... . Bob is
grown + is now at home.' The Prices had been 'to the Iron Bridge + Colebrook
Dale, much delighted, + Lady Caroline brought me a present of a beautiful cup
+ saucer from Brosely. – She is all kindness + respectful attention ... + we
are very happy all together.'[93]

Lady Caroline Price's letters to Harford Jones demonstrate her great interest
in gardening and farming during this period, but also her interest in politics.
She thanked Harford Jones in December 1799 for offering seeds but hoped
that 'you will not confine your liberality to only beautiful and sweet flowers,
for I am quite of your opinion that the Kitchen Garden should be to the full as

much attended to as the Flower Garden + Conservatory'.[94] When Sarah Jones was away in April 1801, Lady Caroline invited the children round for dinner and recounted

> tho' an unfortunate fall of snow, after they arrived, prevented
> our walking out, + their seeing the Pheasants, + Flower
> Garden, which was a great disappointment: little Sarah trotted
> from one to the other and often sat on M[r]. Price's knee, + the
> Gen[ls], but I was happy to see that I was the greater favorite:
> they went home very safe in our Coach.[95]

General Richard Fitzpatrick continued to be a frequent visitor. Lady Caroline told Jones: 'The Gen[l]. just came here for ten days during the Holidays, + set off this morning for London: the times are too critical for any one to leave his Post', but thought that 'the K. – will recover so far as to make a regency unnecessary, but he has not yet been able to compleat the Ministry. He had got heartily tired of Pitt, and during his derangement often called for Addington.' Her letter goes on to discuss the state of the war and notes that

> Most people think Pitt is glad to have got his neck out of the
> Collar, and certainly when we look at the state to which he has
> brought this Country, he had need to fear; for we are at war
> with France, Spain, and all the Northern powers; are without a
> single Ally, and the French strong enough to insist upon all the
> ports in Europe being shut against us.

In 1803 Lady Caroline 'has a great inclination to shew her year old Bull' at the Agricultural Show on 14 March and Sarah Jones calls her 'a very capital farmer' who 'takes great delight in it'.[96]

The Prices made significant modifications to the house at Foxley in 1803. The only information we have is a brief description by Sarah Jones, who told her husband that the old hall had become a 'Salloon' and that the drawing room was 'new fitted up'. The billiard room had the old ante room 'thrown into it by an Arch under which is a Stove' and a further stove had been put 'in the passage under the stair case'. In addition, the 'entrance to the House is in a small room. That was, dressing room to the State Bed Chamber, it has, improved the House extremely both in appearance, + climate. – They propose improving the library next year.' Caroline Price's health, although much improved, was still uncertain: 'I fear she will never be quite steady as on the slightest illness she, has returns of delirium.'[97] In May 1803 Sarah Jones noted that 'Poor Miss Price is again unsettled in her mind', but she had recovered again the following year.[98]

Sarah Jones's letters convey an impression of a lively social scene at Foxley, tempered with great concern over the health of the young Caroline Price. She thought that 'Robert price is grown a very fine young man + of course all their hopes, are now centred in his welfare.'[99] She clearly liked the Prices a great deal. After four years of being neighbours she noted that 'They continue just as friendly as ever + I shall not soon find in material points such – neighbours as they have been',[100] and a year later she reported that 'if she was my sister she could not ... be more friendly.'

> I shall regret Lady Caroline if a quit this as nothing can, ever,
> occur more invariably agreeable as a neighbour than she has
> been, + since I have been without horses, she takes me out in
> her chair offers her horses to put to my carriage to call at Mrs
> Parry's + offers when I wish to go with her to Hereford.[101]

She did hint at one concern with the Prices: 'there are some things as my Girls grow up, that I could wish otherwise, + perhaps for them; a greater distance would be preferable.' But it is impossible to know whether she is referring to the illness of Caroline Price or a possible liaison between her mother and General Fitzpatrick, which was the subject of gossip. However, she never explicitly mentions this and happily reports the general's political opinions, as when on his return from Paris in February 1803, where he had been with Charles James Fox, that he 'was much pleased with his excursion, but not with the Consul'.[102] Others friends of the Prices were not so lucky and got caught at the breakdown of the Treaty of Amiens. Sarah Jones succinctly reported: 'M[r] M[rs] Peploe, + M[r] + M[rs] Clive + Family are prisoners in France.'[103]

CHARLES JAMES FOX

Price was a dependable confidante of Fox who could be relied upon to cover some of Fox's indiscretions. They frequently discussed literary ideas and jokes and only rarely politics. Fox made several visits to Foxley, one in the 1780s being complicated and clandestine. He told Price that 'I should be extremely obliged to you if you would let me know when you expect Mrs C and Mrs B at Foxley ... + whether my being there at the same time would be any wise inconvenient to you.'[104] Fox tells Price to keep this secret. 'I think I am sure you have kindness enough for me to indulge me in my follies + therefore depend upon your secrecy, for I can assure you your betraying me in this instance would give me very great uneasiness.' He goes on:

> I have been reading some Northern Antiquities where the
> Godess that answers to the Grecian Venus is called Frigga. As
> our language is so much derived from the Saxon I would
> submit to the curious in etymology whether some words
> much in use among the English may not be derived from the
> name of that celebrated wife of Odin.

Later, when his permanent companion was the courtesan Mrs Armitshead, he told Price that he hoped to call on him on his way to Lancashire at the end of August. He could not, however, bring Mrs Armitstead to Foxley if the Prices were there: 'I am setting out in about a week upon a grand giro in the course of which I shall be in Herefordshire but can not go to Foxley as Mrs A. will be with me.' They proposed

> going down the Wye and therefore if you can tell me how we
> are to get boats +c at Ross I shall be obliged to you. Pray let
> me know too if you leave Foxley, when you leave it; because if
> you are not there when we are at Ross, I shall shew it to Mrs A.

Fox hoped to see Price at 'Wentworth where I understand I have a chance of meeting you and Lady Caroline. Pray remember me to her, and tell her that I quite agree with her that an ash-leaved Maple is the prettiest tree that grows'.[105]

From 1797 to 1801 Fox almost completely retired from parliamentary politics (Plate 6). He concentrated on domestic life at St Anne's Hill, and on literature, taking a keen interest in Greek.[106] Most of their letters discuss poetry and plays, mutual friends, especially Fitzpatrick, and family illnesses. Fox sent a note to Price 'at Gen. Fitzpatrick's Sunning Hill' on 20 May 1797 asking him to take 'pot Luck' at half past two. He told Price the following year that he hoped to visit Hawkstone and Powis Castle and that they had recently seen young Robert Price: 'We saw Bob a few days ago who is much grown + very well.'[107] They discussed literature, with Fox claiming that 'the finest passages in Racine's Phedre are very closely imitated' from 'Euripides's Hippolytus'.[108] He read the *Plays on the Passions*, which were published anonymously by Joanna Baillie in 1798 and recommended by Price, and liked parts of de Montfort 'very much and Mrs. A. likes it still more'.[109] Price asked him to compose an epitaph for Fitzpatrick's dog Faddle; Fox declined, yet the writing of canine epitaphs became a craze that winter. On 9 January 1799 Price told Fox:

> A new subject for epitaphs has just arisen, though connected
> with the old one. Little Phillis … was brought here from
> Sunning Hill this Christmas, with strong marks of
> incontinency. A certain cur that lurked about FitzPatrick's gate
> was at first suspected; but lately the suspicion has fallen (+ a
> very curious history it is,) on the poor little posthumous son
> of poor old Faddle. He was seen playing with Phillis in
> something more than a common playful manner + this much
> is certain, that soon after their play, the poor puppy followed
> his father very much emaciated. What confirms the suspicion
> is that Phillis is deliver'd of two puppies that are very much
> the same colour with this very juvenile performer. Phillis was
> safely brought to bed yesterday morning; + the very same
> afternoon FitzPatrick miscarried of an Epitaph on her
> supposed husband, from a very common cause of miscarriage
> – a sudden alarm. He was walking in the turnpike road, wrapt
> up in a long, thick black great coat, full of his epitaph, + on

the very point of bringing it into the world, when a large dog,
taking him perhaps for a bear, seized him by the shoulder +
tore of part of his bear-skin, but did not touch that of his real
person; + then finding probably his mistake, escaped from
the blow which FitzPatrick aimed at him with his stick. We are
now grieving at the accident; not for the great coat, which
may be repaired, but for the verses, which perhaps may never
be so happily put together.[110]

They exchanged epitaphs in Greek, Latin, French, Spanish and Italian, Price
arguing that

I must own that there is something very ludicrous in a Man's
choosing to write poetry in a language in which he can hardly
construe the easiest prose; It is very amusing however when it
is not a task, + certainly as far as it goes, extremely
instructive; especially when my blunders are pointed out.[111]

He told Fox that

Lady Caroline, who was very angry at your sending nothing
but greek epitaphs! was delighted to have some english from
you. The one that begins with two lines you thought were
FitzPatricks (+ which he, like many other supposed fathers of
beautiful children, has taken very kindly to,) was, + is, a great
favourite.

Richard Payne Knight also wrote an epitaph, and 'Notwithstanding the goodness
of his epitaph I hope you and Mrs Armitstead will abuse him for his manner of
speaking of the poor series of plays: My Enthusiam is calmed, but his aversion,
like de Montforts, gets stronger + stronger.' By February Fox and Price were
also discussing an epitaph by Sir Edward Winnington, and Price told Fox

I do not remember to have told FitzPatrick that I wished to
get you into a controversy with Knight but if I did I was quite
right to wish it for both your sakes, + still more for my own,
at least while I continue to be the entrepôt of this great
commerce of criticism that has lately flourished so much. It is
impossible in such a situation not to gain something oneself,
tho' the smallness of my capital is much against me. It is really
very diverting to see a controversy carried on with so much
spirit + eagerness through a third person.[112]

In March 1799 the Prices were about to leave Foxley for London, but 'last
night Lady Caroline burnt her hands very much in saving Miss Price whose
gown was on fire, but who luckily was not injured. I fear she will be detained
here some time longer'.[113] Fox was horrified – 'I am very sorry to hear of Lady
Caroline's accident, but when one considers how great the danger was, perhaps

she is well off. Her fright must have been dreadful' – and offered to look after the Prices' son Robert, 'as his holidays begin in a few days, we will, if you and he like it, send for him and keep him here till your arrival'.[114] Their collection of epitaphs continued to grow, with Price disappointed that Fox had sent him two German ones rather than a Portuguese, but Price told Fox that

> Publishing is certainly out of the question, + printing very
> doubtful, as it must depend on my exertions: but these
> epitaphs have afforded me so much amusement, + have been
> the occasion of so much pleasant + interesting
> correspondence, that I shall wish to preserve them altogether;
> + indeed many of them are so good, that they deserve on
> every account to be preserved.[115]

Lady Caroline had recovered by the end of March and Fox invited Price to visit him at St Anne's Hill, and to bring Knight 'only if you come at the same time'. He still hoped that the epitaphs might be printed for circulation 'unless you can get some very good Copier to make at least a score of good copies of them which would be laborious work'.[116] The meeting with Knight was agreed for May. 'We dine at half past three but if Knight wishes it to be later (I do not suspect you) write a line to say so, for it is indifferent to us.' In the same letter, Fox notes that he has been reading Price's 'letter to Repton'.[117] At the end of 1800 Fox asked about Miss Price: 'By mentioning only your own and the general's ailments I hope Miss Price is got better.'[118] And in the summer of 1801 he agreed to continue to look after Robert:

> If he should be unwell of which I see no prospect, we will
> attend to Lady Caroline's Instructions. We are certainly very
> eager just now about farming and Bob has been reaping with
> me a piece (a small one as you may guess) of wheat this
> morning. But I do not think Farming will be in the way of
> History. Idleness and idle reading more likely.[119]

He was pleased to hear that 'Miss Price is better.' In November the Prices sent Fox a gift of sheep from Lady Caroline's flock:

> I have just time to tell you that your magnificent Present is
> just arrived and to return my thanks to you and Ly Caroline for
> it. We have not had time to give the Animal due examination
> yet, but both Mrs. A. and myself are full of admiration at the
> beautiful <u>faces</u> of the Sheep and especially the Ewe that is si
> bien coeffée.[120]

Regular 'Parcels of cyder' were also sent from Foxley to St Anne's Hill.[121]

Fox and Price continued to correspond about literary and political issues, including Greek epigrams and the works of La Fayette, Montaigne, Cowper, Shakespeare, Homer and Virgil. Fox compared Montaigne's 'natural and just' sentiment to John Baptiste Rousseau's, which is 'absurd to the last degree'. He noted: 'I have read but little of Rousseau, his Ode to Fortune I remember thinking full of fine things (for I have not his works) but I suspect his general character is somewhat like his Namesake; sometimes eloquent, sometimes ingenious, sometimes pathetick, sometimes sublime – but nowhere any <u>good sense</u>.'[122] He thanked Price for his flattery about his speeches but 'My opinion is strong against publishing any Speeches except such as have been premeditated.' In June 1803 Fox complained about 'the Doctors Budget': 'What a potion it is! and all this we must swallow because he has sagaciously discovered that Bonaparte wishes at some time or other, by some means or other to get Egypt for a French Colony. It almost drives me mad... .'[123]

In April 1804 Fox told Price that 'They say the K. is better but there is no depending on his Recovery. Pray tell Dick that he <u>must</u> be in the House the 10th at the very latest';[124] and, in an undated letter written after 1802, Fox complained that he wanted to send Price some verses

> but this cursed H. of Coms. & the real anxiety I feel about
> Peace take up my mind too much, tho' you know I bear these
> things as lightly as another. I am sure that two civil sentences
> from the Ministers would ensure Peace, but they have not the
> spirit to pronounce them. Even without them I think it will do
> but their Timidity and fear of nothing puts it to some
> risqué.'[125]

The same letter provides evidence that Price's scheme for the *Defence of Property* was not entirely forgotten. Fox writes that

> You will be surprized at my renewing our correspondence by a
> question relating to Politicks. I think you published some
> years ago a short paper about arming tenants etc which I had
> and probably now have, but cannot find. There was in it some
> account of Ld Barrington's mode of proceeding in Berkshire.
> Can you either send it me, or let me know where I can get it? I
> remember I liked your plan, and think it might be applicable
> to the present circumstances.[126]

In fact there is no explicit reference to Lord Barrington's Berkshire scheme in Price's *Defence of Property*, but Fox's misplaced memory is interesting, as Price's idea of connection and common interest between property owners, farmers, cottagers and the industrious labourer not only reflected his ideas at Foxley but also his remembrance of Lord Barrington's estate at Beckett, near Shrivenham, where the village bore 'strong marks' of the owner's 'attentions' to 'the comforts and pleasures of its inhabitants'.[127]

CHAPTER 7

'MR PRICE THE PICTURESQUE'

DIALOGUE

By the early years of the nineteenth century Price was in his fifties and well established as a leader of taste and public intellectual. His writings continued to arouse controversy. The argument with Repton was so well known that it was used by the defence in a libel case brought by John Soane against Philip Norris, the author of a critical poem called *The modern Goth*. The poem was printed anonymously in 1796 and Soane did not discover the author until 1799. It attacks his designs for his Bank of England, excoriating his pilasters 'scored like loins of pork' and the 'defiance hurl'd at Rome and Greece'. Mr Law, the counsel for the defence, argued that 'every man had a right to comment on works of art' and there had been many previous literary criticisms by poets such as Pope and Dryden. He went on: 'but without going back to those times had very lately ... the late Horace Walpole's Strictures upon the London buildings; we had Mr. Uvedale Price's Severities on Mr. H. Repton', which had not provoked a prosecution. The case at the King's Bench before Lord Kenyon and a special jury found for the defendant.[1] But it was Price's acrimonious disagreements with his old friend Richard Payne Knight, rather than his published argument with Repton, which were foregrounded in the new century.

Price was working on a lengthy original piece during 1800. This was a *Dialogue* to clarify the differences between his and Knight's views on the picturesque. As usual he circulated drafts to friends, telling Lord Abercorn, for instance,

> At last I believe my Dialogue will get itself printed; when I
> shall begin my operations I don't exactly know, but whenever I
> do, I hope you will allow me to send you the proofs as they
> come out, + not be less kind to this, than to my former
> productions.

It consists of an introductory essay 'on Burke's or Sir Joshua's opinions on beauty' followed by a fictitious discussion between three friends on a day's walk through different types of scenery and a visit to a collection of paintings. Lord Abercorn tried to persuade him to write a second day, but Price decided not to as it would have been difficult to avoid 'a good deal of repetition, + I am terribly afraid of wearing out the subject'.[2] In fact, the printer's tight timetable meant that Abercorn was able to comment only on manuscript drafts, Price's aside 'L^y Caroline will look over the proofs as well as myself' to check 'typographical errors' indicating how closely he worked with his wife.[3] It was published in 1801 as *A Dialogue on the Distinct Characters of The Picturesque and the Beautiful. In answer to the Objections of Mr. Knight. Prefaced by An Introductory Essay on Beauty; with Remarks on the Ideas of Sir Joshua Reynolds & Mr. Burke, upon that Subject*. Again it was printed in Hereford but published in London by Robson.

Price reported Knight's argument that 'the distinction which I have endeavoured to establish between the beautiful and the Picturesque, is an imaginary one.' He wrote the dialogue 'in hopes that after so much discussion upon the subject, something lighter, and more like amusement, might be furnished'.[4] The ideas were debated by Howard, who 'is a partizan of Mr. Knight's', Hamilton, who 'is attached to my opinions', and Seymour, who 'has little acquaintance with the art of painting, or with the application of its principles to that of gardening, or to natural scenery'. Price incorporated 'almost the whole' of Knight's note from the second edition of *The Landscape* of 1795 within the *Dialogue* and also prefixed the whole of Knight's note so the reader could 'view the whole chain of his reasoning as he had arranged it himself'.[5] The three characters walk from an inn to a country house, passing 'a ruinous hovel on the outskirts of a heathy common',[6] a cottage scene, a parsonage, a distant view and an improved park. At each point, the characters representing Price and Knight debate the beautiful and the picturesque with the fictional Seymour.

The appearance of two passing strangers is used by Price to exemplify the picturesque: 'Just at this time, a man, with something of a foreign look, passed by them on the heath, whose dress and appearance they could not help staring at.' Seymour tells Hamilton (Price)

> I hope he is sufficiently ugly for you: I shall not get his image
> out of my head for some time; what a singularly formed nose
> he has, and what a size! What eyebrows! How they, and his
> black raven hair, hung over his eyes, and what a dark
> designing look in those eyes! Then the slouched hat he wore
> on one side, and the sort of cloak he threw across him, as if
> he were concealing some weapon!

Hamilton (Price) retorts 'Need I now explain … why an object peculiarly and strikingly ugly, is picturesque?' He argues that if the figure 'just as you saw him' had been 'expressed by a painter with exactness and spirit' that he would have been struck by it 'as you were now in nature, and from the same reasons'. Hamilton concluded by stating that 'it is not ugliness, it is insipidity … that the painter avoids.' To prove his point, he asked of Seymour whether he remembered another figure who passed them on the heath a little earlier who was 'ugly, if not uglier, than the other; a squat figure, a complexion like tallow;

an un-meaning, pudding face, the marks of small-pox appearing all over it, like bits of suet through the skin of a real pudding: a nose like a potatoe; and dull, heavy, oyster-like eyes'. Hamilton argued that a figure of this sort, 'dressed in a common coat and waistcoat, and a common sort of wig, excites little or no attention'. The appearance of this person could not be termed picturesque as 'neither painters, nor others' would consider it attractive.[7]

Further on in their walk they entered a 'pleasing and chearful' village with a picturesquely sited church. Price emphasises the juxtaposition of trees and buildings as defining characteristics of the composition.

> The church was placed upon a small eminence, and in the
> church-yard were some large elms, and two venerable old yews:
> one of them stood in front, and hung over the road, the top of
> the tower appearing above it; the other behind the church, but
> the great part of its boughs advanced beyond the end of the
> chancel, the window of which was sideways against it.

The parsonage 'exhibited a singular mixture of neatness and irregularity'. Successive incumbents had added a room or a staircase or a passage just as they required and 'there were all kinds of projections; of differently shaped windows and chimneys; of rooms in odd corners; of roofs crossing each other in different directions'. The building was well kept and 'vines, roses, jasmines, and honeysuckles, flourished against the walls', while a 'luxuriant Virginia creeper grew quite to the top of a massy stone chimney'. All these plants, together with shrubs and trees in the garden, helped 'to disguise and connect the extreme irregularity of the building'. This building, Hamilton (Price) argued, had a mixture of the qualities of the beautiful and the picturesque.[8]

The three then go on to compare the appearance of the parson's daughter with her home. Seymour thought her to be 'upright', as were the walls of the house, but her 'features have a little of the same irregularity, and her eyes are somewhat inclined to look across each other, like the roofs of the old parsonage'. Hamilton (Price) agreed, reflecting 'how great a conformity there is between our tastes for the sex, and for other objects.' Howard (Knight) replied that he objected 'to this kind of analogy' and 'did not like the habit men are in, of flying for allusions to the inclinations of the sexes towards each other; for that being the strongest of our inclinations, it draws all others into its vortex, and thus becomes the criterion of pleasures …'. Hamilton (Price) responded that in practice there were few such instances, countering with examples of 'women you have known men to be passionately in love with', some of whom were 'short and fat; some tall and skinny; some with a little turn-up nose, a small gimlet eye, a dusky skin or one covered in freckles'. He could think of no instance where 'one of these lovers' was 'so biased by his particular fancy' that he insisted that she represented 'universal principles of beauty'.[9]

Price sent Joseph Farington a copy of his new publication on 1 May 1801, and later in May Farington 'conversed with him on the subject of the *picturesque*.

He told me Mr. Knight has prepared a work for publication in which He threatens to shew the fallacy of Burkes principles on the Sublime & Beautiful as well as those of Mr. Price.'[10] The next day Price and Farington dined together with the Beaumonts at Grosvenor Square with Thomas Hearne. The *Dialogue* reinforced public interest in the picturesque, and mutual friends of Price and Knight were keen to know the outcome of their philosophical dispute. Relations between the two men, however, continued to be friendly. In 1800, following a disastrous journey back to Foxley from north Wales, Price's 'poor little mare fell with my servant …, + cut both her knees, one of them very badly, so that I fear it will be always a great blemish, if she should recover in other respects'. He was 'forced to walk the last part on foot' but 'found Knight quite alone; we dined rapidly, had coffee early, + took a most delightful walk through the whole valley, + I never saw it in higher beauty. He has done a great deal since I was here, + has opened some very charming scenery which was totally concealed.'[11] In September 1801, several months after the publication of the *Dialogue*, Knight and Price were discussing the merits of John Varley, who had been brought into Herefordshire by Lord Essex. Price met him and saw his drawings at 'the music meeting' in Hereford, and told Lady Beaumont that Varley

> chiefly studies landscape, but draws every thing that comes in
> his way; I never saw so eager a creature, or one so devoted to
> his profession. Lord Essex tells me that Edridge + Hoppner
> have a high opinion of him as a very rising artist; + Knight,
> who saw his drawings at Hereford, was so pleased with them,
> that he has invited him to Downton to meet you + Sir
> George; if after <u>tasting</u> him there, we like him sufficiently, I
> will ask him to come on with us to Foxley. He is a great talker,
> + his ideas are sometimes a little wild; but that is better than
> being too tame.[12]

John Varley (1778–1842) was a prolific landscape painter who took part in drawing lessons with Dr Thomas Monro at the 'Monro academy' in Adelphi Terrace from 1800. There are several surviving paintings of Hereford and Leominster and one of Bodenham and the Malvern Hills, one of the villages on the Hampton Court estate of George Capel-Coningsby, 5th earl of Essex (1757–1839), whose principal estate was Cassiobury, Watford. The discussions that Price had of Varley with John Hoppner and Henry Edridge (1769?–1821), who painted Price's uncle Shute Barrington, bishop of Durham, and was a friend of Dr Thomas Monro, indicates the closely connected world of connoisseurs and British artists in which Price moved.[13]

Price and Knight were both avid collectors and they often discussed what was coming up in the London sales. In 1803 Price discussed what was on offer with Lady Beaumont:

> Sir George talked of buying drawings if any good opportunity
> occurred: I fancy there have been none of any consequence sold

this year or I probably should have heard of them from Knight. Udney's I think he mentioned to me as being upon sale, but, If I remember right, there were not a great many good among them. General Morrison's were to have been sold this spring, + from them Sir George might have made an excellent foundation for a collection. Knight was consulted about their value + therefore should know something of the present General's intention: I am anxious to know what became of them, as I have fixed my eye on a few that I had remarked some thirty years ago in old Knapton's time. I wrote to Knight but the other day, a letter of four sides all about Cyder + water; + quite forgot to ask about Morrison's diarys.[14]

General Morrison's paintings were sold 1–3 April 1803 and his drawings in 1807.[15] Price's relations with Knight were on such a good footing that they planned, rather like Mr Hamilton and Mr Howard in the *Dialogue*, to go on a tour of Dorset. This was to replace a planned tour of Paris and Italy which Knight had to put off on the resumption of the war with France on 18 May 1803. Three days later Price told Sir George Beaumont that Knight and he had long 'talked of into Dorsetshire to see M^r. Willett's drawings. I have proposed, + he has agreed to it, that we should meet at Bath, take a peep at the pictures at Corsham + see how they look in their new gallery.' They then intended to 'visit Fonthill', where he hoped that Benjamin West 'will open every part to us, even, I suppose, the sanctum sanctorum, the magnificent apartment over the stables. I very much wish that West may meet us at Willett's, as one is sure of getting a great deal of information from him on the subject of drawings.'[16] This trip would have been a collector's and connoisseur's delight: John Willett Adye's collection at Merley House, Wimborne, which was largely supported by his West Indian property, had many excellent engravings, drawings and paintings. The collections of William Beckford and John Cobb Methuen were some of the finest in the country and the newly completed galleries at Fonthill and Corsham fascinated Price and Knight.[17]

However, when Knight's response to Price's ideas was finally published in 1805 in *An Analytical Inquiry into the Principles of Taste* it caused a genuine rift to open up between the two friends. Knight rejected Price's distinct 'picturesque' aesthetic category, lying between Edmund Burke's categories of 'sublime' and 'beautiful'. Drawing on Archibald Alison's notion of association of ideas, he argued that sight offers pleasure through colour, light and shade and association with memory, literature and philosophy. Knight made a vehement attack on Price's notions of physically innate concepts of beauty. In many passages, Knight argued, 'my friend equally mistakes ideas for things; and the effects of internal sympathies, for those of external circumstances … and thence grounds the best practical lessons of taste upon false principles, and false philosophy.'[18] This was a devastating blow to Price. Andrew Ballantyne has speculated that an additional source of antagonism between the two old friends was Knight's decision to dwell upon Price's example in the *Dialogue* of the parson's daughter, where Price attempted to show that picturesque beauty could be present in an unusual or irregular face.[19] Knight states that 'My friend, Mr. Price, indeed, admits squinting among the irregular and picturesque charms of the parson's daughter, whom (to illustrate the picturesque in opposition to the beautiful) he wishes to make appear lovely and attractive, though without symmetry or beauty.'[20]

The sensitive point here was that Price's daughter Caroline was herself of an unusual appearance and was prone to fevers and outbursts, as witnessed by Sarah Jones when she lived at Mancel House (Chapter 6). Mrs Jones moved to her old family property The Whittern, Lyonshall, in March 1804, and so we have less intimate descriptions of the Prices after that date, but, if anything, she became more complimentary of the family. In March 1804 she told her husband how the whole Foxley party, including Fitzpatrick and the émigré de Crenolle visited her at The Whittern:

> Lady Caroline, Miss Price, the General, Bob + Mons de
> Crenolle, came on Saturday sennight + passed an hour or two
> with us, nothing could be more kind than Lady C in this visit
> was pleased with the place, + she promises to keep up the
> friendship she has invariably professed towards me.

In April 'Miss Price passed a few days here last week + Lady Caroline slept here one night'; and in July 'the Prices came + dined with me the Genl. Bob + all the party + were so kind + pleased it was really a pleasure for me: to receive them.' There is no mention here of Caroline Price's madness or oddity, but in June 1805 Sarah Jones noted that 'Miss Price is reasonable again but very weak.' Moreover, 'Lady Caroline Price was much afflicted at the death of her brother Lord Tyrconnel which happened suddenly.' More happily, Sarah Jones was delighted with her son Henry's success 'and the great + inestimable benefit' of 'Lady Carolines exertions, through General FitzPatrick + Lord Ossory's interest has done' in getting him a post in India – 'we owe all to her.' Also, the Price's son Robert 'is waiting to get into Christ Church, at Oxford, he is grown a fine young man'.[21]

Robert Smirke, who made several visits to Foxley, told Farington in July 1805 that 'Mr. Price evidently appeared much hurt at Mr. Knight's late attack upon' him in his book.[22] The next year he reported that 'There is insanity in the family of Mr. Price. His eldest daughtr. 22 or 3 years old, has been confined, but now visits with them. She is deformed and has many singularities.'[23] Farington noted that 'Price took what related to Himself in Mr. Knight's "Principles of Taste" so ill that it required the intervention of Lady Oxford to make it up.' Lady Oxford told Robert Smirke that that 'Mr. Knight wrote a letter of explanation to Her to be shewn to Mr. Price, but in His writing as in His conversation, when He means to assume lightness and veracity of remark He becomes satirical.' Lady Oxford concluded that she thought Knight 'very learned', but Price 'more elegant and agreeable and that He has a better taste'.[24] Farington went on to record on 13 October 1806 that

> Price is answering Knight's book – A decided coolness has
> subsisted between them. Lady Oxford was apprehensive of
> Knight remaining with them till price & his family came, which
> she shd. have felt herself obliged to prevent by informing
> Knight of it had he continued with them till near the period. –
> Lay. O. sd. Knight is not liked in the country.[25]

Price and Knight had known each other for many years and it is difficult to know the full extent of the breakdown in friendship. Andrew Ballantyne suggests that Knight and Price were 'not afterwards documented as being in each other's company until 1812'.[26] Certainly, the rift did not stop Price visiting London; he is mentioned several times in Miss Berry's journals. In July 1808, for example, he attended a fete at Wimbledon: 'A fine sunny day; scene beautiful; all London world there Dined in a tent – Lady Rosslyn, Mr Rogers, Lord Erskine, Price (father + son), and Charles Stuart (Blantyre) etc joined us'.[27] The following summer Price was at an evening party with Miss Berry, Mrs Damer, Lord Webb Seymour and Prince Staremberg.[28] Farington reports that Knight and Price dined in London with Charles Long on 7 May 1808, where the other guests included the Beaumonts, the Mulgraves and George Dance.[29] Price also visited Knight for a musical dinner in Soho Square in 1810.[30] It is likely that, although they met socially, there was a fracture in their close friendship which lasted several years. Further evidence of their dispute is provided by a letter from Price to Charles Burney in March 1808.[31] Price wrote that he had 'lately been employed in defending, to the best of my abilities, your old friend Mr Burke, against a very violent, + in my opinion, a most unjust attack, of Mr Knight's'. Price asked for Burney's opinion on his criticism of Knight's 'account of the chromatic scale'.[32] The public argument between Price and Knight caused comment from friends and acquaintances for several years. In 1812 Farington, on a visit to Coleorton, noted a discussion on 'The controversy on matters of taste carried on between Mr Payne Knight and Mr Uvedale Price ... it was mentioned by Lady Beaumont that Lady Susan Bathhurst had said that Mr. Price had the most feeling and Mr. Knight the most acquirement.'[33]

PICTURESQUE PROPAGATION

The dispute between Price and Knight did nothing to stop the spread of their ideas and may have encouraged it. Most readers of their works appear to have paid less attention to differences between their philosophical approach than to their practical guidance on gardening, estate management and architecture. Price influenced several authors and his works were widely read. Robert Southey considered that the *Essays* were 'very satisfactory, and quite as good as they could be for their given purpose'.[34] The writer John Aikin praised Price for regretting

149

'MR PRICE THE
PICTURESQUE'

his destruction of the old-fashioned gardens at Foxley.[35] John Stoddart
(1773–1856), who was a friend of Coleridge and later a leader writer for *The Times*,
published his *Remarks on Local Scenery and Manners in Scotland during the years
1799 and 1800* in 1801. Stoddart described spending an evening with the duchess
of Gordon, 'nor should I forget Mr Price's Essay on the Picturesque, which served
as a text-book to all our discussions on local improvement'. Price sent Stoddart
a 'pretty good dose of criticism' of his work and he replied, acknowledging

> the justness of my remark but shews so much apparent
> concern + humility, + is so very earnest for more remarks, +
> seems so convinced of the many errors + imperfections in his
> book, that I have indulged him to the top of my bent, + have
> sent him a couple of sheets brim full of criticisms ... . I wish
> he may not wince a little.

Price joked that 'if Job had been an author, + his friends critics, he could not
have borne such a dose with more patience.'[36] Coleridge himself wrote in 1804
of his intention to make notes 'on the Picturesque, + the Pleasures of natural
Scenery ... from Garve, Price etc'.[37]

Price's views on picturesque landscape were by the early years of the new
century becoming well established, but still required definition or defence.
Farington made several uses of the term in his diary when travelling. On his
visit to Scotland in October 1801, for example, he noted that

> The scenery as it appears from the road from Dunkeld to Blair is
> uncommonly fine. The Hills enriched with plantations not
> formally made but mixing in a natural manner with the rocks,
> and the banks of the river though artless yet have a sufficiently
> neat & finished appearance to be a pattern for forming such
> Parks & what are called Landscape Garden Grounds.

He thought that 'Mr. Price & Mr. Knight might describe the Tay in this part as
an example.' At Milltown of Fascally he observed 'much beautiful Scenery, and
where I particularly attended to some picturesque parts though perhaps they
wd. not be much noticed by one not in the habit of considering what
assemblages are best calculated for the purpose of an Artist.'[38] Here he uses
the term in a technical and precise way and recognises that some would find
it inappropriate for the landscape he described. The next year, while at
Versailles during the brief period of peace with France, he admired the 'fine
appearance' of the view from the Great Hall along the Grand Walk and thought
that the 'formality of these Gardens which are all artificial, every part being of
a regular design of the taste of the Age of Louis 14th., would be much objected
to by those' such as 'Messrs. Price & Knight', who 'have lately written so much
on the Subject'. They would 'not admit the propriety of departing from the
Landscape of Nature, and substituting fancied and unnatural designs, in the
place of what should appear accidental'. He thought, however, that the formal

gardens were the most appropriate accompaniment to the 'vast Masses of Art' at Versailles. Indeed, 'it would be difficult by any alteration that could be made in the design to impress the mind more with stately magnificence than the present accompaniments of the Palace do, however they may be thought antiquated and unnatural.' He made this point 'while on the spot' to Henry Fuseli and John Hoppner, 'who both appeared to me to agree with me in opinion while contemplating the Scene'.[39]

That the picturesque had become a frequent topic of polite conversation in the 1790s and the first years of the nineteenth century is demonstrated by its appearance in the novels of Jane Austen and Goethe. According to Henry Austen, his sister Jane had been 'at a very early age … enamoured of Gilpin on the Picturesque'.[40] The first version of *Sense and Sensibility*, written in 1795 and published in 1811, contains a debate on picturesque beauty. Edward Ferrars had enjoyed taking a view from the village. Marianne Dashwood questioned him 'minutely on the objects that had particularly struck him', but he replied that 'You must not enquire too far, Marianne; remember I have no knowledge in the picturesque, and I shall offend you by my ignorance and want of taste if we come to particulars.' His idea of a 'fine country' was one that 'unites beauty with utility – and I dare say it is a picturesque one too, because you admire it; I can easily believe it to be full of rocks and promontories, grey moss and brushwood, but these are all lost on me.' Marianne agreed that 'admiration of landscape scenery is become a mere jargon' and, referring to Gilpin, that 'every body pretends to feel and tries to describe with the taste and elegance of him who first defined what picturesque beauty was.' Edward confirmed that he liked

> a fine prospect, but not on picturesque principles. I do not
> like crooked, twisted, blasted trees. I admire them much more
> if they are tall, straight, and flourishing. I do not like ruined,
> tattered cottages … and a troop of happy villagers please me
> better than the finest banditti in the world.[41]

Edward's picturesque is more Pricean than Gilpinesque.

The early version of *Northanger Abbey* was written in 1798–9 (published 1818) and again Austen's characters take the picturesque as a topic. Henry Tilney lectures Catherine Moreland: 'He talked of foregrounds, distances, and second distances – side-screens and perspectives – lights and shades; and Catherine was so hopeful a scholar that when they gained the top of Beechen Cliff, she voluntarily rejected the whole city of Bath as unworthy to make part of a landscape.' The subject was concluded by 'an easy transition from a piece of rocky fragment and the withered oak which he had placed near its summit, to oaks in general, to forests, the enclosure of them, waste lands, crown lands and government, he shortly found himself arrived at politics; and from politics, it was an easy step to silence.' Jane Austen's deep understanding of the relationship between enclosure, improvement and the picturesque is further demonstrated by the incident in *Mansfield Park* (1813) in which the aptly named heroine Fanny Price is disturbed by the proposed employment by Mr Rushworth of Repton at five guineas a day. He thought that 'Repton, or anybody of that sort, would certainly have the avenue at Sotherton down'; Fanny is disturbed and reminded of Cowper's line 'Ye fallen avenues, once more I mourn your fate unmerited', and hopes to visit it 'before it is cut down … to see the place as it is now, in its old state'.[42]

Goethe was well aware of the English debates on the picturesque. One of his friends at Weimar was Charles Gore, the wealthy amateur artist who had accompanied Richard Payne Knight to Sicily in 1777. Goethe published his translation of Knight's *Expedition to Sicily* in 1810 and probably came across Price's *Essay* in its German translation, which was published in Leipzig in 1798.[43] In Goethe's *Elective Affinities* (*Die Wahlverwandtshaften*), first published in 1809, an English visitor to the estate portrayed in the novel was a connoisseur of landscape parks. He enjoyed 'capturing the picturesque views of the park in a portable *camera obscura*', knew 'in advance what the struggling plantations promise' and 'no spot escaped his notice where some kind of beauty might be might be introduced or brought into notice.'[44] The attitudes of Goethe's anonymous landscape enthusiast, apart from his use of the camera obscura, are very like those of Price, and he is probably based on an amalgamation of ideas drawn from William Gilpin, Charles Gore and Price.

The influence of Price was also promulgated by the work of a series of architects. James Malton was influenced by Price in his *Essay on British Cottage Architecture* of 1798.[45] David Laing published *Hints for Dwellings, Consisting of Original Designs for Cottages, Farmhouses, Villas, etc.*, in 1800 and it was reprinted in 1804, 1823 and 1841. Laing writes in his preface that a 'late author, of much celebrity (Price on the Picturesque), has well observed, "The Difference of Expense between good and bad Forms is comparatively trifling; the Difference in their Appearance, immense" and emphasises the importance of "painter-like Effects" in architecture'.[46] In the same period Edward Bartell referred to 'Mr. Price's ingenious Essay' in his book of 1804, *Hints for Picturesque Improvements*.[47] Robert Lugar's *Architectural Sketches for Cottages, Rural Dwellings, and Villas, in the Grecian, Gothic, and Fancy Styles, with plans suitable to persons of genteel life and moderate fortune: preceded by some observations on scenery and character proper for picturesque building* was published in 1805 and reprinted in 1815 and 1823, and was the first book to apply Price's ideas to the design of dwellings. Robert Lugar established 'a very widespread practice as a country-house architect, which extended to Scotland and Wales as well as throughout much of England' after 1799. He later published *Plans and Views of Buildings Executed in England and Scotland, in the Castellated and other styles* (1811; 2nd edn, 1823) and *Villa Architecture: A Collection of Views, with Plans, of Buildings Executed in England, Scotland* (1828). Peter Leach argues that 'Lugar was a practitioner of the Picturesque after the manner of John Nash and Humphry Repton', underestimating the influence of Price.[48] But Price's picturesque ideas were clearly permeating architecture as well as literature and studies of landscape.

CONNOISSEURSHIP AND PUBLIC SERVICE

The friendship between Price and Sir George and Lady Beaumont was encouraged by many interests in common. In addition to his discussions on architecture and the design of the Beaumont's new house at Coleorton (see Chapter 6) they discussed art, artists, gardening and poetry, and Price and Sir George had mutual interests in health. The letters to the Beaumonts, although always addressed to one or the other, are usually meant for both. In a letter of 1803 addressed to Sir George, Price began with an extensive discussion of the poetry of Jacques Delille, who had visited and written about Foxley and whom the Beaumonts thought might have succumbed to influenza, then broke off to say 'Dear Lady Beaumont, It has just occurred to me that all I have been writing about the Abbè + his verses, is to you, + not to Sir George; + therefore I have quitted him for the present.' Then, when he began a discussion about the identification of two Claudes he returns to Sir George: 'but I really must go back to Sir George, for he will think we have been a monstrous time together. These women, Sir George, as you well know, are very seducing creatures, + when they once get hold of a man he never knows how to leave them.'[49]

The discussion about the Claudes indicates how Price thought as a scholar and a connoisseur. He looked 'at the Liber Veritatis for the pictures that were painted for the Duc de Bouillon, but can find only one; that is a seaport N° 114'. Claude recorded the pictures he sold in his *Liber veritatis*, now in the British Museum, to protect himself from forgers such as Sébastien Bourdon. In the 1770s, while in the ownership of the duke of Devonshire, the drawings were engraved by Richard Earlom (1743–1822) and published in two volumes by Boydell in 1777. Price is referring to the published *Liber veritatis* and to a pair of paintings, both now in the National Gallery, which were sold by Claude to the duc de Bouillon (1605–52), general of the papal army. These are *Landscape with dancing figures*, Liber veritatis No. 113 (the painting is known as *Landscape with the Marriage of Isaac and Rebecca* NG12) and *Seaport with the Embarkation of the Queen of Sheba*, Liber veritatis No. 114. Price said that he had 'always admired the composition + the effect in the print; if the picture is of his best time, + painted with rigour I think it must be a most splendid one.' He knew 'they were always reckon'd two of his finest pictures, + therefore I am very curious to hear your opinion of them in all points; as to the time of his life when they appear to have been painted, supposing there to be no date upon them; whether they have more of force, depth, + richness, like your cascade Claude' – *Landscape with a goatherd and goats* – 'or of delicacy + freshness like its companion' – *Landscape with Narcissus and Echo*.[50] He then wanted to know 'the style of composition of the one which is not in the Liber Veritas, at least not 114'. His persistent and detailed questioning of Beaumont is followed by a request for him to 'send me the slightest of all sketches of the form of the composition: I doubt much whether in that respect, or perhaps in most others, it was rival your large Claude.'[51]

In 1803 Price was terribly excited about Beaumont's description of two

Rubens which had recently come on the market from the Balbi collection in Genoa: *An Autumn Landscape with a View of Het Steen in the Early Morning* and *The Rainbow Landscape*.[52] 'Your description of the Rubens's is enough to make any man's mouth water, but mine absolutely ran down with water out each corner the whole time I was reading it.' But even these paintings would not tempt him to 'your hot, dusty, stinking town' from 'this delightful place in this delightful weather', modifying the Bastard in Shakespeare's King John:

> Dust, heat + stenches shall not drive me back,
> When Claude + Rubens beck me to come on.[53]

Lady Caroline was 'as much delighted with your description as I am, + particularly with the duck's rapture at having hit upon something infernally nasty', and he wondered who could be the 'rich fellow that in spite of war + taxes, or perhaps by means of war, will be able to purchase these treasures? they must go amazingly high.'[54] He was fascinated to learn very soon afterwards that Lady Beaumont had purchased one of them, *An Autumn Landscape with a View of Het Steen in the Early Morning*, as a present for Sir George: 'I rejoice that one of the Rubens landscapes is in Sir G.' possession: I am told that it was a present to him from a Lady who has had a long attachment to him: some say indeed that they have been married several years.' He reminded her that 'L^y Caroline had rather a longing (not in the way of buying) for the ducks' in the foreground of the other painting *The Rainbow Landscape* 'but I hear that the partridges and jays in your's are as full of sentiment; + in short that the whole picture is full of it down to the very weeds'.[55]

William Lisle Bowles (1762–1850) published *The Picture*, a poem in praise of Sir George Beaumont's Rubens, and Lady Beaumont then sent Price a copy in June 1803. He considered that many of 'the descriptions (that of the Fowler particularly) are so excellent, that they seem rather original ideas from which a picture might be painted, than images suggested to the Poet by the Painter'. He added that the 'reflexions in the <u>picture</u> are not less beautiful than the descriptions; the team crossing the water, the clown's manner of riding + his insensibility, + the reflexion upon it, are delightful instances of both'. He was so pleased by the poem and by Sir George's description of 'this + the other pictures of Rubens' that he intended to bind 'them both together; + if spirits, as they probably may, understand all languages, Rubens's spirit will often be hovering over the book, wishing to return the compliment + paint a new picture from the descriptions'. He was particularly taken with the line in the poem 'where the Kingfisher steals through the dripping sedge away: I hardly know why, but when I read it, I thought I saw the bird, + that the motion of the verse was like his motion.' He went on to make a comparison with Cowper's poem *Truth*, which he 'copied most literally + faithfully from Hogarth's print of morning, with the old maid going to Covent Garden church, + the starved footboy behind her; + I then thought that if some centuries hence that poem + the print should be preserved, but the dates of them lost, our posterity would be puzzled to say which was the original.' Cowper was one of Price's favourite poets and he felt that 'Mr Bowles certainly need not be offended for being put in company with' him.[56]

Price continued to be very involved in political discussions about the Royal Academy and gossiped about artists with Sir George Beaumont. In 1802 he discussed Benjamin West 'my friend the President' and asked Sir George's view of 'his trying to pass off an old picture for a new one. I should be curious to know what account he gives of it himself + of his motive for so strange an attempt when there were so many watchful + unfriendly eyes in the Academy.' Price had little compunction in questioning West's veracity: 'My conjecture is, that he wished for a little more variety, + perhaps still greater celebrity in a favourite amusement of his, for which there are various round-about + softening terms, but which in plain down right english is called Lying.' Price thought he 'had a mind to be splendide mendax, + thought that by means of a lye connected with his own art, + with the history of the Academy of which he was President, he should be omne nobilis aeuum?'[57]

The following year Price discussed the death of Thomas Jones (1743–1803). 'Do you remember spying him out when we were driving through Leicester square?' Price called him 'poor little Jones of Pencerrig ..., whom you knew better as a painter, than a welch squire'. He had earlier been disparaging about Jones and his Welshness: 'a little stunted man as round as a ball, the honest welch runt, who was a pupil of – Oh Aye, to be sure, Jones who was a pupil of Wilson's + his face as red as his Master's + so he has lands + beeves, go to, + two gowns + every thing handsome about him.' Jones had visited Price at Foxley and was 'delighted to be among pictures + drawings'. Price was well aware that Beaumont was a patron of Jones, whom he had first met at Oldfield Bowles' North Aston in 1772; Beaumont purchased a number of works from Jones, including in 1775 a picture of a storm inspired by a scene from *A Winter's Tale*. Price told Beaumont that he had thought of returning the visit: 'I thought of trying some most famous waters that are about 5 miles from Pencerrig at a place called Llandrindod, which sounds like some of the places in Gullivers travels.' He remembered that 'Poor little Jones was no water drinker, "his brandy face proclaimed it", I find he used to sit up all night alone swigging port.'[58]

Although he was closely connected with many artists, there are very few surviving portraits of Price. The lack of portraits and the fact that his grandfather had the same name still causes confusion, and several works state that Gainsborough's portrait of Uvedale Tomkyns Price is of Uvedale Price. The Lawrence exhibited at the Royal Academy in 1799 is the only secure representation. Another portrait shows a slightly younger Price seated on an extremely picturesque chair made of branches.[59] There is also a pencil and chalk drawing now in the National Portrait Gallery which is inscribed in ink on the original backboard 'Uvedale Price Esq. /1805'. This has been attributed to an artist from the circle of Samuel Lane (1780–1859), who painted a portrait of Price's son Robert, or Joseph Slater (c.1779–1837). However, the correspondence between Price and Lady Beaumont suggests that there is a possibility that it could be the unfinished drawing of Price by George Dance of 1803, although, unlike most of Dance's portraits, it is not in profile.[60]

Joseph Farington continued to meet Price in London. In 1804 he discussed 'the Academy & the sentiments of Mr. Price & Sir G. Beaumont' concerning the Thomas Hope affair with George Dance, who 'continued of Opinion that we shd. go on as if nothing had happened, – that it cd. not in any case be supposed that a body of Nobility &c wd. be affected by the opinion of a few of their number & stay away'. The same year Samuel Lysons told Farington that 'Reynolds the Engraver had met him at Lawrence's & had mentioned a desire to make a work of engravings after ancient and modern pictures, and to publish 4 in each number at 28s. a number. Two to be from Ancient & two from Modern pictures.' He thought there should be 'a Committee of Superintendence over the work and Lawrence recommended that they should be Amateurs as it might better serve His interest. Lawrence proposed Wm. Locke, Mr. Price & Sir G. Beaumont, – to be the committee. – P. Knight was not proposed.' In November 1806 Sir George told Farington that he had taken 'Hearne to Wilkie's to see the Blind Fidler, which Hearne recommended to the highest degree'. Sir George told Farington that there was 'not everywhere a disposition to approve of what Wilkie may do. – Mr. Price mentioned it to Hoppner yesterday, who turned from the subject by saying "we have heard enough of Young Roscie".' The same month Farington told Dance 'Artists are seriously affected by these Critics, who run abt. & in many respects do much harm to the professors. – Dance said He thought Price had no taste or true feeling for works of Art, that it was all assumed.'[61]

Whatever the views of artists, however, Price's reputation as a critic was strengthened in 1807 by his appointment to the Committee of Taste when it was doubled in number. Richard Payne Knight was already a member. It is likely that Price's appointment was facilitated by the formation of the Ministry of All the Talents in February 1806.[62] But the relationship between artist and connoisseur remained a fraught one. Farington recalled a discussion on the role of critics with Sir George Beaumont:

> Our conversation turned upon *Critics* on Art. – He spoke as if
> he thought the real judgement was *with professional men*. – I
> said 'Why shd. it not be so?' – Allowing them to be possessed
> of abilities that upon the whole are upon a par with those of
> *their Critics*, is it not fair to suppose that a constant application
> to a consideration of their particular pursuit must enable
> them to judge more exactly of it. – He admitted it & sd. that
> C. Long's judgement was not to be depended upon; nor that
> of Sir Abraham Hume; & that neither Knight or Price were
> assured in that respect, – though He thought Price was the
> best informed.[63]

Sir Abraham Hume (1749–1838) was a keen collector of old masters and

Titian scholar and a founding director of the British Institution in 1805, along with Sir George Beaumont.[64] Although Price did not have a formal role in the British Institution he had been influential in its formation, Sir George noting that he 'wrote the paper' calling for an establishment of an exhibition of 'deceased English artists'.[65]

There is stronger evidence for Price's second public role: he was appointed, by his old friend Lord Robert Spencer, who was Surveyor General of Woods 1806–7, to the post of Superintendent of the Forest of Dean in May 1806 and remained in post until May 1809.[66] The Forest of Dean had great potential for the production of naval timber but, as Nelson had pointed out in 1802: 'The State of the Forest at this moment is deplorable … there is not 3500 Load of Timber in the whole forest fit for building and none coming forward'.[67] Although the day-to-day management of the Forest was looked after by the full-time deputy surveyors James Davies and his son Edward, there is evidence that Price took his role seriously and that the post was no sinecure. A few months after his appointment in May 1806 he told Lady Beaumont that 'Lord Robert Spencer, who is Surveyor General of the forests, thought that from my experience in planting + managing woods I might be of use in the Forest of Dean, where there has been most shameful waste + mismanagement.' He had been 'appointed Superintendent' of the forest 'on his suggestion' and had 'lately been all over it'. He noted: 'The salary is trifling, little more than will pay for my son's expences at Oxford, but it is an office that suits me, + I shall feel a pleasure + pride if I can contribute to make the forest what it ought to be, a nursery of timber for the navy.' He pointed out, moreover, that he was

> so very much occupied just at the moment in writing on the
> subject of the forest, that this letter must be a short one. I
> have the greatest desire to see your new building + all you
> are doing, but as I must often make excursions to the forest I
> fear it will be impossible.[68]

Unfortunately, none of Price's reports about the Forest survive, but his work will have informed the important Dean Forest Timber Act 1808 (48 Geo. III c. 72), which provided powers to enclose 11,000 acres and was passed during the period when he was Superintendent.[69]

LANDSCAPING AT FOXLEY, COLEORTON AND ELSEWHERE

Price continued to carry out landscape improvements at Foxley in the early years of the new century. In 1800 he started to lay out four pools at Foxley in a bout of 'Hydromania'. This was on a small scale: 'though a prodigious theorist, my whole practice has been confined to one island, not near so large as the room I am sitting in.'[70] The pools in the Yarsop Valley are small and in summer concealed by foliage (Figure 27). He was particularly concerned with the disposition of rocks and vegetation along the banks of the pools. He also continued to plant his favourite trees, such as beeches, planes and cedars (Plates 8 and 10), and improve his estate by buying up neighbouring farms when they came on the market. He gave up a planned trip to Paris in 1802 as he was involved in negotiations to spend £600 on a farm much intermixed with his own at Foxley, telling Sir George Beaumont 'I think you will not disapprove of my having purchased the farm, + sent our excuse to the first Consul.'[71] The following year, however, his financial position was such that he had to abandon his pool-

Fig. 27 Yarsop Valley, Foxley, 2011. This is the core of the Foxley estate and shows the view from near the site of the mansion towards the north west. (Photograph Charles Watkins)

making and must 'pinch to live comfortably'.[72] He managed his old coppice woodlands and plantations carefully to reveal the best views of the surrounding landscape, enhancing the views available from the rides around the estate and opening up what he thought of as a gallery of pictures. He also worked *within* his woods and coppices to make compositions and pictures. He told Lord Abercorn how he was 'clearing some parts among the shrubs, + making glades + openings on a small scale, all which operations + their effects I should have liked extremely to have talked over with you'; he cautioned, however, that

> these experiments can only be tried in one's own place, for I never heard of such liberties having been taken with another person's property, except by Lord Clanbrassill; who got up early one morning at his father-in-law's the old Lord Foley, pruned his whole shrubbery, + then, what was still more vexatious, made him listen to his motive for each particular operation.[73]

Using the analogy that in every block of marble there is a fine statue (it only requires to have the rubbish removed from around it), he told Lord Abercorn 'So it is with this place, there are fine pictures without end, but concealed by rubbish to a degree you could hardly conceive.' In the four years since Lord Abercorn's visit he had 'been busied in clearing away some of the mass of rubbish'. The 'great blocks of marble are three distinct coppice woods; as such most unprofitable, but containing treasures of beauty; for a number of fine timber trees of various sorts have been left in them and likewise a number

Fig. 28 Sir George Beaumont, *Yew Tree at Foxley, Herefordshire*, 20 10 1802. This characteristic drawing by Sir George Beaumont has a distant view of Hay Bluff to the left of one of the ancient yew trees of which Uvedale Price was so proud. (Whitworth Art Gallery, Manchester)

of old yews, thorns, nuts, hollies, maples'.[74] Price made the same analogy in a letter to Beaumont and noted that the coppice woods 'are brim full of beautiful groups and compositions both of a near and distant kind'. His method was to 'Begin by taking away everything that may injure the trees and groups that are likely at last to be left, and I open up the compositions little by little but as I must have an eye to profit I leave a number of trees which do no other harm than that of hiding what is at last to be displayed'.[75] Sir George and Lady Beaumont visited Foxley in October 1802; Price showed them his ancient yews and after the visit hoped that Sir George would 'with chalks, pencil, pen, wash copy their dark masses, their wild cedar like boughs, their deep mysterious shadows, with fern at their feet'[76] (Figure 28).

As well as working on subtle improvements to the Foxley landscape, Price also offered advice to his friends on their estates. From 1803 onwards he was especially active in advising the Beaumonts on their plans for the grounds at Coleorton House in Leicestershire. Price made use of the direct practical experience he had gained at Foxley and took considerable pains in explaining these plans. He told Lady Beaumont that many of his 'experiments have been made long enough for you to judge of their effect, they will be examples of what should be imitated, or avoided, or improved upon', and discussions over 'why they had succeeded or failed, or how they might have been managed better would be very useful'. He emphasised that 'I have lately had a great deal of practice in making walks rides +ca + of disguising the lines of them.' He thought he was 'something of a Philopoemen; you have probably read both in Plutarch + in Sir Joshua's quotation from him how that great General has always been in the habit of examining wherever he went every ravine, defile, + intreau, + every character of ground, + of considering how he should dispose his troops to the greatest advantage in each situation: change troops for trees, + it has been my practice for these many years.'[77]

His approach was to thin and prune his trees with 'a proper mixture of caution + boldness'; he stressed that this was 'at least as necessary as planting' and should be 'exercised when wanting in every assemblage of trees, from the higher to the lower growths, + from the oldest woods (but these with particular caution) to the youngest plantations'. To help in this job he trained one of his workers to be 'a pruner who gets up into the very highest trees (not from my teaching however) + perfectly comprehends + executes my ideas. I employed him in that alone good part of last autumn + winter, + have made a number of memoranda for the ensuing campaign.' The result of this vigilance was that 'single trees + groups' which before were '<u>uniformly</u> heavy + massy' were made 'much more varied, light + airy'. In addition, by 'giving head-room in many places to a principal tree in a group' he was able to ensure that 'there should be a marked + decided superiority in one part' and the other trees 'by being shortened in various degrees' were 'obliged to push sideways + to become subordinate to the leading feature'. In this way 'I have been trying to apply to nature the principles of our art, which Sir George understands infinitely better than I can pretend to do.' This pruning and thinning he found to be 'a source of great interest + amusement both at the time + afterwards'.[78]

Price did more than send instructions by letter; he also recommended James Cranston, who had worked for him at Foxley, to advise on landscaping schemes and make plantations. He told Lady Beaumont that 'I rather think you will be pleased + satisfied with' Cranston, who 'has very attentive + respectful manners, is very far from assuming, yet does not conceal his real opinion from wishing to coincide with that of his employer'. He noted that 'compared with those of his profession in general' Cranston was 'very far from being a fine gentleman'. This was meant as a compliment: he charged less than other professional landscapers.

> I told him what I had written to you with regard to his terms,
> + asked whether he could go the beginning of next month, +
> whether a guinea a day during the time he was from home +
> his expenses would satisfy him: he said most chearfully that
> he should be quite satisfied + should be ready to attend you.

Price told Lady Beaumont that

> One always figures to oneself the sort of looking man one
> expects, + therefore for fear you should have made Cranston
> a rawboned Scotchman six feet high, I will tell you that he is

what the french call un petit frapû, shorter than I am by some
inches + some inches broader, with a broad, good humourd,
but intelligent countenance.

Cranston was going to advice the Beaumonts about a stone quarry and Price
had already discussed with him the 'method of taking away the mould so as to
have a picturesque effect after the quarry has been sufficiently worked: he will
give the workmen very good directions about it'. He would also provide advice
on the lake at Coleorton 'as he is very intelligent about heads + banks of pools:
in short he is a Factotissimum.'[79]

An example of the level of detail provided by Price to the Beaumonts is
given by his discussion in June 1804 of the use of elm stumps for the formation
of banks. He told Lady Beaumont that 'I believe the scheme you propose of
making the soil adhere to the upright bank + cover the roots of the Elm, still
preserving the form of the recess is impracticable but I also believe or at least
hope, unnecessary.' He argued that 'No mould will <u>adhere</u> without a foundation
below + if you make a foundation, that is a sloping projection of earth you
must spoil the most picturesque part of the recess, that where the roots of the
Elm hang over in so picturesque a manner.' He also thought that if

it were a common Elm there might be danger, as they are
generally ill rooted + might be blown down + the whole bank
with them, but the witch Elm like the <u>true</u> flower of Love,

clasps the ground, + round it clings
and fastens by a thousand roots.

I think therefore as it has full room to extend it's roots
backwards that it will protect both the bank + itself.

He goes on recommend a method he had devised 'two years ago, the method of
making which Cranston perfectly understands, tho' he did not see it till it was
done'. This was to make 'a wall of live stumps not quite so perpendicular as a
brick, or stone wall, but with very little slope' on a strong foundation of stone.

The stumps I planted were chiefly witch Elm, ash, birch +
hazle, + tho' they were planted very late in the spring most of
them grow + by taking them up pretty wide, ivy +
honeysuckle roots, besides many herbaceous plants came with
them + of course all the moss upon them so that the whole of
this 'verdurous wall' as Milton calls that of Paradise, has
already a rich + natural appearance.

He also directed the Beaumonts on the making of avenues and the
establishment of a shrub and tree nursery.[80]

Price advised at several other estates in the Midlands but we can know
little in practice of the outcomes, as he provided oral rather than written advice
and specific plans were not drawn up. One of the few such interventions to be
documented, albeit briefly, in his home county is at Holme Lacy, the home of

the duke of Norfolk. He was a regular visitor to the house and had paid a visit with Knight and many others during the Three Choirs Festival of 1798, when 'the music party proceeded in pleasure barges down the Wye from Holme Lacy' and 'the excellence of the vocal performance' added to the delight 'experienced from reviewing the wild and romantic scenery'.[81] David Whitehead has identified a path crossing the lower park named 'Price's Walk' on a fragment of an undated late eighteenth-century map. Price took Sir George on a walk through the 'the giant oaks, fantastic witch Elms +ce.' at Holme Lacy and was later concerned that the heir to the estate, Sir Edwin Stanhope, 'who has a decided aversion to the place', would only be interested in 'how many cords of firewood the monarchs will produce' and that 'my future enjoyment of the sublime, the beautiful + the picturesque, which in that walk we so much enjoyed together' was threatened. When the old duchess of Norfolk died Price reiterated that 'the old oaks were in some danger.'[82] Other places where he provided advice included Lord Aylesford's at Packington, where we 'had numberless discussions about improvements at Packington + some of my suggestions were favourably received; among others, a walk or ride of considerable extent which is to bear my name.' Unfortunately many of the family papers at Packington were destroyed in a fire and there is no other evidence of Price's activity there.[83] Price reported that 'The same honour is to be conferred upon me' at Lord Dartmouth's estate at Sandwell, where 'the whole family are delighted with having one of the most beautiful spots in the place + very near the house brought into the pleasure ground, instead of being made, as it had hitherto been, a place where all the rubbish of the garden was thrown'.[84]

Lord Aylesford (1751–1812) was one of Price's oldest friends. They had met at a tennis match at Oxford immediately after Price's return from the Grand Tour, and had many friends in common and strong mutual interests in painting and landscaping. Lord Aylesford's park at Packington had been laid out by Brown in 1751. He was a pupil of Malchair and a patron of Joseph Bonomi (1739–1808), who was also his drawing master and architect and redecorated the house from 1782 onwards. Aylesford himself was a talented artist and a Trustee of the British Museum 1804–12. In the 1790s Price was trying to get him to modify the lake. Lord Aylesford

> has been altering a small part of his peice of water at
> Packington, which I had some difficulty in persuading him to
> do. He said if he has to begin a new peice of water himself, he
> should have no hesitation, but that he doubted whether one
> that had been made by Brown (as that at Packington was)
> could so well be new modelled.

Aylesford had recently 'written me word however, that he has tried a part, + is excessively pleased with what he has done', and Price was delighted that 'he is staggering over to my opinion.'[85]

Price's dislike of the works of Lancelot Brown did not diminish as the years went by and his landscapes matured. In 1806 he made a special effort to visit Fisherwick Park near Lichfield, which had been laid out by Brown thirty-six years earlier for Arthur Chichester, 1st marquis of Donegal (1739–1799). He told Sir George that 'if I had wanted any confirmation of my opinion of Brown I should have had a most compleat one.' He noted that Brown's 'admirers have always quoted Fisherwick, if not as his greatest work, at least as that where he followed the impulse of his own genius without controul', but, ill as he thought of him, he could

> hardly believe that he could choose the situation of the house though he gave the plan of it, for there is a very pretty river + some very pleasing views of it within two hundred yards, yet it is so contrivd that not a glimpse of the water should be seen from either of the fronts,

both of which looked upon 'a most miserably insipid flat, which has not even the merit of being fertile, for not only the trees are wretched but even the sward'. Price was especially provoked by Brown's blocking of a view of

> one of the noblest ashes I ever saw: he has not only planted about it, but has built the kitchen garden wall, or, what is only less bad, sufferd it to remain, quite close to it, so that it is impossible to enjoy what appears to be one of the finest views of this magnificent tree.[86]

Such visits and thoughts compelled Price to continue writing on the picturesque and to produce a complete edition of his works on the subject.

COMPLETE ESSAYS 1810

Price's collection of *Essays on the Picturesque, as Compared with the Sublime and the Beautiful; and, on the Use of Studying Pictures, for the Purpose of Improving Real Landscape* was published in three volumes by J. Mawman in 1810.[87] The first volume contained the *Essay on the Picturesque*; the second contained three essays which 'though detached from each other and from the Essay on the Picturesque, are, in respect to the matter they contain, and the suite of ideas they present, perfectly connected'.[88] The three pieces were 'Essay on Artificial Water'; 'Essay on Decorations' and 'Essay on Architecture and Buildings'. The third volume contained Repton's *Letter to Uvedale Price Esq.*, Price's *Letter to H. Repton Esq.*, and the *Dialogue on the distinct characters of the Picturesque and the Beautiful in answer to the objections to Mr Knight*. In the preface to the first volume Price noted that the 'general plan and intention' of his first publication had been 'a good deal misunderstood' and that his emphasis on the picturesque was not because he 'only preferred such scenes as were merely rude and picturesque' but because the picturesque 'had been totally neglected and despised by professed improvers: my business therefore, was to draw forth, and to dwell upon those less observed beauties'.[89] He quoted Cicero's exclamation *Quam multa vident pictores in umbris, et in eminentia, quae nos non videmus!*[90] and considered that this 'marks his surprise at the extreme difference which the study of nature, by means of the art of painting, seems to make almost to the sight itself'. Price argued that

> If there were no means of seeing with the eyes of painters, than
> by acquiring the practical skill of their hands, the generality of
> mankind must of course give up the point; but luckily, we may
> gain no little insight into their method of considering nature;
> and no inconsiderable share of their relish for her beauties, by
> an easier process – by studying their works.[91]

One lengthy addition to the *Essay on Architecture and Buildings* was in the form of a note concerning Richard Payne Knight's publication of the second edition of his *Analytical Inquiry*. Price's preface states that a long note had been added to the second volume 'in consequence of a very pointed attack from my friend Mr. Knight, in the second edition of the Analytical Inquiry'. This note was 'almost a controversial dissertation on the temple of Vesta, usually called the Sybill's Temple, at Tivoli'.[92] George Dance had told Farington that he had received a 'letter from Sir George Beaumont inclosing one from Uvedale Price, accompanied with 14 pages of manuscript of an answer to certain passages in Payne Knight's Analytical Enquiry, respecting the Sybil's Temple at Tivoli … . On the whole, Dance after reading Prices observations sd. "What stuff it is".'[93] In the 1810 Preface to his *Essays* Price noted that he had made 'one addition to the Dialogue, of a few *last* words, by way of summing up the points of the controversy, and likewise an appendix, which, like the note just mentioned, was occasioned by some strictures of Mr. Knight's, and almost equals it in length'. He continued

> I am still very largely in his debt, on Mr. Burke's, as well as on
> my own account: and am ashamed of being so long in arrears.
> However slow, I hope at last to leave nothing unpaid; but as I
> have undertaken the defence of such a man as Mr. Burke, I feel
> anxious that it should be as little unworthy of him, as it is in
> my power to make it.[94]

The new edition was discussed at length in the *Quarterly Review* of November 1810. The review noted that 'Mr. Price's opinions have been a considerable time before the public; and if all have not been convinced by his theory, few have failed to receive gratification from the justness of his taste and ingenuity of his remarks.'[95] It argued that the word 'picturesque' should be 'used as an analogical term, not as an essential quality' and favoured Dugald Stewart's views on beauty by association over those of Price. However, the reviewer liked the 'animation' of Price's style, which helped to make 'his book a delightful companion to such as have an acquaintance with paintings, an eye for improvement, or even a taste for rural scenery'.[96] The book was not noticed in the *Edinburgh Review*, but a review of Dugald Stewart's *Philosophical Essays* of 1810 reports that Stewart argued that

> where the objects, which Mr Price has denominated picturesque, are not singly entitled to the appellation of beautiful, they will generally be found to deserve that title, by aiding the impression and effect of adjoining beauties – by the pleasing associations with which they are connected – and by the new sources, as it were, of poetical interest, which they open to the imagination.[97]

The following year, the Edinburgh reviewer considered Archibald Alison's *Essays on the Nature and Principles of Taste* of 1811 to be 'the best and most pleasing work which has yet been produced on the subjects of Taste and Beauty. Less ornate and adventurous than Burke, and less lively and miscellaneous than Price or Knight, the author, we think, has gone deeper into his subject than any of those writers.'[98]

CHAPTER 8

'DISTANT PATHS OF LEAFY SECRETNESS'

WORDSWORTH

Although Price would have known the poetry of Wordsworth and Coleridge earlier, he first heard of their friendship with the Beaumonts in 1803. The Beaumonts had met the Coleridges in lodgings at Greta Hall, Keswick. Price told Sir George that

> Both your's + Lady Beaumont's account of your new poetical
> friends makes me very desirous of being known to them
> whenever an opportunity may offer itself. I had heard that M[r]
> Coleridge was supposed to be tainted with democracy; – what
> you suspect is probably true, that there has been in this, as in
> other cases of the same kind, a good deal of exaggeration.

He felt that many who had been 'tainted' with democratic ideas had since become 'completely cured', as 'luckily the French, without intending it, have administered an antidote not less strong than their poison.' He then taunted Sir George by emphasising that 'As M[r] Coleridge, however he may have been wronged or cured, was under strong suspicion, I acknowledge very willingly your claim of being a liberal fellow.'[1] Over the next two years they became regular topics in their correspondence. He joked about the subject of Coleridge's new poem, telling Lady Beaumont that 'I am naturally anxious about my own immortality', and thanked her for sending him a transcription of a 'part of a letter from Miss Wordsworth, which I read with much pleasure'.[2] Price with Lady Beaumont discussed some of Wordsworth's poems before they were published. In 1806 he emphasised the 'perverse judgment' of Brown and 'any of his followers' in their inability to suffer 'the least variation from the established plan' in landscaping by quoting 'For Daisies will be Daisies still' from *Foresight, or the Charge of a Child to his younger Companion*. This poem was composed on 28 April 1802, but not published until 1807.[3]

William Wordsworth provided a detailed description of Price at Foxley in the autumn of 1810. Wordsworth wrote to Sir George Beaumont that

> when in Wales last autumn I contrived to pass a day and a half
> with your friend Price at Foxley. He was very kind and took
> due pains to shew me all the beauties of his place. I should

have been very insensible not to be pleased with, and grateful for, his attentions; and certainly I was gratified by the sight of the scenes through which he conducted me.

However, Wordsworth was

not in a kindly or genial state of mind while Mr Price was taking so many friendly pains for my entertainment. His daughter put me out of tune by her strange speech, looks and manners; and then, unluckily, Fitzpatrick was there, a torch that once may have burnt bright, but is now deplorably dim. It was to me odd to see a host and a guest who appeared to have so little satisfaction in each other's company, and full as off to see a Host*ess* and a Guest so snugly and peaceably content with each other. But this looks like scandal, which is bad enough from the lip, but in a Letter is intolerable.[4]

Wordsworth was surprised about the close friendship between Lady Caroline and Richard Fitzpatrick, but his interpretation of this friendship, although supported by the gossip of Lord Egremont, is impossible to verify. Whatever the truth of his suspicions, Wordsworth found that 'These things deranged me' and that he was 'less able to do justice in my own mind to the scenery of Foxley'. But he went on to criticise Foxley with 'a strange fault … considering the acknowledged taste of the owner', namely that 'small as it is compared with hundreds of places, the Domain is too extensive for the character of the Country.' It lacked 'variety' as there was no 'rock and water'. Moreover 'in a district of this kind, the portion of a Gentleman's estate which he keeps exclusively to himself, and which he devotes wholly or in part to ornament, may very easily exceed the proper bounds, not indeed as to the preservation of wood, but most easily as to everything else.'

Wordsworth was here criticising Price's detailed estate management, which was designed to please the owner, with little regard for the variety of effect produced by everyday management. The very success of Price's consolidation of his estate at Foxley had, according to Wordsworth, reduced the interest of the landscape. He thought that

A man by little and little becomes so delicate and fastidious with respects to forms in scenery, where he has a power to exercise controul over them, that if they do not exactly please him in all moods, and every point of view, his power becomes his law; he banishes one, and then rids himself of another, impoverishing and monotonizing Landscapes, which, if not originally distinguished by the bounty of Nature, must be ill able to spare the inspiriting varieties which Art, and the occupations and wants of life in a country left more to itself never fail to produce. This relish of humanity Foxley wants, and is therefore to me, in spite of all its recommendations a melancholy spot.

Wordsworth then brought to mind Sir George Beaumont's

> Reubens ... that picture in your possession, where he has brought, as it were, a whole County into one Landscape, and made the most formal partitions of cultivation; hedge-rows of pollard willows conduct the eye into the depths and distances of his picture; and thus, more than by any other means, has given it that appearance of immensity which is so striking.[5]

This is the painting, ironically, which Price so admired. Wordsworth's bleak assessment of Price was later to be substantially modified. And it provides a startling contrast to Price's own published views in his *Essay on the Picturesque*. Remembering his uncle's estate, he recalls the cheerfulness of the scene and contrasts this to estates characterised by 'solitary grandeur.' Price is convinced that 'he who destroys dwellings, gardens and inclosures, for the sake of mere extent, and parade of property, only extends the bounds of monotony, and of dreary, selfish pride; but contracts those of variety, amusement and humanity.' Wordsworth seems to be arguing that Price had achieved at Foxley exactly the opposite of what he intended.[6]

The importance that Price put on gaining control over his landscape was given a precise monetary value in 1812. While Price was engaged in his philosophical debate and dispute with Richard Payne Knight he was also involved with a complicated exchange of land with Thomas Andrew Knight, who had taken over the management of his brother's estate.[7] This included land at Wormsley which adjoined Foxley. It is likely that Price will have discussed this issue with Wordsworth on his visit, and this will have coloured Wordsworth's adverse interpretation of the Foxley estate. A valuation of timber of 1812 shows that Price gained by exchange '87 Pollard Oak Trees; 31 Maiden Oak ditto; 6 Maiden Ash ditto; 9 Pollard Ash ditto; 2 Asp Trees; Sundry oak and Ash saplings etc.', but lost to Thomas Andrew Knight '5 Pollard Oaks; 15 Pollard Ash; 5 Maiden Oaks; 5 Maiden Ash; 23 Elm Timber Trees; Sundry Oak and Elm saplings etc.'.[8] Price told Sir George Beaumont that this exchange gave him 'new lands that are of real consequence to the beauty, connection and comfort of my place'.[9] Indeed, Samuel Birch Peploe, the owner of the Garnstone estate, which adjoined both Foxley and Wormsley, told Knight that Price had indicated that he 'was willing to give up to you in exchange, whatever was not absolutely necessary, in his view of it, to complete the wooded boundary of his property'.[10]

Thomas Andrew Knight took advantage of Price's determination to gain complete control and ownership of his view and his surveyor John Harris was instructed to value fields 'in view of Foxley' at a shilling per acre more than the agricultural value.[11] In the final articles of agreement for the exchange (1813) no extra value was put on land because of its location, but it was stated that:

In regard that some of those lands are in an uncultivated state and that the same have been for some time permitted to continue so by the said Thomas Andrew Knight at the request and for the accommodation of the said Uvedale Price It hath been agreed that such Lands shall be valued as if the same were in a fair and proper state of cultivation according to the nature of the Land but that nothing shall be charged for locality of situation.[12]

As Thomas Andrew took over the estate only in 1808/9 it likely that before the exchange Price had arranged with Richard Payne Knight that some of the latter's land should remain in an uncultivated state. The evidence of the timber valuations suggest that in all probability this was an area of old wood-pasture, as it had a high density of pollarded oaks. Price had therefore been able to extend his influence over the landscape of a portion of a neighbouring estate until an exchange of land brought it fully under his control. The comfortable arrangement established between Uvedale Price and Richard Payne Knight probably came to an end partially as a consequence of his younger brother's enthusiasm for agricultural improvement. However, it is certainly not impossible to see it as a not too distant consequence of the estrangement between Price and Richard Payne Knight.

The Prices continued to receive many visitors at Foxley. In 1810 Lord Aberdeen visited in August, not long before Wordsworth, as part of a tour which had been partially orchestrated by Price himself.[13] The young George Hamilton-Gordon (1784–1860), 4th earl of Aberdeen, had been a protégé of William Pitt (who had died earlier in 1806) and got to know Price in London after his marriage to Catherine Elizabeth (1784–1812), the daughter of Price's friend Lord Abercorn, in 1805. Lord Aberdeen's enthusiasm for Greek architecture and literature made him a convivial intellectual correspondent for Price. Price encouraged Aberdeen to visit south Wales and in so doing demonstrated a considerable knowledge of the 'sights' around Neath and Swansea.[14] The following August, Fitzpatrick and Lord Ossory[15] were expected at Foxley, and there was the usual persuasion and bartering between Price and the Beaumonts as to whom should visit whom, with Price hoping that the Beaumonts would visit with Wordsworth and Dance.[16] In 1812 he abandoned plans to visit Lord Ashburnham at Ashburnham in Sussex because of the complexity of his negotiations with Thomas Andrew Knight over the land exchange.[17]

In May 1812 Wordsworth and 'Mr Price the Picturesque … went to see some pictures of Lord Dunstanville's:[18] among others some very accurate copies of some of the most celebrated Works of Raphael in the Vatican.'[19] A fortnight later, the day after one of Coleridge's lectures, Samuel Rogers held a dinner at which the guests included Wordsworth, Uvedale and Lady Caroline Price and their two children. Wordsworth told Mary Wordsworth he found Robert Price to be a 'very well looking and agreeable Young Man' with whom he could discuss the management of his brother-in-law's farm at Hindwell,

Radnorshire. However, 'Nothing could be more deplorable than the rest of the Party: Miss p. – a little deformed Creature, with a most strange enunciation, sitting by Mr Jekyll[20] a celebrated Wit, and quite pert and to use a coarse word ever rampant upon him.' He agreed with Sir George Beaumont that she was 'in expression of countenance and manner just like the bad Sister who does all the Mischief in a Faery tale'. Moreover, 'Lady Caroline was coquetting away with General Fitzpatrick her old Paramour, who is a most melancholy object, with a complection as yellow as a frog, a tall emaciated Figure and hobbling with the gout. He creeps abroad yet, poor Man, and may fairly be said to have one foot in the grave.' Wordsworth concluded by observing that it was 'lamentable' to see

> poor Price overgorging himself at dinner as he did, and falling
> into a lethargic sleep immediately after, from which he had
> not power to preserve himself two minutes together. This was
> truly a piteous sight for Price is a man of genuine talents, and
> gifted by Nature with a firm Constitution which he is
> destroying by gluttony.[21]

A second letter a couple of days later to Dorothy Wordsworth and Sara Hutchinson reinforces Wordsworth's views of the Prices. Robert Price was 'a truly agreeable young man, but his sister one of the most odious little creatures in the world ...'. Uvedale Price was

> killing himself by overloading his stomach in eating; he
> becomes quite comatose in Mr De Quincey's word, immediately
> after Dinner, that is falls into a death like sleep, and I have no
> doubt that he is all day long terribly uncomfortable in his
> stomach; a warning for me and I will take it.

He thought General Fitzpatrick was 'dying of the Gout', noting 'he has been a most debauched man, and will be little regretted'.[22] Others commented on Price's health at this time. Sir George Beaumont reported that Sir Joseph Banks considered 'Mr. Payne Knight' was 'the person who of all others regulated Himself the best so as to have as much indulgence of every appetite as His constitution would bear witht. suffering injury from it. He would eat, He wd. drink as far as consideration for His health wd. admit but never exceed so as to suffer from it. – Mr Uvedale Price on the contrary sd. Sir George, has not that self command & feels the disadvantage arising from the want of it.'[23]

ILLNESS AND HUMOUR

Whether Wordsworth's strictures and claiming of the moral high ground are entirely justified is a moot point. He found the presence at social events of the Prices' daughter, with her strange looks and lengthy bouts of illness, jarring and unpleasant. A more liberal interpretation would be that the Price family gathered round and assisted their sensitive daughter and refused to hide her away at home, or in a private institution. The criticisms of Price's gluttony cannot be taken with a pinch of salt, however, and it is certainly worth considering the evidence for Price's health. Luckily he was not averse to discussing in detail his various illnesses with his correspondents, and he usually does this in an amusing and self-deprecatory manner. Sarah Jones described Price as being ill and very thin in the early years of the century and this is confirmed by Price, who told Sir George in August 1800 of severe problems with his stomach:

> I have been much worse within these few days + am now under the strictest discipline; I am confined to one sort of plain meal, + that in small quantity. I begged hard as you imagine, for a bit of pudding, which has been granted; it is however to be a very small <u>peice</u>, + not a plum or currant in it, as to fruit, either raw or in tarts, 'Why poison is not half so bad'.

He complains that he has been told that 'I must not expose myself to the sun, or heat myself in any way, + my Physician threatens me, like Moliere's Monsr Purgon, that if I disobey him in one little, I shall fall "de la bradypepsie dans la dyspepsie de la dyspepsie dans l'apepsie".' He concludes:

> Dont imagine, because I write in this jocular manner about my illness, that my illness is a joke; I could have given a very dismal + true detail of all I have suffer'd but I think for my own sake + certainly for your's, it is better to turn the whole to farce, than to write a tragedy.[24]

Things had not improved a few weeks later: 'My Doctor thought he should set me up in a fortnight after I had taken his medicines, + pursued his regimen; + ever since I have been like an Accouchèe who longs for her month to be up that she may go again to plays, operas, concerts, balls Masquerades +ca.' In the three weeks since his last letter he had

> undergone pretty severe discipline, for as there were some apprehensions of my liver being affected I had a blister ordered me, which I believe was a good deal larger than the Doctor intended; + having put it on negligently without securing it in one place, it chose to travel about, + you may imagine what work the spanish flies made when they had the range of my whole side.

Spanish flies was a term for the dried beetle *Cantharis vesicatoria*, which was used externally as a rubefacient and vesicant in this period. Price continued

> The discharge from this wide wound, added to the other evacuations that were thought necessary to prepare me for

strengthening medicines, made those medicines very
necessary indeed: all this too in such a continuance of hot
weather as never was known I believe in this island. I have of
course lost a good deal of flesh + of strength.

He admitted that this was 'a dismal account of myself', but he was 'really
thankful, considering the condition of my stomach + the unremitting heat of
the weather, that I have escaped having a serious illness'. He stressed that
'there never was so kind a comforter in sickness', as with Lady Caroline as a
nurse 'it makes it almost worth while to be ill.'[25]

The repeated problems with his stomach suggest that Price may have been
suffering from ulcers of some sort. This would also explain his need to eat at
unusual times, as a full stomach was one way of reducing the crippling pain.
But he also suffered from other ailments. In 1801, following a visit to the
Bowles's at North Aston, where he met up with the Beaumonts, he suffered a
severe attack of rheumatism.

I could scarcely crawl from chair to chair about my room,
where I was close prisoner; being no more able to get up +
down stairs, than to scale Snowdon. The chief pain was in my
right hip, but I could neither lay on that, nor on my left side
for two minutes, without great pain.

He then made it worse by getting treatment.

I had heard that cupping was good in such cases, + sent to a
very expert surgeon in Hereford who did not come until I was
in bed, + arrayed as usual on my back: when the inhuman
dog, after complimenting on my bearing pain remarkably well,
turned me on my left hip which of itself was great agony, +
then upon the tenderest part of the right hip clapt one glass,
pumping + pressing upon it, + then a second, + then a third;
he left them on a little, with the weight of the atmosphere on
them; then forced them off, scarified them all, + then clapt
them all on + fell a-pumping again.

The pain was agonising and the 'next day I felt worse than before, from the
effect of the pressure, but I believe the operation was of use, + I am now
tolerably upright'. However, as one illness improved, another returned: he did
not know whether 'there is any connection between the Rheumatism + the
Dyspepsia (a hard word for indigestion) but certainly my stomach is worse since
my hip is got better.'[26]

In 1803 he gave a full, excruciating, yet enormously entertaining
description of an attack of piles:

This will probably be a short letter as I am writing rather ill at
ease both from pain + the position in which I am forced to

write, being that in which the old Romans chose to eat. This inveterate enemy has attacked me cæcâ rabie, which in this case is worse than rabie cruenta:[27] in plain english I have had the blind piles for these last six days.

He wonders whether Sir George has any 'idea what sort of a disorder it is' and goes on:

> You know by description what it is to be empaled: this is not so bad as it does not go such lengths, but it is a pretty specimen of the first stage of it. You will really have a very exact idea of the piles when at the worst if you suppose the whole orifice of the anus filled, + stretched out by a burning plug; le n'est pas tout; this plug has a sort of machinery within it by means of which it darts out every now + then little sharp needles, on each side: it is likewise furbished with a kind of pepper box probably filled with Cayenne, which it keeps shaking on the outside of the orifice while the needles are going in + out on the inside. Which two operations it performs at the same time as readily by practice, as those who are used to it can pat one side, + rub the other.

He concludes this agonising description by hoping that Sir George 'will never learn from your own experience how exact this account is'.[28]

Price's diverse illnesses continued to plague him throughout his life, and often caused him to cancel proposed visits. In 1805, for example, he told Sir George that 'The Academy dinner must go on as well as it can without me, for although, as you see, I can manage to write a little, I cannot cut my own meat.' He went on that 'it is true that Knight is generally placed next to me, but there is no trial of friendship I should not sooner put him to than that of cutting another man's meat when he ought to be eating his own.' He was also concerned that the marquis of Abercorn

> in his most eager + cordial manner should seize my right hand, + give me a hearty welcome! As it is, I doubt much whether I shall ever recover the use of my finger. I am at present totally unable to shut my hand; the lower joint I am told may recover it's action, but the upper one, where the swelling + inflammation was, I fear is a poker for life.[29]

Together with his daughter's state of health, these illnesses and accidents encouraged Price to limit his visits to friends across the country and to London, although sometimes they may well have been a convenient excuse for staying at home.

MEMORIALS AND GARDENS

The death of Charles James Fox in September 1806 was a blow to Price, who wrote later of their 'private friendship begun in my very early youth'. Both his friends Richard Fitzpatrick and Robert Spencer were at Fox's side when he died at Chiswick House. Price also developed new friendships and correspondents including Mary Berry (1763–1852), the confidante and literary editor of Horace Walpole (whose circle included Princess Caroline, Joanna Baillie and Mme de Staël). At the end of 1812 Price wrote an ode on the burning of Moscow and circulated it to friends including Lord Aberdeen, Richard Payne Knight and Miss Berry. He told Miss Berry: 'it was composed almost entirely sub Dio and sub Jove frigido, and ancle deep in snow; for it was exactly during the fortnight or three weeks that the snow lay on the ground before Christmas.' He explained that

> I was then very busy, marking and cutting in a wood at some
> distance; and sometimes I drew forth my hacker (for I carry
> my Durindana in a scabbard), and sometimes my paper; now
> gave a coup de hache, and then a coup de crayon; and in this
> manner 'I built the lofty rhyme.' Thus far, indeed, the state of
> the weather and the ground might be of use to me, as I could
> paint dal vero (tho' heaven be praised, from a very diminutive
> scale), the icy blast, the trackless snow, the piercing cold ...[30]

Price considered that the subject of his ode 'is certainly a very fine one; the principal actor one of the most extraordinary men 'that ever lived on the tide of times', the burning of Moscow one of the most extraordinary, unexpected, and striking events that ever took place'. He hoped that Miss Berry would show it to Mrs Damer and 'my friend Sir Harry Englefield'. He noted that he had also sent copies to Richard Fitzpatrick and to Samuel Rogers and that 'One circumstance mentioned in these verses is strikingly confirmed by what my nephew Ld Tyrconnel was an eye-witness of: he saw the late governor of Moscow set fire to his own magnificent palace.'[31] The ode concludes with a celebration of Charles James Fox, but Price told Lord Aberdeen that Richard Payne Knight 'though a friend of Fox's, + upon the whole, friendly to his politics' was 'not satisfied with the conclusion'. Knight thought it was

> perhaps impossible to descend to the praises of an Individual,
> however splendid + illustrious, from a matter of such vast +
> general moment, without the descent being felt as such' and
> that 'a brief + vigorous sketch of the general blessings of
> peace, would afford a more spirited + brilliant conclusion.'

Price's praise for Fox is in the last six lines of the 'Ode to Moscow':

> Europe regret, + ne'er forget
> The Man, who War's oerwhelming stream
> Still firm to oppose, undaunted rose:
> But when a dawn of peace appeard to beam –

His sun untimely set; + Fate laid low
Humanity's best friend, Oppressor's steadiest foe.

Price thought that Knight 'may be right' and it was probable that his friendship with Fox 'may have induced me to pay this tribute to Fox's memory, not less than motives of a public nature'. Price thought that

> Whether, if he had lived longer with restored health he would
> have been able to make a secure + lasting peace, must be
> very doubtful; but upon the supposition that in spite of all
> difficulties both at home + abroad he could have
> accomplished it, his death must be considered as one of the
> most fated events that could happen: for from that time to the
> present, more dreadful scenes of human slaughter + misery
> have been presented to the world, than perhaps were ever
> witnessed during the same period.

He had started the poem with Napoleon, who was

> the military despot, the great scourge + oppressor of
> mankind, [and] I thought I could not do better than end it
> with the opposite character of a mild and humane statesman,
> + who I believe is allowed by all to have been most truly, +
> from his most inmost heart + feelings a friend to Humanity, +
> an enemy to every species of tyranny + oppression.

On a more practical point he told Aberdeen that 'in any case, having shewn the ode to some of Fox's warmest friends, I could not change the conclusion even if I were inclined to do it.'[32]

Tantalisingly, it is not known whether the Prices met Lord Byron on his several lengthy visits to Lord and Lady Oxford at Eywood in 1812 and 1813, when the latter became Byron's mistress. The Prices certainly regularly visited the Oxfords. In October 1812 Byron told Lady Melbourne that 'The Country round this place is wild & beautiful, consequently very delightful' but he was laid up because he had 'received a blow with a stone thrown by accident' by one of Lady Oxford's sons as he was 'viewing the remains of a Roman encampment'.[33] Byron was so delighted by the countryside, and by Lady Oxford, that he arranged to take Kinsham Court, a house owned by Lord Oxford near Presteign, for the following year.[34] However, the break-up of his relationship with Lady Oxford in 1813 meant that this plan came to nothing.

Price continued to be an avid visitor to exhibitions and found in Lord Aberdeen a welcome companion. He hoped to go 'picture hunting' with Lord Aberdeen again and complained of the lack of 'virgin pictures' and the distrust dealers had of people 'with too curious an eye', and was interested in Lord Kinnaird's sale of Titian and Rubens.[35] Price still attended as many concerts as possible and reported to Miss Berry that he turned down an invitation from Robert Spencer to meet Mme de Staël at his house because he wanted to go to a concert 'which, in spite of my passion for music, I should have given up, but it was not only a very choice one, but one to which Lady Douglas[36] was, as a great favour, allowed to carry me'.[37] The joke here was that Lady Douglas was well known for her exceptional laziness.

Price was pleased to be able to attend the exhibition of Sir Joshua Reynolds' paintings at the British Institution in June 1813. He had known Reynolds and later told Samuel Rogers an anecdote about a trip down the river Wye from Monmouth to Chepstow.

> I asked him whether he was not very much struck with the
> inside of Tintern Abbey at the opening of the door. 'I believe,'
> he said, 'it is very striking, but I was so taken up with the
> groups of begging figures round the door, and their look of
> want and wretchedness, that I could not take my eyes from
> them.' The fact is, that he did not care very much about
> landscape of any kind in nature, and had only a high relish for
> it in the works of the greatest masters, particularly in the
> backgrounds of Titian.[38]

Price was seen at the exhibition with Sir George and Lady Beaumont by Farington.[39] Sir George had seen the urn dedicated to Pope on a visit to Lord Lyttleton's Hagley and this inspired him to celebrate Reynolds' life and work at Coleorton in a similar manner. The urn, later shown in John Constable's *The Cenotaph* (1836), was to be approached by an avenue of newly planted lime trees. Wordsworth wrote an inscription for Sir George 'and in his name, for an urn, placed by him at the termination of a newly-planted avenue'.[40]

> YE Lime-trees, ranged before this hallowed Urn,
> Shoot forth with lively power at Spring's return;
> And be not slow a stately growth to rear
> Of pillars, branching off from year to year,
> Till they have learned to frame a darksome aisle;–
> That may recall to mind that awful Pile
> Where Reynolds, 'mid our country's noblest dead,
> In the last sanctity of fame is laid.
> –There, though by right the excelling Painter sleep
> Where Death and Glory a joint sabbath keep,
> Yet not the less his Spirit would hold dear
> Self-hidden praise, and Friendship's private tear:
> Hence, on my patrimonial grounds, have I
> Raised this frail tribute to his memory;
> From youth a zealous follower of the Art
> That he professed; attached to him in heart;
> Admiring, loving, and with grief and pride
> Feeling what England lost when Reynolds died.

Price, ever practical, was concerned that the avenue trees would grow too quickly and that the

> two rows of limes which conduct to Sir Joshua's urn are so
> near each other, that as they seem disposed to obey
> Wordsworths practical command, they will certainly, instead
> of an embowering arch, or gothic aile, form on the inside a
> mere mass of boughs + leaves; while on the outside, the
> branches will be forced outwards from want of room within,
> + consequently the avenue will be all sides, + no middle.

Price also told Sir George that the lime trees would grow into some 'very fine oaks' and 'spoil all the beauty of their forms'. To get over this problem he thought that one row of limes should be removed, but accepted that his suggestion would be not be received favourably and that 'nothing of course could be decided without the consent + approbation of Wordsworth + indeed with all my love for the oaks, I should be sorry that any alteration should interfere with such beautiful verses.' He argued, however, that if he remembered right 'Wordsworth only mentions limes in general + makes no allusion to two rows, in which case the limes will equally suit a single row' and recommended 'a very ancient single row of limes' at Lord Bridgewater's Ashridge as a model.[41]

Price frequently reported on the estates he passed by on his travels to his correspondents. On one journey from Coleorton to Foxley he was able to take in four estates in addition to Kenilworth Castle. The first, between Asbhy de la Zouch and Measham, was owned by Sir Charles Hastings. He spotted it by its 'long line of plantation' which was along the main road. This plantation was 'an unfortunate one for the traveller, as in a year or two it will completely hide the whole of the distance'. Price thought 'a few of the trees in particular parts' should be removed to allow distant views to 'be shown to great advantage + be form'd into many very pleasing compositions'. Further along the road there was another belt of trees hiding Gopsall Hall 'that interrupts much finer compositions; but as it belongs to Baroness Howe the destroyer of Pope's garden at Twickenham, there are no hopes'. She had bought Pope's villa at Twickenham in 1807 and demolished it in 1808 being inconvenienced by the visitors to the garden and grotto. Gopsall Hall itself had previously been owned by Charles Jennens, the librettist of *The Messiah*, and Handel had been a frequent visitor. From these two examples Price made the general points that it was 'an odd sort of contradiction, that while Improvers are so anxious to have their places admired by the traveller, the first thing they do is to prevent him as much as possible from seeing any part of it'. They usually did this, at the same time 'spoiling the inside of their own place', in a Brownian manner, 'by means of a thick uniform boundary'. He argues that while the 'Improvers plea, at least one of them' is that the belts provided seclusion, and that this was 'extremely desirable' near the house, it was not so 'at the extremity of the place', where 'the openings required would scarcely interfere with it.'

The third estate visited was Mr Newdigate's at Arbury. Its owner had inherited it from Sir Roger Newdigate (1719–1806), the colliery owner, antiquary, MP for Oxford and founder of the Newdigate Prize for English verse. Price dismissed the 'place' as 'nothing, the house lies low, + has little effect, + after driving half round it, the entrance is by a stable yard surrounded with high walls'. However, 'on passing through a door into the garden the change is very striking.' Lord Aylesford had recommended the house 'as a good specimen of Gothic' but Price was especially taken with the trees in the garden and the way in which they complemented the house:

> there are a number of Cedars + other exotics of a large size,
> very well disposed, which have had full room to grow without
> being too separate: + the enriched turrets, projecting
> windows + porches of the house, are seen under their boughs
> + variously combined with them from many points.

Moreover, in a

> retired part of the Garden there is a very old avenue (if it may
> be so called) of limes, between the two rows of which there is
> a canal, not very broad but of clear water, this avenue appears
> to me exactly of the proper length + breadth, + forms a
> noble arch over the canal: both the rows have had full room to
> spread on the outer sides + make two fine shady walks.

He thought that the walk on the 'garden side of the water is remarkably solemn' and showed that 'a single strait row of trees may accord with opposite trees, such as those in the garden, irregularly disposed, + of various kinds.' Unfortunately, even the charms of the garden at Arbury had been blighted by unnecessary improvement. Price thought that the walk under a fine cedar towards the avenue 'must have been uncommonly solemn before it was injured (I should suppose since Sir Rogers death) by placing a sort of Chinese seat with a sopha + cushions so as to hide the trunk of the outermost + largest lime.' To make matters worse, 'a vista has been cut to open a view from the seat, which lets in the light full upon it: as you know how apt I am to be irritated by any glare, you may imagine what such a glare must have done.' The final stop on this epic short tour was Mr Greathead's at Guy's Cliff near Warwick, where

> they were just come home + pressed us to dine + sleep
> there, which, though we wish'd to get on, we could not
> refuse: it was lucky for ourselves + still more so for our
> horses that we did so, for the weather was broiling in the day
> + quite suffocating in the evening.

Price told Sir George that 'you positively must see it next time you go that road' but he was 'too tired of writing' to tell Sir George about it, so he may imagine 'the Avon, + cliffs, + trees, + mills +ca, +ca, + arrange them according to your fancy'. The Prices had looked over it 'with very great pleasure: it is on a very small scale, but a little gem.'[42]

Price's *Essays* continued to stimulate wider practical application of his ideas on the picturesque than could be achieved by personal visits and advice. Sir Walter Scott was strongly influenced by Price in his landscaping at Abbotsford in 1813 and he told Lady Abercorn of his extensive tree plantings: 'Forest trees flourish with me at a great rate, and of my whole possession of 120 acres I have reduced about 70 to woodland, both upon principles of taste and economy.' He reported that he had

> been studying Price with all my eyes, and not without hopes
> of converting an old gravel-pit into a bower, and an exhausted
> quarry into a bathing house. So you see, my dear Madam, how
> deeply I am bit with the madness of the picturesque, and if
> your Ladyship hears that I have caught a rheumatic fever in
> the gravel pit, or have drowned in the quarry, I trust you will
> give me credit for dying a martyr to taste.[43]

At the same time he wrote to Joanna Baillie in Hampstead about the work of his man John Winnos, whose 'serious employments are ploughing, harrowing, and overseeing all my premises'. Scott said 'I cannot help singing his praises at this moment, because I have so many old and out-of-the-way things to do, that I believe the conscience of many of our jog-trot countrymen would revolt at being made my instrument in sacrificing good corn-land to the visions of Mr Price's theory.'[44] A few years later, Scott named Price in *Heart of Midlothian*: 'Not indeed beautiful ... but intricate, perplexed, or to use Mr Price's appropriate phrase, picturesque.'[45]

From around 1813 to 1816 Price was working on 'a "Comparative View" of the different opinions respecting visible beauty; other kinds of beauty will of course be often considered, but chiefly in the way of illustration'.[46] He asked several friends, including Miss Berry, for advice, and debated the topic with Lord Aberdeen at some length. Indeed, as he never published this work, the letters to Lord Aberdeen form the principal record of this period of study. He considered Hogarth's *Analysis of Beauty* to be the first book in English on the subject and although 'Many things in it have been laughed at, and are open to ridicule', considered it to contain 'a number of just and original observations, and Burke's theory is in a great degree taken from it, though he has not acknowledged his obligations'. He told Miss Berry that the principal writers after Hogarth and Burke were

> Knight, Dugald Stewart, and Alison, at least I know of no
> others. Alison's theory is at present the most popular; partly I
> believe from its being very flattering to the spiritual part of
> our nature, and partly from its having been very highly spoken
> of, and very ingeniously explained and illustrated, in the
> 'Edinburgh Review' of 1811.

Knight had told Price in a letter 'to set me down as a blockhead' if he did not 'cut up "The Sublime and Beautiful" root and branch', giving Price a 'strong hint that he should serve mine the same sauce'. But Price thought that 'Mr. Alison's theory will be found on examination, in many essential points, more like the baseless fabric of a vision than the strong-based promontory.' He told Miss Berry that he did not 'deny, or do not feel and acknowledge in its fullest extent, the powerful influence of association; I only question the exclusive influence which has been attributed to it.'[47] He went on to ask if there have been later editions of Alison than 1790, and whether Madame de Staël knew of any thing in French on the subject.

In the same letter he reminded Mary Berry of 'that exquisite poem I once read to you' by Fitzpatrick that had 'settled the matter most judiciously' and that 'one might almost think that he had these metaphysicians in view when he makes the Soul say to the Body,

> Yet trust me, I'm willing to waive all dispute;
> For though certain grave doctors, by few understood,
> Think they flatter me much when they call you a brute,
> Those who wish to divide us can mean us no good'.[48]

Fitzpatrick lived in retirement at Beech Grove, Sunninghill, where the Wells had been popular in the late seventeenth and early eighteenth century.[49] According to a late nineteenth-century account he remained a 'gay old chap' but his 'tastes … took a milder turn; he amused himself with botany, and enjoyed the quiet social intercourse with his charming neighbours so near him – the most enviable time of his life.' The Prices regularly stayed with Fitzpatrick, and the place of Lady Caroline was, at least according to a 90-year-old parishioner reporting in 1890, 'a very equivocal one'.[50] However, when Fitzpatrick died in 1813 and left Beech Grove and adjoining property to Lady Caroline for life, the trustees were Uvedale Price and Robert Price and the Prices continued to stay there. Richard Fitzpatrick wrote 'My own Epitaph', which is on his tomb in the churchyard at Sunninghill:[51]

> Whose turn is next? This monitory stone
> Replies, vain passenger, perhaps thy own.
> If idly curious, thou wilt seek to know
> Whose relics mingle with the dust below.
> Enough to tell thee that his destined span
> On earth he dwelt – and like thyself a man.
> Nor distant far th' inevitable day
> When thou, poor mortal, shalt like him be clay.
> Through life he walk'd unemulous of fame,
> Content if friendship o'er his humble bier
> Drop but the heartfelt tribute of a tear;
> Though countless ages should unconscious glide,
> Nor learn that he ever had lived or died.

The Prices were reading Madame de Staël's D'Allemagne[52] in 1814. Both Miss Berry and Lord Holland had asked Price whether he had read the book in the winter, and he reported to Miss Berry in March that 'My neighbour Peploe, who had read it, called upon me just as I had received it. He told me the first volume was highly entertaining; the second less so, though still very amusing; the third very abstruse, and not very entertaining.' He told Price that 'the subject of the third volume was distinct from those of the other two, being entirely on German philosophy.' Price said that

> Lady Caroline and my daughter having eagerly seized on the
> first volume, I began with the third, in which I found so many
> new and striking thoughts and reflections, that, in order to
> recollect and dwell upon them again, I marked them as I went
> on, and a pretty task I set myself!

Referring to his work on Beauty, Price said that although he had been 'obliged to write on metaphysical subjects, mine is not a very metaphysical head, and there are parts of the third volume out of my depth; but whenever I met with anything of that kind, I satisfied myself with applying that excellent maxim, il faut comprendre l'incompréhensible comme tel ... .'[53] He had now completed the three volumes and was going to read the whole through again, but 'As far as I can judge, her thoughts are not less just than brilliant. It must be owned, however, that one is not a very accurate judge.' Most of Price's writing on beauty to Lord Aberdeen, however, did not draw on modern German philosophy, but concentrated rather on an examination of the idea of beauty in ancient Greece, particularly as shown in the study of Homer. He also commented on Aberdeen's views on architecture in his introduction to William Wilkins's edition of *Vitruvius* of 1812.[54]

Price continued to visit London – usually on his own, often staying at Sunning Hill – and friends around the country, including Lord Ashburnham in 1814. His scholarly correspondents included Dr Parr of Hatton, with whom he discussed beauty; they had met at the Greatheads' at Guy's Cliffe in Warwickshire.[55] Parr, who had formerly been a schoolmaster at Harrow, was well known for his propensity to flog children but also had a high reputation as a Latin scholar and had been an avid supporter of Charles James Fox and Joseph Priestley.[56] In Herefordshire, the historian and agricultural writer John Duncumb obtained the vicarage of Mansel Lacy in 1815 from Uvedale Price, although he continued to live in Hereford.[57] The Prices frequently visited neighbours in the county. In March 1816, for example, Mrs Mary Westfalling of Rudhall, Ross, wrote to her friend the Rev. John Webb of Tretire that she was

> expecting Mr Price Lady Caroline, &c this Week. the Clive's
> meet them here Tuesday, + leave me on Thursday; on which
> day it wou'd be estee'd the greatest favor if you wou'd join
> the remaining party ... . I know how much pleasure Mr Price
> will have in your Company, + you in his, there is no one I
> could ask who wou'd be so agreeable to him as yourself no
> flattery.[58]

A SUSCEPTIBILITY TO POETICAL *IMPRESSIONS*[59]

For much of 1815–17 Price was rather ill. On 22 March 1815 he 'received a blow on my eye from a chip of some wood I was cutting'. He at first thought that his sight was damaged, as 'for two days I could see nothing definitely with it, but all appeared confused as through a jelly.' He told Lord Aberdeen 'I am at all times tolerably impatient of confinement' and was 'insulted + tantalised the whole time (almost 3 weeks) with perpetual sunshine, which glared most tormentingly in spite of shutters'. As he was unable to read or write and hardly able to talk 'my only resource, but really a very great one, was that of repeating to myself all the lines I could recollect in Homer, Virgil, Horace +c +c'; without 'this inward library I should have died of pure ennui'. As usual he made fun of himself, saying that he would have been

> very much ashamed of exhibiting myself to any but my own
> family, as my <u>costume</u> during this visitation was not very
> becoming, + not a little ludicrous, as I was forced to wear a sort
> of Fools-cap, from which a green silk shade hung over my eye, +
> a little further back a longer lappet of flannel over my ear.

This accident caused long-term problems and in the following year he consulted the leading eye expert Sir William Adams. He often had to rest and, not being able to read or work on his trees outside, found that reciting memorised poems was his main form of entertainment. One result of this was that he 'quitted all that I had been writing upon, + begun, – but merely a sort of hors d'oevre, on a totally new subject … . On our most barbarous manner of pronouncing greek and latin poetry'.[60]

This became the main focus of his writing for the rest of his life, and he never published his additional work on beauty and the sublime. Sir George Beaumont told Wordsworth that Price was working on 'the mistakes we make in pronouncing the works of the Greek + Latin Poets, mangling the metre and destroying the harmony'. He wondered 'how his pursuits have qualified him for this investigation' but added 'I think it quite impossible for him to take up any thing without shewing much ingenuity + acuteness of remark.'[61] In fact, Price appears to have been spurred on to this topic by discussions with Knight over many years. Knight had published his essay on the Greek alphabet in which he expressed concern over the pronunciation of Greek letters in 1792. Certainly Price had developed his ideas considerably since telling Lady Beaumont early in 1805 that 'Knight came here just before he left the country, + read to me a later dissertation he has written on Homer + on the Iliad + Odyssey.' This piece was later to become Knight's *Carmina, Homerica Ilias et Odyssea*, first published in 1808. Price's next comment, however, is particularly interesting. He says that 'as far as I could judge from hearing a thing read out to me in a language I am not much in the habit of reading, + never of hearing, I should think it a very ingenious dissertation.' From that time onwards he had begun to think very seriously about how Greek and Latin should be pronounced.[62] But Price was beginning to be concerned about Knight's health. He told Lord Aberdeen that 'Knight has absolutely given up his numerous friends on this side of the county: he says he is too old to ride, + cannot endure a carriage: his excuse we think a very flimsy one; but we all very much regret him.' Price was particularly concerned 'as he was my first preceptor on the subject of accent quantity +c, + I am extremely desirous of shewing him what I have written + of talking it over with him.'[63]

Price's health remained problematic: he had stayed at Cheltenham in 1816 and when Farington dined with Sir Thomas Lawrence and Robert Smirke in February 1817 they discussed Price's unusual eating habits. Price was staying at Lord Somers's house Castle Ditch at Eastnor, Herefordshire. He would have discussed the layout of the grounds for the new Eastnor Castle, which was designed by Robert Smirke, the architect and son of the artist Robert Smirke, who had known Price for many years. While at the house he

> lived according to His own plan. He had breakfast carried to
> His own room abt. 8 oClock in the morning, and again at
> Eleven he breakfasted below stairs, after the time of the
> family breakfast. The bread He eat was brought by His own
> Servant from Foxley. At dinner he was so intent on the
> business of eating that he was impatient if any one put a
> question to Him; an interruption He cd. not bear.

Farington estimated, correctly, that Price was nearing 70.[64] Later in the year Price wrote to both Lady Beaumont and Lord Aberdeen of his illness and that he was unlikely to go to town that year. The illness restricted his movements: 'instead of roaming amidst my woods + thickets hacker in hand, I can only crawl about the gravel walks with the help of a stick; + if I prune the dead twig of a rose, I consider it a feat.'[65]

Wordsworth's *The Excursion* had been published in 1814 and Price sent a very detailed critique to Sir George and Lady Beaumont in March 1815. He agrees with them that 'a person who does not admire its various beauties, can have no taste for the sublime, the beautiful or the picturesque.' He also agreed that 'it is too contemplative to be generally popular; + indeed the author himself seems to have been aware of it, + prepared for such a consequence, when he says in his poetical preface "fit audience let me find, though few".' He thought that what is 'produced by such a mind as Wordsworth's on subjects of a lofty [or] of an abstruse nature, will not be relished, even if comprehended, by common minds'. Price was aware that the Beaumonts were 'partial to the author + anxious for his success' and agreed with them that the poem was in places too long but that 'this defect is amply compensated by the beauties of other parts.' He reminded them that 'in speaking to me of Wordsworth's + Coleridge's conversation, you said, "they are sometimes apt to get into the clouds, but one can bring them down with a whistle"', and then argued that when Wordsworth reaches the clouds 'without a whistler, he is so pleased to be in his balloon at such a height, that he is in no hurry to descend to earth; where the reader remains a little impatient from having totally lost sight of him'. Another criticism, perhaps a little rich coming from Price, who had made his reputation through an extremely detailed analysis of landscape, was that Wordsworth, through solitude, had developed 'a habit of analyzing + dwelling on the detail of every thing both visible + intellectual'. He reminded the Beaumonts that he had 'brought Wordsworth's two little volumes to you at Benarth, neither of you having ever seen them' and read to them 'the Woman in the red cloak'. They had been 'a good deal surprised at finding some 8 or 10 stanzas employed in describing a little tump of moss with a decayed stump of a thorn upon it'. Price concluded that

> the description itself is excellent; + such a microscopic kind of
> painting, whether of what we see outwardly, or feel inwardly, is
> very curious + amusing, but as few readers are flies, or have
> either microscopic eyes or minds, a propensity to analyzing is
> one that in poetry requires to be watched + restrained.[66]

The following year Price told Sir George that 'Wordsworth belongs to the Lakes' and asked him who was 'surrounded at Keswick by poets + painters + men of genius + talent' to tell

> Mr Wordsworth how much I wished him, on various accounts,
> to come into this part of the world; among others, I was
> anxious to consult him about a sort of <u>hors d'oeuvre</u> I have
> lately been employed upon: it is on our most barbarous
> manner of pronouncing greek + latin verses; a subject I have
> long had in my mind, + have at last given vent to in writing.[67]

But two years later he had still not sent Wordsworth his piece. He told Sir George that he was pleased Wordsworth had complained 'of my not having sent him this work of mine, which is still on the anvil: he shall have it whenever it is fit for his inspection, I shall feel very grateful for his criticisms.' In December 1818 Lady Beaumont sent him a manuscript copy of 'Wordsworth's highly poetical effusion'. He had

> strictly obeyed Lady Beaumont's orders; no copy has been
> taken of the MS, which I now return after reading it
> repeatedly. It requires some little portion of Wordsworth's
> enthusiasm, of his poetical manner of viewing the effects of
> nature to relish thoroughly what he has so finely painted to
> the mind's eye, + so enriched + embellished with a variety of
> striking + congenial images + reflexions.[68]

By early 1818 Price was much better, and started to work again on the creation of a 'picture gallery' of views from his wooded hills. He had been 'clearing underwood' and 'pruning high trees' to make 'picturesque compositions' and had 'been so busy in that way, + in one walk that I have lately been employed upon, have made such a number of these compositions, that a friend of mine jocosely called it my picture gallery; + the name has stuck to it'. There was also the excitement of his son's election campaign. Price defended his son's Whig politics to Sir George: 'my son is far from being a democrat, or from having any wild notions about reform, as yourself, + with just a little fancy for annual parliaments + universal suffrage.' He jokes with Sir George, telling him that he had implied that 'a contested election' was imprudent and 'that my woods are probably in danger, + an insinuation that the new member is little better than a democrat; + that among them all, the nation, together with my trees, will be tumbled to the ground.' The election was controversial, as Sir George Cornewall wrote a letter claiming that he and his son had no intention to stand for the county, but his son then changed his mind. Price was delighted with Robert Price's election. He was 'very desirous that my son should be in parliament; as his thoughts are very much towards parliamentary affairs, + as, if I may be allowed to say so, he has a remarkably right head, an active + reflecting mind, with cool judgment + firm decision.' Moreover, before his election he

> had no profession, his mind + faculties had little employment;
> they will now be fully employed; I feel very sure, that though,
> perhaps, he may not make a brilliant figure, his conduct will
> be consistent + strictly honourable; + that he will neither do
> or say any thing in parliament that his friends will have reason
> to be ashamed of.

Robert Price became the (Whig) MP for Herefordshire and remained so until 1841.[69]

Work on pronunciation and estate management kept Price very busy over the next few years. He was active throughout his last decade and this perhaps helped him to deal with the loss of friends and advisors such as Lord Abercorn in February 1818.[70] He became interested in researching the change in pronunciation of English poetry between Chaucer's and Shakespeare's time,[71] discussed the best type of sycamore leaves as brought by James Cranston from Lonsdale,[72] and visited Aberystwyth in August with Lady Caroline and his daughter, while his son remained in Herefordshire 'on duty in the county attending races, balls +ca +ca'.[73] He completed the first of many drafts of his work on pronunciation in January 1820 and hoped Sir George would dip into it, and perhaps pass it to Wordsworth. Price was still 'at my usual occupation of picture-making with the materials of nature + with a constantly increasing delight'.[74] Later in 1820 he recommended William Sawrey Gilpin to Lady Beaumont and compared his terms favourably with those of Repton.[75] Price confirmed that he and Beaumont had visited William Sawrey Gilpin when he lived at George Barrett's house in Paddington Green several years before and in December Price stayed at Coleorton for 10 days viewing the improvements.[76]

The friendship between Price and Knight flourished again as they got older. Price was delighted to be able to tell Sir George Beaumont in 1820 that Knight had visited and was 'in excellent health + spirits, + walks as stoutly as ever. He has read as much of my Epitome as was written fair, + talks of putting it into Latin + adding it to his Homer.' Price was even more thrilled when Knight told him that 'Dr Parr mentioned the other day that I had converted him, though he [Knight] had long tried at it in vain: I believe it is the greatest conversion since the time of St Paul.' He told Sir George that this made his 'vanity tide (as Mrs Greville used to call it) … almost overflow all bounds'.[77] Price was very concerned about Knight the following year. He had been

> most seriously ill: instead of carrying a hacker, as I do, he goes
> about his woods with a saw at the end of a long pole: a pretty
> large bough he had sawed off, fell on the nape of his neck; he
> did not feel any great pain or inconvenience from the blow,
> but not long afterwards a carbuncle, of the most virulent kind,
> made it's appearance on the part that had been struck; his
> head swelled to an enormous size, + for the whole night he
> was delirious from the pain: then came on so great a
> discharge, that it was feared his strength must be exhausted,
> + a mortification came on.

Price was pleased to be able to tell Sir George that Knight 'is a man of iron, + the strength of his constitution has gone through it all. He wrote me word some time ago that he was quite recoverd'; Thomas Andrew Knight visited Foxley and told Price that his brother 'had recoverd his strength + his appetite' and that 'he walks 5 or 6 miles a day' – 'a few days before, he had eat a whole goose all but the drum-sticks, without being sick or sorry.' Price commented that this was a 'pretty stout meal for a convalescent', but one not so surprising to Knight's old friends, who 'remember how he used to lade down his throat half a tureen of Macaroni, devour good part of a turbot or stewed lamprey, then dig down to the Pope's eye of a leg of mutton slice after slice, + fill up chinks with game puddings, pies +ce'.[78] He thought that Knight 'may go on to a hundred with all his faculties: in which case extreme old age may be endured, tho' by no means prayed for.' He would have felt Knight's death very strongly, as

> he is a friend of very old standing, of full fifty years, + I think,
> like genuine wine, he improves by age: the harshness goes off,
> + the fullness + flavour remain: the two last times he was
> here, we all agreed that we had never known him so pleasant
> + amiable in all respects.[79]

Knight had retired to live, when he was not at his London house in Soho Square, in the tiny Stonebrook Cottage on the Downton estate in 1808. The cottage has a carved motto, modified from Plato in Greek, meaning 'Leisure is the best of possessions.'[80] He had moved out of the Castle, although he retained a study, to allow his brother and family to live there. Price did not consider this a sensible place to be in his state of health. The cottage was built, he told Sir George, in a spot which

> as a bit of retired scenery you would be much pleased with: it
> is a narrow dingle overhung with trees, + a small brook
> running through it. In dry sunshiny weather it is extremely
> pleasant; but when the sky is lowering, it has a sad look of
> damp + gloominess, which might in some degree be
> counteracted by a [cheerful], comfortable, + well furnished
> tho' small + simple habitation: but the cottage he has built
> consists of one small room, + that hung with green baize!

When Price visited him in his cottage 'he looked quite cheerful + contented' and had been so until 'that terribly painful attack of the carbuncle'. Price thought that only someone with Knight's 'good health + equal spirits, his active mind, his eager literary pursuits, his power of application, + indefatigable eyes' could 'endure this solitary cell in such total seclusion, + without a servant of either sex; for there is only a single bed room over a single sitting room + I believe he always slept there alone.' Price himself could not have endured it and if he 'had been condemned to dwell in such a place, + such habitation quite alone, day + night, in all seasons + weathers, I should very soon have purchased a rope, + been found dangling from some tree in my own little dingle.' Price's competitive spirit in relation to Knight remained strong: he claimed that he had in fact discovered the site years before when they both explored 'every bushy dell + bosky bourn' and when they got to this particular dingle he had asked Knight to make him a path through it. Knight 'in his way' replied 'yes, yes yes, very pretty, but there are so many about the place + much finer', but the next time Price visited he said 'I have made the path you desired.' And this is the path, Price reported with relish, that 'now leads to his residence'.[81]

Price hoped that Knight would stop living at Stonebrook Cottage and 'return to the castle; for he now ought not to be alone'. Knight 'was miserably ill + low before he left the country' and although keen to add to his work on Homer he had 'a dread that his mind would not ever be equal to much exertion: + that he might end by being a card-player + a novel reader'. He complained that his 'former good digestion' had been 'treacherous' in 'encouraging him to eat + laying up seeds of disorder' and that he 'almost envied my bad stomach, which at least cried out'. Price wryly composed a verse on this comparison of their digestions:

> D'un estomac bien sain, l'insensible action
> Sans bruit, + sans effort fait la digestion.
> Mais pour la mien helas 'son train me desespere;
> Toujours il fait du bruit, + jamais ne digere.

Knight lingered on at Soho Square and when Robert Price called on him there he was told that 'he was getting better, + had walked out.'[82] He died of a stroke in April 1824 and was buried at Wormsley church on the old family estate adjoining Price's Foxley in May. Thus ended more than fifty years of intense, intellectual friendship: it was a stormy one, but their differences in outlook certainly sparked off ideas as well as controversy. Price clearly admired Knight enormously. Knight's view of Price is more difficult to pin down, but their competitive friendship was enormously productive.[83]

Knight's ghost continued to haunt Price and he was unfaltering in his research on pronunciation. He employed a local man who was 'the son of our road surveyor' and currently working in a druggist's shop to copy out drafts of his work. He had done such a good job that he recommended him to Lord Aberdeen and wondered whether a place as a clerk in a government office could be found for him.[84] He finished a version of the work in 1821, got Aberdeen to read through it again and tried unsuccessfully to get the Italian poet Ugo Foscolo to read it through as well. Aberdeen sent the manuscript on to Valpy the printer.[85] He recommended William Sawrey Gilpin to Lord Aberdeen for some landscaping at the Priory. He also congratulated Aberdeen on his new publication on architecture, but they continued to differ about Burke.[86] He wrote to the Beaumonts in Rome and longed to be back there after an absence of fifty years.[87] They discussed the character of Canova, whom Beaumont met in Rome, and Price commiserated with Sir George when he heard of Canova's death. Price continued to read the latest literature and recommended Washington Irving's *Sketchbook* and *Bracebridge Hall*. He was still finalising his work on pronunciation, going through different proofs.[88] The Prices continued to visit and receive many visitors through the mid 1820s. Mrs Westfalling stayed at Foxley in March, but found the house too cold:

> I brought a wretched cold home with me which I caught at
> Foxley, the weather was most severe and the house the
> coldest, & most comfortless, I ever was in, Entre Nous, altho'
> they had tolerable fires, the general air of the rooms, was not
> warm. Mem[dm], not to go there in winter again.[89]

However, she was pleased to welcome 'the Foxley family' to her house at Ross in May.[90]

In 1823 Price thanked Samuel Rogers for sending him a copy of the first book of his poem *Italy*; he had delayed replying because 'the foul fiend Dyspepsia, who never quite leaves me, has lately been unusually harassing.' He thought he would view 'Italy even with increased delight after more than fifty years' absence' but 'age and infirmities, were there no other obstacles, forbid any hope of so long a journey.' He hoped to attract Rogers to Foxley again to show him the pictures 'I have been producing' since you saw the place 'working with the materials of nature'. He told him how

I have endeavoured to form with them such compositions,

from the foreground to the most distant objects, as would satisfy the eye of a judicious painter. I have had the satisfaction of seeing more than one excellent artist, and one of them – Lord Aylesford – extremely averse to have anything pointed out to him as a good subject for a drawing, take his stand exactly where I wished, and where I had secretly conducted him, and draw the composition as if he had discovered it himself, tale quale and con amore.

Price was keen to emphasise that 'This picture making (you well know the delight of it in poetry) is a most amusing and interesting operation; it is, however, a very nice one, and the varied frame of each composition, itself an essential part, is to be studied almost to a twig.' He considered that some of the yew trees at Foxley were so ancient that they 'must remember the Conquest, and one or two the Heptarchy'. He thought 'Rembrandt would delight in them and give full effect to their black massy trunks and spreading branches', but he needed 'Claude's assistance for the aerial tint of a distant mountain that I have let in, and that appears in one or two instances, under the solemn canopy. I long to shew you what relief and value they give to each other.'[91]

To provide further temptation for Rogers to visit Foxley, Price offered to show him 'some very good specimens' of 'drawings of the old masters'. He remembered 'one of Giorgione that I envied you. Now I have books full of the old masters which I believe you have scarcely looked into, and though I have no Giorgione I have a Titian or two, and many drawings well worth your notice.' Price then questioned Rogers about sections of his poem, particularly his description of an ancient larch. 'I wish I had been with you, for I never saw an ancient larch and long very much to see one.' The larches at Foxley 'some of them nearly ninety feet high, are mere infants compared with yours, for they were all planted by my father and are probably about my age'. Price thought that several 'have roots above ground of a size and character that seem to belong to trees of at least twice their age' and wondered whether he had noticed 'the roots of your ancient larch, "majestic though in ruins." I am afraid you were occupied with the human figure sitting near it, and scarcely observed them.'[92]

The most important family event of 1823 was the marriage of Robert Price to his first cousin, Mary Anne, daughter of Rev. Robert Price DD, on 8 July.[93] Later in the summer Price and his daughter Caroline made a lengthy tour, taking in the Aberdeens at the Priory and Cassiobury with Lord Essex, then on for a day at Dropmore and four days at St Anne's Hill. But he had to cut short his planned trip to Ashburnham and the Isle of Wight due to a painful recurrence of piles.[94] Miss Caroline Price had a relapse at Lord Essex's Cassiobury and they stayed on a couple of extra days. Price told Rogers that he had worked hard removing self-set ash trees and making paths in 'a little amphitheatre, a hollow, nearly flat in the middle, and surrounded on every side by gently rising ground' where 'Many years ago cedars of Lebanon, red cedars, laurels, laburnums, cockspur thorns, &c. – these last the largest and the most picturesque I have ever seen – were planted.' Price was given 'carte blanche' by Lord Essex 'and though in the midst of the hay, gave me several workmen'. He surmised that Rogers

> would have been amused in seeing the progress of the work; it is, however, only sbozzato, for I had only two days, those very hot, and I not very stout, though 'very eager.' My principal operator in pruning, &c. was a common labourer, but sufficiently intelligent, and who took to it all very kindly: his name is John Elliman, and if you should happen to light upon him at your next trip to Cashiobury, he will be a much better cicerone than the Bostanghi Pacha[95] … but this quite between ourselves.[96]

When Price visited London in 1824 he was delighted with the work of his old protégé John Nash. He had left London with 'Swallow Street, &c., in all their dirt and meanness' and had returned after 'my ten years' rustication' to find 'Waterloo Bridge and all the grand openings from Carlton House to the Regent's Park'. He also enjoyed his day at Dropmore. Grenville had removed an 'ale house' and some other houses, one of which, Price discovered, used to be a school kept 'by our late Dean of Hereford, Dr. Gretton', who 'talked of it with as much indignation as an ancient Greek would have done if the Academy where Plato taught had been destroyed'. Price describes Dr Gretton as the 'arrantest pedagogue that ever wielded a rod; his head, face, wig, and his whole person seemed cut out of wood, and, as some one said, there was syntax in every line of his countenance.'[97] Price's use of syntax here is a curious nod to his old acquaintance William Combe's *The Tour of Doctor Syntax, in Search of the Picturesque*, first published in 1812 with illustrations by Rowlandson and in many subsequent editions. This enormously popular comic poetry, loosely based on a combination of Gilpin and Don Quixote, also had strong resonances with Price and his current interest in pronunciation.

Price was happy to find that dinner at Dropmore was at five rather than 'that absurd fashionable hour of seven, which cuts off the most delightful part of the whole day'. He noted he was 'not less fond of highly ornamented than of wild picturesque scenery' and was shown over the garden by Lord and Lady Essex: 'There is an amusing contrast in their manners: his remarkably placid and calm, though far from cold; hers as strikingly eager.' He found the rockwork, which in most gardens has a 'trifling paltry appearance' here to be 'large and massy' and to have 'a sort of architectural grandeur, and when the various plants and creepers begin to shoot luxuriantly as they promise to do, the effect will be excellent'. The earl had also placed 'large bodies of trees, many of them singularly bent, so as to form arches at various directions at the foot of an artificial mound raised to command a view of the distant country.' This 'hazardous undertaking' had 'of course, a crude appearance, but it is so well designed' that he thought when the plants and creepers became established they would form a 'disguise and an ornament'. After four quiet days at St Anne's, probably staying with Mrs Fox, they gave up the rest of their tour and returned to Foxley, where he was now 'busily employed with my two squirrels, well provided with high ladders and various cutting implements, in retouching my pictures, and clearing away the random foliage, as Mason calls it, that begins to disturb my compositions, and hide some of the distances'.[98]

Wordsworth visited Price again in the autumn of 1824. The Hutchinsons had moved to farm at Brinsop Court, just to the east of Foxley, and Wordsworth told Sir George Beaumont that 'I hope to see Mr Price, at Foxley, in a few days. Mrs Wordsworth's brother is about to change his present residence for a farm close to Foxley.'[99] Wordsworth was much more positive about Price on this visit compared with earlier meetings. He told Samuel Rogers that

> last autumn I saw Uvedale Price, our common friend (so I
> presume to call him, tho' really only having a slight
> acquaintance with him), striding up the steep sides of his
> wood-crowned hills, with his hacker, *i.e.* his Silvan Hanger,
> slung from his shoulder like Robin Hood's bow. He is 77 years
> of age and truly a wonder both for body and mind – especially
> do I feel him to be so when I recollect the deranged state of
> his digestive organs 12 years ago. I dined with him about that
> time at your table and elsewhere.[100]

Price himself was overjoyed by the visit and wrote a positively gushing and breathless account to Lady Beaumont:

> Wordsworths card was brought to me before ten O Clock in
> the morning, +, as you may imagine, I saw it with great
> pleasure + went out to welcome him immediately. M^rs
> Wordsworth I had never seen before; they had come a long
> way, + having set out very early on in the morning, were, I
> believe, very glad to find breakfast on the table.

Price then went with 'M^r + Mrs Wordsworth' to 'a part of the place [where] within these last two years I have formed … a number of compositions in which the Skerrit, a beautifully shaped hill, is the principal feature in the distance'. He thought that Lady Beaumont could 'hardly think more highly' of 'Wordsworth's taste + feeling' than he did following this visit. Moreover,

> his prose work on the scenery of the lakes, + particularly
> what relates to the style of buildings that is + is not suited to
> it, should be the <u>manual</u> of every person who visits those
> parts; above all of those who settle there, + who so often cut
> down plant, + build in such a manner as to call down the
> execrations of every one who has a grain of natural taste or
> feeling, on them + their works.

Lady Caroline and Price also liked Mrs Wordsworth:

> From all I saw of Mrs Wordsworth during a pretty long walk
> through different styles of scenery; her remarks seemed to me
> very just + discriminating; they were never obtrusive, never
> from a wish to attract notice, but simply from what she felt. I
> found that she constantly gained upon me; + – what I hold to
> be a very good sign – Lady Caroline liked her very much: We
> both wished they could have made a longer stay, + shall be
> much pleased to see them again.[101]

Wordsworth was delighted by Lady Caroline's gardens at Foxley. In 1825
Mary Wordsworth apologised for not visiting Lady Beaumont and helping to
'plant your flower borders'; instead she transcribed 'the verses I once
mentioned to you on this subject' for her and sent a copy of Wordsworth's *A
Flower Garden*. This poem was subtitled *At Coleorton Hall* but Mary Wordsworth
made the interesting additional comment that 'This little garden is made out
of Lady Caroline Price's and your own, combining the recommendations of
both', indicating Wordsworth's appreciation of the flower garden at Foxley.[102]
Over the winter of 1825 and the following spring Price was ill for nearly five
months and confined to his room and, while his daughter had 'nearly
recovered', Lady Caroline had a 'painful, + [I] fear, hopeless complaint'.[103] Lady
Caroline died on 16 July 1826. This would have been a terrible wrench for Price,
but the life of the household continued: his daughter Caroline remained at
home and often played music for him, and his son and daughter-in-law had
become leading figures in local society and frequently entertained.

Price's work on the pronunciation of Greek and Latin brought him several
new correspondents. In 1825 E. H. Barker of Thetford, the classical scholar and
author, wrote to Price to enquire for any letters he might have from Dr Parr
for an edition he was working on, and this led to a lengthy correspondence
dealing with literary matters and the pronunciation of Greek. Price told Barker
that he was meeting Dr Parr at the Greatheads' in Warwickshire, and was at
the same time advising Mr Greathead on the grounds at Guy's Cliffe. He
continued to reminisce about Daines Barrington, Sheridan, Robert Price,
Sandwich, Fox and Pitt. In the same letter he mentions 'Kant's theory as stated
by Mr Robinson'.[104] In June Price started to correspond with the young
Elizabeth Barrett, who lived at Hope End near Ledbury, about twenty miles to
the east of Foxley. She had just published her *Essay on Mind*, and Price
congratulated her. Over the next three years they frequently wrote to each
other. Elizabeth Barrett was keen to meet Price and paid a visit to Foxley in
October with her sister Henrietta, becoming friends with Caroline Price.[105] It
seems that Caroline had, by her early forties, overcome some of her earlier
problems which had been cruelly caricatured by Wordsworth. Elizabeth
Barrett's correspondence is mainly about pronunciation, particularly in ancient
Greek. Barrett commented on the final versions of Price's work and they

discussed the merits of the different pronunciations used at Winchester, Eton and Charterhouse, but range over many other literary themes, including Richard Payne Knight's use of 'Voltaire's worst and most common-place style of sneering' in his criticism of Burke's work[106] and 'the stilling effect of an approaching thunderstorm on cattle'.[107]

Sir George Beaumont, one of Price's oldest friends, died on 7 February 1827. Price wrote to Lady Beaumont later that year saying 'how glad we are to hear that you have struggled with the feelings + associations, which at first must have been most painful, + are able to resume, with some degree of interest, your former occupations'. She had asked for advice about the gardens at Coleorton and thought his son Robert or daughter-in-law Mary-Anne could write on his behalf, but Price retorted that 'I was forced to employ my son, the last time, being then very unwell + confined to my bed; but now that I am up, + tolerably well, I will not part with the pleasure of writing to you myself.' Lady Beaumont asked about the thinning of trees that had been planted almost twenty years earlier and were now too close together. Price was 'much flatterd by your recollecting an observation of mine on the Winter garden: I had forgotten it'; he had 'often fallen into the same sort of error, + know how much resolution it requires to cut down beautiful + flourishing trees, because they have flourished too much, + grown so as to mar the planter's intention'. If the planter was not careful there would be 'no variety, no play of form or of outline, but a mere crowd of plants, a uniform mass of foliage'. He argued that as 'the Winter Garden is of small extent, I should, as far as I can judge, be most inclined to part with the firs', otherwise they would damage her best plants. Lady Beaumont had offered him 'some choice specimens of my beloved + ever regretted friends drawings for my collection: were it ever so full + the drawings ever so select, they should make way for his: I shall be proud of shewing them to those who are worthy, as his performance, + as your gift.' He advises her that 'a certain number of those that have most effect, you probably will be inclined to frame, + hang up: the rest cannot be better than in portfolios'.[108] One of the paintings Price received from Lady Beaumont was *Peele Castle in a Storm* (Plate 11). Wordsworth later commented that he had seen it at Foxley 'rather grudgingly I own' as Mrs Wordsworth had been promised it by Sir George, but Lady Beaumont 'interfered' after his death and gave it to Price.[109]

On his eightieth birthday Price was delighted to receive some verses from Miss Barrett:

> My eyes pain me + I write by candlelight: I therefore can only
> shortly tell you that I was in every way, + on every account
> delighted with your verses on my birthday; + not a little vain
> of being celebrated at eighty, by a Muse in the very prime of
> life. I had the pleasure of seeing Mr Barrett for a few minutes
> at Hereford, + thought him looking remarkably well: I wished
> to have a longer conversation, but my carriage was at the
> door + Mrs R. Price in it.[110]

The poem *To Uvedale Price, Esqr. On his birthday, March 26, 1827* celebrates both Price's work on pronunciation and landscape:

> Thy distant paths of leafy secretness, –
> Where Nature welcomes man in Nature's gear, –
> Freed from the tyrant's chain, and bondslave's
>   fear –
> Freed by thy generous hand, from which was ta'en
> The zone of painting, to replace the chain![111]

He continued to correspond about his work on pronunciation, stayed in London in June and early July while his work was printed at Oxford, and returned to Foxley in July via the Grenvilles at Dropmore.[112] He met Lady Beaumont in London and she reported to Mrs Wordsworth: 'When I saw him in town he seemed unwearied in his pursuits, and as much alive at 80 to all that music painting or the fine arts in general can afford as in youth, an unusual gift.' She spotted that 'except a little weakness in the knees, which does not prevent his attending every concert, I scarcely saw a difference.'[113]

The essay on the modern pronunciation of the Greek and Latin languages was finally printed in September 1827 by Baxter of Oxford, and Price sent copies to friends. He paid particular thanks 'to persons of undoubted and extensive erudition, particularly my much regretted friends, Mr Knight and Dr Parr' who had 'looked over a great part of what I had written'.[114] He compared this new essay with his *Essays on the Picturesque*, in which

> I endeavoured to shew that our English system of laying out
> grounds, or, as it has lately been called, of *Landscape
> Gardening*, is at variance with all the principles of landscape
> painting, and with the practice of all the most eminent
> masters: in the present publication it has been my endeavour
> to shew, that our system of pronouncing the ancient
> languages is equally at variance with the principles and
> established rules of ancient prosody, and the practice of the
> best poets.[115]

In both essays he stressed 'the destruction of variety and connection. These two qualities are equally indispensable in the composition and arrangement of scenery, and of versification; and a succession of clumps, unconnected with one another, and with all other objects has [a close analogy with] a succession of trochees uncombined with one another.' He also pointed out that 'I rather flatter myself, that since the publication of the Essays, fewer distinct clumps have been planted, and fewer clumps of trees made as clump-like, as their originally varied character would allow of … .'[116]

The autumn of 1827 was again a busy one for Price, with the 'house brimful of company'.[117] He also continued to pay visits, staying at Lord Essex's Hampton Court, Herefordshire.[118] Back at Foxley, he wrote to Lady Beaumont expressing his hope to be with her the following year, if both were still alive. He told her: 'Although upon the whole I am pretty stout for an octogenaire yet I have certain infirmities that make travelling very inconvenient + uncomfortable, but if they do not get worse, they shall not stop me.'[119] Lady Beaumont told Mrs Wordsworth that her 'chief amusement out of doors' was 'what is commonly called improving Nature' but that she was concerned that this would 'attach her to the visible world I must so soon quit', especially when she saw 'how seductive the amusement becomes by the proof in my friend Mr Price who from early youth to fourscore, is as ardent in the pursuit as ever'.[120] In September Price lent a Reynolds to a local exhibition of paintings held in a room in the churchyard at Ross-on-Wye.[121] Barker asked Price about Mr Uvedale Price's 'Catechism for Young Ladies', but Price claimed to know nothing of it and speculated that it must have been his grandfather's.[122] In December he wrote to Elizabeth Barrett about her comments on his essay. He noted 'I need not answer your enquiries about Caroline as it is so long since you made them + she has written to you herself. You may imagine what pleasure it gives me to see her well + in spirits + to hear her music every night as usual.' He had had to give up a visit to Eastnor Castle, the enormous newly constructed mansion of Lord Somers, 'very reluctantly', as he had thought of it with so much pleasure. He thanked her for the 'moor-game' which 'notwithstanding its long journey, brought with it no *travelled airs: it was excellent* ...'.[123]

Price was created a baronet on 12 February 1828. He wrote to Archer Clive, a neighbour at Whitfield, Herefordshire: 'You probably heard from Bob how very unexpectedly the offer of a baronetcy came upon me: in honest truth I had never had a thought (much less wish) of being anything more than a Squire.'[124] Wordsworth stayed a few days with 'Sir Uvedale Price, one of the last batch of Baronets' in January 1828 and noted that he 'is in his 81st year, and as active in ranging around his woods as a setter dog. We talked much of Sir George Beaumont, to whom he was very strongly attached.' Wordsworth was impressed by Price's work on pronunciation:

> He has just written a most ingenious work on ancient metres,
> and the proper mode of reading Greek and Latin verse. If he is
> right, we have all been wrong; and I think he is. It is a strange
> subject for a man of his age, but he is all life and spirits ...[125]

Wordsworth sent William Whewell a paper by Price on some comments by Whewell on the *Essay on pronunciation*, noting 'I cannot but think you will be pleased by the Paper now sent, as an indication of extraordinary activity of mind, and clearness also, in a Person now in his 81st or 82nd year.' He thought the subject 'dry', but Whewell responded that

> Your strong impression of the dryness of the subject
> somewhat reminds me of a tenet of Sedgwick's who maintains
> sometimes that a person may be too good a mineralogist for
> it to be possible for him to be a good geologist. In the same

way I suppose a person may be too good a writer of verses to
be a good critic of versification, or rather I should say a good
anatomist of verse.[126]

Price was extremely pleased with Wordsworth's comments on his essay.
He told Barker that

Wordsworth, when he was here the other day, told me he had
paid little attention to the subject, took little interest in it, +,
from want of use, at the first reading puzzled with several
parts of the Essay: he persevered, however, took to it kindly,
+ professed himself a convert.[127]

Lady Beaumont thought that Wordsworth 'must have admired the stately groves
and fine scenery at Foxley, so long the object of Sir Uvedale's affections, and a
monument to his paternal care'.[128] But Price was wary of being 'puffed up with
vanity' from the comments of critics and reviewers.[129] He reported to Elizabeth
Barrett that the responses varied 'from unmixed praise + complete coincidence
of opinion, to a mixture of praise + censure in various degrees + proportions,
+ again to reprobation + contempt, almost to abuse, without any
commendation.' He was particularly amused by a comment from the German
scholar Hermann: 'Pricii librum, magna cum voluptate legi, velimque ei, meo
nomine plurimas a te agi gratias. Videtur ille mihi pleraque omnia, non subtiliter
tantum, sed etiam vere disputasse, paucaque sunt, in quibus ab illo dissentiam.'
Price adds 'I never could have expected (nor could you) to see my name in the
genitive case with a latin termination!' Price notes that the nominative case must
be Pricius, and feels 'exalted to the rank of a "Savant en *us*," as that scoffer
Voltaire ludicrously call those Erudits'.[130] A correspondent of Barker felt, however,
'The Pronunciation of Latin than wch. I know not a more frivolous, useless, Topic.
Whether we call the voluminous writer before me Sisero; – or with the Italians
Tchischero; – or, as we ought, Kikero, deserves not a Thought'.[131]

Elizabeth Barrett herself told Hugh Boyd that

I owe Sir Uvedale Price much gratitude, and have a high
respect for taste, which so entirely deserves Mr. Barker's
epithet – 'exquisite.' I never met with a mind equally poetical,
– OUT *of a poet!* And I am surprised, that, where nature gave
such a susceptibility to poetical *impressions*, she should have
denied the *impresive* poetical faculty.

She recommended the *Essay on the Picturesque* for its style. She read it 'without
feeling an interest in the subject' and thought 'The style has not much
eloquence brilliancy or energy, – but is natural, chaste, graceful and
harmonious, to a captivating degree.'[132] Price's enthusiasm for Elizabeth
Barrett's poem came when she was suffering from her father's displeasure and
she recorded that 'Mr Price's friendship has given me more continued
happiness than any single circumstance ever did.'[133]

Price continued to be interested in architecture and wrote to Barker about Bowles on modern castellated mansions. He described John Nash's Garnstone Castle built for Mr Peploe as a 'modern castle' that had

> within a very few years been built by my nearest neighbour whose grounds join to mine: + I never look a it from any point, without rejoicing that it was not an unvaried lump of brick like most of the houses throughout the county. The two leading characters of Architecture, to speak in very general terms, are the Grecian + the Gothic: the first is to us, a beautiful exotic; the other comparatively indigenous; + even in respect to association, accords more with ours.[134]

The fashion for new castles was indeed dominant at this time, and Price was fascinated by the fruitful influence that Knight's Downton Castle and his own Castle House at Aberystwyth were having on modern architecture, with the examples of Garnstone and Eastnor close at hand. He reported that the architect Charles Cockerell liked his *Essay on Architecture*.[135] He considered that 'Mr Laing Meason's work on the landscape architecture of the great painters' was influenced by both himself and Knight.[136] In October 1828 he was 'employed professionally' at Lord Talbot's Ingestre Hall, Staffordshire, and stayed there almost a month. This was a park that had been designed by Lancelot Brown and so Price will have been delighted to suggest improvements.[137]

He paid a final visit to Lady Beaumont at Coleorton in 1828, where he also advised on the grounds. In January, however, Robert Price told Barker that his father 'is confined to his room by a severe cold combined with Erysipelas' but that he was happy to present Mr Long with a copy of the book.[138] Price recovered somewhat, and told Barker in May that he had been very ill with a bad pain in the eyebrow and been 'bound up, poulticed, cabbaged, fomented'.[139] He died at Foxley on 14 September 1829, aged 82. His obituary in the *Hereford Journal* (16 September 1829) referred to his 'learning, his sagacity, his exquisite taste, his indefatigable ardour' and was confident that 'the obituary of 1829 will not record a name more gifted or more dear'.[140] He was buried against the east wall of Yazor church, in the churchyard, under a simple table tomb. 'It survives today, albeit in ruins.'[141] Elizabeth Barrett wrote that 'Literature and his literary and personal friends have lost much – his poor daughter has lost everything. I had a letter from her and from his son yesterday, and I have the satisfaction of knowing that they are as resigned as human nature can be under such a blow.'[142] She wrote an elegy on his death 'To the Memory of Sir Uvedale Price, Bart';[143] and noted in her diary in 1831 'Sir Uvedale Price was as eloquent and imaginative at eighty ... than he was at eighteen.'[144]

TO THE MEMORY OF
SIR UVEDALE PRICE, BART.

FAREWELL!–a word that human lips bestow
On all that human hearts delight to know:
On summer skies, and scenes that change as fast;
On ocean calms, and faith as fit to last;
On Life, from Love's own arms that breaks away;
On hopes that blind, and glories that decay!

And ever thus, "farewell, farewell," is said,
As round the hills of lengthening time we tread;
As at each step the winding ways unfold
Some untried prospect which obscures the old;–
Perhaps a prospect brightly coloured o'er,
Yet not with brightness that we loved before;
And dull and dark the brightest hue appears
To eyes like ours, surcharged and dim with tears.

Oft, oft we wish the winding road were past,
And yon supernal summit gained at last;
Where all that gradual change removed, is found
At once, for ever, as you look around;
Where every scene by tender eyes surveyed,
And lost and wept for, to their gaze is spread–
No tear to dim the sight, no shade to fall,
But Heaven's own sunshine lighting, charming all.

Farewell!–a common word–and yet how drear
And strange it soundeth as I write it here!
How strange that *thou* a place of death shouldst fill,
Thy brain unlighted, and thine heart grown chill!
And dark the eye, whose plausive glance to draw,
Incited Nature brake her tyrant's law!
And deaf the ear, to charm whose organ true,
Mœonian Music tuned her harp anew!
And mute the lips where Plato's bee hath roved;
And motionless the hand that genius moved!–
Ah, friend! thou speakest not!–but still to me
Do Genius, Music, Nature, speak of *thee*!–

CONCLUSION

U VEDALE PRICE'S NINETEENTH-CENTURY REPUTATION rested on his *Essays on the Picturesque* and their influence on literary figures, especially Wordsworth and Scott, and practising architects and landscapers. It has already been shown that the debates in which Price engaged figured in the novels of Jane Austen and Sir Walter Scott. Jane Austen was fully aware of the picturesque debate and her sympathies in *Mansfield Park* (1814) clearly lie with Price.[1] Walter Scott not only discussed Price in his correspondence and novels but used his ideas directly in the creation of his own landscape at Abbotsford. Thomas Love Peacock, in *Headlong Hall* (1816), wrote entertainingly of the debate over picturesque landscaping, with Sir Patrick O'Prism representing Price and Mr Milestone, Repton. In 1826 the poet Thomas Moore found Price's *Essay on the Picturesque* 'a good companion over Salisbury Downs' in the chaise on a journey from Salisbury to Devizes.[2]

The relationship between William Wordsworth and Price is particularly interesting. Wordsworth took on board many of Price's ideas on picturesque landscape and Price greatly admired Wordsworth's prose on Lakeland scenery. Their acquaintance, which developed through their mutual friendship with Sir George and Lady Beaumont, was a fruitful channel through which Price's classically informed understanding of landscape and poetry engaged with the poet's vernacular vision. When Price thanked Lady Beaumont for the gift of Wordsworth's poems *The River Duddon, a Series of Sonnets* of 1820 he particularly mentioned the prose work annexed to the poems, *A Topographical Description of the Country of the Lakes in the North of England*.[3] Price argued that Wordsworth's 'account of the Lakes should be in every house all around them'. This was not just because it described so well 'their characteristic beauties' but because it pointed out 'in a most impressive manner all that ought not, + all that ought to have been done'. He felt that the piece was 'dictated by the truest taste + feeling' and that the principles were 'so just + comprehensive' that 'it should be the <u>Manual</u> of Improvers in every part of the kingdom'.[4] Nigel Everett has pointed out that Wordsworth's approach to the improvement of landscape was 'broadly similar to that of Price' and that the values of the picturesque espoused in Wordsworth's *Guide through the District of the Lakes* (1810) was 'was no more than a reader of Price would expect'.[5]

But Price also advised directly on the layout of grounds and gardens. The

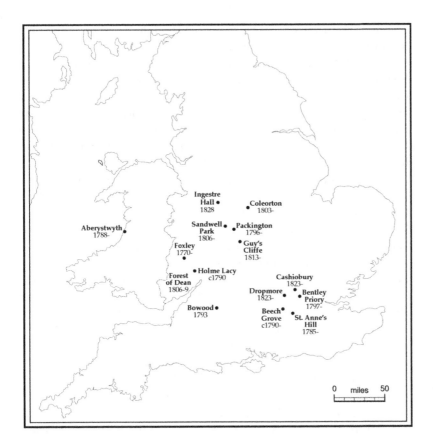

Map 2 Map of estates and places where Uvedale Price advised on landscape.

evidence we have is slim, and derived mainly from his correspondence, but we do know that he advised, among others, Charles James Fox at St Annes' Hill, Lord Aylesford at Packington, Lord Dartmouth at Sandwell Park, Lord Abercorn at Bentley Priory, Lord Essex at Cassiobury, Lord Grenville at Dropmore, Mr Greathead at Guy's Cliffe and Lord Talbot at Ingestre Hall (Map 2). The best-documented practical advice is that given to Sir George and Lady Beaumont, where his letters demonstrate a deep knowledge of horticulture and forestry which had been developed over a lifetime working at his own Herefordshire estate. He advised on very different landscapes. At Coleorton there was a need to establish plantations to disguise the surrounding coal mines. At other places, such as Packington, he modified landscapes which had been planted many years before, just as his own estate at Foxley had been. Indeed, one of Price's most important original contributions to landscape management was his understanding of how to deal effectively with maturing plantations through subtle thinning and pruning. His practical knowledge of tree establishment was also drawn on in a public capacity in 1806–9 when he was government advisor on the reinvigoration of the silviculture of the Forest of Dean for the improvement of future timber for the Royal Navy.

Although Price found this personal advice fascinating and enjoyable, there is little remaining evidence through maps or plans of what precisely he did. His detailed advice on the Winter Garden at Coleorton is one of the few instances where his writings can be linked to a surviving landscape. In some places his ideas survive as a distant memory, as with Price's Walk at Holme Lacy in Herefordshire. In others the landscapes he advised on have been so heavily changed, as with Lord Dartmouth's Sandwell Park, through which the M5 now runs, or Guy's Cliffe, which is in ruins, that it is difficult to identify what he achieved. The estate papers for Lord Aylesford's Packington, where Price advised on the modification of a Brown landscape, were destroyed in a fire. More important than this somewhat fleeting and ephemeral advice was Price's influence, through personal acquaintance, discussion and his published works, on the architects John Nash and Robert Smirke and the landscapers Humphry Repton and John Claudius Loudon. Indeed, he was regularly quoted and referred to by a wide range of architects and landscapers and his direct effect on landscaping in the nineteenth century is difficult to overestimate.

John Claudius Loudon (1783–1843) and William Sawrey Gilpin (1762–1843) stand out as Price's greatest champions in the decades after his death. Loudon was taught by Professor Andrew Coventry at Edinburgh University, where the works he studied included those of William Gilpin, Price, Knight and Repton.[6] He published in 1804, at the age of 21, *Observations on the Formation and Management of Useful and Ornamental Plantations* and *Observations on the Theory and Practice of Landscape Gardening* in a single volume. In both he made extensive reference to the works of Price and in the second he emphasised that: 'I believe I am the first who has set out as a landscape gardener, professing to follow Mr. Price's principles. How far I shall succeed in executing my plans, and introducing more of the picturesque into improved places, time alone must determine.' He considered that Price and Knight pointed out 'the distinguishing errors of the present system of laying out grounds, and contain the best ideas that can be imagined for those who practice this art', and argued that the 'ineffectual attempts' of 'modern professors ... to confute the reasoning of these gentlemen ... had only the happy effect of rousing the landed interest to see the absurdity of Brown's whimsical system'.[7] Melanie Louise Simo, Loudon's biographer, argues that Loudon was 'drawn to the elegant writings' of Price and that Price's aesthetic views had 'a profound influence on Loudon's early practice'.[8]

It is ironic that the other person who did most to implement Price's ideas practically through commissioned landscape schemes in the early nineteenth century was William Gilpin's nephew, William Sawrey Gilpin (1761/2–1843), the second son of the animal painter Sawrey Gilpin (1733–1807). Price had been familiar with his work for many years and he will have known the plates he etched based on his uncle's drawings for William Gilpin's *Observations on* the *River Wye* in 1782.[9] Sophieke Piebenga notes that at the Royal Academy exhibition of 1799 'Gilpin's work caught the attention of the art patron Sir George Beaumont', who introduced him to Price. 'This introduction was to prove crucial to Gilpin's later career as a landscape gardener.'[10] He was third drawing master at the Royal Military College 1806–1820, losing his position owing to post-Napoleonic Wars cutbacks. He almost immediately 'actively sought to renew his acquaintance with Price',[11] who was pleased because he had long wished 'that such a person as Mr Gilpin might be induced to take up the profession'.[12] His career as a landscape gardener, which he took up as his principal profession at the age of 58, flourished and he advised on many properties, about 70 of which have recently been identified.[13]

Gilpin proclaimed himself a disciple of Price in his *Practical Hints on Landscape Gardening* of 1832, with a second edition in 1835. He wrote 'This little work may probably, at first sight, appear superfluous to those who have read the Essays of Sir Uvedale Price upon this department of taste; where the subject is so ably and fully discussed as to leave no room for improvement, no ground for dissent.' He aimed to 'to concentrate, and to render practically useful the ideas of Uvedale Price' and his book contained many lengthy quotations from Price.[14] Gilpin was also concerned to remove the 'charge of *bitterness of controversy* from the Essays' and to 'rescue the memory of their author from an imputation which, from personal knowledge' he knew 'did not attach to him'. Gilpin asserted that 'Whatever may appear severe throughout the work in question, is attributable to an uncommon quickness of perception, joined to a keenness of expression that delighted all who had the pleasure of his acquaintance.'[15] By the late 1830s he had advised on several hundred properties, such as Wolterton Hall, Norfolk, Sudbury Hall, Derbyshire, and Clumber, Nottinghamshire, for the duke of Newcastle. He often seemed to act 'as a kind of gentleman adviser to the owner of a property, steering the ideas of his employer and assisting with staking out plantations and drives', such that Ralph Sneyd at Keele referred to him as 'my man of taste'. This is reminiscent of Price's approach, though, of course, Gilpin was paid for his advice. Gilpin's plantations were characteristically 'irregularly shaped ... with bold projections and recesses' and such intricacy was also 'found in the architectural details of Gilpin's terrace walls with overhanging copings, vases, and protruding buttresses'. Sophieke Piebenga concludes that 'Gilpin was at the forefront of this reintroduction of formality into the garden.'[16]

Other writers, too, were influenced by the heat of the picturesque debate. Price himself thought that both he and Knight had influenced Gilbert Laing Meason's *On the Landscape Architecture of the great Painters of Italy* of 1828.[17] Richard Morris wrote in 1825 that on the subject of the picturesque 'the Essays of Mr. Price may be considered to stand unrivalled.' Morris believed that the controversy had served to contribute 'important information on the subject; and also on the ever-varying beauties connected with landscape scenery and picturesque effect'.[18] Price also joined William Gilpin in the roster of names associated with touring the Wye. Thomas Dudley Fosbrooke's popular tourist guide to the Wye was first published in 1818 and by the third edition Price's name had been added to that of Gilpin's as one of the key interpreters of the river.[19] More importantly, David Watkin has identified Price as a key influence on the remodelling by Thomas Hope of his influential mansion The Deepdene, near Dorking, in the 1820s. He suggests that 'grouping the offices so that they form with the house itself an irregular and Picturesque composition is doubtless inspired by Uvedale Price's observations' on the beneficial contribution made to the 'variety' and 'consequence' of the 'principal building' by the 'accompaniment, and, as it were, the attendance of the inferior parts in their different gradations'. Watkin points out that Loudon, writing in the *Gardener's Magazine* in 1829, thought that 'in the house and offices' Thomas Hope had 'combined in them all the finest parts of what might be called the landscape architecture and sculpture of Italy, has formed a whole, the greatest praise that we can bestow on which, is to say that it will delight such men as Sir Uvedale Price and Gilbert Laing Meason.'[20]

The international reach of Price's *Essay*, following earlier notice in France and Germany, extended to, America where his work influenced Andrew Jackson Downing (1815–52) and Frederick Olmsted (1822–1903). Downing published his *A Treatise on the Theory and Practice of Landscape Gardening Adapted to North America* in New York in 1841. The book was aimed at the improvement of American country residences and Downing argued that domestic architecture should exist harmoniously with its natural surroundings. He referred favourably to Price's ideas, noting that 'Those who have perused, Price's "Essay on the Picturesque," can not fail to be entertained with the vigour with which he advocates the picturesque … .' In 1844 Downing published *Cottage Residences; or A Series of Designs for Rural Cottages and Cottage Villas, and Their Gardens and Grounds Adapted to North America*, which was influential in the spread of cottage and villa architecture in the United States. Downing's friend, the landscape architect Frederick Olmsted, similarly pursued a strong interest in Price's theories on the picturesque, having made a visit to Herefordshire on his tour of England in 1850 'with the specific intention of soaking up the countryside which nurtured Uvedale Price'.[21] In this way, Price can be said to have had a transatlantic influence on landscape design, such that his ideas directly helped to shape Olmsted's plan for Central Park in New York in 1858.[22]

Sir Thomas Dick Lauder edited and published a new edition of Price's *Essays* in 1842, with illustrations by Montagu Stanley.[23] The edition became an important reference point, helping to keep Price's name and reputation alive even as the Price family fortune was heading into decline. In an essay on 'the origin of taste', Lauder argued of Price that 'the acuteness of his perception, the nicety of his discrimination, and the highly cultivated delicacy of his taste' enabled him to 'give us the happiest selection of the liveliest and most pleasing pictures'. Lauder called for all those who had landed estates to 'contribute to the general improvement of the face of the country', since despite the richness of the natural scenery, in his view there was still 'much ... to be done, and, perhaps, not a little to be undone' when it came to the national landscape. For Lauder, careful improvement of 'the face of the country' was a duty borne by owners of landed estates, who must do all in their power to enrich the features of their property, 'whether it be small, or whether it be great'. While the improvement of estates by individual owners was a form of 'self-gratification', it produced effects that 'must give the widest pleasure to all the rest of mankind who may have an opportunity of looking upon them', and, moreover, 'not only in our own time, but for generations to come'. Therefore Lauder concluded by asserting that every landowner 'ought to feel that the eyes of his country are upon him and upon his place' and that it was a patriotic duty for them to ensure that that their estates were 'a feature worthy of British landscape'.[24]

Lauder's aim in reprinting Price's essays in a single volume was therefore to remind landowners of their landscape responsibilities; but it was also to provide a running commentary on, and update of, Price's theories. For example, to Price's chapter on the definition of the picturesque Lauder drew attention to a new word in circulation – *sculpturesque* – referring to objects that were 'best fitted for displaying the powers of the sculpture'. Lauder took issue with Price's objections to buildings painted bare white, giving his experiences travelling through Italy as his justification, though he acknowledged Price's line of reasoning. Lauder also used the opportunity of his role as editor to insert his own extended passages on topics loosely connected with those being discussed by Price – as, for example, in his discussion of the houses of old Scotland or the examples he gives of different planting regimes on Scottish estates, or in his confession that 'after considerable experience, I have been completely cured of my romantic attachment to thatch.'[25]

Lauder's call for estate and village improvement was certainly one which many landowners took to heart in the mid nineteenth century. One of the great transformations of British landed estates in the nineteenth century was the provision of new cottages and villages by landowners and aristocrats whose incomes became vastly increased through the development of industry and international trade. Price's ideas and writings played a crucial role in this transformation of the design and appearance of rural housing. This continued after his death: in 1830, for example, Peter Frederick Robinson published *Village Architecture: Being a Series of Designs for the Inn, the Schoolhouse, Almshouses, Markethouse, Shambles, Workhouse, Parsonage, Town Hall, and Church: Illustrative of the Observations contained in the Essay on the Picturesque, by Sir Uvedale Price: and as a Supplement to a Work on Rural Architecture.*[26] Price was not alone in arguing that there was a link between picturesque landscaping and design and rural improvement and benevolence. Thomas Ruggles, most famous for his work on *The History of the Poor* (1793/4), had also written on picturesque agriculture and William Gilpin's sale of his picturesque writings and drawings helped to fund his charitable undertakings at Boldre in the New Forest. Nigel

204

Everett has argued that 'The writings of Uvedale Price and Richard Payne Knight suggested, albeit from a generally secular point of view, that the improvement of landscape and society were essentially related.'[27] He also points out that Price's uncle Shute Barrington, the bishop of Durham, worked closely with Sir Thomas Bernard on the establishment in 1796 of the Society for Bettering the Condition and Increasing the Comforts of the Poor. One of the aims of this society was to 'carry domestic comforts into the recesses of every cottage'. Landowners should adorn 'the skirts of their parks and paddocks, of their farms and commons, with picturesque and habitable cottages and fruitful gardens; so as to increase every Englishman's affection for an island replete with beauty and happiness'.[28] Price's ideas of a benevolent yet strongly and even pedantically controlled countryside became entrenched in this period as the ideal for many landowners.

By the mid-nineteenth-century the picturesque ways of seeing the landscape had become so normal and natural that Uvedale Price's contribution to the debate began to be forgotten. No further editions of his work were published after 1842. He became relegated, usually paired with Knight, to the footnotes of garden histories. David Whitehead has argued that for a time Price's *Essays* became 'a manifesto for a new movement in painting' and 'an ideology for British romanticism'. He notes that

> Thomas Hearne responded in the 1790s to Price's theory by his rejection of prospects and espousal of intimate scenes. David Cox went to live in Herefordshire in 1814 because it was the county of the picturesque, and his adoption of 'the broken tint style' was designed to capture the texture of the countryside admired by Price. Cox painted a Scene at Foxley Park which was engraved by G. Hunt in 1823.[29]

But the world of British art criticism was to change radically with the publication in 1846, only four years after Lauder's edition of Price, of John Ruskin's second volume of *Modern Painters*, in which he established 'the ground plan of his critical and aesthetic theories' and challenged the 'aesthetic orthodoxy derived from Sir Joshua Reynolds and Sir George Beaumont'.[30] John Ruskin had divergent view on the picturesque. In *Of the Turnerian Picturesque* he argued against a heartless lower picturesque in which pleasure was derived from viewing 'fallen cottage – desolate villa – deserted village – blasted heath – mouldering castle –' which did not take account of the 'feverish misery' and 'helpless darkness' of the inhabitants.[31] He traced this 'modern feeling of the picturesque, which, so far as it consists in a delight in ruin, is perhaps the most suspicious and questionable of all the characters distinctively belonging to our temper, and art' back to Claude. But he set against this a higher type of picturesque. He recollected

> the intense pleasure I have always in first finding myself … at the foot of the old tower of Calais church. The large neglect,

the noble unsightliness of it; the record of its years written so
visibly, yet without sign of weakness or decay; its stern
wasteness and gloom, eaten away by the Channel winds, and
overgrown with the bitter sea grasses; its slates and tiles all
shaken and rent, and yet not falling; its desert of brickwork
full of bolts, and holes, and ugly fissures, and yet strong, like a
bare brown rock; its carelessness of what any one thinks or
feels about it, putting forth no claim, having no beauty or
desirableness, pride, nor grace; yet neither asking for pity;
not, as ruins are, useless and piteous, feebly or fondly
garrulous of better days; but useful still, going through its
own daily work.[32]

Ruskin could be paraphrasing Price in this section, though he does not refer
to him.

In the *Seven Lamps of Architecture* Ruskin celebrated the 'actual beauty in the
marks' of age in buildings which could be 'loosely expressed by the term
"picturesque"'. He recognised that the term had been the subject of frequent
and 'prolonged dispute' and 'yet none remain more vague in their acceptance'.
He felt that picturesqueness was '*Parasitical sublimity*' and that the 'characters of
line or shade or expression' productive of picturesqueness that 'are generally
acknowledged' are 'angular and broken lines, vigorous oppositions of light and
shaded and grave, deep, or boldly contrasted colour …'. When applied to
buildings, he argued that 'picturesque … architecture is an exponent of age, of
that in which … . The greatest glory of the building consists … . I think a building
cannot be considered as in its prime until four or five centuries have passed over
it.'[33] John Macarthur points out that the dominance of a picturesque sensibility
in the early nineteenth century meant that 'the picturesque is the premise of
Ruskin's work … . He read Price and Reynolds, and through the remainder of his
architectural and art writing, the affects of seeing are foundational to much of
his commentary' and he 'writes as if the aesthetic reception of art and nature
does in fact begin for all … in a picturesque sensibility'.[34]

The late-nineteenth-century preoccupation with Ruskin put Price's
contribution into the shade, and this obscurity was furthered by the end of the
direct Price family line: there were to be no filial appreciations. His son Sir
Robert Price became heavily involved in industrial investments in the mid-
nineteenth-century and was eventually made bankrupt. This caused the sale
of the Foxley estate and the collections of paintings and drawings. The family
papers became dispersed and in many cases lost. The fact that Robert Price
produced no heir exacerbated this situation; there were few likely 'keepers of
the flame' who would wish to encourage a biography. The sale of Foxley, the
break-up of the family archive and the dispersal of his library and art collections
resulted in an arid and desolate field for biographical investigation. There was
little chance for friends or members of the family to write a biography in the
middle years of the nineteenth century.

An early attempt was made by E. H. Barker to collect Price's letters for publication.[35] The young Elizabeth Barrett received 'a curious and memorable application on the subject of Sir Uvedale Price's letters' from Barker.[36] Barrett's father, a well-known exponent of parental power, was put in a passion by the suggestion, stating that 'the giving … possession of the correspondence in opposition or in ignorance of the wishes of the family upon the subject would be a dereliction of all I know you to feel towards the memory of Sir U.P.'[37] Elizabeth Barrett's elegy was published in 1833.[38] Mr Barrett's response may have been characteristic of other correspondents of Price. For whatever reason, the idea of collecting Price's letters at that time was still-born. A few of Price's letters were published in collections later in the nineteenth century, however. Lady Theresa Lewis's *Extracts from the Journals and Correspondence of Miss Berry, from the year 1783 to 1852*, published in three volumes in 1865, contained quotations from three letters. A single letter to E. H. Barker was published in *Literary Anecdotes and Contemporary Reminiscences of Professor Porson and Others; from the Manuscript Papers of the Late E.H. Barker Esq. of Thetford, Norfolk*, published in London in two volumes in 1852. P. W. Clayden's compilation *Rogers and His Contemporaries*, published in two volumes in 1889, contained another three letters. No letters from Price survive in public collections earlier than that written when he was aged 45 to Lord Abercorn in 1792, and no other letters appear to have been published in the nineteenth century. The great majority of his private correspondence to members of his family, to local landowners and to literary figures appears to be lost, or possibly remains hidden in private collections. Perhaps it is not so surprising that a nineteenth-century biography was not completed.

The Prices continued to live at Foxley for almost thirty years after Uvedale Price's death. Sir Robert Price remained MP for Herefordshire until 1841 and then became MP for Hereford City from 1845 to 1857.[39] The foundation stone of a new church at Yazor was laid by Mary Anne Price in 1843 but the building was not consecrated until 1851. Some have attributed the decision to build a new church, and its position, 'a spot at some distance from the old building, commanding an extensive prospect', to Uvedale Price, but his lifetime lack of interest in Christianity makes this unlikely: it is more likely that his enthusiastically religious nephew Uvedale Shudd Price was the person responsible.[40] In 1829, the year Uvedale Price died, Sir Robert Price became 'the largest proprietor of the Duffryn, Llynfi, & Porthcawl Railway, a horse-drawn tramroad connecting the coal and iron areas of Maesteg and the Llynfi valley to a new harbour at Porthcawl on the Glamorgan coast'.[41] He also set up the Glamorgan Iron and Coal Company and borrowed £25,000 using Foxley as security. Although Sir Robert invested heavily in iron and coal works in South Wales he left the management of these interests largely in the hands of agents while he pursued his political career in London. Recessions in the iron trade in the 1840s, and the loss of a schooner chartered by Price's company to carry ore to the ironworks at Tondu in Glamorgan, gave rise to mounting debts. The company failed and he went bankrupt in 1855, when the estate was sold 'to satisfy claims caused by a craze of [Robert Price] to obtain additional wealth in commercial investments, from which losses instead of profits accumulated'.[42] Sir Robert Price's tramway and the iron works at Tondu Iron Park are now a tourist attraction. Uvedale Price's daughter Caroline had died in 1853. Caroline Duff Gordon noted in 1856 'Gilbert & I drove over to call at Foxley, it made me sad to think of the changes there! Sir Robert & Lady Price are still there, but the house belongs to a Mr Davenport ... . Shade of Sir Uvedale what must you feel?'[43] Sir Robert died in 1857, and his wife, 'who retired to London and managed to pay off all her husband's debts', died in March 1878.[44]

The Price collections of paintings and drawings were sold in three sales, two in the 1850s and one in the 1890s. The first sale of 320 lots over two days was by Sotheby's in May 1854.[45] It was advertised as 'the most Valuable and Interesting Collection of Ancient Drawings of the Italian, German, Dutch, Flemish and French Schools formed with the greatest taste and care, in a Continental Tour undertaken during the years 1767–8 by the late Uvedale Price Esq., Author of "Essays on the Picturesque"'. The catalogue pointed out that 'these drawings have been buried from the public eye' since the days of 'Sir Joshua Reynolds, Gainsborough, and Benjamin West, who were frequent visitors at Mr. Price's house, enjoying a sight of his folios'. The second sale, in fifty-five lots, was by Foster and Son on 11 June 1856. It described the 'Foxley Collection of Pictures' as including 'several fine works exhibited at the British Institution in the years 1837, 1838, 1839 and 1840.' The pictures

> have long adorned the walls of the old mansion at Foxley. So many original works are rarely found in so small a collection: this may, in great measure, be attributed to the fact that more than one ancestor of Sir Robert Price had fine taste and knowledge of the Arts; and, in particular, Sir Uvedale Price not only distinguished himself as a connoisseur, but established a lasting reputation by his well-known work on the Picturesque. The pictures are to be found in a state so much coveted by amateurs, the Berghem was cleaned some years ago by the late Mr. Seguier.[46]

The final sale was in 1893, when the Price family portraits were sold by Christies on the death of their last owner, Mr Thomas Price, of Albany Chambers.[47]

A reinvigorated interest in Uvedale Price's importance in the development of landscape aesthetics began in the 1920s, when Christopher Hussey identified the picturesque 'point of view' at Scotney Castle. Hussey described how his 'eye, ranging the mellow shelves beside me, fell on ... *Sir Uvedale Price on the Picturesque*' and he had a sudden realisation that the view from the library at Scotney Castle was not the result of 'natural good taste'. Indeed, the scene before him 'so far from being a happy coincidence, must have been planned on picturesque principles'.[48] The idea of the picturesque as something planned and sensitive to local context equally appealed to Nikolaus Pevsner, who was much influenced by Hussey. He was encouraged to write and explore the relationship between Price's ideas and modern planning by Hubert de Cronin Hastings.[49] During the war Pevsner published a series of articles in *The Architectural Review* that drew explicitly on Price and the picturesque. He argued in 'Price on Picturesque planning' that Price's ideas 'assume a new importance in conjunction with the problems of large-scale visual planning which face us today'. He felt that Price had 'left behind the accepted dogmas and fashions of his generation' and that his 'latitude of aesthetic sensibility raises him out of the eighteenth century to an undated position in the history of aesthetic theory'.[50]

Hubert de Cronin Hastings, writing under the pseudonym Ivor de Wolfe, went so far as to write 'A plea for an English visual philosophy founded on the true rock of Sir Uvedale Price' in *The Architectural Review* of December 1949.[51] He argued that the publication of Price's *Essay* 'was a key moment in art history since Price actually succeeded, despite the handicap of eighteenth-century art-jargon, in isolating what had not been isolated before – a way of looking at the world that might be called perennially English'. He felt that knowledge of the picturesque 'could revolutionize our national contribution to architecture and town-planning by making possible our own regional development of the International style.' He further emphasised the 'radical canon' of the 'Picturesque doctrines' of Price: compared to Kent and Brown who 'conceived it their duty to *improve* the environment, Price argued that it should be *made*.'[52] Hasting's essay is followed by a 'Townscape Casebook' by Gordon Cullen, which includes examples of good practice for architects and planners such as 'eye as agoraphobe' (enclosure and exposure); 'eye as articulator' (incident; flowing lines; undulation; projection and recession) and 'eye as poet' (metaphor, individuality and nostalgia).[53]

Pevsner's Reith lectures of 1955, reprinted as *The Englishness of English Art*, contained a whole lecture devoted to 'Picturesque England'.[54] Pevsner was here using the picturesque as a shorthand for the eighteenth-century English landscaping tradition as a whole, but he made a particular reference to the value of 'improvers' such as Price and Knight as the inspiration for a 'healthy, attractive, acceptable town planning'. For Pevsner, Pope's instruction to 'Consult the genius of the place in all' had lessons for a country that was still trying to rebuild its bombed-out cities after six years of war, where the *genius loci*, 'in modern planning terms, is the character of the site'. This amounted, in Pevsner's view, to the need for sensitivity to place and a recognition that planning needed to be flexible enough to accommodate the different requirements of places as diverse as the City of London, Cambridge, small towns with character (such as Blandford) and towns 'with little character, such as Slough'. Pevsner recognised this as a typically English approach to treating each place 'on its own merit', even if, as he acknowledged, the English had somehow forgotten this way of doing things at some point in the preceding century. The townscapes Pevsner most admired were either those that had developed 'by accident', or those that had irregularity and variety built into their design, such as John Wood's design for Bath and Wren's City of London. By contrast, the Victorian period had seen a *laissez faire* attitude develop which, ironically, had inspired nothing more than a bland uniformity of architecture. Pevsner noted that the reaction against this uniformity at the end of the nineteenth century had been to return to the picturesque, in the form of the garden suburb and garden city, and he called for this spirit to rise again among English planners, both in the enhancement of existing urban areas and in the planning of new towns. To illustrate his point Pevsner included a photograph of a model of Frederick Gibberd's design for the centre of Harlow New Town, which in later decades was to become the very epitome of everything that the picturesque was not: bland, characterless, repetitious.

There is now an extensive literature on the picturesque debate and on Price's role in it. The classic studies are by Hussey (1927) and Hipple (1957). Following the bicentenary of the publication of the *Essay* and *The Landscape* in 1994 there has been more interest in the relationship between Price's ideas on landscape history and practice.[55] It is generally accepted, and Price would have surely have agreed with this himself, that his contribution to the history of aesthetics and landscaping is more practical than theoretical. His theoretical originality lay in his definition of the picturesque as a third aesthetic category lying between Burke's sublime and beautiful. Price's ideas on the theory of landscape aesthetics were undoubtedly rooted in a deep understanding of classical authors and modern poets rather than contemporary theoreticians such as Kant and Alison. His practical understanding of the creation and management of landscapes and the relationship between architecture and landscape, however, was at the forefront of contemporary knowledge. His critical engagements with John Nash, Richard Payne Knight, Humphry Repton, John Claudius Loudon, William Sawrey Gilpin and William Wordsworth brought about a novel understanding of the way that landscapes could be made, managed and enjoyed. Price undoubtedly knew how to look after his own interests, and took his role as an owner of a landed estate seriously. His views on benevolent landownership were strongly influenced by those of his father and his Barrington uncles, as well as practical self-interest and the experiments and innovations of Benjamin Stillingfleet and Nathaniel Kent. His enthusiasm for writing was engendered by his grandfather's scholarly interests and the eclectic essays of Daines Barrington.

Price's character and personality are intriguing and contradictory. The lack of surviving correspondence for much of his early life means that a great deal remains conjectural. We have only tantalising glimpses of his life in London before his marriage and we know little of aspects of life, such as his keen interest in music and membership of the Society of Dilettanti, which were clearly of great importance to him. Some contemporaries, such as Lord

Egremont, found him a selfish and almost laughable character. Others, such as Wordsworth, were at times critical of his mode of living and his family life, but at other times complimentary of his character, stamina and ideas. The evidence provided by lengthy friendships with Charles James Fox and the Beaumonts strongly suggests that he was an entertaining and generally benevolent person, an impression reinforced by the lengthy support provided by Price and his wife for his daughter Caroline through her periods of intense illness. The early death of his father and mother may have been factors encouraging a demand for the safety of scholarship, precision and control which he showed throughout his life, whether in estate management, gardening or art criticism. He was equivocal about his Welsh ancestry, joking about his 'welch temper' and the Welsh idioms of acquaintances such as the painter Thomas Jones, yet retaining a deep appreciation of the Welsh mountains and coast. The importance of his family inheritance of land, property and art cannot be overestimated. He gained enormous practical knowledge of tree and woodland management and the plantations made by his father meant that he was able to experiment widely in the creation and management of woodland views. He was always interested in sharing ideas, as shown by his mode of circulating drafts of his writings among friends such as Lord Abercorn and the Beaumonts for critical appraisal. But he was never afraid to make a judgment and it can be argued that he was one of those who invented the role of public intellectual in early nineteenth-century Britain. Price's picturesque aesthetic remains powerful and influential today, and his role in identifying, elucidating and classifying the picturesque and transforming the way we understand and appreciate landscape should be celebrated.

NOTES TO THE TEXT

INTRODUCTION (pages 1–3)

[1] D. Watkin, 1982, *The English Vision. The Picturesque in Architecture, Landscape and Garden Design*. London, p. vii.

[2] John Macarthur, 2007, *The Picturesque. Architecture, Disgust and other Irregularities*. London, p. 1.

[3] Christopher Hussey, 1927, *The Picturesque*. London.

[4] Nikolaus Pevsner, 1963, *Herefordshire*. London, p. 328.

[5] Walter Hipple, 1957, *The Beautiful, the Sublime and the Picturesque in Eighteenth Century Aesthetic Theory*. Carbondale.

[6] Stephen Daniels and Charles Watkins (eds), 1994, *The Picturesque Landscape: Visions of Georgian Herefordshire*. Nottingham, catalogues the exhibition held to celebrate the bicentenary of the 1794 publication of Price's *Essay on the Picturesque* and Richard Payne Knight's *The Landscape*.

[7] Charles Watkins and Ben Cowell (eds), 2006, *Letters of Uvedale Price*, Walpole Society, 68. The principal correspondents are Lord Abercorn, Lord Aberdeen and Sir George and Lady Beaumont.

[8] Lars E. Troide, 1988, *The Early Journals and Letters of Fanny Burney*. London: 8 May 1771, p. 148 and 4 May 1772, p. 218.

[9] Uvedale Price to Samuel Rogers, 25 May 1823. In P.W. Clayden (ed.), 1889, *Rogers and His Contemporaries*. London, vol. 1, pp. 355–61.

[10] Examples of this type of research include Stephen Daniels, 1999, *Humphry Repton: Landscape Gardening and the Geography of Georgian England*. New Haven and London; John Bonehill and Stephen Daniels (eds), 2009, *Paul Sandby: Picturing Britain*. London; Sandrine Petit and Charles Watkins, 2003, 'Pollarding trees: changing attitudes to a traditional land management practice in Britain 1600–1900', *Rural History*, 14, pp. 157–76; Susanne Seymour and Rupert Calvocoressi, 2007, 'Landscape parks and the memorialisation of empire: the Pierreponts' "naval seascape" in Thoresby Park, Nottinghamshire during the French Wars (1793–1815)', *Rural History*, 18, pp. 95–118.

[11] Macarthur 2007, p. 11.

[12] Stephen Daniels and Charles Watkins, 1991, 'Picturesque landscaping and estate management', *Rural History*, 2, pp. 141–69; Denis A. Lambin, 1987, 'Foxley; the Price's estate in Herefordshire', *Journal of Garden History*, 7, pp. 244–70; Susanne Seymour, Stephen Daniels and Charles Watkins, 1998, 'Estate and empire: Sir George Cornewall's management of Moccas, Herefordshire and La Taste, Grenada, 1771–1829', *Journal of Historical Geography*, 24, pp. 313–51.

[13] Susan Sloman, 2002, *Gainsborough in Bath*. New Haven and London.

[14] Felicity Owen and David Blayney Brown, 1988, *Collector of Genius: A Life of Sir George Beaumont*. New Haven and London; Andrew Ballantyne, 1997, *Architecture, Landscape and Liberty: Richard Payne Knight and the Picturesque*. Cambridge.

CHAPTER 1: 'THE GREATEST VARIETY OF PROSPECTS' (pages 4–23)

[1] James Joel Cartwright (ed.), 1888, *The Travels through England of Dr Richard Pococke during 1750, 1751 and later years*. London, pp. 224–5.

[2] E. Cruikshank, S. Handley and D. W. Hayton, 2002, *History of Parliament. The House of Commons 1690–1715*. vol. V: Members O–Z. London, p. 204.

[3] Stuart Handley, *ODNB*. An important source is Edmund Curll, 1734, *The Life of the Late Honourable Robert Price, Esq; one of the Justices of His Majesty's Court of Common-Pleas*. London. This was printed 'by Appointment of the Family' by Edmund Curll, who dedicated the biography 'To Uvedale Tomkyns Price, Esq; member of parliament for Weobly in the County of Hereford and only son and heir to the late Hon. Mr. Justice Price'. He noted 'Having obtained the Honour, and Friendship of your Commands, for Compiling, Publishing, and Addressing these Papers to You; I hope, all the Mistrust of a censorious Age, as to their Genuineness, will be looked upon as groundless' (Curll 1734, p. iii). Curll's defence was necessary as 'Pope's depiction of him as a loathsome dunce and crook has been powerful – leading not least to his becoming known as the Unspeakable Curll' but 'scholars more recently have begun to question that image … he was also inventive, energetic, and always alive to the value of publicity and the need to create a market for one's product'. Raymond N. MacKenzie, *ODNB*.

[4] Edward Foss, 1870, *A Biographical Dictionary of the Judges of England*. London, p. 539.

[5] Douglas B. Hague, 1958, 'Giler, Cerrig-y-drudion, Denbighshire', *Denbighshire Historical Society Transactions*, 7, pp. 67–85. See also E. Hubbard, 1986, *Buildings of Wales: Clwyd*. Harmondsworth, p. 261.

[6] Curll 1734, p. 59. He accompanied Robert Sutton (1661–1723), second Baron Lexington of Averham Park, Nottinghamshire, who succeeded as second baron while still a child, in October 1668.

[7] Curll 1734, p. 3. Anna Sophia Rodd's mother Lucy was the daughter of William Uvedale of Wickham in Hampshire, and remarried Sir Thomas Tomkins, MP for Weobley. Their son, Uvedale Tomkins, might have followed his father into a political career, and indeed was nominated for the seat of Weobley by Robert Price in 1691, but took little interest in politics and died a year later. This is the origin of the use of Uvedale as a Christian name by the Prices.

[8] Cruikshank *et al.* 2002, p. 204.

[9] See letter quoted in B. Henning, 1983, *History of Parliament. The House of Commons 1660–1690*, vol. 3. London, p. 286. Also P. Jenkins, 1983, *The Making of a Ruling Class: The Glamorgan Gentry 1640–1790*. Cambridge, pp. 145 and 165 for Price as supporter of 1st duke. See also Sloman 2002, p. 43, and p. 226 note 54.

[10] Sloman 2002, p. 148.

[11] Joseph Hillaby, 1967, 'The parliamentary borough of Weobley, 1628–1708', *Transactions of the Woolhope Naturalists' Field Club*, 39, 1, pp. 104–51.

[12] Curll 1734, Stuart Handley, *ODNB*; See also Francis James Rennell, 1958, *Valley on the March*. London.

[13] Curll 1734, p. 37. The speech was reprinted by Walter Scott, 1814, *Somers' Tracts*, vol. 11. London, pp. 387–93.

[14] George Sherburn (ed.), 1956, *The Correspondence of Alexander Pope*, vol. III. Oxford. Pope to Earl of Oxford 16 Nov. 1730, pp. 149–50.

[15] Cruikshank *et al.* 2002. Colourful though inaccurate accounts are given by William Henry Cooke, 1892, *Collections towards the History and Antiquities of the County of Hereford: In Continuation of Duncumb's History. vol. 4 Hundred of Grimsworth*. London, p. 190 and Rennell 1958.

[16] Curll 1734, pp. 40–41.

[17] Curll 1734, p. 42. A member of the Cornewall family of Moccas, Herefordshire.

[18] Curll 1734, p. 43.

[19] Curll 1734, Appendix, Thomas Price to his mother, 19 October 1705.

[20] Curll 1734, Appendix, Thomas Price to his mother, 12 March 1706.

[21] Curll 1734, pp. 45–7.

[22] Curll 1734, Appendix, Thomas Price to his mother, 12 March 1706.

[23] Curll 1734, p. 53.

[24] Curll 1734, p. 59.

[25] Curll 1734, p. 58.

[26] Curll 1734, p. 7.

[27] Curll 1734, p. 4.

[28] See Daniels and Watkins 1991.

[29] Lambin 1987, pp. 246–8.

[30] Proverbs 19.7 'All the brethren of the poor do hate him: how much more do his friends go far from him? he pursueth them with words, yet they are wanting to him'; Tobit 4.7 'Give alms from your possessions. Do not turn your face away from any of the poor, and God's face will not be turned away from you.' Luke 14.13–14 'But when thou makest a feast, call the poor, the maimed, the lame, the blind: And thou shalt be blessed; for they cannot recompense thee: for thou shalt be recompensed at the resurrection of the just.'

[31] Anne Price to Lady Anne Coventry 18 June n.d. Letters from Anne Price to Lady Anne Coventry Poston Hereford, Badminton Muniments 1715–1738 FM T/B 1/2/23, transcribed by Susan Sloman. See also Sloman 2002, p. 149.

[32] The architectural historian Bryan Little made a radio broadcast for the *Midlands Miscellany* programme of the Midlands Home Service Friday 18 May 1956. He sent a copy of the script with a 'written record' of changes at Foxley he had made on 20 May 1956 to the Manuscripts Collection of Hereford City Library in 1970. Charles Watkins found this transcript in 1987 and contacted Bryan Little, who wrote on 5 February 1988 that he had found a copy of James Gibbs' *Book of Architecture* in the bookshop of Mr H. D. Lyon of 11 Pitt Street, Kensington, while researching *The Life and Works of James Gibbs 1682–1754*, 1955. 'The book was bought, at the Foxley sale in 1856, by Robert Biddulph Phillips, and Mr Lyon bought it in 1954 from the heirs of the Phillips family'. Judge Robert Price was one of the subscribers to the *Book of Architecture* in 1728. No one knows the current whereabouts of the book. There were manuscript notes on the fly page of the book made by Uvedale Tomkyns Price, Robert Price and Uvedale Price. These notes transcribed by Bryan Little are referred to as the 'Little Transcript'. The architectural history of the mansion at Foxley is fully described by David Whitehead, Foxley House, Yazor, in *The Country Houses of Herefordshire*, forthcoming.

[33] Anne Price to Lady Anne Coventry 18 June n.d. Letters from Anne Price to Lady Anne Coventry Poston Hereford, Badminton Muniments 1715–1738 FM T/B 1/2/23, transcribed by Susan Sloman.

[34] Andor Harvey Gomme, 2000, *Smith of Warwick: Francis Smith, Architect and Master-builder*. Stamford.

[35] Gomme 2000, pp. 159–6.

[36] Gomme 2000, p. 529.

[37] Daines Barrington in an unpublished paper on 'Architects & Architecture in this Kingdom' to the Society of Antiquaries 20 January 1785. S.A.L. Minute Book 18/11/1784 to 10/11/1785, vol. XX, 1784, pp. 84–8.

[38] Uvedale Price to E. H. Barker, 5 June 1828.

[39] Udal ap Rhys, 1749, *An Account of the Most Remarkable Places and Curiosities in Spain and Portugal*. London, p. 2.

[40] 'Little transcript'; Gomme 2000, p. 529. There was a loose sheet of paper inserted in Uvedale Tomkyns Price's copy of *Vitruvius Britannicus* 1717 which has a plan probably by Uvedale Tomkyns Price. Whitehead, Foxley House, Yazor, in *The Country Houses of Herefordshire*, forthcoming; Lambin 1987, p. 247.

[41] Curll notes 'The whole' of Robert Price's life was 'in a great Measure confined to Westminster-Hall'. He left his daughter in law Anne 'one of my best Clocks in my Chambers in Searjeants-Inn' and to his grandson Robert 'my own Picture, his Father and Mother, and his own, and Sister Hester's Picture, at Searjeants-Inn'. Curll 1734, p. 63.

[42] 'Little transcript'.

[43] 'Little transcript'.

[44] See Jack Callow, 2001, '"The Ragged Castle": an architectural feature on the Foxley estate, Herefordshire', *The Picturesque*, 34, pp. 1–14.

[45] Sloman 2002, p. 156.

[46] Sloman 2002, p. 149.

[47] Although Denis Lambin argues that 'Uvedale Tompkins does not seem to have had time enough to leave his imprint on the place' and downplays his involvement at Foxley, he does note that the horticultural interests of both father and son is shown by them both being subscribers to Furber's Catalogue of 1730–32. Lambin 1987, p. 247.

[48] Lambin 1987, p. 248, p. 251, p. 267 n. 24.

[49] Sloman 2002, p. 148, Lambin 1987, p. 248, John Ingamells, 1997, *A Dictionary of British and Irish Travellers in Italy 1701–1800*. New Haven and London, p. 787.

[50] Gomme 2000, p. 159.

[51] 'Little transcript'.

[52] Uvedale Price was sent a copy by Archdeacon Wrangham of Chester in 1828. He was unaware of its existence and noted 'From what is written on the blank leaf, I have no doubt that this parody, tho' anonymously printed, must have been written by my Grandfather; + having satisfied my curiosity, + repeating my thanks to you for having indulged it, I now return this little scarce article: + altogether am not sorry that it should be so scarce, + so little known'. Price to Wrangham 9 January 1828, tipped into 1733 edition held in British Library. It was republished in 1740 with 'Another Psalm for the Use of a Young Lady, by Mr Pope'.

[53] Sherburn 1956. Martha Blount to Mrs Price; Pope to Mrs Price, 8 September 1740. 265–6. Martha Blount (1690–1763) was a long-standing friend of Alexander Pope.

[54] *London Evening Post*, 20 May 1731; 16 June 1741.

[55] E. I. Carlyle, *ODNB*.

[56] Louise Lippincott, *ODNB*.

[57] Louise Lippincott, 1983, *Selling Art in Georgian London. The Rise of Arthur Pond*. London, p. 175, n. 50.

[58] Lippincott 1983, p. 57.

[59] The earliest references in the list are to 'Mr Price', but this must refer to Uvedale Price as his son Robert was then on his visit to France, Italy and Switzerland.

[60] National Library of Wales LW 1. Court Rolls and Court Books. No. 1,709. 11 April 1744 to 12 May 1756 Uvedale Price Lord of Manor 1744–1755.

[61] He subscribed to Andrew Ramsay's *A New Cyropædia: or the Travels of Cyrus, with a Discourse on the Theology & Mythologie of the Ancients*, 1730; Guido Bentivoglio's *A Collection of Letters written by Cardinal Bentivoglio*, 1753 and Sarah Fielding's *The Lives of Cleopatra and Octavia*, 1757.

[62] Uvedale Price, 1739, Translation of Antonio Palomino de Castro y Velasco, *An Account of the Lives and Works of the Most Eminent Spanish Painters, Sculptors and Architects from the Musæum Pictorium*. London.

[63] Udal ap Rhys 1749, p. 2, p. 271.

[64] Philip Thicknesse, 1778, *A Year's Journey through France and Part of Spain*. London, p. 338. Thicknesse is described by Katherine Turner in the *ODNB* as 'easily the most irascible individual within the arena of late eighteenth-century print culture'. We would like to thank Dr Rogério Puga of the New University of Lisbon for discussing Uvedale Price's authorship of this book.

[65] There was an important family link in that Margaret Burr was the natural daughter of Henry Somerset, the 3rd duke of Beaufort (1707–1745). She married Gainsborough in 1746 and received an annuity from the Beaufort estate for the rest of her life. Uvedale Tomkyns Price's wife Anne Somerset (1698–1741) was a cousin of the 3rd duke of Beaufort. Sloman 2002, p. 43, p. 147.

[66] William Coxe, 1811, *Literary Life and Select Works of Benjamin Stillingfleet, Several of Which have Never Before been Published*. London, II, part II, p. 161.

[67] Beryl Hartley, 1994, 'Naturalism and sketching, Robert Price at Foxley and on Tour', in Stephen Daniels and Charles Watkins (eds), *The Picturesque Landscape: Visions of Georgian Herefordshire*. Nottingham, pp. 34–7, p. 34.

[68] Uvedale Price, 1810, *Essays on the Picturesque*. London, II, pp. 234–5.

[69] Coxe 1811, II, part II, pp. 160–61; R. W. Ketton-Cremer, 1962, *Felbrigg: The Story of a House*. London, p. 116.

[70] For a detailed account of the Tour see Coxe 1811, I, pp. 73–81.

[71] William Windham (1717–1761) was father of William Windham (1750–1810) Secretary at War 1794–1801 and godparent to Robert Price's third son William Price.

[72] Coxe 1811, II, part II, p. 170.

[73] Ketton-Cremer 1962, p. 114.

[74] Coxe 1811, II, part II, p. 170.

[75] Coxe 1811, II, part II, p. 171.

[76] Ingamells 1997, pp. 787–8.

[77] Coxe 1811, I, p. 74.

[78] Coxe 1811, I, pp. 74–9.

[79] Hartley 1994, p. 34.

[80] Coxe 1811, I, p. 81.

[81] Pierre Martel and William Windham, 1774, *An Account of the Glacieres, or Ice Alps, in Savoy, in two Letters; One from an English Gentleman* [W. Windham, assisted by R. Price and B. Stillingfleet] … *the Other from P. Martel, Engineer… With a Map and Two Views* [from drawings by R. Price and P. Martel], etc. London. See also Ketton-Cremer 1962, pp. 119–20.

[82] Jacques-Phillipe Le Bas (1707–1783) was a French engraver who concentrated on plates based on Dutch and Flemish painters including David Teniers (II), Philips Wouwerman and Salomon van Ruysdael. Coxe 1811, II, p. 123.

[83] Hartley 1994, p. 35, Colin Harrison, 1998, 'Malchair the Artist', in Colin Harrison (ed.), *John Malchair of Oxford: Artist and Musician*. Oxford, p. 10.

[84] André Laurent (1708–1747) was an English-born engraver who was apprenticed to Le Bas and later 'refused an offer from Arthur Pond to return to London'. Grove, *Dictionary of Art*, 1996; Francis W. Hawcroft, 1958, 'The "Cabinet" at Felbrigg', *Connoisseur*, CXLI, pp. 216–19, letter from Price in Paris to William Windham in Geneva, 9 November 1741. Pierre Soubeyran, Swiss artist and engraver (1709–1775). See also Francis W. Hawcroft, 'Giovanni Battista Busiri', *Gazette des Beaux-Arts*, LIII, 1959, pp. 295–304.

[85] Hawcroft 1958, letter from Price in London to Lord Haddington 19 December 1741. Arline J. Meyer, 'Wootton, John (1681/2–1764)', *ODNB*.

[86] Hawcroft 1958, pp. 216–19. Letter from Price in London to Lord Haddington in Geneva, 19 December 1741.

[87] C. H. Collins Baker, 1938, '*The Price Family* by Bartholomew Dandridge', *Burlington Magazine*, 72, pp. 132–9.

[88] Christie's, Portraits and other Pictures chiefly of the early English School. The property of Thomas Price, Esq, deceased, late of the Albany. Saturday 6 May 1893.

[89] Sloman 2002, p. 150. Collins Baker identifies the young Robert Price as the figure seated at the left; Susan Sloman and the 1893 catalogue as the figure third from the left.

[90] 'Benjamin Stillingfleet', *ODNB*.

[91] See Daniels and Watkins 1991 and Lambin 1987.

[92] 'Little transcript'.

[93] Coxe 1811, I, p. 98.

[94] Coxe 1811, I, pp. 108–17.

[95] First edition 1759, second 1762, third 1775.

[96] Coxe 1811, I, p. 125.

[97] See F. McCarthy, 1964, 'Some newly discovered drawings by Robert Price of Foxley', *National Library of Wales Journal*, 13, 3, pp. 289–94, quotation p. 293. Isaac Basire (1704–1768), printmaker and draughtsman.

[98] Richard Neville Aldworth (1717–1793), diplomatist and politician.

[99] Coxe 1811, I, p. 155.

[100] Coxe 1811, I, p. 174, fn. 2.

[101] Stillingfleet to Windham 12 December 1757 transcribed for Denis Lambin by R. W. Ketton-Cremer. MSS Felbrigg Hall, Lambin 1987, p. 268.

[102] Coxe 1811, II, part II, pp. 176–7.

[103] Isaac Taylor publicly thanks Robert Price and Theophilus Lane for 'many particular favours' in the Cartouche of his Map of Hereford, 1757.

[104] See Cartwright 1888, pp. 224–5. Pococke also noted 'They have a quarry here of the most beautiful freestone; it has a green cast, and works extremely well'.

[105] See Charles Watkins, Stephen Daniels and Susanne Seymour, 1995, 'Picturesque woodland management: the Prices at Foxley', in D. Arnold (ed.), *The Picturesque in Late Georgian England*. London, pp. 27–34, 69–70. The Lady Lift clump has been variously interpreted as a marker for drovers and a symbol of Jacobite sympathies.

106 Coxe 1811, II, part II, p. 232. Although Coxe records that Stillingfleet had formed the beginnings of a companionship with Anne Scudamore, the sister of a neighbour in Herefordshire, and continued to meet her in London (at the house of Mr Torriano, who had married her sister), the lack of any great fortune on either side ultimately meant that 'love gradually subsided into friendship, and the lady, like Mr Stillingfleet, died unmarried'. He was buried at St James's Church, Piccadilly, and his memorial tablet can be seen on the staircase of the church.

107 Coxe 1811, II, part II, p. 161.

108 Coxe 1811, II, part II, p. 175, note.

109 Coxe 1811, I, p. 121.

110 Nathaniel Kent, 1775, *Hints to a Gentleman of Landed Property*. London, pp. 37–42.

111 Coxe 1811, II, part II, p. 180.

112 Coxe 1811, II, part II, p. 172, note. Metastasio's oratorio Guiseppe Riconosciuto was originally performed in the Imperial Chapel, Vienna, 12 March 1733. See also Charles Burney, 1789, *A General History of Music from the Earliest Ages to the Present Period*, London (ed. Frank Mercer, 1957), vol. II, p. 855. Jamie Croy Kassler in the *Grove Dictionary of Music*, 1980, states that arias by Robert Price were performed at the King's Theatre, London on 22 February 1743, 9 December 1755 and 11 December 1755. In William Coxe's 1799 *Anecdotes of George Frederick Handel and John Christopher Smith with Select Pieces of Music Composed by J. C. Smith Never Before Published*, Smith calls Price 'an excellent composer' who 'encouraged him in his labours, and wrote the poetry for the Oratorio Judith' (p. 46). The list of subscribers to Coxe 1799 includes the Hon. Daines Barrington; Admiral Barrington; Mr Crotch, Oxford; the Hon. and Right Rev. the Lord Bishop of Durham; the Earl of Egremont; Thomas Pennant, Esq.; Uvedale Price, Esq.; Rev. Robert Price D.D. Prebendary of Durham; William Price, Esq.; Mrs A. Scudamore, Hereford, and Samuel Whitbread, Esq.

113 Michael Burden, *ODNB*. Daniel Lysons (1812, *History of the Origin and Progress of the Meeting of the Three Choirs of Gloucester, Worcester and Hereford*. Gloucester, p. 189) states 'Malchair, who is living, but in a state of blindness and infirmity, was a drawing master at Oxford for many years, led the band at the Music-room in that city, and was much respected by the members of the university.' He performed at the Three Choirs music festival at least ten times between 1759 and 1775. Robert Price was a steward of the festival in 1759, Lysons 1812, pp. 141–57.

114 T. B. Healey, *ODNB*.

115 Colin Harrison considers that Malchair was 'no doubt employed as a musician [at Foxley] but must also have taken informal drawing lessons from his patron'. Harrison 1998, p. 10.

116 Sloman 2002, p. 154.

117 Coxe 1811, II, part II, p. 171.

118 Cooke 1892, p. 197.

119 The wall tablet is number 464. See typescript by Tim Woods, 1992. 'A guide to the wall tablets of Bath Abbey as they appear today', unpublished typescript, Bath. Information provided by Susan Sloman who verified the text on the monument in 1998.

120 The Portsmouth Bookshop, New Hampshire, 1999 catalogue. Lambin notes that 'The only surviving copy of the 5 January 1762 sale catalogue of Uvedale Tompkins's collections ..., auctioned by Langford, was destroyed in a raid over Berlin during the last war. It was in the Kupferstichkabinett, Staatbibliotheck'. Lambin 1987, p. 267 n. 19. Lugt 1214, states, however, that the catalogue was 'transported to Russia in 1945'. The collection consisted of 161 drawings and 123 prints and books of prints. Some of Uvedale Tompkins Price's collection was sold in 1772. James Robson, 1772, *A Catalogue of a very Large and Capital Collection of Books....* London, Lot 19. More drawings from his collection were sold in 1787: Mr Greenwood, 1787, *A Catalogue of that Superb and well known Cabinet of Drawings of John Barnard....* 16 February, London.

CHAPTER 2: 'MACARONY OF THE AGE' (pages 24–45)

1 Troide 1988, p. 218, 4 May 1772.

2 Uvedale Price to Lord Aberdeen, 18 August 1816, Watkins and Cowell 2006b, pp. 250–53. This was part of a discourse on beauty, in which Price tried to show that subjective beauty accorded to familiar scenes of youth did not necessarily equate with beauty as defined by Burke.

[3] Uvedale Price to E. H. Barker, 26 October 1827.

[4] Uvedale Price to E. H. Barker, 24 March 1827, in E. H. Barker, 1852, *Literary Anecdotes and Contemporary Reminiscences of Professor Porson and Others; from the Manuscript Papers of the Late EH Barker Esq of Thetford, Norfolk*. London, vol. II, pp. 36–7.

[5] Horace Walpole to Montague Thursday 22 January 1761. In W. S. Lewis (ed.), 1941, *Horace Walpole's Correspondence*. New Haven, vol. 9, p. 335.

[6] Lord Egremont (3rd earl 1751–1837) to Lord Holland (Henry Richard Fox, 3rd Baron Holland 1773–1840) BM Add Ms 51725, 25 December 1827.

[7] Price 1810, II, p. 368. The influence of Gainsborough on Price's ideas of the picturesque has been discussed by Christopher Hussey, John Hayes and Susan Sloman.

[8] Price 1810, I, p. 15.

[9] Lord Barrington and his brother Daines Barrington were trustees for Uvedale Price from March 1765 until November 1769, Goslings Bank 03594.

[10] Uvedale Price, 1794, *An Essay on the Picturesque*. London, pp. 279–80.

[11] Ingamells 1997, pp. 787–8.

[12] Uvedale Price to E. H. Barker, 24 March 1827, in Samuel Rogers, 1856, *Recollections of the Table-talk of Samuel Rogers*. London, p. 76–7, fn. William Wentworth Fitzwilliam, second Earl Fitzwilliam in the peerage of Great Britain, and fourth Earl Fitzwilliam in the peerage of Ireland (1748–1833), Whig politician and landowner of Milton House, Peterborough and Wentworth House, Yorkshire. 'His time in Italy had a profound and lasting influence on him and stimulated his love of art.' *ODNB*.

[13] Fox to Price, 27 October 1767, BM Add Ms 47576.

[14] Susan Sloman, 2008, pers comm.

[15] John Skippe, notebook, HRO, B38/324. The notebook provides travel costs and prices paid for his pictures. He stayed in Venice until September 1767 and was back in Ledbury, Herefordshire, in January 1768.

[16] Fox to Price, 24 February 1768, BM Add Ms 47576.

[17] Sir Horatio Mann (1706–1786), diplomatist, British resident in Florence 1740–1786 and correspondent of Horace Walpole. 'William, second Earl Fitzwilliam … wrote that: Sir Horace is the most finical man in the world: if you speak a little loud, he can't bear it, it hurts his nerves, he dies – and he v–m–ts if you eat your petite patee before your soup; take him as he is, without the least notice, he is perfect character for the stage. He has been so long out of England, that he had lost the manliness of an Englishman, and has borrowed the effeminacy of Italy. But with all his little airs, he is a good kind of man, and is very civil. (Fitzwilliam MSS) His close friendships with the homosexual painter Thomas Patch and the effete John, second Earl Tylney, adds weight to this description.' Hugh Belsey, *ODNB*.

[18] Fox to Price, Nice, 24 February 1768.

[19] Uvedale Price to Sir George Beaumont, 12 January 1822, Watkins and Cowell 2006b, pp. 299–300.

[20] Uvedale Price to Sir George Beaumont, 12 January 1822, Watkins and Cowell 2006b, pp. 299–300. Gavin Hamilton (1723–1798), painter, archaeologist, and dealer: 'a central figure in the artistic life of Rome in the latter half of the eighteenth century and a key influence on the formation of neo-classical taste in Europe.' Julia Lloyd Williams, *ODNB*.

[21] Uvedale Price to E. H. Barker, 24 March 1827 in Barker 1852, vol. II pp. 36–7.

[22] Johann-George Wille, 1857, *Mémoires et Journal de J-G Wille, Graveur du Roi*, 2 vols. Paris, pp. 387–8; 404: 9 November 1768; 17 November 1768 and 23 April 1769.

[23] Susan Sloman, 2008, pers comm. She notes that 'Roos, a follower of Salvator Rosa, created a rather sinister brand of wild rocky landscape (usually occupied by sheep or goats) very much in the Rosa tradition. Perhaps Wille's additional gift to Price of a painting or drawing of Roman ruins by January Both was a sign of a guilty conscience, but Price was no fool and he may have had second thoughts about his Raphael during his journey from Italy …'.

[24] Uvedale Price to Sir George Beaumont, 11 November 1812, Watkins and Cowell 2006b, pp. 204–6.

[25] HRO, D 344.

[26] Lambin 1987, pp. 244–70 and Daniels and Watkins 1991, pp. 141–69.

[27] *Public Advertiser*, 18 August 1773.

[28] John Nichols, 1828, *Illustrations of the Literary History of the Eighteenth Century*, vol. V. London, Daines Barrington to Richard Gough 2 September 1770, p. 585. Edward Lhwyd (1659/60–1709), naturalist and philologist.

[29] 'Little transcript'.

[30] James Cranston (1748–1835). Brian S. Smith, 2004, *Herefordshire Maps 1577–1800*. Hereford, p. 189.

[31] 'Little transcript'. Robert Price and Uvedale Price (Price's father and grandfather) are both listed as subscribers to Robert Adam's *Ruins of the Palace of the Emperor Diocletian at Spalatro in Dalmatia*, published in 1764 (London).

[32] HRO, BH 97/9 From H. Davies, Henbury, to Miss Davies at Mr Poole's, Widemarsh St, Hereford, 16 May 1772.

[33] David Whitehead, pers comm, 2004. See also David Whitehead, 2009, 'Artisan attitudes to Gothic in Georgian Herefordshire', *The Georgian Group Journal*, 17, pp. 61–76.

[34] *Hereford Journal*, 6 July 1780. Symonds was later replaced as architect of the Infirmary by William Parker. Reference provided by David Whitehead.

[35] Ballantyne 1997. Knight intended to publish a description of his 'Expedition into Sicily' of 1777. A version was eventually published in translation by Goethe in 1810, and the original English version was rediscovered by Claudia Stumpf in Weimar in 1980 and published in 1986. See Richard Payne Knight (ed. Claudia Stumpf), 1986, *Expedition into Sicily*. London.

[36] Other members elected in 1770 included Henry Fox-Strangways (earl of Ilchester), the duke of Devonshire and John and William Hanger. Lionel Cust and Sidney Colvin, 1898, *History of the Society of Dilettanti*. London, p. 267.

[37] *ODNB*.

[38] Sir Thomas Clarges (1751–1782), 3rd baronet, was a cousin of Uvedale Price, his mother Anne being the sister of Uvedale Price's mother Sarah Price née Barrington. John Nichols, 1812, *Literary Anecdotes of the Eighteenth Century*, vol. VI, p. 452. He later married Louisa Skrine (1760–1809). Her portrait was painted by Gainsborough in 1778. There is also a reference to Clarges travelling in Italy in 1773, accompanied by a Mr Price: Ingamells 1997, p. 227.

[39] Troide 1988, 8 May 1771, p. 148.

[40] Troide 1988, 4 May 1772, p. 218.

[41] Uvedale Price to Samuel Rogers, Foxley, 6 October 1824, Clayden 1889, I, pp. 385–90.

[42] The drawings are inscribed by Malchair: 'A view of Lady Lift from a Meadow by Yazor. Herefordshire wednesday 16 of Sept: 1772 /1', 44; 'at Mr Price's at Foxley. Herefordshire. wednesday Sepʳ: 16 1772', 45; 'A view of Foxley in Herefordshire belongin to Uvedal Price Esqʳ Septʳ 16 1772/6', 46; 'A view from Foxley Garden. Mr Prices. Herefordshire Friday 18 of Sepr. 1772/7', 51. Corpus Christi College, Oxford, MS CCC 443 (III).

[43] Malchair led the band at the Oxford Music Room until 1792, 'when an orange thrown at the orchestra during an undergraduate disturbance broke his Cremona violin'. T. B. Healey, *ODNB*.

[44] A large collection of colour engravings by Skippe after Michaelangelo, Rubens and others dated between 1770 and 1773 is in the British Museum. L. H. Cust, *ODNB*.

[45] Lysons 1812, p. 205. Price was also one of the subscribers to the meeting many years later in 1811: Lysons 1812, p. 267.

[46] *St James's Chronicle*, 25 August 1774.

[47] Lysons 1812, p. 151.

[48] J. H. Gladstone, Guy Boas and Harald Christopherson, 1996, *Noblemen and Gentlemen's Catch Club: three essays towards its history*. London. The other members elected in 1770 were Henry Drummond; Lord le Spencer; Lord Pigot; the earl of Ancram and the duke of Buccleuch. The club met at Almack's in St James's. See also Brian Robins, 2006, *Catch and Glee Culture in Eighteenth-Century England*. Woodbridge.

[49] *London Chronicle*, 28 April 1774.

[50] Lady Caroline Price portrait by George Romney (1734–1802). Painted for the sitter's husband. Herbert Maxwell, 1902, *George Romney*. London, p. 187, no. 319. Royal Academy, London, 'Old Masters Exhibition', 1891, no. 27.

[51] He had been nominated as George I's ambassador to Vienna but the 1715 Jacobite rising

caused him to be made commander of all forces in northern England instead. He was created Baron Carpenter of Killaghy in the kingdom of Ireland in 1719: H. M. Stephens, *ODNB*.

[52] Memorial in Dilwyn Church: 'Near this place are interred the remains of FRANCES Countess Dowager of TYRCONNEL who died at the HOMME ON THE 8TH day of November 1786 in the 56th year of her age'.

[53] She was the daughter of Baron Delaval of Redford (1783), later of Seaton Delaval (1786). His son John (1756–1775) died 'having been kicked in the testicles by a laundry maid to whom he was paying his advances'. *Burke's Complete Peerage*, 1916.

[54] Sir N. W. Wraxall, 1836, *Posthumous Memoirs of his Own Time*. London, vol. III pp. 192–3.

[55] *The London Magazine*, 1747, p. 260. Almeria Carpenter was frequently referred to in verse. See, for example, John Huddlestone Wynne, 1773, *The Four Seasons*. London, and Earl of Chesterfield, 1773, *Lord Chesterfield's Witticisms*. London, p. 130.

[56] M. J. Levy (ed.), 1994, *Perdita: The Memoirs of Mary Robinson*. London, p. 160.

[57] Wraxall 1836, vol. III, pp. 192–3.

[58] Sir Herbert Croft, 1788, *The Abbey of Kilkhampton*. London, p. 93.

[59] *The Female Jockey Club*, 1794, pp. 186–192.

[60] Matthew Kilburn, *ODNB*. Lady Almeria died unmarried 5 October 1809.

[61] Charles Maynard, 7th Baron and 2nd Viscount Maynard, 1751–1824; Sir John Stepney, 8th baronet of Llanelly House, died 1811, was a diplomat and envoy to Dresden and Berlin; Edward Smith-Stanley (1752–1834) 12th Earl and 'leader of the glittering circle of London society. He was an inveterate and extravagant gambler, a close associate of Charles James Fox and the prince of Wales (afterwards George IV), and perhaps the greatest sportsman of his day, a devotee of cricket and hunting as well as racing and cockfighting'. Alan G. Crosby, *ODNB*.

[62] Probably Hon Elizabeth Venables-Vernon (1746–1826), wife of 2nd Earl Harcourt.

[63] Uvedale Price to Lady Beaumont, Foxley, 21 April 1804, Watkins and Cowell 2006b, pp. 177–8.

[64] *London Courant and Westminster Chronicle*, 16 March 1780.

[65] Letters from Price to Skippe in material in the possession of E. Holland Martin of Overbury Court December 1961 noted when on loan to the Department of Prints and Drawings, BM: Brinsley Ford Archive, Paul Mellon Centre, London.

[66] A small vellum-bound notebook: A list of *Pictures painted at Ledbury and elsewhere* by John Skippe in material in the possession of E. Holland Martin of Overbury Court December 1961 noted when on loan to the Department of Prints and Drawings, BM: Brinsley Ford Archive, Paul Mellon Centre, London. See also Ian Fleming-Williams, 1965, 'John Skippe', *Master Drawings*, III, pp. 268–75. John Skippe owned some drawings by Busiri including 'Landscape with mountain village and water-fall': see Hawcroft 1959, p. 297.

[67] Owen and Brown 1988, p. 59.

[68] Uvedale Price to E. H. Barker, March 24, 1827. From Barker 1852, vol. II, pp. 36–7.

[69] Uvedale Price to Samuel Rogers, 6 October 1824, Clayden 1889, I, pp. 385–90.

[70] 'With a growing reputation for scholarly excellence, wit, and social polish, during the early 1770s he became a much sought-after guest.' Philip Carter, *ODNB*.

[71] This visit must have been in the mid 1780s as Caroline Price was born in January 1783. This date ties in with a letter to Mrs Sheridan from Mary Tickell 25 November 1785 in which she writes 'I have no doubt Foxley has its comforts.' Cecil Price (ed.), 1966, *The Letters of Richard Brinsley Sheridan*. Oxford, p. 165.

[72] Lord Egremont (3rd earl 1751–1837) to Lord Holland (Henry Richard Fox, 3rd Baron Holland 1773–1840), Add Ms 51725, 25 December 1827.

[73] Uvedale Price to Samuel Rogers, Foxley, 6 October 1824, Clayden 1889, I, pp. 385–90.

[74] Henry Temple, second viscount Palmerston (1739–1802), politician and traveller.

[75] Brian Connell, 1957, *Portrait of a Whig Peer: Compiled from the Papers of the Second Viscount Palmerston, 1739–1802*. London, p. 174, Lord Palmerston to Lady Palmerston, 4 December 1787.

[76] Rogers 1856.

[77] John St John (1746–1793), politician and fop, published *Mary, Queen of Scots, a tragedy*, which was performed at the Theatre Royal, Drury Lane in 1789.

[78] Uvedale Price to Samuel Rogers, Foxley, 6 October 1824, Clayden 1889, I, pp. 385–90; Philip Carter, *ODNB*.

[79] Daniels 1999.

[80] Rogers 1856, pp. 113–14.

[81] Owen and Brown 1988.

[82] Price 1810, II, pp. 118–19. Price states 'If I have detained the reader so long in relating what personally concerns myself, I did it, because there is nothing so useful to others, however humiliating to ourselves, as the frank confession of our errors, and of their causes', p. 126.

[83] Price 1810, II, p. 120.

[84] Price 1810, II, p. 128.

[85] Price 1810, II, p. 122.

[86] Price 1810, II, p. 124.

[87] Price 1810, II, p. 126. For employment of James Cranston (1748–1835), see Smith 2004, p. 189.

[88] Dorothy Stroud, 1975, *Capability Brown*. London, p. 189; Jane Brown, 2011, *The Omnipotent Magician: Lancelot 'Capability' Brown, 1716–1783*. London, p. 247–9.

[89] Son of the third duke of Marlborough, a lifelong friend of Charles James Fox and Price.

[90] Fox to Price, Newmarket 9 July 1781.

[91] Fox to Price, St Anne's Hill near Chertsey, 14 November 1785.

[92] Fox to Price, St Anne's Hill near Chertsey, 14 November 1785.

[93] Uvedale Price, *An Account of the Statues, Pictures, and Temples in Greece; Translated from the Greek of Pausanias*, 1780. T. Evans (1738/9–1803), Michael T. Davis, *ODNB*. See Elsner, Jaś 'Pictureque and sublime: impacts of Pausanias in late-Eighteeenth- and early-Nineteenth-Century Britain' *Classical Receptions Journal*, 2, pp. 219–253.

[94] Uvedale Price to E. H. Barker, 19 May 1825 and 4 June 1825. He told Barker 'You perhaps never saw a copy, only heard of the book, and the name of the author.'

[95] David Philip Miller, *ODNB*.

[96] Daines Barrington, 1785, 'On the progress of gardening', read at Society of Antiquaries London 13 June 1782, published in *Archaeologia*, XIII, p. 130. Lambin 1987, p. 257; Sloman 2002, p. 159.

[97] HRO, Mansel Lacy Parish, AB69/2.

CHAPTER 3: 'THE IMPROVEMENT OF REAL LANDSCAPE' (pages 46–60)

[1] From the full title of Price's *Essay on the Picturesque*, 1794.

[2] HRO, D 344.

[3] See Pamela Horn, 1982, 'An eighteenth century land agent: the career of Nathaniel Kent (1737–1810)', *Agricultural History Review*, 30, pp. 1–16.

[4] This survey was discovered by Major David Davenport at Foxley in 1988.

[5] Kent 1775; Horn 1982. In Herefordshire he also surveyed the Kyre Park estate (1774); the Hampton Court estate (1786–87) and the Hellens estate, Much Marcle (1787–90). Smith 2004, pp. 50–51. Ronald Bayne, 'Kent, Nathaniel (1737–1810)', rev. Anne Pimlott Baker, *ODNB*.

[6] John Lodge, 1793, *Introductory Sketches Towards a Topographical History of the County of Hereford*. Kington.

[7] See Daniels and Watkins 1991 for a fuller discussion.

[8] F. M. L. Thompson, 1963, *English Landed Society in the Nineteenth Century*. London.

[9] WRO, Berington Collection 705:24/1205, 1 November 1775.

[10] HRO, B 47 D220–22.

[11] Kent 1775, p. 194.

[12] Joan Thirsk notes that the central Herefordshire plain had a large number of smallholders in the eighteenth century and that this persisted well into the nineteenth century. Joan Thirsk (ed.), 1984, *The Agrarian History of England and Wales: Volume V, 1640–1750, I Regional Farming Systems*. Cambridge.

[13] Kent 1775, p. 208.

[14] Daniels and Watkins 1991.

[15] Kent, Foxley Survey 1774.

[16] Kent, Foxley Survey 1774.

[17] *Hereford Journal*, 18 March 1795. David Whitehead kindly provided this reference.

[18] HRO, B 47/- D97.

[19] HRO, B47/- D303–07.

[20] HRO, B47/- D70–1 D97.

[21] John Clark, 1794, *General View of the Agriculture of the County of Hereford*, London.

[22] Clark 1794; John Duncumb, 1805, *General View of the Agriculture of the County of Hereford*, London.

[23] Duncumb 1805.

[24] Kent, Foxley Survey 1774.

[25] Kent, Foxley Survey 1774.

[26] Thirsk 1984, pp. 192–4.

[27] HRO, B 47/- D97, 1.7.1774.

[28] HRO, B 47/- D97, 2.2.1781.

[29] Uvedale Price, 1786, 'On the bad effects of stripping and cropping trees', *Annals of Agriculture*, 5, pp. 241–50.

[30] Price 1786, p. 241.

[31] Price 1786, p. 243.

[32] Price 1786, pp. 241–2.

[33] John Skippe (1741–1812), *ODNB*. John Skippe's sister Penelope (1740–1830) married James Martin (1738–1810) and the estate remained in the Martin family until the early twentieth century, subsequently becoming Ledbury Grammar School and then being converted to flats.

[34] Price 1786, p. 243.

[35] Price 1786, p. 244.

[36] Price 1786, p. 247.

[37] Price 1786, p. 247.

[38] HRO, BC 986A.

[39] Price 1786, p. 248–9.

[40] For a full discussion see Petit and Watkins 2003, pp. 157–76, and Daniels and Watkins 1991.

[41] *Hereford Journal*, 11 December 1783. Reference kindly supplied by David Whitehead.

[42] Lodge 1793, p. 23.

[43] Price 1810, I, pp. 26–7.

[44] HRO, B 47/- H70–1 D97 31.7.1799.

[45] Alvaro Ribeiro (ed.), 1991, *The letters of Dr Charles Burney*, vol. I 1754–84. Oxford, p. 399, fn. 66.

[46] Richard Muir, 2001, 'The Burgage-house, otherwise known as the Lodge', unpublished notes from Haslemere Educational Museum.

[47] A. Aspinall (ed.), 1964, *Correspondence of George, Prince of Wales 1770–1812*. London, vol. 6, p. 23, Letter 2348. Later he lived at the Burgage house in High Street Haslemere, with 120 acres of land. See Surrey History Centre, G85/2/1/1/176 Sales Particulars, 28 September 1827.This house had a picturesque garden and is currently Haslemere Educational Museum. It is likely that his brother Robert Price lived at this house for some years. Both brothers were Life Subscribers to The Royal Institution of Great Britain.

[48] Rogers 1856, pp. 259–60.

[49] F. McKno Bladon (ed.), 1930, *The Diaries of Colonel the Hon Robert Fulke Greville Equerry to His Majesty King George III*. London, p. 270.

[50] Bladon 1930, pp. 269–70.

[51] Bladon 1930, p. 329.

[52] Bladon 1930, p. 344.

[53] Neil Chambers (ed.), 2007, *Scientific Correspondence of Sir Joseph Banks 1767–1820*. London. Dr James Lind Winsor to Sir Joseph Banks Revesby Abbey; 681, October 1786; 692, 19 October 1786.

[54] Aspinall 1964, vol. 2, p. 396, Letter 790, 4 October 1790.

[55] Jane Roberts, 1997, *Royal Landscape: The Gardens and Parks of Windsor*. New Haven and London, pp. 221–2.

[56] Royal Archives, Windsor Castle, RA GEO/7831.

[57] Roberts 1997, p. 226.

[58] Uvedale Price to Lord Abercorn, 14 July 1792, Watkins and Cowell 2006b, p. 79. See Daniels 1999 for a full account of Repton's Herefordshire commissions and his relationship with Knight and Price.

[59] Uvedale Price to Lord Abercorn, 14 July 1792, Watkins and Cowell 2006b, p. 79.

[60] William Petty (1737–1805), 2nd Earl of Shelburne and 1st Marquess of Lansdowne, prime minister 1782–83. In 1763 he employed Capability Brown to construct the lake at Bowood and Robert Adam to enlarge the house. John Cannon, *ODNB*.

[61] Wife of the duc de Levis 1764–1830.

[62] Uvedale Price to Samuel Rogers, Foxley, 6 October 1824, Clayden 1889, I, pp. 385–90.

CHAPTER 4: 'THE GREAT GUNS OF TASTE' (pages 61–86)

[1] D. Watkin, 1982, *The English Vision. The Picturesque in Architecture, Landscape and Garden*

[1] Uvedale Price to Lord Abercorn, 14 July 1792, Watkins and Cowell 2006b, p. 79.

[2] Uvedale Price to Sir George Beaumont, 12 February 1802, Watkins and Cowell 2006b, p. 147.

[3] Sloman 2002, p. 159; Lambin 1987, p. 257.

[4] Price 1810, I, p. 40.

[5] William Shenstone, 1764, *Unconnected Thoughts on Gardening*, in *The Works in Verse and Prose of William Shenstone*, vol. II. London, p. 94 and fn.

[6] William Hogarth, 1754, *Analysis of Beauty*. London, p. 52.

[7] William Chambers, 1772, *A Dissertation on Oriental Gardening*. London, Preface, pp. vii–ix.

[8] Jules Smith, William Mason, *ODNB*.

[9] Horace Walpole, 1771, *Anecdotes of Painting in England*, Works III, London, p. 438.

[10] The island of Tinian had been praised for 'the excellency of its landskips' in W. H. Dilworth's 1759 *Lord Anson's Voyage Around the World Performed in the Years 1740, 41, 42, 43, 44*, 4th edn. London, p. 89, and influenced Jean-Jacques Rousseau's descriptions in *Julie ou La nouvelle Héloïse*, 1761.

[11] Horace Walpole (ed. Isabel Chase), 1943, *The History of the Modern Taste in Gardening*. Princeton, p. 4, p. 22 fn.

[12] Walpole 1943, pp. 35–6.

[13] Walpole 1943, pp. 25–7, 31, 35–7.

[14] William Gilpin, 1768, *An Essay upon Prints, containing Remarks upon the Principles of Picturesque Beauty*.... London, pp. 2–3.

[15] Carl Paul Barbier, 1963, *William Gilpin: His Drawings, Teaching, and Theory of the Picturesque*. Oxford, pp. 101–2.

[16] William Gilpin, 1798, *Observation on the Western Parts of Britain ... Chiefly Relative to Picturesque Beauty*.... London, p. 328.

[17] Gilpin, William, 1782, *Observations on the River Wye*. London, p. 1.

[18] Barbier 1963, p. 161.

[19] William Gilpin to William Mason, 12 July 1755, Barbier 1963, p. 53.

[20] William Gilpin to William Mason 23 April 1787, Barbier 1963, pp. 71–2, fn. 3.

[21] William Gilpin to W. Clarke 9 July 1787, Barbier 1963, p. 162.

[22] Barbier 1963, p. 173.

[23] Harrison 1998, p. 23.

[24] George Mason (1795, *An Essay on Design in Gardening*. London, p. 3, fn.) noted that 'Our great dictionary writer (DR JOHNSON) settles this point with great ease to himself: for the word *picturesque* is quite omitted by him'. Johnson's *Dictionary*, 1801 edition, quoted in John Dixon Hunt and Peter Willis (eds), 1975, *The Genius of the Place: The English Landscape Garden 1620–1820*. London, p. 337.

[25] Uvedale Price to Samuel Rogers, Foxley, 6 October 1824, Clayden 1889, I, pp. 385–90.

[26] *Morning Chronicle*, 28 February 1794; *Morning Chronicle*, 4 June 1794.

[27] Price 1794, Preface, pp. iii–iv.

[28] Knight 1986, p. 31.

[29] Richard Payne Knight, 1791, *An Analytical Essay on the Greek Alphabet*. London. See Ballantyne 1997, p. 74.

[30] Charles-Alphonse Dufresnoy, 1783, *The Art of Painting of Charles Alphonse Du Fresnoy. Translated into English verse by William Mason, M.A. with annotations by Sir Joshua Reynolds....* York.

[31] Price 1794, Preface, pp. iv–v.

[32] Farington, 8 September 1794. All references to the Farington Diary are from Joseph Farington (eds K. Garlick and A. Macintyre), 1978–1998, *The Diary of Joseph Farington*. New Haven and London.

[33] Horace Walpole to William Mason, 22 March 1796; W. S. Lewis, Grover Cronin Jr and Charles H. Bennett, 1955, *Horace Walpole's correspondence with William Mason*. New Haven, 29, p. 339; Ballantyne 1997, p. 104.

[34] Ballantyne 1997, p. 74.

[35] Price 1810, I, p. 2.

[36] Price 1810, I, p. 14.

[37] Price 1810, I, p. 345.

[38] Andrew Ballantyne, 1992, 'Genealogy of the Picturesque', *British Journal of Aesthetics*, 32, 4, pp. 320–29.

[39] Price 1810, I, pp. 22–3, 50.

[40] Price 1810, I, p. 114.

[41] Price 1810, I, p. 22, 55, 57.

[42] Price 1810, I, p. 3.

[43] Price 1810, I, p. 244.

[44] Price 1810, I, p. 325, 327.

[45] Edmund Burke to Price, 1 June 1794, transcribed by Price and sent to Sir George Beaumont. See also P. J. Marshall and J. A. Woods, 1968, *Correspondence of Edmund Burke. Vol. 7: January 1792–August 1794*. Cambridge, pp. 547–8.

[46] Edmund Burke, *ODNB*, Paul Langford.

[47] Edmund Burke to Uvedale Price, 1 June 1794, transcribed by Price and sent to Sir George Beaumont. See also Marshall and Woods 1968, pp. 547–8.

[48] Frances Anne Crewe, 1862–3, 'Extracts from Mr. Burke's Table–Talk, at Crewe Hall. Written down by Mrs. Crewe', *Miscellanies of the Philobiblon Society*, VII, pp. 42–3.

[49] Farington, 14 December 1794.

[50] The Diaries of Anna Margaretta Larpent, Huntingdon Library, 21, 22, 25 July; 1, 6, 7, 8 August 1794.

[51] William Marshall, 1795, *A Review of the Landscape, A Didactic Poem: Also of An Essay on the Picturesque: Together with Practical Remarks on Rural Ornament*. London, p. 106.

[52] Uvedale Price to Sir George Beaumont, 3 June 1795, Watkins and Cowell 2006b, pp. 83–4.

[53] Farington, 31 August 1794.

[54] George Mason, 1795, *An Essay on Design in Gardening*. London, p. 205. George Mason, *ODNB*, James Samford.

[55] Mason, 1795, p. 209.

[56] George Mason, 1798, *An Appendix to An Essay on Design in Gardening*. London.

[57] William Mason, 1797, *Poems*, vol. III. York. Sonnet XI, *Occasioned by a Didactic POEM on the Progress of CIVIL SOCIETY*, is a strong attack on Richard Payne Knight.

[58] Lewis *et al.* 1955, II, Appendix 1, 'Walpole's quarrel with Mason and Lord Harcourt', pp. 347–66. The correspondence was only very briefly revived; they both died in 1797.

[59] Thomas James Mathias, 1798, *Pursuits of Literature*, Second Dialogue, 8th edn. London, p. 116. The poem was 'a wide-ranging satire with extensive notes on the conceit and licence of contemporary authors, appeared anonymously in four dialogues, the first on 7 June 1794, the second and third on 14 July 1796, and the fourth on 19 July 1797. The poem was issued as a whole in a 'fifth edition revised' in 1798 … The attacks on Payne Knight's *Worship of Priapus* and Lewis's *The Monk* are concerned with obscenity', Paul Baines, *ODNB*.

[60] Uvedale Price to Lord Aberdeen, September 1816, Watkins and Cowell 2006b, p. 260.

[61] NAO DD.SY 169/17, 27 March 1796.

[62] Humphry Repton, 1794, *A Letter to Uvedale Price, Esq.* London, in Price 1810, III, p. 10. At the end of the *Letter* Repton advertised his forthcoming work: 'Mr Repton takes this opportunity to acquaint the Subscribers to his Work on Landscape Gardening, that the publication has been delayed on account of the Plates …'.

[63] Uvedale Price to Lady Beaumont, 2 February 1795, Watkins and Cowell 2006b, pp. 82–3.

[64] Farington, 30 September 1794; Farington, 1 July 1795.

[65] Uvedale Price to Sir George Beaumont, 3 June 1795, Watkins and Cowell 2006b, pp. 83–4.

[66] Printed for Robson, London. The second edition in 1798 was printed by Walker in Hereford for Robson.

[67] Uvedale Price to Sir George Beaumont, 28 November 1794, Watkins and Cowell 2006b, pp. 79–81.

[68] Uvedale Price to Sir George Beaumont, 4 December 1794, Watkins and Cowell 2006b, p. 81.

[69] Uvedale Price to Lady Beaumont, 2 February 1795, Watkins and Cowell 2006b, pp. 82–3.

[70] Price 1810, III, p. 178.

[71] Price 1810, I, p. 375.

[72] See Daniels 1999, pp. 122–6, who provides a full discussion of the relationship between Repton and Price. William Windham (1750–1810) had broken with Charles James Fox in 1793 in response to the French massacres, and became Secretary at War 1794–1801 under Pitt. He was the son of William Windham (1717–1761), who was a friend of Robert Price: David Wilkinson, *ODNB*.

[73] Uvedale Price to Lady Beaumont, 2 February 1795, Watkins and Cowell 2006b, pp. 82–3.

[74] Uvedale Price to Sir George Beaumont, 28 November 1797, Watkins and Cowell 2006b, p. 108.

[75] Uvedale Price to Sir George Beaumont, 4 December 1794, Watkins and Cowell 2006b, p. 81.

[76] Richard Payne Knight, 1795, *The Landscape, a Didactic Poem, in Three Books. Addressed to Uvedale Price*, 2nd edn. London, pp. 17–24.

[77] Uvedale Price to Sir George Beaumont, 4 December 1794, Watkins and Cowell 2006b, p. 81.

[78] Knight 1795, p. vii.

[79] Ballantyne 1997, pp. 84–5.

[80] Ballantyne 1997, pp. 79–80.

[81] Uvedale Price to Sir George Beaumont, 28 November 1797, Watkins and Cowell 2006b, p. 108.

[82] Uvedale Price to Sir George Beaumont, 28 November 1794, Watkins and Cowell 2006b, pp. 79–81. Elizabeth Bridget Cane (1750–1842), known as Mrs Armstead, Armistead or Armitstead, had been Fox's mistress since 1783. She was to marry him on 28 September 1795 but this was not publicly known until 1802. In Laurence Sterne's *The Life and Opinions of Tristram Shandy* (1769–67, York and London), Uncle Toby would whistle or hum Lillabullero in response to any kind of argument or issue he felt was nonsense or in a situation where he was shocked or embarrassed by the subject at hand. Johann Hasse (1699–1783), German composer; Giovannii Paisello (1740–1816), Italian composer.

[83] Farington, 10 May 1796.

[84] Uvedale Price to Lord Abercorn, 31 May 1796, Watkins and Cowell 2006b, pp. 84–5.

[85] Uvedale Price to Lord Abercorn, 12 June 1796, Watkins and Cowell 2006b, p. 86.

[86] Farington, 7 March 1797.

[87] Uvedale Price to Lord Abercorn, 13 January 1797, Watkins and Cowell 2006b, p. 95.

[88] Uvedale Price to Sir George Beaumont, 28 December 1797, Watkins and Cowell 2006b, pp. 111–13.

[89] Uvedale Price to Sir George Beaumont, 28 January 1798, Watkins and Cowell 2006b, pp. 117–18.

[90] Uvedale Price to Sir George Beaumont, 28 November 1797, Watkins and Cowell 2006b, p. 108.

[91] Price 1810, II, pp. 218–19.

[92] Uvedale Price to Sir George Beaumont, 28 November 1797, Watkins and Cowell 2006b, p. 108; Owen and Brown 1988, p. 88.

[93] Uvedale Price to Sir George Beaumont, 28 January 1798, Watkins and Cowell 2006b, p. 116.

[94] Uvedale Price to Sir George Beaumont, 8 March 1798, Watkins and Cowell 2006b, pp. 120–21. *Middlesex Victoria County History*, IV, p. 62. William Gilpin, 1791, *Remarks on Forest Scenery*. London, I, pp. 77–8. J. C. Loudon, 1854, *Arboretum et Fruticetum Britannicum*. London, IV, p. 2417. Mr Cocker refers to Edward Cocker (1631–1675), arithmetician.

[95] Uvedale Price to Sir George Beaumont, 15 January 1798, Watkins and Cowell 2006b, pp. 115–16; 17 February 1798, Watkins and Cowell 2006b, p. 118. The note is in *Essay on Architecture and Buildings*. 1810, II, p. 319. See *'Noble and Patriotic' the Beaumont Gift 1828*, National Gallery, 1988.

[96] Uvedale Price to Sir George Beaumont, 8 March 1798, Watkins and Cowell 2006b, pp. 120–21.

[97] Price 1810, *Essays*, II, pp. xiv–xv. Philips Wouwerman (1619–1668) Dutch painter most famous for his horses and battle and hunting scenes. He was very popular in the eighteenth and early nineteenth centuries.

[98] Richard Owen Cambridge (1717–1802): 'his friends laughed at his dedication to the collection and dissemination of news and gossip, a practice that led Gibbon to call him "the Cambridge Mail".' James Sambrook, *ODNB*.

[99] Price 1810, II, pp. xix–xx. Ovid, *Metamorphoses*, line 6.

[100] Uvedale Price to Lord Abercorn, 25 February 1798, Watkins and Cowell 2006b, p. 119.

CHAPTER 5: PICTURESQUE DESIGNS (pages 87–111)

[1] James Baker, 1795, *A Picturesque Guide through Wales and the Marches…*, 2nd edn. Worcester, pp. 208–11.

[2] John Campbell, 1774, *A Political Survey of Britain: Being a Series of Reflections on the Situation, Lands, Inhabitants, Revenues, Colonies and Commerce of this Island*. London, vol. 1, p. 183.

[3] G. H. Jenkins, 1993, *The Foundations of Modern Wales, 1642–1780*. Oxford, pp. 296, 299.

[4] By the early nineteenth century guide *An Excursion from the Source of the Wye* (undated) states that there were exports of lead, calamine and manufactured goods, such as flannels and stockings, to Liverpool and Bristol and imports of cast iron goods, coal and porter.

[5] W. J. Lewis, 1980, *Born on a Perilous Rock*. Aberystwyth, pp. 195, 197. Henry Wigstead, 1799, *Remarks on a Tour to North and South Wales in the year 1797*. London, p. 50.

[6] Aberystwyth was by no means the only Welsh resort to develop in this period; the vogue for sea bathing encouraged the development of Tenby and Swansea, also described as the Brighton of Wales in 1786, to the detriment of inland spas. See David Boorman, 1986, *The Brighton of Wales. Swansea as a Fashionable Seaside Resort, c1780–c1830*. Swansea, p. 1.

[7] Benjamin Heath Malkin, 1804, *The Scenery, Antiquities and Biography of South Wales*. London, pp. 367–7, 376–7.

[8] Anon, 1830, *The Cambrian Tourist, or Post-Chaise Companion, through Wales*, 7th edn. London, pp. 104–5.

[9] George Eyre Evans, 1902, *Aberystwyth and its Court Leet*. Aberystwyth, p. 147.

[10] Thomas Johnes (1748–1816), Richard Moore-Colyer, *ODNB*.

[11] Richard Moore-Colyer, 1992, *A Land of Pure Delight. Selections from the letters of Thomas Johnes of Hafod, Cardiganshire (1748–1816)*. Llandysul, pp. 10–12; Elisabeth Inglis-Jones, 1950, *Peacocks in Paradise*. London, p. 70.

[12] Uvedale Price to Lord Aberdeen, 29 June 1810, Watkins and Cowell 2006b, p. 199; Moore-Colyer 1992; Inglis-Jones 1950, pp. 88–101.

[13] Willett 1810, pp. 20, 93–4.

[14] Moore-Colyer 1992, pp. 138; 198.

[15] Evans 1902, p. 147.

[16] James Lees-Milne, 1992, *People and Places*. London, p. 54.

[17] Lewis 1980, pp. 121–2.

[18] Moore-Colyer 1992, pp. 122, 198.

[19] D. J. V. Jones, 1973, *Before Rebecca: Popular Protests in Wales 1793–1835*. London, pp. 20; 57; 48–9.

[20] Lewis 1980, p. 9.

[21] Evans 1902, p. 49.

[22] Richard Suggett, 1995, *John Nash: Architect in Wales*. Aberystwyth, p. 55.

[23] Uvedale Price to Sir George Beaumont, 18 March 1798, Watkins and Cowell 2006b, p. 122.

[24] R. C. Gaut, 1939, *A History of Worcestershire Agriculture and Rural Evolution*. Worcester, p. 200.

[25] Suggett 1995, pp. 107–28; David Whitehead, 1992, 'John Nash and Humphry Repton: an encounter in Herefordshire 1785–98', *Transactions of the Woolhope Naturalists Field Club*, 47, pp. 221–7.

[26] Suggett 1995, p. 65; p. 76.

[27] John Summerson, in Terence Davies, 1960, *The Architecture of John Nash*. London, p. 10.

[28] Uvedale Price to Sir George Beaumont, 18 March 1798, Watkins and Cowell 2006b, pp. 121–2; Uvedale Price to Lord Aberdeen, 29 June 1810, Watkins and Cowell 2006b, pp. 198–200; Uvedale Price to Sir George Beaumont, 5 August 1819, Watkins and Cowell 2006b, pp. 278–9.

[29] Uvedale Price to Sir George Beaumont, 15 January 1798, Watkins and Cowell 2006b, p. 115.

[30] Uvedale Price to Sir George Beaumont, 28 January 1798, Watkins and Cowell 2006b, p. 116.

[31] Suggett 1995, p. 112. Frederick J. Ladd, 1978, *Architects at Corsham Court. A Study in Revival Style Architecture and Landscaping, 1749–1849*. London, p. 110. Nash was also working at this time at Attingham for Lord Berwick.

[32] HRO, 7750 Mancel 17 November 1798.

[33] RIBA GSR cottage for U. Price. See Nigel Temple, 1979, *John Nash and the Village Picturesque*, Gloucester.

[34] Uvedale Price to Sir George Beaumont, 8 March 1798, Watkins and Cowell 2006b, p. 121.

[35] Ladd 1978, p. 111.

[36] Uvedale Price to Sir George Beaumont, 18 March 1798, Watkins and Cowell 2006b, p. 121.

[37] Suggett 1995, p. 121.

[38] Uvedale Price to Sir George Beaumont, 18 March 1798, Watkins and Cowell 2006b, pp. 121–2.

[39] Price 1810, II, pp. 268–9.

[40] Suggett 1995, p. 71.

[41] Uvedale Price to Sir George Beaumont, 29 June 1810, Watkins and Cowell 2006b, p. 199.

[42] Samuel Ireland, 1797, *Picturesque Views on the River Wye*. London, p. 19.

[43] Uvedale Price to Sir George Beaumont, 18 March 1798, Watkins and Cowell 2006b, p. 123.

[44] Uvedale Price to Lord Aberdeen, 29 June 1810, Watkins and Cowell 2006b, p. 199; George Lipscomb, 1802, *Journey into South Wales*. London, p. 163.

[45] Malcolm Andrews, 1989, *The Search for the Picturesque: Landscape Aesthetics and Tourism in Britain, 1760–1800*. Aldershot, p. 145.

[46] Lipscomb 1802, p. 163.

[47] Sir Samuel Rush Meyrick, 1810, *The History and Antiquities of the County of Cardigan*. London, p. 417.

[48] T. I. Llewellyn, 1824, *The New Aberystwyth Guide*. Aberystwyth, pp. 22–3, 27.

[49] Price 1810, II, pp. 263–5.

[50] Andrews 1989, p. 145.

[51] M. W. Thompson, *The Journeys of Sir Richard Colt Hoare through Wales and England 1793–1810*, 1983, p. 63.

[52] Ireland 1797, p. 18.

[53] Turner, *Aberystwyth Castle*, 1798, Finberg XL 56a Tate Gallery; J. P. Neale, *Engraving of Castle House 1818–29* in Michael Mansbridge, 1991, *John Nash. A Complete Catalogue 1752–1835*. Oxford, p. 59; pottery model of Castle House, mid nineteenth-century, Aberystwyth University; drawing c.1800.

[54] Inglis-Jones 1950, pp. 107–8.

[55] Moore-Colyer 1992, p. 140; Thomas Johnes to George Cumberland, 21 January 1799.

[56] *Cambrian Tourist*, 1830, p. 104.

[57] Lewis 1980, 124.

[58] John Glasse to the Right Honourable Lady Camelford, Cheltenham. Pencombe, Sunday Evening 20 September 1795, BL Add MS 69306.

[59] Uvedale Price to Lord Abercorn, 25 July 1796, Watkins and Cowell 2006b, p. 89.

[60] Uvedale Price to Sir George Beaumont, 18 March 1798, Watkins and Cowell 2006b, p. 122.

[61] Lewis 1980, fn.

[62] John Eisel pointed out this reference.

[63] HRO, Kentchurch AL 40 7764, 7 October 1799.

[64] Evans 1902, p. 39; Oliver 1986, p. 285.

[65] Suggett 1995, p. 112.

[66] Uvedale Price to Sir George Beaumont, 18 March 1798, Watkins and Cowell 2006b, p. 122.

[67] Uvedale Price to Sir George Beaumont, 5 August 1819, Watkins and Cowell 2006b, p. 278.

[68] Uvedale Price to Sir George Beaumont, 5 August 1819, Watkins and Cowell 2006b, p. 278–9.

[69] National Library of Wales, St Michael's Church (Aberystwyth), 69 October 21 1825; 70 November 18 1825; Evans 1902, pp. 46, 49.

[70] Llewellyn 1824, pp. 11–112.

[71] A full treatment of the later development of the house is provided by Roger Webster, 1995, *Old College Aberystwyth. The Evolution of a High Victorian Building*. Cardiff. See also Evans 1902, pp. 39; 121; Suggett 1995, p. 119.

[72] Price 1810, II, p. 268.

[73] Charles Eastlake (ed. J. M. Crook), 1970, *A History of the Gothic Revival*. p. 47.

[74] William Wordsworth to Sir George Beaumont, 28 August 1811 in Ernest de Selincourt (ed.), 1937, *The Letters of William and Dorothy Wordsworth: The Middle Years*. Oxford, p. 467.

[75] Price 1810, I, pp. 259–61.

[76] Uvedale Price to Lord Aberdeen, 29 June 1810, Watkins and Cowell 2006b, p. 199.

[77] Price 1810, I, pp. 100–101.

[78] Uvedale Price to Sir George Beaumont, 18 March 1798, Watkins and Cowell 2006b, p. 123.

[79] Alain Corbain, 1994, *The Lure of the Sea*, p. 97.

[80] Corbain 1994, pp. 106, 126, 142.

[81] Owen and Brown 1988, pp. 108–14.

[82] Uvedale Price to Lady Beaumont, 4 December 1801, Watkins and Cowell 2006b, p. 144; Uvedale Price to Sir George Beaumont, 12 February 1802, Watkins and Cowell 2006b, pp. 145–6.

[83] Price 1794, pp. 47–9.

[84] Uvedale Price to Sir George Beaumont, 12 February 1802, Watkins and Cowell 2006b, pp. 147.

[85] Farington, 7 November 1802.

[86] Farington, 17 October 1803; 6 November 1803.

[87] Uvedale Price to Lady Beaumont, 31 January 1804, Watkins and Cowell 2006b, pp. 172–4.

[88] Farington, March 1804.

[89] Farington, 29 April; 12 May; 15 May; 16 May; 10 June. In February 1804 Thomas Hope had caused a sensation by inviting 60 members of the Royal Academy to his Duchess Street mansion by admission ticket. He also published a plea for the Greek revival in relation to

Downing College, Cambridge which contained an attack on Wyatt. For the Thomas Hope affair in detail see David Watkin, 1968, *Thomas Hope 1769–1831*. London, pp. 9–15.

[90] Uvedale Price to Lady Beaumont, 9 June 1804, Watkins and Cowell 2006b, p. 180.

[91] Uvedale Price to Lady Beaumont, 9 June 1804, Watkins and Cowell 2006b, p. 180.

[92] Uvedale Price to Lady Beaumont, 26 June 1804, Watkins and Cowell 2006b, p. 181.

[93] Uvedale Price to Lady Beaumont, 26 June 1804, Watkins and Cowell 2006b, p. 181.

[94] Uvedale Price to Sir George Beaumont, 10 July 1804, Watkins and Cowell 2006b, p. 182.

[95] Uvedale Price to Lady Beaumont, 24 August 1804, Watkins and Cowell 2006b, p. 183.

[96] Farington, 19 July 1804.

[97] Uvedale Price to Lady Beaumont, 13 October 1804, Watkins and Cowell 2006b, p. 185.

[98] Owen and Brown 1988, p. 120.

[99] Roger Bowdler, 'Dance, George, the younger (1741–1825)', *ODNB*; Owen and Brown 1988, p. 120; See also A. Peter Fawcett and Neil Jackson (1998, *Campus critique. The Architecture of the University of Nottingham*. Nottingham) for related work by Wilkins at Lenton Hall and Highfield House, Nottingham.

[100] John Throsby, 1792, *The Supplementary Volume to the Leicestershire Views: Containing a Series of Excursions in the Year 1790....* London, p. 454.

CHAPTER 6: PROPERTY AND LANDSCAPE (pages 112–141)

[1] George Hanger (1751–1824), 4th baron Coleraine of Driffield Hall, Gloucestershire. 'Long-nosed but reportedly considered handsome when young, he was irascible, violent, dissipated, extravagant, and individualistic sometimes to eccentricity. He fought three duels before he was twenty-one.' Stuart Reid, *ODNB*. He was a captain in the Hessian Jäger corps and served throughout the American War of Independence. He was appointed major in Tarleton's light dragoons in 1782. He was a 'beau and clubman – in both senses – who affected the manners of the French court ... Hanger assisted Tarleton with his faro bank at Daubigney's Tavern, London, lounging at the entrance with a huge rattan he called "the Infant". He became one of the dissipated companions of the prince of Wales, indulging in gambling, racing, and pugilism. In 1787 he and Tarleton organized "bludgeon men" for the whigs at the Westminster by-election.' *ODNB*. In 1791 he was appointed equerry to the Prince of Wales; in 1800 he became a coal merchant. In 1801 William Combe compiled *The Life, Adventures, and Opinions of Colonel George Hanger, written by himself.*

[2] General Sir Banastre Tarleton (1754–1833). 'Tarleton's fame and notoriety reached their peaks in the southern campaigns of 1780 and 1781, by which time he was lieutenant-colonel commanding the British Legion, a mid infantry and cavalry unit of American loyalists.' Stephen Conway *ODNB*. When he returned to England in 1782 he was feted as a hero and became a friend of the Prince of Wales. He was painted by Reynolds and Gainsborough. He was obsessed by gambling and had a long affair with Mary (Perdita) Robinson from 1782 to 1797. His 'prevailing foible' was 'vanity': *ODNB*. In 1798 he married Priscilla Susan Bertie, illegitimate daughter of Robert Bertie, 4th duke of Ancaster. He was made a baronet in 1816 and on retirement they lived at Leintwardine House, Herefordshire, where he died in 1833, survived by his wife.

[3] Uvedale Price to Lord Abercorn, 6 August 1796, Watkins and Cowell 2006b, p. 90.

[4] Austin Gee, 2003, *The British Volunteer movement 1794–1814*. Oxford, pp. 1, 56.

[5] Uvedale Price to Lord Abercorn, 11 March 1797, Watkins and Cowell 2006b, p. 98.

[6] Uvedale Price to Lord Abercorn, 15 March 1797, Watkins and Cowell 2006b, p. 99.

[7] Uvedale Price to Lord Abercorn, 20 March 1797, Watkins and Cowell 2006b, pp. 99–100.

[8] Uvedale Price to Lord Abercorn, 14 April 1797, Watkins and Cowell 2006b, p. 100.

[9] *The Times*, 2 June 1798. This is the same day that the 1798 edition of *Essays on the Picturesque* was published by J. Robson, and they both receive separate advertisements in *The Times*.

[10] Uvedale Price, 1797, *Thoughts on the Defence of Property. Addressed to the County of Hereford.* Hereford, pp. 1, 5, 11.

[11] Price 1797, pp. 6–7.

[12] Price 1797, pp. 16, 9.

[13] L. G. Mitchell, 1997, *Charles James Fox*. London, p. 32.

[14] Price 1797, pp. 19–20; 17–18.

[15] Price 1797, pp. 27–8.

[16] Price 1797, pp. 27–8.

[17] Thomas Beddoes, 1797, *Alternatives Compared: or What shall the Rich do to be Safe?* London, pp. 73–4.

[18] Uvedale Price to Lord Abercorn, 3 May 1798, Watkins and Cowell 2006b, pp. 123–4.

[19] HRO, Kentchurch AL 40 7764 7 October 1799.

[20] The Rev. Stebbing Shaw, 1789, *A Tour to the West of England, in 1788.* London, p. 165.

[21] *ODNB*, Britton, John (1771–1857). John Britton, 1850, *The Autobiography of John Britton*. London, p. 150.

[22] Britton 1850, p. 150.

[23] E. W. Brayley and J. Britton, 1805, *The Beauties of England and Wales*. *Vol. VI*. London, pp. 581–2.

[24] James Plumptre (1771–1832). Ian Ousby (ed.), 1992, *James Plumptre's Britain. The Journals of a Tourist in the 1790s*. London, pp. 171–4.

[25] James Plumptre, 1990, *The Lakers*. Oxford and New York, Introduction and p. 19.

[26] M. W. Thompson, 1983, *The Journeys of Sir Richard Colt Hoare through Wales and England 1793–1810*. Gloucester, p. 201.

[27] Uvedale Price to Sir George Beaumont, 30 September 1796, Watkins and Cowell 2006b, pp. 91–2.

[28] Alexandre de Laborde, 1808, *Description des nouveaux jardins de la France, et de ses anciens châteaux, mêlée d'observations sur la vie de la campagne et la composition des jardins*, Paris. The quotation is at p. 15.

[29] Jaques Delille (1738–1813), a French poet frequently called de Lisle by contemporaries. Note that Delille combines Downton and Bowood to make Bowton.

[30] Jean de Dieu-Raymond de Cucé de Boisgelin (1732–1804) was a member of the French Academy from 1776 and his works include *Traduction des Héroïdes d'Ovide*, 1784; *L'art de juger d'après l'analogie des idées*, 1789; *Considérations sur la paix publique adressées de la Révolution*, 1791. His complete works were published in Paris in 1818. Some letters to Lord Carnarvon 1786–1800 are in the Hampshire Record Office: 75M91/A6–7. He also corresponded with Burke (Cobban and Smith 1967, VI, p. 293). See Nigel Aston, 1999, 'Burke, Boisgelin and the politics of the émigré bishops', in Kirsty Carpenter and Philip Mansel (eds), *The French Émigrés in Europe and the Struggle against Revolution, 1789–1814*. London.

[31] Uvedale Price, 1798. *Essays on the Picturesque. Essay on Artificial Water. Essay on Decorations. Essay on Architecture and Buildings*. Hereford and London, p. 83, fn.

[32] Uvedale Price to Lady Beaumont, June 1800, Watkins and Cowell 2006b, p. 129.

[33] Farington, 13 August 1799.

[34] Uvedale Price to Sir George Beaumont, 22 September 1799, Watkins and Cowell 2006b, pp. 127–9.

[35] Farington, 16 October 1799. Benjamin West (1760–1841) made a tour of the Wye in September 1799. At least one painting and one drawing survive from West's tour: 'The Ruins of Tintern Abbey, on the Banks of the River Wye', shown at the Royal Academy in 1800. Helmut von Erffa and Allen Stanley, 1986, *The Paintings of Benjamin West*. New Haven and London, pp. 428–9 and 'Weeping rock on River Wye, September 13 1799', Ruth S. Kraemer, 1975, *Drawings by Benjamin West and his son Raphael Lamar West*. Boston.

[36] Uvedale Price to Sir George Beaumont, 22 September 1799, Watkins and Cowell 2006b, pp. 127–9. The Foleys lived at Stoke Edith Park, which was remodelled by Humphry Repton. The Red Book is dated 1792.

[37] Susan Burney journal, 4 April 1790.

[38] Charles Burney to Madame D'Arblay, 25 May 1799, BL Egerton 3690 fos. 100^r–101^v.

[39] Farington, April 1796.

[40] Farington, April 1796.

[41] John Wilson, John Hoppner (1758–1810) *ODNB*.

[42] Farington, 16 May 1797. Farington also noted that 'Price engaged pictures of Discovery, & Fortune Teller for Genll. Fitzpatrick for 50 gs.' Robert Smirke (1753–1845).

[43] Farington, 20 May 1797.

[44] Farington, 10 November 1797.

45 Uvedale Price to Lord Abercorn, 15 July 1797, Watkins and Cowell 2006b, pp. 104–5.

46 Uvedale Price to Sir George Beaumont, 5 September 1797, Watkins and Cowell 2006b, pp. 106–7.

47 Uvedale Price to Sir George Beaumont, 7 December 1797, Watkins and Cowell 2006b, pp. 109–11.

48 R. Paulson, 1971, *Hogarth: His Life, Art, and Times*. London, p. 558 n. 36; J. Burke and C. Caldwell, 1968, *Hogarth: The Complete Engravings*. London, p. 181.

49 Richard Wyatt (1731–1813). JP. Held estates in Surrey (mostly Egham and Thorpe), Middlesex, Somerset and Sussex. An active collector of pictures and patron of contemporary artists including John Opie, Paul Sandby and John Thomas Smith. Said by George III to be 'a very good man. I have a high regard for him and all his family.' Elizabeth Silverthorne, 1976, 'Deposition Book of Richard Wyatt, J.P.', *Surrey Record Society*, 30, pp. vii–viii; Sir Joseph Mawbey (1730–1798), vinegar distiller, landed proprietor and politician. He was a supporter of John Wilkes and was satirised in the Rolliad. His Palladian mansion Botleys was at Chertsey, where he was a neighbour of Richard Wyatt: W. P. Courtney, *ODNB*.

50 Probably John Wallop (1690–1762), 1st earl of Portsmouth, or possibly his grandson, John, 2nd earl of Portsmouth (1742–1797).

51 Uvedale Price to Sir George Beaumont, 7 December 1797, Watkins and Cowell 2006b, pp. 109–11.

52 Farington, June 1798.

53 Farington, 23 April 1799.

54 The Royal Academy of Arts, 1095, *A Complete Dictionary of Contributors and their Work from its Foundation in 1769 to 1904*. London.

55 Farington, 9 May 1799.

56 Farington, 11 May 1799.

57 Farington, 29 April 1799. Nathaniel Dance (1735–1811), artist.

58 Farington, 24 May 1799. William Dance (1755–1840), pianist and violinist.

59 Farington, 7 May 1800.

60 John Glasse to the Lady Camelford, 20 September 1795.

61 Uvedale Price to Sir George Beaumont, 30 September 1796, Watkins and Cowell 2006b, pp. 91–2.

62 Uvedale Price to Lord Abercorn, 6 August 1796, Watkins and Cowell 2006b, pp. 91–2. Adam Walker (1730/31–1821), author, inventor and lecturer, had three sons, William (1767–1816), Adam John (?–1839) and Deane Franklin Walker (1778–1865). He published *Remarks made in a tour from London to the Lakes of Westmoreland and Cumberland, in the summer of M,DCC,XCI*. in 1792. 'Adam Walker with his wife, daughter, and three sons' by George Romney, RA, National Portrait Gallery. E. I. Carlyle, *ODNB*.

63 David Whitehead, 2001, *A Survey of Historic Parks and Gardens in Herefordshire*. Hereford, p. 30.

64 John Barrell, 2006, *The Spirit of Despotism: Invasions of Privacy in the 1790s*. Oxford. Charles James Fox's reply to Pitt, pp. 155, 178.

65 Francis Russell, 5th duke of Bedford (1765–1802), was the leading Whig in the House of Lords in the late eighteenth century and a leading promoter of agricultural and urban estate improvement. E. A. Smith, *ODNB*.

66 Lord Monboddo, James Burnett (1714–1799), Scottish judge. He wrote *Of the Origin and Progress of Language*, 6 vols, 1773–92. He was influenced by J. J. Rousseau and maintained that the Orangutang (chimpanzee) was a class of human species and that its want of speech was merely an accident. 'Burnett was preoccupied with his health, and, like other primitivists, also with what he saw as modern luxury and decadence. Extremely abstemious, he exercised naked in the open air, took cold baths, and – as the ancients did not use coaches – rode to London regardless of the weather.' Iain Maxwell Hammett, *ODNB*.

67 *Paradise lost*, Book 9, line 633. Uvedale Price to Lord Abercorn, 28 November 1796, Watkins and Cowell 2006b, pp. 93–94.

68 *Paradise lost*, Book 4, line 506.

69 Uvedale Price to Sir George Beaumont, 5 September 1797, Watkins and Cowell 2006b, pp. 106–7. Edward Harley was 5th earl of Oxford and Mortimer (1773–1849). He married in

1794 Jane-Elizabeth, daughter of Rev. James Scott (d. 1824). The reference is to *Henry IV Part 1*, Act I, Scene 4.

[70] Uvedale Price to Lord Abercorn, 6 September 1797, Watkins and Cowell 2006b, pp. 106–7.

[71] Uvedale Price to Sir George Beaumont, 28 January 1798, Watkins and Cowell 2006b, pp. 116–17.

[72] Uvedale Price to Sir George Beaumont, 17 February 1798, Watkins and Cowell 2006b, p. 118.

[73] Sir Harford Jones Brydges (1764–1847), diplomatist and author, married Sarah, widow of Robert Whitcomb, of the Whittern, Herefordshire, on 1 February 1796. He assumed the additional name of Brydges in 1826. He worked for the East India Company as assistant and factor at Basrah, 1783–94, and was its president in Baghdad, 1798–1806. T. F. Henderson, *ODNB*.

[74] HRO, Kentchurch AL 40, 7743–7853. AL 40 also contains three letters from Lady Caroline Price to Harford Jones, two letters from Price to Harford Jones and a few letters in letter books from Harford Jones to Price.

[75] HRO, AL 40 7744 15 July 1798.

[76] HRO, AL 40 7752 17 December 1798.

[77] HRO, AL 40 7779 2 August 1800.

[78] HRO, AL 40 7756 20 April 1799.

[79] HRO, AL 40 7762 14 July 1799.

[80] HRO, AL 40 7764 7 October 1799.

[81] HRO, AL 40 7763 4 August 1799. 'Lady Caroline says the Major has heard we are very comfortable with the Foxley family, + that he does not like that. I think that is rather severe.'

[82] HRO, AL 40 7773 15 March 1800.

[83] HRO, AL 40 7770 4 February 1800.

[84] HRO, AL 40 7783 4 October 1800.

[85] Uvedale Price to Lord Abercorn, 28 December 1797, Watkins and Cowell 2006b, p. 113.

[86] Uvedale Price to Lord Abercorn, January 1798, Watkins and Cowell 2006b, p. 115.

[87] HRO, AL 40 7779 2 August 1800.

[88] HRO, AL 40 7784 23 November 1800.

[89] HRO, AL 40 7785 1 December 1800.

[90] HRO, AL 40 7788 4 January 1801.

[91] HRO, AL 40 7789 24 January 1801.

[92] HRO, AL 40 7794 28 April 1801.

[93] HRO, AL 40 7800 20 September 1801.

[94] HRO, AL 40 6443 Uvedale and Lady Caroline Price to Harford Jones, Bath 31 December 1799.

[95] HRO, AL 40 7704 Lady Caroline Price to Harford Jones, Foxley 13 April 1801.

[96] HRO, AL 40 7820 3 March 1803.

[97] HRO, AL 40 7820 3 March 1803.

[98] HRO, AL 40 7842 28 October 1804.

[99] HRO, AL 40 7822 6 May 1803.

[100] HRO, AL 40 7810 28 May 1802.

[101] HRO, AL 40 7820 3 March 1803.

[102] HRO, AL 40 7820 3 March 1803.

[103] HRO, AL 40 7826 20 September 1803.

[104] Sent from Kingsgate, near Margate, August 11, Sunday, probably 1782 but possibly 1776.

[105] Undated letter from Fox to Price. Before 1802 when he married Mrs Armitshead.

[106] Mitchell 1997.

[107] Fox to Price, 19 July 1798.

[108] Fox to Price, 19 December 1798.

[109] Fox to Price, 21 December 1798. The *Plays on the Passions* were published anonymously by Joanna Baillie (1762–1851) in 1798.

[110] Price to Fox, 9 January 1799.

[111] Price to Fox, 17 January 1799.

[112] Price to Fox, 19 February 1799.

[113] Price to Fox, 4 March 1799.

[114] Fox to Price, 10 March 1799.

[115] Price to Fox, 13 March 1799.

[116] Fox to Price, 20 March 1799. The Prices were staying at 62 Lower Grosvenor St.

[117] Fox to Price, 6 May 1799.

[118] Fox to Price, 30 December 1800.

[119] Fox to Price, 7 August 1801.

[120] Fox to Price, 20 November 1801.

[121] Fox to Price, 15 June 1803.

[122] Fox to Price, 6 June 1802.

[123] Fox to Price, 15 June 1803.

[124] Fox to Price, 5 April 1804.

[125] 1802 or later because Fox sends Price 'Mrs F's compliments'. Fox publicly announced his marriage to Mrs Armitshead in 1802.

[126] Fox to Price, 5 April 1804.

[127] Price 1794, pp. 279–80.

CHAPTER 7: 'MR PRICE THE PICTURESQUE' (pages 142–164)

[1] *Star*, Monday, May 20, 1799; issue 3330. Some newspapers give William Norris as the author.

[2] Uvedale Price to Lord Abercorn, 21 December [1800], Watkins and Cowell 2006b, pp. 136–7.

[3] Uvedale Price to Lord Abercorn, 20 January 1801, Watkins and Cowell 2006b, pp. 137–8.

[4] Price 1810, *Dialogue, Essays*, III, p. 243.

[5] Price 1810, *Dialogue, Essays*, III, pp. 244–5.

[6] Price 1810, *Dialogue, Essays*, III, p. 262.

[7] Price 1810, *Dialogue, Essays*, III, pp. 276–8.

[8] Price 1810, *Dialogue, Essays*, III, pp. 284–8.

[9] Price 1810, *Dialogue, Essays*, III, pp. 291–4.

[10] Farington, 21 May 1801.

[11] Uvedale Price to Sir George Beaumont, undated c.1800, Watkins and Cowell 2006b, pp. 134–6.

[12] Uvedale Price to Lady Beaumont, 21 September 1801, Watkins and Cowell 2006b, pp. 143–4.

[13] M. Kauffmann, 1984, *John Varley, 1778–1842*, London.

[14] Uvedale Price to Lady Beaumont, 29 April 1803, Watkins and Cowell 2006b, pp. 156–7.

[15] John Udney of Teddington, merchant and art collector. His collection was not sold until 15 May 1829, at Christie's (Lugt 12047) John Robert Udney, and John Udney, 'Valuable collection of Italian Pictures'. General George Morrison (1704–1799) was Quartermaster General of the British army until 1795. He surveyed roads in Scotland under Marshall Wade. There was a sale of his paintings 1–2 April 1803, Farebrother (Lugt 6586a) and another of drawings 25 May and 5 June 1807, Philipe (Lugt 7253). George Knapton (1698–1778) portrait painter and antiquarian. He was in Rome 1725–32 and his report on excavations in Herculaneum was published in 1740. He was a founding member of the Society of Dilettanti and painted portraits of its members (1741–49). He catalogued the Royal Collection and was appointed Keeper of the King's Pictures in 1765.

[16] Uvedale Price to Sir George Beaumont, 21 May 1803, Watkins and Cowell 2006b, pp. 157–8.

[17] John Willett Adye (1745–1815) MP for New Romney (1796–1806), of Merley House, Wimborne, inherited the collections of his second cousin Ralph Willett (1719–1795). 'With the depreciation of West Indian property in the early years of the nineteenth century Willett's collections were dispersed, and the two pairs of balancing wings he had added to Merly, including the library building, were torn down. The bulk of his extensive collections of prints and drawings was sold by Thomas Philipe in eight sales between June 1808 and

May 1814 …. A large part of the engravings had been purchased by Willett at the Mariette sale of 1775, and the finest examples were acquired by William Beckford. Willett's paintings, from the Orleans Gallery and other fine collections, were auctioned by Peter Co over three days commencing on 31 May 1813. Although a number of the 128 lots were bought in, the sale realized over £7000.' Marc Vaulbert de Chantilly, *ODNB*. See Lugt 8342.

[18] Richard Payne Knight, 1805, *An Analytical Inquiry into the Principles of Taste*. London, p. 200, fn.

[19] Andrew Ballantyne, 1994–95, 'The Prices' daughter', *The Picturesque*, 9, pp. 1–2.

[20] Knight 1805, p. 198.

[21] HRO, AL 40 7834 March 1804; 7835 14 April 1804; 7841 1 August 1804; 7849 7 February 1805; 7857 10 June 1805.

[22] Farington, 16 July 1805.

[23] Farington, 13 October 1806.

[24] Farington, 21 June 1806.

[25] Farington, 13 October 1806.

[26] Ballantyne 1997, p. 18.

[27] Lady Theresa Lewis (ed.), 1865, *Extracts from the Journals and Correspondence of Miss Berry from the year 1783 to 1852*, 3 vols. London, II, 2 July 1808, p. 353. Robert Price had been at the University of Edinburgh in 1807 where he came to the attention of Walter Scott with 'several other young men of good family and great expectation'. Walter Scott to Lady Abercorn, 1808: H. J. C. Grierson (ed.), 1932, *The Letters of Sir Walter Scott 1808–1811*. London, p. 133.

[28] Lewis 1865, II, 10 July 1809, p. 385.

[29] Farington, 7 May 1808.

[30] Uvedale Price to Lord Aberdeen, May 1810, Watkins and Cowell 2006b, p. 198.

[31] Uvedale Price to Charles Burney, Sunning Hill, 9 March 1808, James Marshall and Marie-Louise Osborn Collection, Beinecke Rare Book and Manuscript Library, Yale University, Burney Family Collection, OSB MSS 3, box 14, folder 1044.

[32] The point at issue is the use of the term 'delight' in Knight's *An Analytical Inquiry into the Principles of Taste*, 1805, part 1, chapter 3, line 13.

[33] Farington, 27 October 1812 [at Coleorton; at breakfast].

[34] Robert Southey to Miss Barker, 24 December 1805, John Wood Warter (ed.), 1856, *Selections from the Letters of Robert Southey*. London, p. 303.

[35] John Aikin, 1800, *Letters from a Father to his Son* …. London, pp. 99–101.

[36] Uvedale Price to Sir George Beaumont, 16 June 1801, Watkins and Cowell 2006b, pp. 138–9; 11 July 1801, Watkins and Cowell 2006b, pp. 139–40.

[37] Kathleen Coburn (ed.), 1957, *The Notebooks of Samuel Taylor Coleridge. Vol. 1, 1794–1804*. London, 21 November 1803, Monday, 4 a.m. Christian Garve (1742–98), professor of philosophy at Leipzig, had translated Burke into German in 1773.

[38] Farington, 3 October 1801.

[39] Farington, 21 September 1802.

[40] Jane Austen (ed. R. Ballaster), 2003. *Sense and Sensibility*. London/Harmondsworth, note p. 401.

[41] Austen 1811, Chapter 18.

[42] Jane Austen, *Mansfield Park*, Chapter 6.

[43] Price's essay was translated in 1798 as *Über den guten Geschmack bei ländlichen Kunst- und Garten-Anlagen und verbesserung wirklicher Landschaften*, Leipzig. For Goethe's translation of Knight see Claudia Stumpf's edition of *Expedition into Sicily* (1986). See also John Hennig, 1951, 'A note on Goethe and Charles Gore', *Monatshefte*, 43, pp. 27–37.

[44] Johann von Goethe (trans. R. J. Hollingdale), 1971, *Elective Affinities*. Harmondsworth, pp. 231–4.

[45] James Malton, 1798, *Essay on British Cottage Architecture*, London.

[46] David Laing, 1800, *Hints for Dwellings, Consisting of Original Designs for Cottages, Farmhouses, Villas, etc.* London, p. iv. David Laing (1775–1856) was articled to John Soane in 1790 and established his own practice in 1796. There was a scandal over his building of the custom house on Thames Street in London in 1817 and his career never recovered. Steven Brindle, *ODNB*.

47 David Whitehead, *ODNB*.

48 Robert Lugar (1772/3–1855) Peter Leach, *ODNB*, notes that Lugar 'was among the first to introduce the picturesquely asymmetrical castle form into Scotland; but he was a designer of only limited ability, who frequently reduced the process of picturesque composition to a meagrely detailed routine formula of only marginal asymmetry'.

49 Uvedale Price to Sir George Beaumont, 23 April 1803, Watkins and Cowell 2006b, pp. 153–6.

50 Claude, c.1636, National Gallery, NG58; Claude, 1644, National Gallery, NG19.

51 Michael Kitson, 1978, *Claude Lorrain: Liber Veritatis*. London, pp. 121–4; Uvedale Price to Sir George Beaumont, 23 April 1803, Watkins and Cowell 2006b, pp. 153–6.

52 National Gallery, NG66; Wallace Collection, P63.

53 *King John*, Act III, Scene 3: BASTARD: Bell, book, and candle shall not drive me back/ When gold and silver becks me come on.

54 Uvedale Price to Sir George Beaumont, 21 May 1803, Watkins and Cowell 2006b, pp. 157–8.

55 Uvedale Price to Lady Beaumont, 31 May 1803, Watkins and Cowell 2006b, pp. 158–60; National Gallery, *'Noble and patriotic' The Beaumont Gift 1828*, 1988.

56 Uvedale Price to Lady Beaumont, 28 June 1803, Watkins and Cowell 2006b, pp. 163–4. The description is in Cowper's 'Truth'; see John D. Baird and Charles Ryskamp (eds), 1980, *The Poems of William Cowper. Vol. I, 1748–1782*. Oxford, pp. 280–96, ll. 131–154. The print is Hogarth's *The four times of the day* (c.1736).

> Yon antient prude, whose wither'd features show
> She might be young some forty years ago,
> Her elbows pinion'd close upon her hips,
> Her head erect, her fan upon her lips,
> Her eye-brows arch'd, her eyes both gone astray
> To watch yon am'rous couple in their play,
> With boney and unkerchief'd neck defies
> The rude inclemency of wintry skies,
> And sails with lappet-head and mincing airs
> Duely at clink of bell, to morning pray'rs.
> To thrift and parsimony much inclin'd,
> She yet allows herself that boy behind;
> The shiv'ring urchin, bending as he goes,
> With slipshod heels, and dew drop at his nose,
> His predecessor's coat advanc'd to wear,
> Which future pages are yet doom'd to share,
> Carries her bible tuck'd beneath his arm,
> And hides his hands to keep his fingers warm.

57 Benjamin West (1738–1820) PRA 1791–1805; 1806–1820. The quotations are from Horace, *Odes* Book III, 11:

> 'una de multis face nuptiali
> digna periurum fuit in parentem
> splendide mendax et in omne uirgo
> nobilis aeuum,'
> One alone there was who deserved the wedding-
> Torch, a brilliant liar towards her perjured
> Father and a virgin for every future
> Era ennobled

58 Uvedale Price to Sir George Beaumont, 21 May 1803; 3 June 1795, Watkins and Cowell 2006b, p. 158; p. 84; 'Memoirs of Thomas Jones, Penkerrig, Radnorshire 1803', *Walpole Society*, XXXII, 1946–48, p. 26, 35, 121.

59 Private collection.

60 Uvedale Price to Lady Beaumont, 9 June 1804, Watkins and Cowell 2006b, p. 180.

61 Farington, 11 June 1804; 23 June 1804; 14 November 1806; 12 November 1806.

[62] Farington, 9 March 1807 [Wm Locke called and informed F that] 'the *Committee of Taste* is doubled in number & adjudge to whom the monuments shall be given. The Marquess of Buckingham – Thos Hope – The Marquiss of Stafford – Uvedale Price – Lord Carlisle are added to the Committee, – which before consisted of C Long Sir G Beaumont Wm. Locke H Bankes Payne Knight R P Carew'. See also Holger Hoock, 2003, *The King's Artists. The Royal Academy of Arts and Politics of British Culture 1760–1840*. Oxford, pp. 263–74 and Frederick A. Whiting, 1967, 'The Committee of Taste', *Apollo*, 82, pp. 326–30.

[63] Farington, 13 April 1806.

[64] His sister married James Hare (1747–1804) and his daughter Amelia married Charles Long (1760–1838), and he was a close friend of Reynolds. Christopher Lloyd, *ODNB*.

[65] Farington, 7 May 1800.

[66] TNA L. R. 4 20/5–8 1806–9 provides details of his salary, which over three years was £1,200. Dr Cyril Hart kindly provided this information. For a full discussion of the Forest of Dean see Cyril Hart, 1966, *Royal Forest: A History of Dean's Woods as Producers of Timber*. Oxford, and Cyril Hart, 1995, *The Forest of Dean: New History 1550–1818*. Stroud. Price's involvement has formerly been ignored.

[67] Nelson's *Report on the Forest of Dean*, 1802, Nelson Museum and Local History Centre, Monmouth.

[68] Uvedale Price to Lady Beaumont, 16 July 1806, Watkins and Cowell 2006b, pp. 196–7.

[69] Price's business in the Forest of Dean may partially account for the gap of almost five years in the correspondence with the Beaumonts from October 1806 to August 1811. Alternatively, the letters may simply not have survived. There is no evidence of a dispute with Beaumont, and Price continued to visit Beaumont in London.

[70] Uvedale Price to Lord Abercorn, 21 December 1800, Watkins and Cowell 2006b, pp. 136–7.

[71] Uvedale Price to Sir George Beaumont, 12 February 1802, Watkins and Cowell 2006b, pp. 145–8.

[72] Uvedale Price to Lady Beaumont, April 1803, Watkins and Cowell 2006a, pp. 73–4.

[73] Uvedale Price to Lord Abercorn, 31 May 1796, Watkins and Cowell 2006b, pp. 84–5. James Hamilton (1730–1798), 2nd earl of Clanbrassil, Tollymore Park, County Down, Ireland. He married Grace Foley in 1774. He was a landscape improver and the dwarf conifer *Picea abies* 'Clanbrassiliana', planted by him in 1798 at Tollymore Park, is named after him.

[74] Uvedale Price to Lord Aberdeen, 6 February 1818, Watkins and Cowell 2006b, p. 274. Price may have come across this analogy via Joseph Addison who, in *The Spectator* 215, 6 November 1706, stated that Aristotle in his *Doctrine of Substantial Forms* tells us that 'a Statue lies hid in a Block of Marble'.

[75] Uvedale Price to Sir George Beaumont, 11 November 1812, Watkins and Cowell 2006b, pp. 204–6.

[76] Uvedale Price to Sir George Beaumont, 28 October 1802, Watkins and Cowell 2006b, pp. 151–2.

[77] Uvedale Price to Lady Beaumont, August 1803, Watkins and Cowell 2006b, pp. 164–5. Plutarch, *Lives, Philopoemen*, IV, 5: 'Even in speculations on military subjects it was his habit to neglect maps and diagrams, and to put the theorems to practical proof on the ground itself. He would be exercising his thoughts and considering as he travelled, and arguing with those about him of the difficulties of steep or broken ground, what might happen at rivers, ditches, or mountain-passes, in marching in close or in open, in this or in that particular form of battle.' Dryden's translation of Plutarch's *Philopoemen*. The quotation is in Sir Joshua Reynolds' *Second Discourse*, 1778, in R. R. Wark (ed.), 1959, *Sir Joshua Reynolds: Discourses on Art*, San Marino, pp. 35–6. Reynolds refers to both Plutarch and Livy, but quotes from Livy's History of Rome.

[78] Uvedale Price to Lady Beaumont, August 1803, Watkins and Cowell 2006b, pp. 164–5.

[79] Uvedale Price to Lady Beaumont, 8 June 1803, Watkins and Cowell 2006b, pp. 160–62.

[80] Uvedale Price to Lady Beaumont, 9 June 1804, Watkins and Cowell 2006b, pp. 179–80. The common elm is *Ulmus procera*, the wych elm *Ulmus glabra*. *Paradise Lost*, 4, l. 143: 'Yet higher then their tops The verdurous wall of Paradise upsprung'.

[81] David Whitehead, 2007, 'Veterans in the arboretum: planting exotics at Holme Lacy, Herefordshire, in the late Nineteenth Century', *Garden History*, 35, 2, p. 103, quoting *Hereford Journal*, 12 September 1798.

[82] Uvedale Price to Sir George Beaumont, 16 September 1820; 5 November 1820, Watkins and Cowell 2006b, pp. 288–9, 290–91.

[83] Lord Guernsey, pers comm, 2010.

[84] Uvedale Price to Sir George Beaumont, 17 October 1806, Watkins and Cowell 2006b, pp. 197–8. Fragments of the park and the kitchen gardens remain at Sandwell, although the house has gone and much of the landscape has been destroyed by the M5.

[85] Uvedale Price to Sir George Beaumont, 6 September 1797, Watkins and Cowell 2006b, pp. 107–8.

[86] Uvedale Price to Sir George Beaumont, 17 October 1806, Watkins and Cowell 2006b, pp. 197–8.

[87] Joseph Mawman of 22 Poultry was a leading London publisher who had purchased the long-established bookselling business of Charles Dilly (1739–1807) in 1800. Mawman was publisher of the *Critical Review* and handled the first number of the *Edinburgh Review* in 1802.

[88] Price 1810, II, Preface, p. v.

[89] Price 1810, I, Preface, p. x.

[90] Cicero *Academica*, II, 7.

[91] Price 1810, I, Preface xiii.

[92] Price 1810, I, p. xviii and II, pp. 383–406.

[93] Farington, 4 March 1810.

[94] Price 1810, I, Preface, p. xix.

[95] *Quarterly Review*, 1810, pp. 372–82, 372.

[96] *Quarterly Review*, 1810, p. 381.

[97] *Edinburgh Review*, 1810, pp. 167–211, 202.

[98] *Edinburgh Review*, 1811, pp. 1–45, 1.

CHAPTER 8: 'DISTANT PATHS OF LEAFY SECRETNESS' (pages 165–197)

[1] Uvedale Price to Sir George Beaumont, 23 August 1803, Watkins and Cowell 2006b, pp. 166–7. Owen and Brown 1988, p. 114.

[2] Uvedale Price to Lady Beaumont, 18 February 1804; Uvedale Price to Sir George Beaumont, 13 January 1805, Watkins and Cowell 2006b, pp. 174–5, 187–8.

[3] See H. de Selincourt (ed.), 1940/1952, *Poetical Words of William Wordsworth: Poems Written in Youth, Poems Referring to the Period of Childhood*. Oxford, pp. 227–8. Uvedale Price to Sir George Beaumont, 17 October 1806, Watkins and Cowell 2006b, pp. 197–8.

[4] Wordsworth to Sir George Beaumont, de Selincourt 1937, Letter 437, pp. 466–7.

[5] William Wordsworth to Sir George Beaumont, de Selincourt 1937, Letter 437, pp. 466–7.

[6] Price 1794, pp. 279–80.

[7] Thomas Andrew Knight (1759–1838), younger brother of Richard Payne Knight. In 1808/9 he took over the management of his brother's estate at Downton and moved into his Downton Castle. He was president of the Horticultural Society (1811–38). He was 'a whig of the old school, a lax Christian, and an engaging host'. Janet Browne, *ODNB*.

[8] HRO, T74 Knight Papers exchange of land between Uvedale Price and Thomas Andrew Knight, 25/2/1812; valuation of timber.

[9] Uvedale Price to Sir George Beaumont, 24 July 1812, Watkins and Cowell 2006b, pp. 202–4.

[10] HRO, Knight Papers T74 728.

[11] HRO, Knight Papers T74 728 5. John Harris (1753–1829) of Wickton Court, Stoke Prior, was a leading Herefordshire surveyor, Smith 2004, p. 192.

[12] HRO, Knight Papers T74 590.

[13] Uvedale Price to Lord Aberdeen, Foxley, 14 August 1810, Watkins and Cowell 2006b, pp. 200–201.

[14] Uvedale Price to Lord Aberdeen, Sunning Hill, 29 June 1810, Watkins and Cowell 2006b, pp. 198–200.

[15] John Fitzpatrick (1745–1818), the elder brother of Richard Fitzpatrick, was MP for Bedfordshire from 1767 to 1794, when he was created Baron Upper Ossory in the British peerage.

[16] Uvedale Price to Sir George Beaumont, 10 August 1811, Watkins and Cowell 2006b, pp. 201–2.

[17] Uvedale Price to Sir George Beaumont, 24 July 1812, Watkins and Cowell 2006b, pp. 202–4.

[18] Francis Basset (1757–1835), Baron de Dunstanville and Baron Basset, politician and landowner.

[19] William Wordsworth to Dorothy Wordsworth, 15 May 1812, Alan Hill (ed.), 1993, *The Letters of William and Dorothy Wordsworth, vol. 8, A Supplement of New Letters*. Oxford.

[20] Joseph Jekyll (1754–1837) was a lawyer and politician remembered mainly as a wit, but this 'which consisted in large measure of excruciating puns, has not lasted well'. Stephen Lee, *ODNB*.

[21] William Wordsworth to Mary Wordsworth, 1 June 1812, Hill 1993.

[22] William Wordsworth to Dorothy Wordsworth and Sara Hutchinson, 4–5 June 1812, Hill 1993.

[23] Farington, 22 October 1812 [at Coleorton].

[24] Uvedale Price to Sir George Beaumont, 4 August 1800, Watkins and Cowell 2006b, p. 131. The quotation is from *Paulo Purganti and his Wife* by Matthew Prior (1664–1721). Monsieur Purgon is the doctor in Moliere's *Le Malade Imaginaire*, 1673, Act 3, Scene 5.

[25] Uvedale Price to Sir George Beaumont, 22 August 1800, Watkins and Cowell 2006b, pp. 132–3.

[26] Uvedale Price to Sir George Beaumont, 16 June 1801, Watkins and Cowell 2006b, pp. 138–9.

[27] With blind rage; bloody madness.

[28] Uvedale Price to Sir George Beaumont, 23 August 1803, Watkins and Cowell 2006b, pp. 166–7.

[29] Uvedale Price to Sir George Beaumont, 24 April 1805, Watkins and Cowell 2006b, pp. 191–2.

[30] Uvedale Price to Miss Berry, Foxley, 19 January, 1813; from Lewis 1865, II, pp. 528–9. The reference is to Milton, Lycidas, 1.

[31] Uvedale Price adds 'You may happen to have seen in the papers that Ld Tyrconnel has been with Admiral Tchesagoff: it is an odd circumstance, though certainly not of a lyrical kind, that the parson of my parish was the man who married this amphibious hero to a daughter of Commissioner Proby's; and, to finish the history, the ceremony was performed at Paddington.' John Joshua Proby (1751–1828), 1st earl of Carysfort, was Commissioner of the Board of Control 1806–8 in the ministry of all the talents, G. F. R. Barker, *ODNB*.

[32] Uvedale Price to Lord Aberdeen, 10 February 1813, Watkins and Cowell 2006b, pp. 206–11.

[33] Lord Byron to Lady Melbourne, 30 October 1812, Leslie A. Marchand (ed.), 1973, *Byron's Letters and Journals*. London, vol. 2, p. 237.

[34] Lord Byron to Lady Melbourne, 4 November 1812, Marchand 1973, vol. 2, p. 239.

[35] Uvedale Price to Lord Aberdeen, 27 February 1813, Watkins and Cowell 2006b, pp. 211–13. Charles Kinnaird (1780–1826), 8th Lord Kinnaird of Inchture, politician and art collector, 'travelled much on the continent and was an avaricious buyer of works of art dispersed during the Napoleonic wars; in particular he bought much of the collection of Philippe Égalité, duke of Orléans … He was said to have given extravagant sums for what he regarded as his best pictures (which included works by Titian, Poussin, Teniers, and Rubens), with the result that in 1813 he was forced to sell his London possessions.' A. H. Millar, *ODNB*.

[36] Frances Douglas, Lady Douglas (1750–1817), of Bothwell Castle, Lanarkshire and Grosvenor Square. She is thought to have been memorialised by Scott in the character of Jeanie Deans in *The Heart of Midlothian* (Edinburgh, 1818). 'Her only fault, mentioned by all, was her laziness.' Alison Rosie, *ODNB*.

[37] Uvedale Price to Miss Berry, Foxley, 18 December 1813, Lewis 1865, II, pp. 547–9.

[38] Uvedale Price to Samuel Rogers, Foxley, 25 May 1823, Clayden 1889, I, pp. 355–61.

[39] Farington, 18 June 1813. He also saw 'Mr U Price Junr' at the evening exhibition of Sir J. Reynolds' pictures, 2 July 1813.

[40] Owen and Brown 1988, p. 208.

[41] Uvedale Price to Sir George Beaumont, 4 August 1813, Watkins and Cowell 2006b, pp. 214–6.

[42] Uvedale Price to Sir George Beaumont, 4 August 1813, Watkins and Cowell 2006b, pp. 214–16.

[43] Scott to Lady Abercorn 23 March 1813, D. Douglas (ed.), 1894, *Familiar Letters of Sir Walter Scott*. Edinburgh, vol. 1, p. 278.

[44] Scott to Baillie, 13/21 March, 1813, J. G. Lockhart (ed.), 1837, *Memoirs of the Life of Sir Walter Scott*. Edinburgh, vol. 3, p. 51.

[45] Scott 1818, Chapter 32.

[46] Uvedale Price to Miss Berry, Foxley 18 December 1813, Lewis 1865, II, pp. 547–9.

[47] Uvedale Price to Miss Berry, Foxley 18 December 1813, Lewis 1865, II, pp. 547–9.

[48] Uvedale Price to Miss Berry, Foxley 18 December 1813, Lewis 1865, II, pp. 547–9.

[49] G. M. Hughes, 1890, *A History of Windsor Forest Sunninghill and the Great Park*. London and Edinburgh, states a frequent visitor to the Wells was Benjamin Stillingfleet, 'the great friend of Mr Aldworth Neville of Stanlake, and of Mr Uvedale Price … It was of him that Mrs. Montague said he attempted to destroy "the false shame that attended the devotee to ornithology"', p. 266.

[50] 'Both he and Fox, ardent admirers of French institutions, had imbibed the free-thinking irreligious notions so prevalent then; they paid but little thought to the conventionalities of life, and their domestic arrangements were alike irregular.' Lady Lade 'was Caroline Price's particular friend'. After Lady Caroline's death, the property went to Fitzpatrick's niece Caroline Fox, daughter of his sister, Lady Mary Holland: Hughes 1890, pp. 240–44.

[51] 'THE RIGHT HONOURABLE RICHARD FITZPATRICK, second son of John, Earl of Upper Ossory, and Evelyn Leveson Gower, his wife, General of His Majesty's Forces, Colonel of the 47th Regiment of Foot, Privy Councillor in both Kingdoms, and at different times Member of Parliament for the borough of Tavistock and the county of Bedford. He twice held the important office of Secretary at War, and once that of Secretary to the Lord-Lieutenant of Ireland, and was during forty years the intimate friend of Mr Fox. He was an inhabitant and proprietor in the parish. Born 30 January 1749, died 25 April 1813': Hughes 1890, p. 436.

[52] This book was first published in 1810 in Paris but the entire edition, except for three proof copies ending with page 240 of the third volume, was seized and destroyed on the orders of Napoleon. The title page of the 1813 edition, which is therefore in practice the first edition, has 'Paris, H. Nicolle. la Librairie Stéréotype, 1810. Ré-imprimée par John Murray, Albemarle Street, Londres, 1813'. There were three volumes in 8vo. Mme de Staël explains in the introduction that, although the text had already been submitted and passed after certain excisions, the minister of police had all 10,000 copies destroyed on the grounds that the book was 'un-French'.

[53] Uvedale Price to Miss Berry, Foxley, 29 March 1814, Lewis 1865, III, pp. 67–9.

[54] Uvedale Price to Aberdeen, 9 December 1814; Price to Aberdeen, 5 February 1815, Watkins and Cowell 2006b, pp. 230–41.

[55] Uvedale Price to the Rev Dr Parr Hatton, Foxley, 27 July 1814.

[56] Samuel Parr (1747–1825). 'When he was in a whipping mood he would birch boys in advance, promising them that their next fault would go unpunished, an often forgotten assurance … The boys even boasted of his prowess with the rod, and he was popular with them.' Leonard W. Cowie, *ODNB*.

[57] *Gentleman's Magazine*, lxxv, pt 1, p. 561. John Duncumb (1765–1839). 'Duncumb was secretary to the Herefordshire Agricultural Society from its formation in 1797, and published works on agriculture, including a General View of the Agriculture of the County of Hereford (1805) as well as sermons.' The first volume of his history of Herefordshire was published in 1804, the second in 1812. Gordon Goodwin, rev. Robin Whittaker, *ODNB*.

[58] HRO, BD/11 44, Mrs Mary Westfaling to The Rev John Webb, Tretire, Ross Rudhall, 3 March 1816.

[59] Elizabeth Barrett to Hugh Boyd, Hope End, 28 May 1828. McCarthy 1955, pp. 43–4.

[60] Uvedale Price to Lord Aberdeen, Foxley, 22 July 1816, Watkins and Cowell 2006b, pp. 248–50.

[61] Sir George Beaumont to William Wordsworth, 8 January 1817.

[62] Uvedale Price to Lady Beaumont, 9 February 1805, Watkins and Cowell 2006b, pp. 190–91.

[63] Uvedale Price to Lord Aberdeen, 4 August 1817, Watkins and Cowell 2006b, pp. 266–8.

[64] Farington, 2 February 1817.

[65] Uvedale Price to Lady Beaumont, 13 June 1817, Watkins and Cowell 2006b, pp. 265–6; Uvedale Price to Lord Aberdeen, 4 August 1817, Watkins and Cowell 2006b, pp. 266–8.

[66] Uvedale Price to Sir George and Lady Beaumont, 18 March 1815, Watkins and Cowell 2006b, pp. 242–3. 'The Thorn', first published in 1798 in *Lyrical Ballads*, republished in 1800. *Poems in Two Volumes* was published in 1807.

[67] Uvedale Price to Sir George Beaumont, 27 October 1816, Watkins and Cowell 2006b, pp. 256–9.

[68] Uvedale Price to Sir George Beaumont, 7 December 1818, Watkins and Cowell 2006b, pp. 276–7.

[69] Uvedale Price to Sir George Beaumont, 31 October 1818, Watkins and Cowell 2006b, pp. 275–6.

[70] Uvedale Price to Lord Aberdeen, 6 February 1818, Watkins and Cowell 2006b, p. 274.

[71] Uvedale Price to Sir George Beaumont, 7 December 1818, Watkins and Cowell 2006b, pp. 276–7.

[72] Uvedale Price to Lady Beaumont, 21 December 1818, Watkins and Cowell 2006b, pp. 277–8.

[73] Uvedale Price to Sir George Beaumont, 5 August 1819, Watkins and Cowell 2006b, pp. 278–9.

[74] Uvedale Price to Sir George Beaumont, 10 January 1820, Watkins and Cowell 2006b, pp. 280–82.

[75] Uvedale Price to Lady Beaumont, 10 August 1820, Watkins and Cowell 2006b, pp. 286–7.

[76] Uvedale Price to Sir George Beaumont, 5 November 1820, Watkins and Cowell 2006b, pp. 290–91. Gilpin used the London address of his close friend, the landscape painter George Barret junior (1767–1842), at 50 Upper Berkeley Street, Portman Square, Paddington Green. Sophieke Piebenga, *ODNB*. His father George Barret (1732?–1784), also a landscape painter, was born in Dublin and was a friend of Edmund Burke. 'By tradition Burke introduced him to the wild scenery of the Dargle valley and the Powerscourt estate (notably its waterfall) in co. Wicklow and influenced him to paint in a remarkably Romantic style for the date'. See Huon Mallalieu and W. C. Monkhouse, *rev.* Anne Crookshank, *ODNB*.

[77] Uvedale Price to Sir George Beaumont, 5 November 1820, Watkins and Cowell 2006b, pp. 290–91. Mrs Greville is possibly Mrs Frances Greville née Macartney (c.1724–89), author of *A Prayer for Indifference*.

[78] Uvedale Price to Sir George Beaumont, 12 January 1822, Watkins and Cowell 2006b, pp. 299–301.

[79] Uvedale Price to Lord Aberdeen, 22 November 1821, Watkins and Cowell 2006b, pp. 298–9.

[80] Ballantyne 1997, p. 38.

[81] Uvedale Price to Sir George Beaumont, 11 March 1823, Watkins and Cowell 2006b, pp. 305–7.

[82] Uvedale Price to Sir George Beaumont, 11 March 1823, Watkins and Cowell 2006b, pp. 305–7.

[83] There was gossip about Knight's sexuality, and his interest and support of young artists such as John Robert Cozens and Richard Westall was noticed: G. S. Rousseau, 1987, 'The sorrows of Priapus: anticlericalism, homosocial desire, and Richard Payne Knight', in G. S Rousseau and Roy Porter (eds), *Sexual Worlds of the Enlightenment*. Manchester, pp. 101–53.

[84] Uvedale Price to Lord Aberdeen, 3 May 1821, Watkins and Cowell 2006b, pp. 292–3.

[85] Uvedale Price to Lord Aberdeen, 1 August 1821 and August 1821, Watkins and Cowell 2006b, pp. 294–5.

[86] Uvedale Price to Lord Aberdeen, 20 May [1822], Watkins and Cowell 2006b, pp. 301–2.

[87] Uvedale Price to Sir George Beaumont, 12 January 1822, Watkins and Cowell 2006b, pp. 299–301.

[88] Uvedale Price to Sir George Beaumont, 2 December 1822, Watkins and Cowell 2006b, pp. 303–5.

[89] HRO, BD/11 47 Mrs Mary Westfaling to the Rev. John Webb, Tretire, Ross Rudhall, 10 March 1824.

[90] HRO, BD/11 48 To Webb, 10 May 1824 'The Foxley family are coming to me on the 19th Wednesday Senight and I do hope you will contrive to join them. They stay with me till Saturday 22d.'

[91] Uvedale Price to Samuel Rogers, Foxley, 25 May 1823, Clayden 1889, I, pp. 355–61.

[92] Uvedale Price to Samuel Rogers, Foxley, 25 May 1823, Clayden 1889, I, pp. 355–61.

[93] Uvedale Price to Sir George Beaumont, 20 August 1823, Watkins and Cowell 2006b, pp. 308–9; Thorne, *The House of Commons 1790–1820*; IV Members G-P p. 888.

[94] Uvedale Price to Sir George Beaumont, 12 September 1824, Watkins and Cowell 2006b, pp. 309–11.

[95] Turkish palace guard: Lord Essex.

[96] Uvedale Price to Samuel Rogers, Foxley, 26 July 1824, Clayden 1889, I, pp. 379–84.

[97] Uvedale Price to Samuel Rogers, Foxley, 26 July 1824, Clayden 1889, I, pp. 379–84; George Gretton was Dean of Hereford 1809–20.

[98] Uvedale Price to Samuel Rogers, Foxley, 26 July 1824, Clayden 1889, I, pp. 379–84.

[99] William Wordsworth to Sir G. Beaumont, Radnor, 20 September 1824, de Selincourt 1937, p. 155.

[100] William Wordsworth to Samuel Rogers, Rydal Mount, 21 January 1825, de Selincourt 1937, p. 175.

[101] Uvedale Price to Lady Beaumont, 8 October 1824, Watkins and Cowell 2006b, pp. 311–12. Wordsworth's *A Description of the Scenery of the Lakes in the North of England* was first published in 1820.

[102] Mrs Wordsworth to Lady Beaumont, 25 February 1825. 'A Flower garden' was published in *Poems of the Fancy II*, 1827.

[103] Uvedale Price to E. H. Barker, 9 February 1826; 11 May 1826.

[104] Uvedale Price to E. H. Barker, 24 March 1827; 17 April 1827.

[105] Elizabeth Berridge (ed.), 1974, *The Barretts at Hope End: The Early Diary of Elizabeth Barrett Browning*. London; Margaret Forster, 1988, *Elizabeth Barrett Browning*. London, p. 34.

[106] Uvedale Price to Elizabeth Barrett, 11 January 1827.

[107] Uvedale Price to Elizabeth Barrett, 20 December 1826.

[108] Uvedale Price to Lady Beaumont, 19 August 1827, Watkins and Cowell 2006b, pp. 314–15.

[109] William Wordsworth, *Elegiac Stanzas suggested by a Picture of Peel Castle painted by Sir George Beaumont*. Wordsworth had seen the painting at the Beaumonts' house in Grosvenor Square, and his poem written in 1806 and published in 1807 laments the death of his brother in a shipwreck.

[110] Uvedale Price Uvedale to Elizabeth Barrett, 7 April 1827.

[111] Elizabeth Barrett Browning, 1914, *The Poet's Enchiridion with an Inedited Address to Uvedale Price on his eightieth birthday....* Boston, pp. 41–3.

[112] Uvedale Price to E. H. Barker, 4 June 1827; 18 June 1827; 7 July 1827; 20 July 1827.

[113] Lady Margaret Beaumont to Mrs Wordsworth, 28 June, Coleorton.

[114] Uvedale Price, 1827, *An Essay on the Modern Pronunciation of the Greek and Latin Languages*. Oxford, p. vii.

[115] Price 1827, p. 240.

[116] Price 1827, p. 241.

[117] Uvedale Price to E. H. Barker, 25 September 1827.

[118] Uvedale Price to E. H. Barker, 26 October 1827.

[119] Uvedale Price to Lady Beaumont, 31 October 1827, Watkins and Cowell 2006b, pp. 314–15.

[120] Lady Margaret Beaumont to Mrs Wordsworth, September 1827.

[121] The exhibition of 200 paintings was organised by Ross Society for the Encouragement of the Progress of Fine Arts, 12 September 1827. John Tisdall, 1996, *Joshua Cristall*

1768–1847: In Search of Arcadia. Hereford. Price owned two Reynolds portraits: Lady Caroline Price, Mannings, 1482; and Lady Almeria Carpenter, Mannings, 313.

[122] Uvedale Price to E. H. Barker, 11 November 1827.

[123] Uvedale Price to Elizabeth Barrett, 11 December 1827.

[124] Uvedale Price to Archer Clive, Private collection.

[125] William Wordsworth to Lord Lonsdale, Liverpool, 25 January 1828, Alan G. Hill, 1988. *The Letters of William and Dorothy Wordsworth, vol. 3, The Later Years Part 1 1821–1828*. Oxford.

[126] William Wordsworth to William Whewell, 4 December 1828. William Whewell (1794–1866) scientist and philosopher was later Master of Trinity. Hill, 1988.

[127] Uvedale Price to E. H. Barker, 29 March 1828.

[128] Lady Margaret Beaumont to Mrs Wordsworth, 30 January 1828.

[129] Uvedale Price to E. H. Barker, 5 March 1828.

[130] Uvedale Price to Elizabeth Barrett, 14 April 1828. Gottfried Hermann (1772–1848), Leipzig.

[131] Quayle to Barker, 15 October 1829. Thomas Quayle wrote these comments on hearing of Price's death, prefacing them with 'Poor Sir Uvedale! – Sic transit'.

[132] Elizabeth Barrett to Hugh Boyd, Hope End, 28 May 1828. McCarthy 1955, 43–4.

[133] Dorothy Mermin, 1989, *Elizabeth Barrett Browning: The Origins of a New Poetry*. Chicago, p. 42.

[134] Uvedale Price to E. H. Barker, 5 June 1828.

[135] Charles Robert Cockerell (1788–1863), architect.

[136] G. L. Meason, 1828, *On the Landscape Architecture of the Great Painters of Italy*. London. Price to Barker, 18 August 1828.

[137] Charles Chetwynd Talbot (1777–1849), 2nd Earl Talbot. The park at Ingestre had been modified by Brown.

[138] Robert Price to E. H. Barker, 31 January 1829.

[139] Uvedale Price to E. H. Barker, 2 May 1829.

[140] *Hereford Journal*, 16 September 1829.

[141] David Whitehead, *ODNB*. There is no legible inscription, although there is one to Thomas White who was steward thirty years with Sir Uvedale Price and died 22 November 1829 aged 56.

[142] Elizabeth Barrett to Hugh Boyd, Hope End, Wednesday [1829]. McCarthy 1955, p. 81.

[143] Elizabeth Barrett to Hugh Boyd, Hope End, Wednesday morning [1829]. McCarthy 1955, p. 85.

[144] Berridge 1974. Tuesday, 25 October 1831, p. 207.

CONCLUSION (pages 198–210)

[1] Seymour *et al.* 1998.

[2] Lord John Russell (ed.), 1853, *Memoirs, Journal and Correspondence of Thomas Moore*. London, V, 26 July 1826, p. 96.

[3] This included material he had contributed to Joseph Wilkinson's 1810 *Select Views in Cumberland, Westmoreland and Lancashire*. W. J. B. Owen and J. M. Smyser, 1974, *The Prose Works of William Wordsworth*. Oxford, II.

[4] Uvedale Price to Lady Beaumont, 6 August 1820, Watkins and Cowell 2006b, pp. 285–6.

[5] Nigel Everett, 1994, *The Tory View of Landscape*. London, pp. 158–9.

[6] Andrew Coventry (1764–1832), first Professor of Agriculture at the University of Edinburgh (1790–1831).

[7] J. Loudon, 1804, *Observations on the Formation and Management of Useful and Ornamental Plantations*. Edinburgh, and *Observations on the Theory and Practice of Landscape Gardening*, pp. 214–15. Loudon picks out the 'fine woods at Foxley, U. Price, Esq.' for praise in his *Encyclopaedia of Agriculture* of 1825, p. 1101.

[8] Melanie Louise Simo, 1988, *Loudon and the Landscape*. New Haven and London, pp. 4, 38.

[9] Barbier 1963, p. 70.

[10] Sophieke Piebenga, *ODNB*.

242

UVEDALE PRICE
1747–1829
DECODING THE
PICTURESQUE

11 Sophieke Piebenga, 2004, 'William Sawrey Gilpin (1761/62–1843): watercolour artist and landscape gardener', *The Picturesque*, 48, p. 15.

12 Uvedale Price to Lady Beaumont, 6 August 1820, Watkins and Cowell 2006b, pp. 285–6.

13 Sophieke Piebenga, 1994, 'William Sawrey Gilpin: picturesque improver', *Garden History*, 22, pp. 176–96; Piebenga 2004.

14 William S. Gilpin, 1832, *Practical Hints upon Landscape Gardening: With Some Remarks on Domestic Architecture as Connected with Scenery*. London, pp. v–vi.

15 Gilpin 1832, p. 145.

16 Sophieke Piebenga, William Sawrey Gilpin, *ODNB*.

17 Uvedale Price to E. H. Barker, 18 August 1828.

18 Richard Morris, 1825, *Essays on Landscape Gardening and on Uniting Picturesque Effect with Rural Scenery: Containing Directions for Laying Out and Improving the Grounds Connected with a Country Residence*. London, pp. vi–vii.

19 Thomas Dudley Fosbrooke (1770–1842) was elected to the Society of Antiquaries in 1799. He published *British Monachism, or, Manners and Customs of the Monks and Nuns of England*, in 1802. He became curate of Walford, near Ross, on the river Wye, in 1811 and continued to write on historical topics. Brian S. Smith, *ODNB*.

20 Watkin 1968, p. 175, quoting *Gardener's Magazine*, V, pp. 783–4.

21 David Whitehead, *ODNB*.

22 See also J. Conron, 2000, *American Picturesque*. Pennsylvania; C. E. Beveridge and P. Rocheleau, 1998, *Frederick Law Olmsted: Designing the American Landscape*. New York.

23 Sir Thomas Dick Lauder (1784–1848) lived at Relugas on the River Findhorn, near Forres. 'The scenery and legends of the district gave a special bent to his scientific and literary studies.' He wrote papers on scientific and literary themes and contributed to Blackwood's *Edinburgh* magazine. His most original work was 'An Account of the Great Moray Floods of 1829' (1830), which is 'an exceptional record of the geography of a highland area'. In 1832 he moved to Edinburgh. He was described as 'a tall, gentleman-like Quixotic figure, [with] a general picturesqueness of appearance'. H. C. G. Matthew, *ODNB*.

24 Sir Thomas Dick Lauder, 1842, *Sir Uvedale Price on the Picturesque, With an Essay on the Origin of Taste and much Original Matter*. Edinburgh, p. 57–8.

25 Lauder 1842, pp. 89, 130–32; 166–75; 205–12; 398.

26 Peter Frederick Robinson (1776–1858) first exhibited at the Royal Academy in 1795. He subsequently worked for Henry Holland (including the Royal Pavilion, Brighton, c.1801–04) and on his own account in 1807. 'In his love of the picturesque and in his eclecticism Robinson was highly representative of his age; he designed buildings in the Greek revival, Gothic, Norman, Tudor, Elizabethan, Egyptian, and "Swiss cottage" styles', including a 'Swiss Cottage' in Regent's Park. He developed a successful practice working on villas in Leamington and on the Duke of Newcastle's Park Estate at Nottingham, 1–12 Park Terrace (c.1831). An obituarist noted that 'some pecuniary difficulties a few years ago led him to select Boulogne for his residence'. Steven Brindle, *ODNB*.

27 Everett 1994, p. 124.

28 Everett 1994, p. 137; 142.

29 David Whitehead, *ODNB*, quoting J. Murdoch, 1983, *David Cox, 1783–1859*. Birmingham, p. 12.

30 Robert Hewison, *ODNB*.

31 John Ruskin, 1856/1904, *Modern Painters*. London, part V, 'Of the Turnerian Picturesque', p. 10.

32 Ruskin 1856/1904, part V, 'Of the Turnerian Picturesque', pp. 2–3. John Macarthur makes the interesting point that Ruskin's contrast between windmills painted by Turner and Stanfield has a close antecedent in Price's contrast between the watermills by Bourdon and Boucher, Macarthur, 2007, p. 98.

33 John Ruskin, 1883, *The Seven Lamps of Architecture, The Lamp of Memory*, 4th edn. Orpington, pp. 188–92.

34 Macarthur 2007, p. 103.

[35] E. H. Barker (1788–1839) published the pamphlet *The Claims of Sir Philip Francis to the Authorship of Junius Disproved: in a Letter addressed to Uvedale Price…* (Thetford) in 1827.

[36] Elizabeth Barrett to Hugh Boyd, Hope End, 29 January 1830; McCarthy 1955, p. 96.

[37] Forster 1988, p. 54.

[38] Elizabeth Barrett's *Prometheus Bound. Translated from the Greek of Aescylus. And Miscellaneous Poems* was published in 1833 by A. J. Valpy of London. 'To the memory of Sir Uvedale Price, Bart.' pp. 126–30.

[39] Robert Price was at Eton 1793–1802; Christ Church 1805; Edinburgh University 1807–8.

[40] Cooke 1892, p. 196, suggested that Price selected the spot but that, owing to his death, the work was delayed until 1843.

[41] R. W. D. Fenn and J. B. Sinclair, 2000, *The Herefordshire Bowmeeting*. Kington, p. 146.

[42] Cooke 1892, p. 191. Sheffield Archives Wentworth Woodhouse muniments WWM: Failure of Strahan, Paul and Bates, bankers, 1855–1856; affairs of Sir Robert Price of Foxley, 1847–1855.

[43] Duff Gordon Diaries, 19 September 1856, Hampton Court in Fenn and Sinclair 2000, p. 63.

[44] Fenn and Sinclair 2000, p. 146.

[45] S. Leigh Sotheby & John Wilkinson 3 and 4 May 1854, National Art Library, Victoria and Albert Museum, Lugt 21889.

[46] Foster and Son 11 June 1856, National Art Library, Victoria and Albert Museum, Lugt 23050.

[47] Lugt 51714.

[48] Hussey 1927, pp. 3–4.

[49] Susan Lasdun, 1996, 'H. de C. reviewed – the importance of architect Hubert de Cronin Hastings to *The Architectural Review*' *The Architectural Review*, September.

[50] Nikolaus Pevsner, 1944, 'Price on Picturesque planning', *The Architectural Review*, 95, pp. 47–50, pp. 47, 50; Nikolaus Pevsner, 1944, 'The genesis of the Picturesque', *The Architectural Review*, 96, pp. 139–46.

[51] *Architectural Review*, 106, December 1949, pp. 354–62.

[52] *Architectural Review*, 106, December 1949, p. 344.

[53] *Architectural Review*, 106, December 1949, p. 363–74.

[54] Nikolaus Pevsner, 1956, *The Englishness of English Art*. London.

[55] Everett 1994, pp. 103–15; Daniels and Watkins 1994; Ballantyne 1997, pp. 86–109; Daniels 1999, pp. 103–47. See also Stephen Copley and Peter Garside (eds), 1994, *The Politics of the Picturesque: Literature, Landscape and Aesthetics since 1770*, Cambridge, and Macarthur 2007.

BIBLIOGRAPHY

Adam, Robert, 1764. *Ruins of the Palace of the Emperor Diocletian at Spalatro in Dalmatia.* London.

Addison, Joseph, 1706. *The Spectator*, 215, 6 November.

Aikin, John, 1800. *Letters from a Father to his Son* …. London.

Andrews, Malcolm, 1989. *The Search for the Picturesque: Landscape Aesthetics and Tourism in Britain, 1760–1800.* Aldershot.

Anon, 1794. *The Female Jockey Club.* London.

Anon, 1830. *The Cambrian Tourist, or Post-Chaise Companion, through Wales*, 7th edn. London.

Arnold, Dana, 2000. *Re-presenting the Metropolis. Architecture, Urban Experience and Social Life in London 1800–1840.* Aldershot.

Aspinall, A. (ed.), 1964. *Correspondence of George, Prince of Wales 1770–1812.* London.

Aston, Nigel, 1999. 'Burke, Boisgelin and the politics of the émigré bishops', in Kirsty Carpenter and Philip Mansel (eds), *The French Émigrés in Europe and the Struggle against Revolution, 1789–1814.* Basingstoke, pp. 197–213.

Austen, Jane (ed. R. Ballaster), 2003. *Sense and Sensibility.* London/Harmondsworth.

Baillie, Joanna, 1798. *Plays on the Passions.* London.

Baird, John D. and Ryskamp, Charles (eds), 1980. *The Poems of William Cowper. Vol. I, 1740–1782.* Oxford.

Baker, James, 1795. *A Picturesque Guide through Wales and the Marches…*, 2nd edn. Worcester.

Ballantyne, Andrew, 1992. 'Genealogy of the Picturesque', *British Journal of Aesthetics*, 32, 4, pp. 320–29.

Ballantyne, Andrew, 1994–95. 'The Prices' daughter', *The Picturesque*, 9, pp. 1–2.

Ballantyne, Andrew, 1997. *Architecture, Landscape and Liberty: Richard Payne Knight and the Picturesque.* Cambridge.

Barbier, Carl Paul, 1959. *Samuel Rogers and William Gilpin. Their Friendship and Correspondence.* Oxford.

Barbier, Carl Paul, 1963. *William Gilpin: His Drawings, Teaching, and Theory of the Picturesque.* Oxford.

Barker, E. H., 1827. *The Claims of Sir Philip Francis to the Authorship of Junius Disproved: in a Letter Addressed to Uvedale Price….* Thetford.

Barker, E. H., 1852. *Literary Anecdotes and Contemporary Reminiscences of Professor Porson and Others; from the Manuscript Papers of the Late EH Barker Esq. of Thetford, Norfolk.* London.

Barrell, John, 2006. *The Spirit of Despotism: Invasions of Privacy in the 1790s.* Oxford.

Barrett, Elizabeth, 1833. *Prometheus Bound. Translated from the Greek of Aeschylus, and Miscellaneous Poems*, London.

Barrett Browning, Elizabeth, 1914. *The Poet's Enchiridion with an Inedited Address to Uvedale Price on his Eightieth Birthday….* Boston.

Barrington, Daines, 1785. 'On the progress of gardening', *Archaeologia*, XIII, pp. 113–130.

Beddoes, Thomas, 1797. *Alternatives Compared: or What shall the Rich do to be Safe?* London.

Bentivoglio, Guido, 1753. *A Collection of Letters written by Cardinal Bentivoglio.* London.

Berridge, Elizabeth (ed.), 1974. *The Barretts at Hope End: The Early Diary of Elizabeth Barrett Browning.* London.

Bevan, G. P., 1887. *Tourists' Guide to the Wye and its Neighbourhood.* London.

Beveridge, C. E. and P. Rocheleau, 1998. *Frederick Law Olmsted: Designing the American Landscape.* New York.

Bladon, F. McKno (ed.), 1930. *The Diaries of Colonel the Hon Robert Fulke Greville Equerry to His Majesty King George III.* London.

Boden, A., 1992. *Three Choirs: A History of the Festival: Gloucester, Hereford, Worcester.* Stroud.

Bonehill, J. and Daniels, S. (eds), 2009. *Paul Sandby: Picturing Britain*. London.

Boorman, David, 1986. *The Brighton of Wales. Swansea as a Fashionable Seaside Resort, c1780–c1830*. Swansea.

Brayley, E. W. and Britton, J., 1805. *The Beauties of England and Wales. Vol. VI*. London.

Brigstocke, H., 1982. *William Buchanan and the 19th-Century Art Trade: 100 Letters to his agents in London and Italy*. London.

Britton, John, 1850. *The Autobiography of John Britton*. London.

Brown, Jane, 2011. *The Omnipotent Magician: Lancelot 'Capability' Brown, 1716–1783*. London.

Buonaiuti, B. Serafino, 1806. *Italian Scenery: Representing the Manners, Customs, and Amusements of the Different States of Italy*. London.

Burke, Edmund, 1797. *A Third Letter to a Member of the Present Parliament, on the Proposals for Peace with the Regicide Directory of France*. London.

Burke, J. and Caldwell, C., 1968. *Hogarth: The Complete Engravings*. London.

Burney, Charles, 1789. *A General History of Music from the Earliest Ages to the Present Period*. London.

Callow, Jack, 2001. '"The Ragged Castle": an architectural feature on the Foxley estate, Herefordshire', *The Picturesque*, 34, pp. 1–14.

Campbell, John, 1774. *A Political Survey of Britain: Being a Series of Reflections on the Situation, Lands, Inhabitants, Revenues, Colonies and Commerce of this Island*. London.

Cartwright, James Joel (ed.), 1888. *The Travels through England of Dr Richard Pococke during 1750, 1751 and Later Years*. London.

Chambers, Neil (ed.), 2007. *Scientific Correspondence of Sir Joseph Banks 1767–1820*. London.

Chambers, William, 1772. *A Dissertation on Oriental Gardening*. London.

Chesterfield, Earl of, 1773. *Lord Chesterfield's Witticisms*. London.

Clark, John, 1794. *General View of the Agriculture of the County of Hereford*. London.

Clarke, Michael and Penny, Nicholas, 1982. *The Arrogant Connoisseur: Richard Payne Knight, 1751–1824*. Manchester.

Clayden, P. W., 1889. *Rogers and His Contemporaries*. London.

Cobban, A. and Smith, R. A. (eds.) 1967. *The Correspondence of Edmund Burke*. Cambridge.

Coburn, Kathleen (ed.), 1957. *The Notebooks of Samuel Taylor Coleridge. Vol. 1, 1794–1804*. London.

Collins Baker, C. H., 1938. 'The Price Family by Bartholomew Dandridge', *Burlington Magazine*, 72, pp. 132–9.

Combe, William, 1801. *The Life, Adventures, and Opinions of Col. George Hanger, Written by Himself*. London.

Connell, Brian, 1957. *Portrait of a Whig Peer: Compiled from the Papers of the Second Viscount Palmerston, 1739–1802*. London.

Conron, J., 2000. *American Picturesque*. University Park, Pennsylvania.

Cooke, William Henry, 1892. *Collections towards the History and Antiquities of the County of Hereford: In Continuation of Duncumb's History. Vol. 4 Hundred of Grimsworth*. London.

Copley, Stephen and Garside, Peter (eds), 1994. *The Politics of the Picturesque: Literature, Landscape and Aesthetics since 1770*. Cambridge.

Corbain, Alain, 1994. *The Lure of the Sea*. London.

Coxe, William, 1799. *Anecdotes of George Frederick Handel and John Christopher Smith with Select Pieces of Music Composed by J. C. Smith Never Before Published*. London.

Coxe, William, 1811. *Literary Life and Select Works of Benjamin Stillingfleet, Several of Which have Never Before been Published*. London.

Crewe, Frances Anne, 1862–3. 'Extracts from Mr. Burke's Table–Talk, at Crewe Hall. Written down by Mrs. Crewe', *Miscellanies of the Philobiblon Society*, VII, 5, pp. 1–62.

Croft, Sir Herbert, 1788. *The Abbey of Kilkhampton*. London.

Cruikshank, E., Handley, S. and Hayton, D. W. (eds), 2002. *The History of Parliament. The House of Commons 1690–1715*. London.

Curll, Edmund, 1734. *The Life of the Late Honourable Robert Price, Esq; one of the Justices of His Majesty's Court of Common-Pleas*. London.

Cust, Lionel and Colvin, Sidney, 1898. *History of the Society of Dilettanti*. London.

Daniels, Stephen, 1999. *Humphry Repton: Landscape Gardening and the Geography of Georgian England*. New Haven and London.

Daniels, Stephen and Watkins, Charles, 1991. 'Picturesque Landscaping and Estate Management', *Rural History*, 2, pp. 141–69.

UVEDALE PRICE
1747–1829
DECODING THE
PICTURESQUE

Daniels, Stephen and Watkins, Charles (eds), 1994. *The Picturesque Landscape: Visions of Georgian Herefordshire*. Nottingham.

Davies, Terence, 1960. *The Architecture of John Nash: Introduced with a Critical Essay by John Summerson*. London.

de Laborde, Alexandre, 1808. *Description des Nouveaux Jardins de la France et de ses Anciens Châteaux*. Paris.

de Selincourt, E., 1937. *The Letters of William and Dorothy Wordsworth: The Middle Years*. Oxford.

de Selincourt, E. (ed.), 1940/1952. *The Poetical Words of William Wordsworth: Poems Written in Youth, Poems Referring to the Period of Childhood*. Oxford.

Dilworth, W. H. (ed.), 1759. *Lord Anson's Voyage Around the World Performed in the Years 1740, 41, 42, 43, 44*. London.

Dixon Hunt, John and Willis, Peter (eds), 1975. *The Genius of the Place: The English Landscape Garden 1620–1820*. London.

Douglas, D. (ed.), *Familiar Letters of Sir Walter Scott*. Edinburgh.

Dufresnoy, Charles-Alphonse, 1783. *The Art of Painting of Charles Alphonse Du Fresnoy. Translated into English verse by William Mason, M.A. with annotations by Sir Joshua Reynolds,…*. York.

Duncumb, John, 1805. *General View of the Agriculture of the County of Hereford*. London.

Eastlake, Charles (ed. J. M. Crook), 1970. *A History of the Gothic Revival*. London.

Elsner, Jaś. 'Picturesque and Sublime: Impacts of Pausanias in Late-Eighteenth- and Early-Nineteenth-Century Britain', *Classical Receptions Journal*, 2, pp. 219–53.

Elwin, Malcolm (ed.), 1950. *The Autobiography and Journals of Benjamin Robert Haydon*. London.

Evans, George Eyre, 1902. *Aberystwyth and its Court Leet*. Aberystwyth.

Everett, Nigel, 1994. *The Tory View of Landscape*. New Haven and London.

Farington, Joseph (eds K. Garlick and A. Macintyre), 1978–1998. *The Diary of Joseph Farington*. New Haven and London.

Fawcett, A. Peter and Jackson, Neil, 1998. *Campus Critique. The Architecture of the University of Nottingham*. Nottingham.

Fenn, R. W. D. and Sinclair, J. B., 2000. *The Herefordshire Bowmeeting*. Kington.

Fielding, Sarah, 1757. *The Lives of Cleopatra and Octavia*. London.

Fleming-Williams, Ian, 1965. 'John Skippe', *Master Drawings*, III, pp. 268–75.

Forster, Margaret, 1988. *Elizabeth Barrett Browning*. London.

Fosbrooke, Thomas Dudley, 1802. *British Monachism, or, Manners and Customs of the Monks and Nuns of England*, London.

Foss, Edward, 1870. *A Biographical Dictionary of the Judges of England*. London.

Garlick, Kenneth, 1989. *Sir Thomas Lawrence. A Complete Catalogue of the Oil Paintings*. Oxford.

Gaut, R. C., 1939. *A History of Worcestershire Agriculture and Rural Evolution*. Worcester.

Gee, Austin, 2003. *The British Volunteer Movement 1794–1814*. Oxford.

Gilpin, William, 1768. *An Essay upon Prints, containing Remarks upon the Principles of Picturesque Beauty…*. London.

Gilpin, William, 1782. *Observations on the River Wye*. London.

Gilpin, William, 1791. *Remarks on Forest Scenery*. London.

Gilpin, William, 1798. *Observation on the Western Parts of Britain … Chiefly Relative to Picturesque Beauty…*. London.

Gilpin, William S., 1832. *Practical Hints upon Landscape Gardening: With Some Remarks on Domestic Architecture as Connected with Scenery*. London.

Gladstone, J. H., Boas, Guy and Christopherson, Harald, 1996. *Noblemen and Gentlemen's Catch Club: Three Essays Towards its History*. London.

Goethe, Johann von (trans. R. J. Hollingdale), 1971. *Elective Affinities*. Harmondsworth.

Gomme, Andor Harvey, 2000. *Smith of Warwick: Francis Smith, Architect and Masterbuilder*. Stamford..

Greater London Council, 1977. *Survey of London, Vol. 39, The Grosvenor Estate in Mayfair*. London.

Grierson, H. J. C. (ed.), 1932. *The Letters of Sir Walter Scott 1808–1811*. London.

Hague, Douglas B., 1958. 'Giler, Cerrig-y-drudion, Denbighshire', *Denbighshire Historical Society Transactions*, 7, pp. 67–85.

Hamilton, George Gordon (Lord Aberdeen), 1822. *An Inquiry into the Principles of Beauty in Grecian Architecture an Historical View of the Rise and Progress of the Art in Greece*. London.

Hare, Augustus (ed.), 1894. *The Life and Letters of Maria Edgeworth*. London.

Harrison, Colin, 1998. 'Malchair the Artist', in Colin Harrison (ed.), *John Malchair of Oxford: Artist and Musician*. Oxford.

Hart, Cyril, 1966. *Royal Forest: A History of Dean's Woods as Producers of Timber*. Oxford.

Hart, Cyril, 1995. *The Forest of Dean: New History 1550–1818*. Stroud.

Hartley, Beryl, 1994. 'Naturalism and sketching, Robert Price at Foxley and on Tour', in Stephen Daniels and Charles Watkins (eds), *The Picturesque Landscape: Visions of Georgian Herefordshire*. Nottingham, pp. 34–7.

Hawcroft, Francis W., 1958. 'The "Cabinet" at Felbrigg', *Connoisseur*, CXLI, pp. 216–19.

Hawcroft, Francis W., 1959. 'Giovanni Battista Busiri' *Gazette des Beaux-Arts*, LIII, pp. 295–304.

Hayes, John, 1982. *The Landscape Paintings of Thomas Gainsborough*. London.

Hennig, John, 1951. 'A note on Goethe and Charles Gore', *Monatshefte*, 43, pp. 27–37.

Henning, Basil, 1983. *History of Parliament. The House of Commons, 1660–1690*. London.

Hill, Alan (ed.), 1988. *The Letters of William and Dorothy Wordsworth, The Later Years, Part 1, 1821–1828*.

Hill, Alan (ed.), 1993. *The Letters of William and Dorothy Wordsworth, vol. 8, A Supplement of New Letters*. Oxford.

Hillaby, Joseph, 1967. 'The parliamentary borough of Weobley, 1628–1708', *Transactions of the Woolhope Naturalists' Field Club*, 39, 1, pp. 104–51.

Hipple, Walter John, 1957. *The Beautiful, the Sublime and the Picturesque in Eighteenth Century British Aesthetic Theory*. Carbondale.

Hogarth, William, 1753. *The Analysis of Beauty*. London.

Hoock, Holger, 2003. *The King's Artists. The Royal Academy of Arts and Politics of British Culture 1760–1840*. Oxford.

Horn, Pamela, 1982. 'An eighteenth century land agent: the career of Nathaniel Kent (1737–1810)', *Agricultural History Review*, 30, pp. 1–16.

Hubbard, E. 1986. *Buildings of Wales: Clwyd*. Harmondsworth.

Hughes, G. M., 1890. *A History of Windsor Forest, Sunninghill, and the Great Park*. London and Edinburgh.

Hussey, Christopher, 1927. *The Picturesque: Studies in a Point of View*. London.

Ingamells, John, 1997. *A Dictionary of British and Irish Travellers in Italy 1701–1800*. New Haven and London.

Inglis-Jones, Elisabeth, 1950. *Peacocks in Paradise*. London.

Ireland, Samuel, 1797. *Picturesque Views on the River Wye*. London.

Irving, Washington (ed. S. Manning), 1998. *The Sketch-Book of Geoffrey Crayon, Gent.* Oxford.

Jenkins, G. H., 1993. *The Foundations of Modern Wales, 1642–1780*. Oxford.

Jenkins, Philip, 1983. *The Making of a Ruling Class: The Glamorgan Gentry 1640–1790*. Cambridge.

Jones, D. J. V. 1973. *Before Rebecca: Popular Protests in Wales 1793–1835*. London.

Kauffmann, M., 1984. *John Varley, 1778–1842*. London.

Kent, Nathaniel, 1775. *Hints to a Gentleman of Landed Property*. London.

Ketton-Cremer, R. W., 1962. *Felbrigg: The Story of a House*. London.

Kitson, Michael, 1978. *Claude Lorrain: Liber Veritatis*. London.

Knight, Richard Payne (ed. Claudia Stumpf), 1777/1986. *Expedition into Sicily*. London.

Knight, Richard Payne, 1786. *An Account of the Remains of the Worship of Priapus*. London.

Knight, Richard Payne, 1791. *An Analytical Essay on the Greek Alphabet*. London.

Knight, Richard Payne, 1794. *The Landscape, a Didactic Poem, in Three Books. Addressed to Uvedale Price*. London.

Knight, Richard Payne, 1805. *An Analytical Inquiry into the Principles of Taste*. London.

Kraemer, Ruth S., 1975. *Drawings by Benjamin West and his son Raphael Lamar West*. Boston.

Ladd, Frederick J., 1978. *Architects at Corsham Court. A Study in Revival Style Architecture and Landscaping, 1749–1849*. London.

Laing, David, 1880. *Hints for Dwellings, Consisting of Original Designs for Cottages, Farmhouses, Villas, etc*. London.

Lambin, Denis A., 1987. 'Foxley: the Price's estate in Herefordshire', *Journal of Garden History*, 7, pp. 244–70.

Lasdun, Susan, 1996. 'H. de C. reviewed – the importance of architect Hubert de Cronin Hastings to *The Architectural Review*', *The Architectural Review*, September, pp. 68–72.

UVEDALE PRICE
1747–1829
DECODING THE
PICTURESQUE

Lauder, Sir Thomas Dick, 1842. *Sir Uvedale Price on the Picturesque, With an Essay on the Origin of Taste and much Original Matter*. Edinburgh.

Lees-Milne, James, 1992. *People and Places*. London.

Levy, M. J. (ed.), 1994. *Perdita: The Memoirs of Mary Robinson*. London.

Lewis, Lady Theresa (ed.), 1865. *Extracts from the Journals and Correspondence of Miss Berry, from the Year 1783 to 1852*. London.

Lewis, W. J., 1980. *Born on a Perilous Rock*. Aberystwyth.

Lewis, W. S. (ed.), 1941. *Horace Walpole's Correspondence*. New Haven.

Lewis, W. S., Cronin, Grover Jr and Bennett, Charles H. (eds), 1955. *Horace Walpole's Correspondence with William Mason*. New Haven.

Lippincott, Louise, 1983. *Selling Art in Georgian London. The Rise of Arthur Pond*. London.

Lipscomb, George, 1802. *Journey into South Wales*. London.

Llewellyn, T. I., 1824. *The New Aberystwyth Guide*. Aberystwyth.

Lockhart, J. G. (ed.), 1837. *Memoirs of the Life of Sir Walter Scott, Bart*. Edinburgh.

Lodge, John, 1793. *Introductory Sketches Towards a Topographical History of the County of Hereford*. Kington.

Loudon, J. C., 1804. *Observations on the Formation and Management of Useful and Ornamental Plantations*. Edinburgh.

Loudon, J. C., 1825. *Encyclopaedia of Agriculture*. London.

Loudon, J. C., 1854. *Arboretum et Fruticetum Britannicum*. London.

Lysons, Daniel, 1812. *History of the Origin and Progress of the Meeting of the Three Choirs of Gloucester, Worcester and Hereford*. Gloucester.

Macarthur, John, 2007. *The Picturesque: Architecture, Disgust and Other Irregularities*. London.

McCarthy, B. (ed.), 1955. *Elizabeth Barrett to Mr. Boyd*. London.

McCarthy, F., 1964. 'Some newly discovered drawings by Robert Price of Foxley', *National Library of Wales Journal*, 13, 3, pp. 289–94.

Magne, Émile, 1930. *Voiture et l'Hotel de Rambouillet*. Paris.

Malkin, Benjamin Heath, 1804. *The Scenery, Antiquities and Biography of South Wales*. London.

Malton, James, 1798. *An Essay on British Cottage Architecture*. London.

Mannings, David, 2000. *Sir Joshua Reynolds: A Complete Catalogue of his Paintings*. New Haven and London.

Mansbridge, Michael, 1991. *John Nash. A Complete Catalogue 1752–1835*. Oxford.

Marchand, Leslie A. (ed.), 1973. *Byron's Letters and Journals*. London.

Marshall, P. J. and Woods, J. A., 1968. *Correspondence of Edmund Burke. Vol. 7: January 1792–August 1794*. Cambridge.

Marshall, William, 1795. *A Review of the Landscape, A Didactic Poem: Also of An Essay on the Picturesque: Together with Practical Remarks on Rural Ornament*. London.

Martel, Pierre and Windham, William, 1774. *An Account of the Glacieres, or Ice Alps, in Savoy...*. London.

Martineau, Yzabelle, 2002. *Le Faux Littéraire. Plagiat Littéraire, Intertextualité et Dialogisme*. Québec.

Mason, George, 1795. *An Essay on Design in Gardening*. London.

Mason, George, 1798. *An Appendix to An Essay on Design in Gardening*. London.

Mason, William, 1773. *An Heroic Epistle to Sir William Chambers*. London.

Mason, William, 1772–81. *The English Garden*. London.

Mason, William, 1797. *Poems*, vol. III. York.

Mathias, Thomas James, 1798. *Pursuits of Literature*. London.

Maxwell, Herbert, 1902. *George Romney*. London.

Meason, G. L., 1828. *On the Landscape Architecture of the Great Painters of Italy*. London.

Mermin, Dorothy, 1989. *Elizabeth Barrett Browning: The Origins of a New Poetry*. Chicago.

Meyrick, Sir Samuel Rush, 1810. *The History and Antiquities of the County of Cardigan*. London.

Mitchell, L. G., 1997. *Charles James Fox*. London.

Moore-Colyer, Richard, 1992. *A Land of Pure Delight. Selections from the Letters of Thomas Johnes of Hafod, Cardiganshire (1748–1816)*. Llandysul.

Morris, David, 1989. *Thomas Hearne and his Landscape*. London.

Morris, Richard, 1825. *Essays on Landscape Gardening and on Uniting Picturesque Effect with Rural Scenery: Containing Directions for Laying Out and Improving the Grounds Connected with a Country Residence*. London.

Muir, Richard, 2001. 'The Burgage-house, otherwise known as the Lodge', unpublished notes from Haslemere Educational Museum.

Murdoch, J., 1983. *David Cox, 1783–1859*. Birmingham.

Nichols, John, 1812. *Literary Anecdotes of the Eighteenth Century*, vol. VI. London.

Nichols, John, 1828. *Illustrations of the Literary History of the Eighteenth Century*, vol. VI. London.

Norton, Lucy, 1972. *Historical Memoirs of the Duc de Saint Simon*, London.

Oliver, R. C. B., 1986. 'Holidays at Aberystwyth 1798–1823', *Ceredigion*, pp. 269–86.

Oppe, A. P. (ed.), 1951. 'Memoirs of Thomas Jones', *Walpole Society*, 32.

Ousby, Ian (ed.), 1992. *James Plumptre's Britain. The Journals of a Tourist in the 1790s*. London.

Owen, Felicity, 1988. *'Noble and patriotic' – The Beaumont Gift 1828*. London.

Owen, Felicity and Blayney Brown, David, 1998. *Collector of Genius: A Life of Sir George Beaumont*. New Haven and London.

Owen, W. J. B. and Smyser, J. M. (eds), 1974. *The Prose Works of William Wordsworth*. Oxford.

Paulson, R., 1971. *Hogarth: His Life, Art, and Times*. London.

Petit, Sandrine and Watkins, Charles, 2003. 'Pollarding trees: changing attitudes to a traditional land management practice in Britain 1600–1900', *Rural History*, 14, pp. 157–76.

Pevsner, Nikolaus, 1944a. 'Price on Picturesque planning', *The Architectural Review*, 95, pp. 47–50.

Pevsner, Nikolaus, 1944b. 'The genesis of the Picturesque', *The Architectural Review*, 96, pp. 139–46.

Pevsner, Nikolaus, 1956. *The Englishness of English Art*. London.

Pevsner, Nikolaus, 1963. *Herefordshire*. London.

Piebenga, Sophieke, 1994. 'William Sawrey Gilpin: picturesque improver', *Garden History*, 22, pp. 176–96.

Piebenga, Sophieke, 2004. 'William Sawrey Gilpin (1761/2–1843): watercolour artist and landscape gardener', *The Picturesque*, 48, pp. 2–28.

Plomer, W. (ed.), 1938. *Kilvert's Diary: Selections from the Diary of the Reverend Francis Kilvert, 1 January 1870–19 August 1871*. London.

Plumptre, James, 1798/1990 *The Lakers*. London/Oxford and New York.

Price, Cecil (ed.), 1966. *The Letters of Richard Brinsley Sheridan*. Oxford.

Price, Uvedale, 1733. *A New Catechism for the Fine Ladies*. Paris.

Price, Uvedale (trans. of Antonio Palomino de Castro y Velasco), 1739. *An Account of the Lives and Works of the Most Eminent Spanish Painters, Sculptors and Architects from the Musæum Pictorium*. London.

Price, Uvedale, 1740. *A New Catechism for the Fine Ladies: With a Specimen of a New Version of the Psalms, by Mr. Pope, &c,*. London.

Price, Uvedale, 1749. *An Account of the Most Remarkable Places and Curiosities in Spain and Portugal*. London.

Price, Uvedale, 1780. *An Account of the Statues, Pictures, and Temples in Greece; Translated from the Greek of Pausanias*. London.

Price, Uvedale, 1786. 'On the bad effects of stripping and cropping trees', *Annals of Agriculture*, 5, pp. 241–50.

Price, Uvedale, 1794. *An Essay on the Picturesque*. London.

Price, Uvedale, 1795. *A Letter to H. Repton, Esq*. London.

Price, Uvedale, 1796. *An Essay on the Picturesque … A New Edition, with Considerable Additions*. London.

Price, Uvedale, 1797. *Thoughts on the Defence of Property. Addressed to the County of Hereford*. Hereford.

Price, Uvedale, 1798a. *Essays on the Picturesque. Essay on Artificial Water. Essay on Decorations. Essay on Architecture and Buildings*. Hereford and London.

Price, Uvedale, 1798b. *Über den guten Geschmack bei ländlichen Kunst- und Garten-Anlagen und verbesserung wirklicher Landschaften* [Concerning good taste in landscape art and landscape gardening and the improvement of real landscape with examples]. Leipzig.

Price, Uvedale, 1801. *A Dialogue on the Distinct Characters of the Picturesque and the Beautiful. In answer to the Objections of Mr. Knight. Prefaced by An Introductory Essay on Beauty; with Remarks on the Ideas of Sir Joshua Reynolds & Mr. Burke, upon that Subject*. London.

Price, Uvedale, 1810. *Essays on the Picturesque*. London.

Price, Uvedale, 1827. *An Essay on the Modern Pronunciation of the Greek and Latin Languages*. Oxford.

Ramsay, Andrew, 1730. *A New Cyropædia: or the Travels of Cyrus, with a Discourse on the Theology & Mythologie of the Ancients*. London.

Rennell, Francis James, 1958. *Valley on the March*. London.

Repton, Humphry, 1794. *A Letter to Uvedale Price, Esq*. London.

Rhys, Udal ap, 1749. *An Account of the Most Remarkable Places and Curiosities in Spain and Portugal*. London.

Ribeiro, Alvaro (ed.), 1991. *The Letters of Dr Charles Burney*, vol. I 1754–84. Oxford.

Roberts, Jane, 1997. *Royal Landscape: The Gardens and Parks of Windsor*. New Haven and London.

Robins, Brian, 2006. *Catch and Glee Culture in Eighteenth-Century England*. Woodbridge.

Robinson, Jancis, 1999. *The Oxford Companion to Wine*. Oxford.

Rogers, Samuel, 1856. *Recollections of the table-talk of Samuel Rogers, to which is added, Porsoniana*. London.

Rousseau, G. S., 1987. 'The sorrows of Priapus: anticlericalism, homosocial desire, and Richard Payne Knight', in G. S. Rousseau and Roy Porter (eds), *Sexual Worlds of the Enlightenment*. Manchester, pp. 101–53.

Rousseau, Jean-Jacques, 1761. *Lettres de deux amans habitans d'une petite ville au pied des Alpes [Julie ou La nouvelle Héloïse]*. Amsterdam.

Royal Academy of Arts, 1905. *A Complete Dictionary of Contributors and their Work from its Foundation in 1769 to 1904*. London.

Ruskin, John, 1883. *The Seven Lamps of Architecture, The Lamp of Memory*, 4th edn. Orpington.

Ruskin, John, 1856/1904. *Modern Painters*. London.

Russell, Lord John (ed.), 1853–56. *Memoirs, Journal and Correspondence of Thomas Moore*. London.

Scott, Jonathan, 1995. *Salvator Rosa: His Life and Times*. New Haven and London.

Scott, Walter, 1814. *Somers' Tracts*, vol. 11. London.

Scott, Walter, 1818. *Heart of Midlothian*. Edinburgh.

Seymour, Susanne and Calvocoressi, Rupert, 2007. 'Landscape parks and the memorialisation of empire: the Pierreponts' "naval seascape" in Thoresby Park, Nottinghamshire during the French Wars (1793–1815)', *Rural History*, 18, pp. 95–118.

Seymour, Susanne, Daniels, Stephen and Watkins, Charles, 1998. 'Estate and empire: Sir George Cornewall's management of Moccas, Herefordshire and La Taste, Grenada, 1771–1829', *Journal of Historical Geography*, 24, pp. 313–51.

Shaw, Rev. Stebbing, 1789. *A Tour to the West of England, in 1788*. London.

Shenstone, William, 1764. *Unconnected Thoughts on Gardening*, in *The Works in Verse and Prose of William Shenstone*, vol. II. London.

Sherburn, George (ed.), 1956. *The Correspondence of Alexander Pope*, 4 vols. Oxford.

Silverthorne, Elizabeth, 1976. 'Deposition Book of Richard Wyatt, J.P.', *Surrey Record Society*, 30, pp. vii–viii.

Simo, Melanie Louise, 1988. *Loudon and the Landscape*. New Haven and London.

Sloman, Susan, 2002. *Gainsborough in Bath*. New Haven and London.

Smith, Brian S., 2004. *Herefordshire Maps 1577–1800*. Hereford.

Staël, Madame de, 1813. *De l'Allemagne*, Paris and London.

Sterne, Laurence, 1760–67. *The Life and Opinions of Tristram Shandy, Gentleman*. York and London.

Stoddart, John, 1801. *Remarks on Local Scenery and Manners in Scotland During the Years 1799 and 1800*. London.

Stone, George Winchester (ed.), 1962. *The London Stage 1660–1800, Part 4 1747–1776*. Carbondale.

Stroud, Dorothy, 1975. *Capability Brown*. London.

Suggett, Richard, 1995. *John Nash: Architect in Wales*. Aberystwyth.

Sumner, Ann and Smith, Greg (eds), 2003. *Thomas Jones (1742–1803) An artist Rediscovered*. New Haven and London.

Tancock, Leonard (ed.), 1982. *Madame de Sévigné. Selected letters*. London.

Temple, Nigel, 1979. *John Nash and the Village Picturesque*. Gloucester.

Thicknesse, Philip, 1778. *A Year's Journey through France and Part of Spain*. London.

Thirsk, Joan (ed.), 1984. *The Agrarian History of England and Wales. Volume V, 1640–1750, I Regional Farming Systems*. Cambridge.

Thompson, F. M. L., 1963. *English Landed Society in the Nineteenth Century*. London.

Thompson, M. W. (ed.), 1983. *The Journeys of Sir Richard Colt Hoare through Wales and England 1793–1810*. Gloucester.

Thorne, R. G., 1986. *The House of Commons 1790–1820*. London.

Throsby, John, 1792. *The Supplementary Volume to the Leicestershire Views: Containing a Series of Excursions in the Year 1790....* London.

Tisdall, John, 1996. *Joshua Cristall 1768–1847: In Search of Arcadia*. Hereford.

Trefman, Simon, 1971. *Sam. Foote, Comedian 1720–1777*. New York.

Trevelyan, Sir George, 1901. *The Early History of Charles James Fox*. London.

Troide, Lars E. (ed.), 1988. *The Early Journals and Letters of Fanny Burney*. Oxford.

von Erffa, Helmut and Stanley, Allen, 1986. *The Paintings of Benjamin West*. New Haven and London.

Walker, Adam, 1792. *Remarks made in a Tour from London to the Lakes of Westmoreland and Cumberland....* London.

Walpole, Horace, 1771. *Anecdotes of Painting in England*. London.

Walpole, Horace (ed. Isabel Chase), 1943. *The History of the Modern Taste in Gardening*. Princeton.

Wark, R. R. (ed.), 1959. *Sir Joshua Reynolds: Discourses on Art*. San Marino.

Warter, John Wood (ed.), 1856. *Selections from the Letters of Robert Southey*. London.

Watkins, Charles and Cowell, Ben, 2006a. '"Mr Price the Picturesque": critic, connoisseur and landscape enthusiast', *Walpole Society*, 68, pp. 1–77.

Watkins, Charles and Cowell, Ben, 2006b. *Letters of Uvedale Price*, Walpole Society, 68.

Watkins, Charles, Daniels, Stephen and Seymour, Susanne, 1995. 'Picturesque woodland management: the Prices at Foxley', in Dana Arnold (ed.), *The Picturesque in Late Georgian England*. London, pp. 27–34.

Watkins, Charles, Daniels, Stephen and Seymour, Susanne, 1996. 'Uvedale Price's marine Picturesque at Aberystwyth, 1790–1829', *The Picturesque*, 14, pp. 1–12.

Watkin, D., 1968. *Thomas Hope 1769–1832 and the Neo-Classical Idea*. London.

Watkin, D., 1982. *The English Vision. The Picturesque in Architecture, Landscape and Garden Design*. London.

Webster, J. Roger, 1995. *Old College Aberystwyth. The Evolution of a High Victorian Building*. Cardiff.

Whately, Thomas, 1770. *Observations on Modern Gardening*. London.

Whitehead, David, 1992. 'John Nash and Humphry Repton: an encounter in Herefordshire 1785–98', *Transactions of the Woolhope Naturalists Field Club*, 47, pp. 221–7.

Whitehead, David, 2001. *A Survey of Historic Parks and Gardens in Herefordshire*. Hereford.

Whitehead, David, 2007. 'Veterans in the arboretum: planting exotics at Holme Lacy, Herefordshire, in the late nineteenth century', *Garden History*, 35, 2, pp. 96–112.

Whitehead, David, 2009. 'Artisan attitudes to Gothic in Georgian Herefordshire', *The Georgian Group Journal*, 17, pp. 61–76.

Whiting, Frederick A., 1967. 'The Committee of Taste', *Apollo*, 82, pp. 326–30.

Wigstead, Henry, 1799. *Remarks on a Tour to North and South Wales in the year 1797*. London.

Wille, Johann-George, 1857. *Mémoires et Journal de J-G Wille, Graveur du Roi*, 2 vols. Paris.

Willett, Mark, 1810. *An Excursion from the Source of the Wye*. Chepstow.

Williams, Harold (ed.), 1963. *The Correspondence of Jonathan Swift*, 5 vols. Oxford.

Woods, Tim, 1992. 'A guide to the wall tablets of Bath Abbey as they appear today', unpublished typescript, Bath.

Wordsworth, William, 1807. *Poems in Two Volumes*. London.

Wordsworth, William and Coleridge, Samuel Taylor, 1798. *Lyrical Ballads*. London.

Wordsworth, William and Coleridge, Samuel Taylor, 1800. *Lyrical Ballads*, 2 vols. London.

Wraxall, Sir N. W., 1836. *Posthumous Memoirs of His Own Time*. London.

Wynne, John Huddlestone, 1773. *The Four Seasons*. London.

INDEX

Printed and bound by CPI Group (UK) Ltd, Croydon, CR0 4YY

13/04/2025

14656527-0002